Applied Data Mining

Applied Data Mining

Statistical Methods for Business and Industry

PAOLO GIUDICI

Faculty of Economics
University of Pavia
Italy

WILEY

Other Wiley Editorial Offices

John Wiley & Sons Inc., 111 River Street, Hoboken, NJ 07030, USA

Jossey-Bass, 989 Market Street, San Francisco, CA 94103-1741, USA

Wiley-VCH Verlag GmbH, Boschstr. 12, D-69469 Weinheim, Germany

John Wiley & Sons Australia Ltd, 33 Park Road, Milton, Queensland 4064, Australia

John Wiley & Sons (Asia) Pte Ltd, 2 Clementi Loop #02-01, Jin Xing Distripark, Singapore 129809

John Wiley & Sons Canada Ltd, 22 Worcester Road, Etobicoke, Ontario, Canada M9W 1L1

Wiley also publishes its books in a variety of electronic formats. Some content that appears
in print may not be available in electronic books.

Library of Congress Cataloging-in-Publication Data

Giudici, Paolo.
     Applied data mining : statistical methods for business and industry / Paolo Giudici.
        p. cm.
     Includes bibliographical references and index.
     ISBN 0-470-84678-X (alk. paper) – ISBN 0-470-84679-8 (pbk.)
        1. Data mining. 2. Business – Data processing. 3. Commercial statistics. I. Title.

     QA76.9.D343G75 2003

                                                                      2003050196

British Library Cataloguing in Publication Data

A catalogue record for this book is available from the British Library

ISBN 0-470-84678-X (Cloth)
ISBN 0-470-84679-8 (Paper)

Typeset in 10/12pt Times by Laserwords Private Limited, Chennai, India
Printed and bound in Great Britain by Biddles Ltd, King's Lynn, Norfolk
This book is printed on acid-free paper responsibly manufactured from sustainable forestry
in which at least two trees are planted for each one used for paper production.

Contents

Preface

The increasing availability of data in the current information society has led to the need for valid tools for its modelling and analysis. Data mining and applied statistical methods are the appropriate tools to extract knowledge from such data. Data mining can be defined as the process of selection, exploration and modelling of large databases in order to discover models and patterns that are unknown a priori. It differs from applied statistics mainly in terms of its scope; whereas applied statistics concerns the application of statistical methods to the data at hand, data mining is a whole process of data extraction and analysis aimed at the production of decision rules for specified business goals. In other words, data mining is a business intelligence process.

Although data mining is a very important and growing topic, there is insufficient coverage of it in the literature, especially from a statistical viewpoint. Most of the available books on data mining are either too technical and computer science oriented or too applied and marketing driven. This book aims to establish a bridge between data mining methods and applications in the fields of business and industry by adopting a coherent and rigorous approach to statistical modelling.

Not only does it describe the methods employed in data mining, typically coming from the fields of machine learning and statistics, but it describes them in relation to the business goals that have to be achieved, hence the word 'applied' in the title. The second part of the book is a set of case studies that compare the methods of the first part in terms of their performance and usability. The first part gives a broad coverage of all methods currently used for data mining and puts them into a functional framework. Methods are classified as being essentially computational (e.g. association rules, decision trees and neural networks) or statistical (e.g. regression models, generalised linear models and graphical models). Furthermore, each method is classified in terms of the business intelligence goals it can achieve, such as discovery of local patterns, classification and prediction.

The book is primarily aimed at advanced undergraduate and graduate students of business management, computer science and statistics. The case studies give guidance to professionals working in industry on projects involving large volumes of data, such as in customer relationship management, web analysis, risk management and, more broadly, marketing and finance. No unnecessary formalisms and mathematical tools are introduced. Those who wish to know more should consult the bibliography; specific pointers are given at the end of Chapters 2 to 6.

The book is the result of a learning process that began in 1989, when I was a graduate student of statistics at the University of Minnesota. Since then my research activity has always been focused on the interplay between computational and multivariate statistics. In 1998 I began building a group of data mining statisticians and it has evolved into a data mining laboratory at the University of Pavia. There I have had many opportunities to interact and learn from industry experts and my own students working on data mining projects and doing internships within the industry. Although it is not possible to name them all, I thank them and hope they recognise their contribution in the book. A special mention goes to the University of Pavia, in particular to the Faculty of Business and Economics, where I have been working since 1993. It is a very stimulating and open environment to do research and teaching.

I acknowledge Wiley for having proposed and encouraged this effort, in particular the statistics and mathematics editor and assistant editor, Sian Jones and Rob Calver. I also thank Greg Ridgeway, who revised the final manuscript and suggested several improvements. Finally, the most important acknowledgement goes to my wife, Angela, who has constantly encouraged the development of my research in this field. The book is dedicated to her and to my son Tommaso, born on 24 May 2002, when I was revising the manuscript.

I hope people will enjoy reading the book and eventually use it in their work. I will be very pleased to receive comments at giudici@unipv.it and www.datamininglab.it. I will consider any suggestions for a subsequent edition.

Paolo Giudici
Pavia, 28 January 2003

CHAPTER 1

Introduction

Nowadays each individual and organisation – business, family or institution – can access a large quantity of data and information about itself and its environment. This data has the potential to predict the evolution of interesting variables or trends in the outside environment, *but so far that potential has not been fully exploited.* This is particularly true in the business field, the subject of this book. There are two main problems. Information is scattered within different archive systems that are not connected with one another, producing an inefficient organisation of the data. There is a lack of awareness about statistical tools and their potential for information elaboration. This interferes with the production of efficient and relevant data synthesis.

Two developments could help to overcome these problems. First, software and hardware continually, offer more power at lower cost, allowing organisations to collect and organise data in structures that give easier access and transfer. Second, methodological research, particularly in the field of computing and statistics, has recently led to the development of flexible and scalable procedures that can be used to analyse large data stores. These two developments have meant that data mining is rapidly spreading through many businesses as an important intelligence tool for backing up decisions.

This chapter introduces the ideas behind data mining. It defines data mining and compares it with related topics in statistics and computer science. It describes the process of data mining and gives a brief introduction to data mining software. The last part of the chapter outlines the organisation of the book and suggests some further reading.

1.1   What is data mining?

To understand the term 'data mining' it is useful to look at the literal translation of the word: to mine in English means to extract. The verb usually refers to mining operations that extract from the Earth her hidden, precious resources. The association of this word with data suggests an in-depth search to find additional information which previously went unnoticed in the mass of data available. From the viewpoint of scientific research, data mining is a relatively new discipline that has developed mainly from studies carried out in other disciplines such as computing, marketing, and statistics. Many of the methodologies used in data mining

Applied Data Mining.   Paolo Giudici
© 2003 John Wiley & Sons, Ltd   ISBNs: 0-470-84679-8 (Paper); 0-470-84678-X (Cloth)

come from two branches of research, one developed in the machine learning community and the other developed in the statistical community, particularly in multivariate and computational statistics.

Machine learning is connected to computer science and artificial intelligence and is concerned with finding relations and regularities in data that can be translated into general truths. The aim of machine learning is the reproduction of the data-generating process, allowing analysts to generalise from the observed data to new, unobserved cases. Rosenblatt (1962) introduced the first machine learning model, called the perceptron. Following on from this, neural networks developed in the second half of the 1980s. During the same period, some researchers perfected the theory of decision trees used mainly for dealing with problems of classification. Statistics has always been about creating models for analysing data, and now there is the possibility of using computers to do it. From the second half of the 1980s, given the increasing importance of computational methods as the basis for statistical analysis, there was also a parallel development of statistical methods to analyse real multivariate applications. In the 1990s statisticians began showing interest in machine learning methods as well, which led to important developments in methodology.

Towards the end of the 1980s machine learning methods started to be used beyond the fields of computing and artificial intelligence. In particular, they were used in database marketing applications where the available databases were used for elaborate and specific marketing campaigns. The term knowledge discovery in databases (KDD) was coined to describe all those methods that aimed to find relations and regularity among the observed data. Gradually the term KDD was expanded to describe the whole process of extrapolating information from a database, from the identification of the initial business aims to the application of the decision rules. The term 'data mining' was used to describe the component of the KDD process where the learning algorithms were applied to the data.

This terminology was first formally put forward by Usama Fayaad at the First International Conference on Knowledge Discovery and Data Mining, held in Montreal in 1995 and still considered one of the main conferences on this topic. It was used to refer to a set of integrated analytical techniques divided into several phases with the aim of extrapolating previously unknown knowledge from massive sets of observed data that do not appear to have any obvious regularity or important relationships. As the term 'data mining' slowly established itself, it became a synonym for the whole process of extrapolating knowledge. This is the meaning we shall use in this text. The previous definition omits one important aspect – the ultimate aim of data mining. In data mining the aim is to obtain results that can be measured in terms of their relevance for the owner of the database – business advantage. Here is a more complete definition of data mining:

Data mining is the process of selection, exploration, and modelling of large quantities of data to discover regularities or relations that are at first unknown with the aim of obtaining clear and useful results for the owner of the database.

In a business context the utility of the result becomes a business result in itself. Therefore what distinguishes data mining from statistical analysis is not so much the amount of data we analyse or the methods we use but that we integrate what we know about the database, the means of analysis and the business knowledge. To apply a data mining methodology means following an integrated methodological process that involves translating the business needs into a problem which has to be analysed, retrieving the database needed to carry out the analysis, and applying a statistical technique implemented in a computer algorithm with the final aim of achieving important results useful for taking a strategic decision. The strategic decision will itself create new measurement needs and consequently new business needs, setting off what has been called 'the virtuous circle of knowledge' induced by data mining (Berry and Linoff, 1997).

Data mining is not just about the use of a computer algorithm or a statistical technique; it is a process of business intelligence that can be used together with what is provided by information technology to support company decisions.

1.1.1   Data mining and computing

The emergence of data mining is closely connected to developments in computer technology, particularly the evolution and organisation of databases, which have recently made great leaps forward. I am now going to clarify a few terms.

Query and reporting tools are simple and very quick to use; they help us explore business data at various levels. Query tools retrieve the information and reporting tools present it clearly. They allow the results of analyses to be transmitted across a client-server network, intranet or even on the internet. The networks allow sharing, so that the data can be analysed by the most suitable platform. This makes it possible to exploit the analytical potential of remote servers and receive an analysis report on local PCs. A client-server network must be flexible enough to satisfy all types of remote requests, from a simple reordering of data to ad hoc queries using Structured Query Language (SQL) for extracting and summarising data in the database.

Data retrieval, like data mining, extracts interesting data and information from archives and databases. The difference is that, unlike data mining, the criteria for extracting information are decided beforehand so they are exogenous from the extraction itself. A classic example is a request from the marketing department of a company to retrieve all the personal details of clients who have bought product A and product B at least once in that order. This request may be based on the idea that there is some connection between having bought A and B together at least once but without any empirical evidence. The names obtained from this exploration could then be the targets of the next publicity campaign. In this way the success percentage (i.e. the customers who will actually buy the products advertised compared to the total customers contacted) will definitely be much higher than otherwise. Once again, without a preliminary statistical analysis of the data, it is difficult to predict the success percentage and it is impossible to establish whether having better information about the customers' characteristics would give improved results with a smaller campaign effort.

Data mining is different from data retrieval because it looks for relations and associations between phenomena that are not known beforehand. It also allows the effectiveness of a decision to be judged on the data, which allows a rational evaluation to be made, and on the objective data available. Do not confuse data mining with methods used to create multidimensional reporting tools, e.g. online analytical processing (OLAP). OLAP is usually a graphical instrument used to highlight relations between the variables available following the logic of a two-dimensional report. Unlike OLAP, data mining brings together all the variables available and combines them in different ways. It also means we can go beyond the visual representation of the summaries in OLAP applications, creating useful models for the business world. Data mining is not just about analysing data; it is a much more complex process where data analysis is just one of the aspects.

OLAP is an important tool for business intelligence. The query and reporting tools describe what a database contains (in the widest sense this includes the data warehouse), but OLAP is used to explain why certain relations exist. The user makes his own hypotheses about the possible relations between the variables and he looks for confirmation of his opinion by observing the data. Suppose he wants to find out why some debts are not paid back; first he might suppose that people with a low income and lots of debts are high-risk categories. So he can check his hypothesis, OLAP gives him a graphical representation (called a multidimensional hypercube) of the empirical relation between the income, debt and insolvency variables. An analysis of the graph can confirm his hypothesis.

Therefore OLAP also allows the user to extract information that is useful for business databases. Unlike data mining, the research hypotheses are suggested by the user and are not uncovered from the data. Furthermore, the extrapolation is a purely computerised procedure; no use is made of modelling tools or summaries provided by the statistical methodology. OLAP can provide useful information for databases with a small number of variables, but problems arise when there are tens or hundreds of variables. Then it becomes increasingly difficult and time-consuming to find a good hypothesis and analyse the database with OLAP tools to confirm or deny it.

OLAP is not a substitute for data mining; the two techniques are complementary and used together they can create useful synergies. OLAP can be used in the preprocessing stages of data mining. This makes understanding the data easier, because it becomes possible to focus on the most important data, identifying special cases or looking for principal interrelations. The final data mining results, expressed using specific summary variables, can be easily represented in an OLAP hypercube.

We can summarise what we have said so far in a simple sequence that shows the evolution of business intelligence tools used to extrapolate knowledge from a database:

QUERY AND REPORTING $\longrightarrow$ DATA RETRIEVAL $\longrightarrow$ OLAP

$\longrightarrow$ DATA MINING

Query and reporting has the lowest information capacity and data mining has the highest information capacity. Query and reporting is easiest to implement and data mining is hardest to implement. This suggests a trade-off between information capacity and ease of implementation. The choice of tool must also consider the specific needs of the business and the characteristics of the company's information system. Lack of information is one of the greatest obstacles to achieving efficient data mining. Very often a database is created for reasons that have nothing to do with data mining, so the important information may be missing. Incorrect data is another problem.

The creation of a data warehouse can eliminate many of these problems. Efficient organisation of the data in a data warehouse coupled with efficient and scalable data mining allows the data to be used correctly and efficiently to support company decisions.

1.1.2 Data mining and statistics

Statistics has always been about creating methods to analyse data. The main difference between statistical methods and machine learning methods is that statistical methods are usually developed in relation to the data being analysed but also according to a conceptual reference paradigm. Although this has made the statistical methods coherent and rigorous, it has also limited their ability to adapt quickly to the new methodologies arising from new information technology and new machine learning applications. Statisticians have recently shown an interest in data mining and this could help its development.

For a long time statisticians saw data mining as a synonymous with 'data fishing', 'data dredging' or 'data snooping'. In all these cases data mining had negative connotations. This idea came about because of two main criticisms. First, there is not just one theoretical reference model but several models in competition with each other; these models are chosen depending on the data being examined. The criticism of this procedure is that it is always possible to find a model, however complex, which will adapt well to the data. Second, the great amount of data available may lead to non-existent relations being found among the data.

Although these criticisms are worth considering, we shall see that the modern methods of data mining pay great attention to the possibility of generalising results. This means that when choosing a model, the predictive performance is considered and the more complex models are penalised. It is difficult to ignore the fact that many important findings are not known beforehand and cannot be used in developing a research hypothesis. This happens in particular when there are large databases.

This last aspect is one of the characteristics that distinguishes data mining from statistical analysis. Whereas statistical analysis traditionally concerns itself with analysing primary data that has been collected to check specific research hypotheses, data mining can also concern itself with secondary data collected for other reasons. This is the norm, for example, when analysing company data that comes from a data warehouse. Furthermore, statistical data can be experimental data (perhaps the result of an experiment which randomly allocates all the statistical units to different kinds of treatment), but in data mining the data is typically observational data.

Berry and Linoff (1997) distinguish two analytical approaches to data mining. They differentiate top-down analysis (confirmative) and bottom-up analysis (explorative). Top-down analysis aims to confirm or reject hypotheses and tries to widen our knowledge of a partially understood phenomenon; it achieves this principally by using the traditional statistical methods. Bottom-up analysis is where the user looks for useful information previously unnoticed, searching through the data and looking for ways of connecting it to create hypotheses. The bottom-up approach is typical of data mining. In reality the two approaches are complementary. In fact, the information obtained from a bottom-up analysis, which identifies important relations and tendencies, cannot explain why these discoveries are useful and to what extent they are valid. The confirmative tools of top-down analysis can be used to confirm the discoveries and evaluate the quality of decisions based on those discoveries.

There are at least three other aspects that distinguish statistical data analysis from data mining. First, data mining analyses great masses of data. This implies new considerations for statistical analysis. For many applications it is impossible to analyse or even access the whole database for reasons of computer efficiency. Therefore it becomes necessary to have a sample of the data from the database being examined. This sampling must take account of the data mining aims, so it cannot be performed using traditional statistical theory. Second many databases do not lead to the classic forms of statistical data organisation, for example, data that comes from the internet. This creates a need for appropriate analytical methods from outside the field of statistics. Third, data mining results must be of some consequence. This means that constant attention must be given to business results achieved with the data analysis models.

In conclusion there are reasons for believing that data mining is nothing new from a statistical viewpoint. But there are also reasons to support the idea that, because of their nature, statistical methods should be able to study and formalise the methods used in data mining. This means that on one hand we need to look at the problems posed by data mining from a viewpoint of statistics and utility, while on the other hand we need to develop a conceptual paradigm that allows the statisticians to lead the data mining methods back to a scheme of general and coherent analysis.

1.2   The data mining process

Data mining is a series of activities from defining objectives to evaluating results. Here are its seven phases:

A.   Definition of the objectives for analysis
B.   Selection, organisation and pretreatment of the data
C.   Exploratory analysis of the data and subsequent transformation
D.   Specification of the statistical methods to be used in the analysis phase
E.   Analysis of the data based on the chosen methods

F. Evaluation and comparison of the methods used and the choice of the final model for analysis

G. Interpretation of the chosen model and its subsequent use in decision processes

Definition of the objectives

Definition of the objectives involves defining the aims of the analysis. It is not always easy to define the phenomenon we want to analyse. In fact, the company objectives that we are aiming for are usually clear, but the underlying problems can be difficult to translate into detailed objectives that need to be analysed. A clear statement of the problem and the objectives to be achieved are the prerequisites for setting up the analysis correctly. This is certainly one of the most difficult parts of the process since what is established at this stage determines how the subsequent method is organised. Therefore the objectives must be clear and there must be no room for doubts or uncertainties.

Organisation of the data

Once the objectives of the analysis have been identified, it is necessary to select the data for the analysis. First of all it is necessary to identify the data sources. Usually data is taken from internal sources that are cheaper and more reliable. This data also has the advantage of being the result of experiences and procedures of the company itself. The ideal data source is the company data warehouse, a storeroom of historical data that is no longer subject to changes and from which it is easy to extract topic databases, or data marts, of interest. If there is no data warehouse then the data marts must be created by overlapping the different sources of company data.

In general, the creation of data marts to be analysed provides the fundamental input for the subsequent data analysis. It leads to a representation of the data, usually in a tabular form known as a data matrix, that is based on the analytical needs and the previously established aims. Once a data matrix is available it is often necessary to carry out a preliminary cleaning of the data. In other words, a quality control is carried out on the available data, known as data cleansing. It is a formal process used to highlight any variables that exist but which are not suitable for analysis. It is also an important check on the contents of the variables and the possible presence of missing, or incorrect data. If any essential information is missing, it will then be necessary to review the phase that highlights the source.

Finally, it is often useful to set up an analysis on a subset or sample of the available data. This is because the quality of the information collected from the complete analysis across the whole available data mart is not always better than the information obtained from an investigation of the samples. In fact, in data mining the analysed databases are often very large, so using a sample of the data reduces the analysis time. Working with samples allows us to check the model's validity against the rest of the data, giving an important diagnostic tool. It also reduces the risk that the statistical method might adapt to irregularities and lose its ability to generalise and forecast.

Exploratory analysis of the data

Exploratory analysis of the data involves a preliminary exploratory analysis of
the data, very similar to OLAP techniques. An initial evaluation of the data's
importance can lead to a transformation of the original variables to better understand the phenomenon or it can lead to statistical methods based on satisfying
specific initial hypotheses. Exploratory analysis can highlight any anomalous
data – items that are different from the rest. These items data will not necessarily be eliminated because they might contain information that is important to
achieve the objectives of the analysis. I think that an exploratory analysis of the
data is essential because it allows the analyst to predict which statistical methods
might be most appropriate in the next phase of the analysis. This choice must
obviously bear in mind the quality of the data obtained from the previous phase.
The exploratory analysis might also suggest the need for new extraction of data
because the data collected is considered insufficient to achieve the set aims. The
main exploratory methods for data mining will be discussed in Chapter 3.

Specification of statistical methods

There are various statistical methods that can be used and there are also many
algorithms, so it is important to have a classification of the existing methods.
The choice of method depends on the problem being studied or the type of data
available. The data mining process is guided by the applications. For this reason
the methods used can be classified according to the aim of the analysis. Then we
can distinguish three main classes:

- *Descriptive methods*: aim to describe groups of data more briefly; they are
  also called symmetrical, unsupervised or indirect methods. Observations may
  be classified into groups not known beforehand (cluster analysis, Kohonen
  maps); variables may be connected among themselves according to links
  unknown beforehand (association methods, log-linear models, graphical models). In this way all the variables available are treated at the same level and
  there are no hypotheses of causality. Chapters 4 and 5 give examples of
  these methods.
- *Predictive methods*: aim to describe one or more of the variables in relation
  to all the others; they are also called asymmetrical, supervised or direct methods. This is done by looking for rules of classification or prediction based on
  the data. These rules help us to predict or classify the future result of one or
  more response or target variables in relation to what happens to the explanatory or input variables. The main methods of this type are those developed
  in the field of machine learning such as the neural networks (multilayer perceptrons) and decision trees but also classic statistical models such as linear
  and logistic regression models. Chapters 4 and 5 both illustrate examples of
  these methods.
- *Local methods*: aim to identify particular characteristics related to subset
  interests of the database; descriptive methods and predictive methods are
  global rather than local. Examples of local methods are association rules for

analysing transactional data, which we shall look at in Chapter 4, and the iden- tification of anomalous observations (outliers), also discussed in Chapter 4.

I think this classification is exhaustive, especially from a functional viewpoint. Further distinctions are discussed in the literature. Each method can be used on its own or as one stage in a multistage analysis.

Data analysis
Once the statistical methods have been specified, they must be translated into appropriate algorithms for computing calculations that help us synthesise the results we need from the available database. The wide range of specialised and non-specialised software for data mining means that for most standard applica- tions it is not necessary to develop ad hoc algorithms; the algorithms that come with the software should be sufficient. Nevertheless, those managing the data mining process should have a sound knowledge of the different methods as well as the software solutions, so they can adapt the process to the specific needs of the company and interpret the results correctly when taking decisions.

Evaluation of statistical methods
To produce a final decision it is necessary to choose the best model of data analysis from the statistical methods available. Therefore the choice of the model and the final decision rule are based on a comparison of the results obtained with the different methods. This is an important diagnostic check on the validity of the specific statistical methods that are then applied to the available data. It is possible that none of the methods used permits the set of aims to be achieved satisfactorily. Then it will be necessary to go back and specify a new method that is more appropriate for the analysis.

When evaluating the performance of a specific method, as well as diagnostic measures of a statistical type, other things must be considered such as time constraints, resource constraints, data quality and data availability. In data mining it is rarely a good idea to use just one statistical method to analyse the data. Different methods have the potential to highlight different aspects, aspects which might otherwise have been ignored.

To choose the best final model it is necessary to apply and compare various techniques quickly and simply, to compare the results produced and then give a business evaluation of the different rules created.

Implementation of the methods
Data mining is not just an analysis of the data, it is also the integration of the results into the decision process of the company. Business knowledge, the extraction of rules and their participation in the decision process allow us to move from the analytical phase to the production of a decision engine. Once the model has been chosen and tested with a data set, the classification rule can be applied to the whole reference population. For example we will be able to distinguish beforehand which customers will be more profitable or we can

calibrate differentiated commercial policies for different target consumer groups, thereby increasing the profits of the company.

Having seen the benefits we can get from data mining, it is crucial to implement the process correctly to exploit its full potential. The inclusion of the data mining process in the company organisation must be done gradually, setting out realistic aims and looking at the results along the way. The final aim is for data mining to be fully integrated with the other activities that are used to back up company decisions.

This process of integration can be divided into four phases:

- *Strategic phase*: in this first phase we study the business procedure being used in order to identify where data mining could give most benefits. The results at the end of this phase are the definition of the business objectives for a pilot data mining project and the definition of criteria to evaluate the project itself.

- *Training phase*: this phase allows us to evaluate the data mining activity more carefully. A pilot project is set up and the results are assessed using the objectives and the criteria established in the previous phase. The choice of the pilot project is a fundamental aspect. It must be simple and easy to use but important enough to create interest. If the pilot project is positive, there are two possible results: the preliminary evaluation of the utility of the different data mining techniques and the definition of a prototype data mining system.

- *Creation phase*: if the positive evaluation of the pilot project results in implementing a complete data mining system, it will then be necessary to establish a detailed plan to reorganise the business procedure to include the data mining activity. More specifically, it will be necessary to reorganise the business database with the possible creation of a data warehouse; to develop the previous data mining prototype until we have an initial operational version; and to allocate personnel and time to follow the project.

- *Migration phase*: at this stage all we need to do is prepare the organisation appropriately so the data mining process can be successfully integrated. This means teaching likely users the potential of the new system and increasing their trust in the benefits it will bring. This means constantly evaluating (and communicating) the efficient results obtained from the data mining process.

For data mining to be considered a valid process within a company, it needs to involve at least three different people with strong communication and interactive skills:

- Business experts, to set the objectives and interpret the results of data mining
- Information technology experts, who know about the data and technologies needed
- Experts in statistical methods for the data analysis phase

1.3 Software for data mining

A data mining project requires adequate software to perform the analysis. Most software systems only implement specific techniques; they can be seen as specialised software systems for statistical data analysis. But because the aim of data mining is to look for relations that are previously unknown and to compare the available methods of analysis, I do not think these specialised systems are suitable.

Valid data mining software should create an integrated data mining system that allows the use and comparison of different techniques; it should also integrate with complex database management software. Few such systems exist. Most of the available options are listed on the website www.kdnuggets.com/.

This book makes many references to the SAS software, so here is a brief description of the integrated SAS data mining software called Enterprise Miner (SAS Institute, 2001). Most of the processing presented in the case studies is carried out using this system as well as other SAS software models.

To plan, implement and successfully set up a data mining project it is necessary to have an integrated software solution that includes all the phases of the analytical process. These go from sampling the data, through the analytical and modelling phases, and up to the publication of the resulting business information. Furthermore, the ideal solution should be user-friendly, intuitive and flexible enough to allow the user with little experience in statistics to understand and use it.

The SAS Enterprise Miner software is a solution of this kind. It comes from SAS's long experience in the production of software tools for data analysis, and since it appeared on the market in 1998 it has become worldwide leader in this field. It brings together the system of statistical analysis and SAS reporting with a graphical user interface (GUI) that is easy to use and can be understood by company analysts and statistics experts.

The GUI elements can be used to implement the data mining methods developed by the SAS Institute, the SEMMA method. This method sets out some basic data mining elements without imposing a rigid and predetermined route for the project. It provides a logical process that allows business analysts and statistics experts to achieve the aims of the data mining projects by choosing the elements of the GUI they need. The visual representation of this structure is a process flow diagram (PFD) that graphically illustrates the steps taken to complete a single data mining project.

The SEMMA method defined by the SAS Institute is a general reference structure that can be used to organise the phases of the data mining project. Schematically the SEMMA method set out by the SAS consists of a series of 'steps' that must be followed to complete the data analysis, steps which are perfectly integrated with SAS Enterprise Miner. SEMMA is an acronym that stands for 'sample, explore, modify, model and assess:

- *Sample*: this extracts a part of the data that is large enough to contain important information and small enough to be analysed quickly.

- *Explore*: the data is examined to find beforehand any relations and abnormalities and to understand which data could be of interest.
- *Modify and model*: these phases seek the important variables and the models that provide information contained in the data.
- *Assess*: this assesses the utility and the reliability of the information discovered by the data mining process. The rules from the models are applied to the real environment of the analysis.

1.4 Organisation of the book

This book is divided into two complementary parts. The first part describes the methodology and systematically treats data mining as a process of database analysis that tries to produce results which can be immediately used for decision making. The second part contains some case studies that illustrate data mining in real business applications. Figure 1.1 shows this organisation. Phases B, C, D

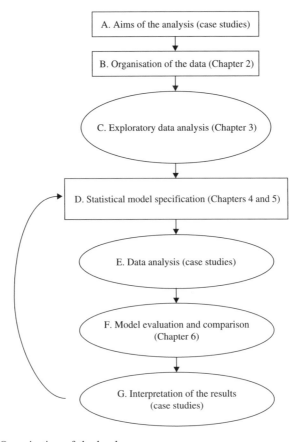

Figure 1.1 Organisation of the book.

and F receive one chapter each in the first part of the book; phases A, E and G will be discussed in depth in the second part of the book. Let us now look in greater detail at the two parts.

1.4.1   Chapters 2 to 6: methodology

The first part of the book illustrates the main methodologies. Chapter 2 illustrates the main aspects related to the organisation of the data. It looks at the creation of a ready-to-analyse database, starting from examples of available structures – the data warehouse, the data webhouse, and the data mart – which can be easily transformed for statistical analysis. It introduces the important distinction between types of data, which can be quantitative and qualitative, nominal and ordinal, discrete and continuous. Data types are particularly important when specifying a model for analysis. The data matrix, which is the base structure of the statistical analysis, is discussed. Further on we look at some transformations of the matrix. Finally, other more complex data organisation structures are briefly discussed.

Chapter 3 sets out the most important aspects of exploratory data analysis. It explains concepts and illustrates them with examples. It begins with univariate analysis and moves on to multivariate analysis. Two important topics are reducing the size of the data and analysing qualitative data.

Chapters 4 and 5 describe the main methods used in data mining. We have used the 'historical' distinction between methods that do not require a proba-bilistic formulation (computational methods), many of which have emerged from machine learning, and methods that require a probabilistic formulation (statistical models), which developed in the field of statistics.

The main computational methods illustrated in Chapter 4 are cluster analysis, decision trees and neural networks, both supervised and unsupervised. Finally, 'local' methods of data mining are introduced, and we will be looking at the most important of these, association and sequence rules. The methods illustrated in Chapter 5 follow the temporal evolution of multivariate statistical methods: from models of linear regression to generalised linear models that contain models of logistic and log-linear regression to reach graphical models.

Chapter 6 discusses comparison and evaluation of the different models for data mining. It introduces the concept of discrepancy between statistical methods then goes on to discuss the most important evaluation criteria and the choice between the different models: statistical tests, criteria based on scoring functions, Bayesian criteria, computational criteria and criteria based on loss functions.

1.4.2   Chapters 7 to 12: business cases

There are many applications for data mining. We shall discuss six of the most frequent applications in the business field, from the most traditional (customer rela-tionship management) to the most recent and innovative (web clickstream analysis).

Chapter 7 looks at market basket analysis. It examines statistical methods for analysing sales figures in order to understand which products were bought together. This type of information makes it possible to increase sales of products by improving the customer offering and promoting sales of other products associated with that offering.

Chapter 8 looks at web clickstream analysis. It shows how information on the order in which the pages of a website are visited can be used to predict the visiting behaviour of the site. The data analysed corresponds to an e-commerce site and therefore it becomes possible to establish which pages influence electronic shopping of particular products.

Chapter 9 looks at web profiling. Here we analyse data referring to the pages visited in a website, leading to a classification of those who visited the site based on their behaviour profile. With this information it is possible to get a behavioural segmentation of the users that can later be used when making marketing decisions.

Chapter 10 looks at customer relationship management. Some statistical methods are used to identify groups of homogeneous customers in terms of buying behaviour and socio-demographic characteristics. Identification of the different types of customer makes it possible to draw up a personalised marketing campaign, to assess its effects and to look at how the offer can be changed.

Chapter 11 looks at credit scoring. Credit scoring is an example of the scoring procedure that in general gives a score to each statistical unit (customer, debtor, business, etc.) In particular, the aim of credit scoring is to associate each debtor with a numeric value that represents their credit worth. In this way it is possible to decide whether or not to give someone credit based on their score.

Chapter 12 looks at prediction of TV shares. Some statistical linear models as well as others based on neural networks are presented to predict TV audiences in prime time on Italian TV. A company that sells advertising space can carry out an analysis of the audience to decide which advertisements to broadcast during certain programmes and at what time.

1.5   Further reading

Since data mining is a recent discipline and is still undergoing great changes there are many sources of further reading. As well as the large number of technical reports about the commercial software available, there are several articles available in specialised scientific journals as well as numerous thematic volumes. But there are still few complete texts on the topic. The bibliography lists relevant English-language books on data mining. Part of the material in this book is an elaboration from a book in Italian by myself (Giudici, 2001b). Here are the texts that have been most useful in writing this book.

For the methodology

- Jiawei Han and Micheline Kamber, *Data Mining: Concepts and Techniques*, Morgan Kaufmann, 2001

- David J. Hand, Heikki Mannila and Padhraic Smyth, *Principles of Data Mining*, MIT Press, 2001
- Trevor Hastie, Robert Tibshirani and Jerome Friedman, *The Elements of Statistical Learning: Data Mining, Inference and Prediction.* Springer-Verlag, 2001

For the applications

- Olivia Par Rudd, *Data Mining Cookbook*, John Wiley & Sons, 2001
- Michael Berry and Gordon Lindoff, *Data Mining Techniques for Marketing, Sales and Customer Support*, John Wiley & Sons, 2000
- Michael Berry and Gordon Lindoff, *Mastering Data Mining*, John Wiley & Sons, 1997

One specialised scientific journal worth mentioning is *Knowledge Discovery and Data Mining*; it is the most important review for the whole sector. For introductions and synthesis on data mining see the papers by Fayyad *et al.* (1996), Hand *et al.* (2000) and Giudici, Heckerman and Whittaker (2001).

The internet is another important source of information. There are many sites dedicated to specific applications of data mining. This can make research using search engines quite slow. These two websites have a good number of links:

- www.kdnuggets.com/
- www.dmreview.com/

There are many conferences on data mining that are often an important source of information and a way to keep up to date with the latest developments. Information about conferences can be found on the internet using search engines.

PART I

Methodology

CHAPTER 2

Organisation of the data

Data analysis requires that the data is organised into an ordered database, but I do not explain how to create a database in this text. The way data is analysed depends greatly on how the data is organised within the database. In our information society there is an abundance of data and a growing need for an efficient way of analysing it. However, an efficient analysis presupposes a valid organisation of the data.

It has become strategic for all medium and large companies to have a unified information system called a data warehouse; this integrates, for example, the accounting data with data arising from the production process, the contacts with the suppliers (supply chain management), and the sales trends and the contacts with the customers (customer relationship management). This makes it possible to get precious information for business management. Another example is the increasing diffusion of electronic trade and commerce and, consequently, the abundance of data about websites visited along with any payment transactions. In this case it is essential for the service supplier, through the internet, to understand who the customers are in order to plan offers. This can be done if the transactions (which correspond to clicks on the web) are transferred to an ordered database, usually called a webhouse, that can later be analysed.

Furthermore, since the information that can be extracted from a data mining process (data analysis) depends on how the data is organised, it is very important to involve the data analyst when setting up the database. Frequently, though, the analyst finds himself with a database that has already been prepared. It is then his job to understand how it has been set up and how best it can be used to meet the needs of the customer. When faced with poorly set up databases it is a good idea to ask for them to be reviewed rather than trying laboriously to extract information that might be of little use.

This chapter looks at how database structure affects data analysis, how a database can be transformed for statistical analysis, and how data can be classified and put into a so-called data matrix. It considers how sometimes it may be a good idea to transform a data matrix in terms of binary variables, frequency distributions, or in other ways. Finally, it looks at examples of more complex data structures.

Applied Data Mining.   Paolo Giudici
© 2003 John Wiley & Sons, Ltd   ISBNs: 0-470-84679-8 (Paper); 0-470-84678-X (Cloth)

2.1   From the data warehouse to the data marts

The creation of a valid database is the first and most important operation that must be carried out in order to obtain useful information from the data mining process. This is often the most expensive part of the process in terms of the resources that have to be allocated and the time needed for implementation and development. Although I cover it only briefly, this is an important topic and I advise you to consult other texts for more information, e.g. Berry and Linoff (1997), Han and Kamber (2001) and Hand, Mannila and Smyth (2001). I shall now describe examples of three database structures for data mining analysis: the data warehouse, the data webhouse and the data mart. The first two are complex data structures, but the data mart is a simpler database that usually derives from other data structures (e.g. from operational and transactional databases, but also from the data warehouse) that are ready to be analysed.

2.1.1   The data warehouse

According to Immon (1996), a data warehouse is 'an integrated collection of data about a collection of subjects (units), which is not volatile in time and can support decisions taken by the management'.

From this definition, the first characteristic of a data warehouse is the orientation to the subjects. This means that data in a data warehouse should be divided according to subjects rather than by business. For example, in the case of an insurance company the data put into the data warehouse should probably be divided into Customer, Policy and Insurance Premium rather than into Civil Responsibility, Life and Accident. The second characteristic is data integration, and it is certainly the most important. The data warehouse must be able to integrate itself perfectly with the multitude of standards used by the different applications from which data is collected. For example, various operational business applications could codify the sex of the customer in different ways and the data warehouse must be able to recognise these standards unequivocally before going on to store the information.

Third, a data warehouse can vary in time since the temporal length of a data warehouse usually oscillates between 5 and 10 years; during this period the data collected is no more than a sophisticated series of instant photos taken at specific moments in time. At the same time, the data warehouse is not volatile because data is added rather than updated. In other words, the set of photos will not change each time the data is updated but it will simply be integrated with a new photo. Finally, a data warehouse must produce information that is relevant for management decisions.

This means a data warehouse is like a container of all the data needed to carry out business intelligence operations. It is the main difference between a data warehouse and other business databases. Trying to use the data contained in the operational databases to carry out relevant statistical analysis for the business (related to various management decisions) is almost impossible. On the other hand, a data warehouse is built with this specific aim in mind.

There are two ways to approach the creation of a data warehouse. The first is based on the creation of a single centralised archive that collects all the company information and integrates it with information coming from outside. The second approach brings together different thematic databases, called data marts, that are not initially connected among themselves, but which can evolve to create a perfectly interconnected structure. The first approach allows the system administrators to constantly control the quality of the data introduced. But it requires careful programming to allow for future expansion to receive new data and to connect to other databases. The second approach is initially easier to implement and is therefore the most popular solution at the moment. Problems arise when the various data marts are connected among each other, as it becomes necessary to make a real effort to define, clean and transform the data to obtain a sufficiently uniform level. That is until it becomes a data warehouse in the real sense of the word.

In a system that aims to preserve and distribute data, it is also necessary to include information about the organisation of the data itself. This data is called metadata and it can be used to increase the security levels inside the data warehouse. Although it may be desirable to allow vast access to information, some specific data marts and some details might require limited access. Metadata is also essential for management, organisation and the exploitation of the various activities. For an analyst it may be very useful to know how the profit variable was calculated, whether the sales areas were divided differently before a certain date, and how a multiperiod event was split in time. The metadata therefore helps to increase the value of the information present in the data warehouse because it becomes more reliable.

Another important component of a data warehouse system is a collection of data marts. A data mart is a thematic database, usually represented in a very simple form, that is specialised according to specific objectives (e.g. marketing purposes).

To summarise, a valid data warehouse structure should have the following components: (a) a centralised archive that becomes the storehouse of the data; (b) a metadata structure that describes what is available in the data warehouse and where it is; (c) a series of specific and thematic data marts that are easily accessible and which can be converted into statistical structures such as data matrices (Section 2.3). These components should make the data warehouse easily accessible for business intelligence needs, ranging from data querying and reporting to OLAP and data mining.

2.1.2   The data webhouse

The data warehouse developed rapidly during the 1990s, when it was very successful and accumulated widespread use. The advent of the web with its revolutionary impact has forced the data warehouse to adapt to new requirements. In this new era the data warehouse becomes a web data warehouse or, more simply, data webhouse. The web offers an immense source of data about people who use their browser to interact on websites. Despite the fact that most of the data related to the flow of users is very coarse and very simple, it gives detailed information about how internet users surf the net. This huge and undisciplined source can be transferred to the data webhouse, where it can be put together with more conventional sources of data that previously formed the data warehouse.

Another change concerns the way in which the data warehouse can be accessed. It is now possible to exploit all the interfaces of the business data warehouse that already exist through the web just by using the browser. With this it is possible to carry out various operations, from simple data entry to ad hoc queries through the web. In this way the data warehouse becomes completely distributed. Speed is a fundamental requirement in the design of a webhouse. However, in the data warehouse environment some requests need a long time before they will be satisfied. Slow time processing is intolerable in an environment based on the web. A webhouse must be quickly reachable at any moment and any interruption, however brief, must be avoided.

2.1.3 Data marts

A data mart is a thematic database that was originally oriented towards the marketing field. Indeed, its name is a contraction of marketing database. In this sense it can be considered a business archive that contains all the information connected to new and/or potential customers. In other words, it refers to a database that is completely oriented to managing customer relations. As we shall see, the analysis of customer relationship management data is probably the main field where data mining can be applied. In general, it is possible to extract from a data warehouse as many data marts as there are aims we want to achieve in a business intelligence analysis. However, a data mart can be created, although with some difficulty, even when there is no integrated warehouse system. The creation of thematic data structures like data marts represents the first and fundamental move towards an informative environment for the data mining activity. There is a case study in Chapter 10.

2.2 Classification of the data

Suppose we have a data mart at our disposal, which has been extracted from the databases available according to the aims of the analysis. From a statistical viewpoint, a data mart should be organised according to two principles: the statistical units, the elements in the reference population that are considered important for the aims of the analysis (e.g. the supply companies, the customers, the people who visit the site) and the statistical variables, the important characteristics, measured for each statistical unit (e.g. the amounts customers buy, the payment methods they use, the socio-demographic profile of each customer).

The statistical units can refer to the whole reference population (e.g. all the customers of the company) or they can be a sample selected to represent the whole population. There is a large body of work on the statistical theory of sampling and sampling strategies; for further information see Barnett (1975). If we consider an adequately representative sample rather than a whole population, there are several advantages. It might be expensive to collect complete information about the entire population and the analysis of great masses of data could waste a lot of time in analysing and interpreting the results (think about the enormous databases of daily telephone calls available to mobile phone companies).

The statistical variables are the main source of information to work on in order to extract conclusions about the observed units and eventually to extend these conclusions to a wider population. It is good to have a large number of variables to achieve these aims, but there are two main limits to having an excessively large number. First of all, for efficient and stable analyses the variables should not duplicate information. For example, the presence of the customers' annual income makes monthly income superfluous. Furthermore, for each statistical unit the data should be correct for all the variables considered. This is difficult when there are many variables, because some data can go missing; missing data causes problems for the analysis.

Once the units and the interest variables in the statistical analysis of the data have been established, each observation is related to a statistical unit, and a distinct value (level) for each variable is assigned. This process is known as classification. In general it leads to two different types of variable: qualitative and quantitative. Qualitative variables are typically expressed as an adjectival phrase, so they are classified into levels, sometimes known as categories. Some examples of qualitative variables are sex, postal code and brand preference. Qualitative data is nominal if it appears in different categories but in no particular order; qualitative data is ordinal if the different categories have an order that is either explicit or implicit.

The measurement at a nominal level allows us to establish a relation of equality or inequality between the different levels ($=$, $\neq$) . Examples of nominal measurements are the eye colour of a person and the legal status of a company. Ordinal measurements allow us to establish an order relation between the different categories but they do not allow any significant numeric assertion (or metric) on the difference between the categories. More precisely, we can affirm which category is bigger or better but we cannot say by how much ($=$, $>$, $<$). Examples of ordinal measurements are the computing skills of a person and the credit rate of a company.

Quantitative variables are linked to intrinsically numerical quantities, such as age and income. It is possible to establish connections and numerical relations among their levels. They can be divided into discrete quantitative variables when they have a finite number of levels, and continuous quantitative variables if the levels cannot be counted. A discrete quantitative variable is the number of telephone calls received in a day; a continuous quantitative variable is the annual revenues of a company.

Very often the ordinal level of a qualitative variable is marked with a number. This does not transform the qualitative variable into a quantitative variable, so it is not possible to establish connections and relations between the levels themselves.

2.3 The data matrix

Once the data and the variables have been classified into the four main types (qualitative nominal, qualitative ordinal, quantitative discrete and quantitative continuous), the database must be transformed into a structure that is ready for statistical analysis. In the case of thematic databases this structure can be described by a data matrix. The data matrix is a table that is usually two-dimensional, where the rows represent the n statistical units considered and the columns represent the p statistical variables considered. Therefore the generic element (i, j) of the matrix ($i = 1, \ldots, n$ and $j = 1, \ldots, p$) is a classification of the data related to the statistical unit i according to the level of the jth variable, as in Table 2.1.

The data matrix is the point where data mining starts. In some cases, such as a joint analysis of quantitative variables, it acts as the input of the analysis phase. Other cases require pre-analysis phases (preprocessing or data transformation). This leads to tables derived from data matrices. For example, in the joint analysis of qualitative variables, since it is impossible to carry out a quantitative analysis directly on the data matrix, it is a good idea to transform the data matrix into a contingency table. This is a table with as many dimensions as there are qualitative variables considered. Each dimension is indexed by the level observed by the corresponding variable. Within each cell in the table we put the joint frequency of the corresponding crossover of the levels. We shall discuss this in more detail in the context of representing the statistical variables in frequency distributions.

Table 2.2 is a real example of a data matrix. Lack of space means we can only see some of the 1000 lines included in the table and only some of the 21 columns. Chapter 11 will describe and analyse this table.

Table 2.1 The data matrix.

	1	$\cdots$	j	$\cdots$	p
1	$X_{1,1}$		$X_{1,j}$		$X_{1,p}$
$\vdots$					
i	$X_{i,1}$		$X_{i,j}$		$X_{i,p}$
$\vdots$					
n	$X_{n,1}$		$X_{n,j}$		$X_{n,p}$

Table 2.2 Example of a data matrix.

	Y	X1	X2	$\cdots$	X3	$\cdots$	X20
N 1	1	1	18	$\cdots$	1049	$\cdots$	1
$\vdots$							
N 34	1	4	24	$\cdots$	1376	$\cdots$	1
$\vdots$							
N 1000	0	1	30	$\cdots$	6350	$\cdots$	1

Table 2.3 Example of binarisation.

	Y	X1	X2	X3
1	1	1	0	0
2	3	0	0	1
3	1	1	0	0
4	2	0	1	0
5	3	0	0	1
6	1	1	0	0

2.3.1 Binarisation of the data matrix

If the variables in the data matrix are all quantitative, including some continuous ones, it is easier and simpler to treat the matrix as input without any pre-analysis. But if the variables are all qualitative or discrete quantitative, it is necessary to transform the data matrix into a contingency table (with more than one dimension). This is not necessarily a good idea if p is large. If the variables in the data matrix belong to both types, it is best to transform the variables into the minority type, bringing them to the level of the others. For example, if most of the variables are qualitative and there are some quantitative variables, some of which are continuous, contingency tables will be used, preceded by the discretisation of the continuous variables into interval classes. This results in a loss of information.

If most of the variables are quantitative, the best solution is to make the qualitative variables metric. This is called binarisation. Consider a binary variable set to 0 in the presence of a certain level and 1 if this level is absent. We can define a distance for this variable, so it can be seen as a quantitative variable. In the binarisation approach, each qualitative variable is transformed into as many binary variables as there are levels of the same type. For example, if a qualitative variable X has r levels, then r binary variables will be created as follows: for the generic level i, the corresponding binary variable will be set to 1 when X is equal to i, otherwise it will be set to 0. Table 2.3 shows a qualitative variable with three levels (indicated by Y) transformed into the three binary variables X_1, X_2, X_3.

2.4 Frequency distributions

Often it seems natural to summarise statistical variables by the co-occurrence of their levels. A summary of this type is called a frequency distribution. In all procedures of this kind, the summary makes it easier to analyse and present the results, but it also leads to a loss of information. In the case of qualitative variables, the summary is justified by the need to carry out quantitative analysis on the data. In other situations, such as with quantitative variables, the summary is essentially to simplify the analysis and presentation of results.

2.4.1 Univariate distributions

First we will concentrate on univariate analysis, the analysis of a single variable. This simplifies presentation of results but it also simplifies the analytical method. It is easier to extract information from a database by beginning with univariate analysis and then moving on to multivariate analysis. Determining the univariate distribution frequency from the data matrix is often the first step in a univariate exploratory analysis. To create a frequency distribution for a variable it is necessary to know the number of times each level appears in the data. This number is called the absolute frequency. The levels and their frequencies give the frequency distribution.

The observations related to the variable being examined can be indicated as follows: $x_1, x_2, \ldots, x_N$, omitting the index related to the variable itself. The distinct values between the N observations (levels) are indicated as $x_1^*, x_2^*, \ldots, x_k^*$ ($k \leq N$). The frequency distribution is shown as in Table 2.4 where n_i indicates the number of times level x_i^* appears (its absolute frequency). Note that $\sum_{i=1}^{k} n_i = N$, where N is the number of classified units. Table 2.5 shows an example of a frequency distribution for a binary qualitative variable that will be analysed in Chapter 10.

It can be seen from Table 2.5 that the data at hand is fairly balanced between the two levels.

To make reading and interpretation easier, frequency distribution is usually presented with relative frequencies. The relative frequency of the level x_i^*, indicated by p_i, is defined by the relationship between the absolute frequency n_i and the total number of observations: $p_i = n_i/N$. Note that we have $\sum_{i=1}^{k} p_i = 1$.

Table 2.4 Univariate frequency distribution.

Levels	Absolute frequencies
x_1^*	n_1
x_2^*	n_2
$\vdots$	$\vdots$
x_k^*	n_k

Table 2.5 Example of a frequency distribution.

Levels	Absolute frequencies
0	1445
1	1006

Table 2.6 Univariate relative frequency distribution.

Levels	Relative frequencies
x_1^*	p_1
x_2^*	p_2
$\vdots$	$\vdots$
x_k^*	p_k

Table 2.7 Example of a univariate relative frequency distribution.

Modalities	Relative frequencies
0	0.59
1	0.41

The results are shown in Table 2.6. For the frequency distribution in Table 2.5 we obtain the relative frequencies in Table 2.7.

2.4.2 Multivariate distributions

Now we shall see how it is possible to create multivariate frequency distributions for the joint examination of more than one variable. We will look particularly at qualitative or discrete quantitative variables. For continuous quantitative multivariate variables, it is better to work directly with the data matrix. Multivariate frequency distributions are represented by a contingency table. For clarity, we will mainly consider the case where two variables are examined at a time. This creates a bivariate distribution having a contingency table with two dimensions.

Let X and Y be the two variables collected for N statistical units, which take on h levels for X, $x_1^*, \ldots, x_h^*$, and k levels for Y, $y_1^*, \ldots, y_k^*$. The result of the joint classification of the variables into a contingency table can be summarised by the pairs $\{(x_i^*, y_j^*), n_{xy}(x_i^*, y_j^*)\}$ where $n_{xy}(x_i^*, y_j^*)$ indicates the number of statistical units, among the N considered, where the level pair (x_i^*, y_j^*) is observed. The value indicated by $n_{xy}(x_i^*, y_j^*)$ is called the absolute joint frequency which refers to the (x_i^*, y_j^*) pair. For simplicity we will often refer to $n_{xy}(x_i^*, y_j^*)$ with the symbol n_{ij}.

Note that since $N = \sum_i \sum_j n_{xy}(x_i^*, y_j^*)$ is equal to the total number of classified units, we can get relative joint frequencies from the equation

$$p_{xy}(x_i, y_j) = \frac{n_{xy}(x_i^*, y_j^*)}{N}$$

Table 2.8   A two-way contingency table.

$X \backslash Y$	y_1^*	y_2^*	$\cdots$	y_j^*	$\cdots$	y_k^*	
x_1^*	$n_{xy}(x_1^*, y_1^*)$	$n_{xy}(x_1^*, y_2^*)$	$\cdots$	$n_{xy}(x_1^*, y_j^*)$	$\cdots$	$n_{xy}(x_1^*, y_k^*)$	$n_x(x_1^*)$
x_2^*	$n_{xy}(x_2^*, y_1^*)$	$n_{xy}(x_2^*, y_2^*)$	$\cdots$	$n_{xy}(x_2^*, y_j^*)$	$\cdots$	$n_{xy}(x_2^*, y_k^*)$	$n_x(x_2^*)$
$\vdots$	$\vdots$	$\vdots$	$\vdots$	$\vdots$	$\vdots$	$\vdots$	$\vdots$
x_i^*	$n_{xy}(x_i^*, y_1^*)$	$n_{xy}(x_i^*, y_2^*)$	$\cdots$	$n_{xy}(x_i^*, y_j^*)$	$\cdots$	$n_{xy}(x_i^*, y_k^*)$	$n_x(x_i^*)$
$\vdots$	$\vdots$	$\vdots$	$\vdots$	$\vdots$	$\vdots$	$\vdots$	$\vdots$
x_h^*	$n_{xy}(x_h^*, y_1^*)$	$n_{xy}(x_h^*, y_2^*)$	$\cdots$	$n_{xy}(x_h^*, y_j^*)$	$\cdots$	$n_{xy}(x_h^*, y_k^*)$	$n_x(x_h^*)$
	$n_y(y_1^*)$	$n_y(y_2^*)$	$\cdots$	$n_y(y_j^*)$	$\cdots$	$n_y(y_k^*)$	N

To classify the observations into a contingency table, we could mark the level of the variable X in the rows and the levels of the variable Y in the columns. In the table we will therefore include the joint frequencies, as shown in Table 2.8. Note that from the joint frequencies it is easy to get the marginal univariate frequencies of X and Y using the following equations:

$$n_X(x_i^*) = \sum_j n_{xy}(x_i^*, y_j^*)$$

$$n_Y(y_j^*) = \sum_i n_{xy}(x_i^*, y_j^*)$$

Table 2.8 reports absolute frequencies. It can also be expressed in terms of relative frequencies. This will lead to two analogous equations that determine marginal relative univariate frequencies.

From a joint frequency distribution it is also possible to determine h frequency distributions of the variable Y, conditioned on the h levels of X. Each of these, indicated by $(Y|X = x_i^*)$, shows the distribution frequency of Y only for the observations where $X = x_i$. For example, the frequency with which we observe $Y = y_1^*$ conditional on $X = x_i^*$ can be obtained from the ratio

$$p_{Y|X}(y_1^*|x_i^*) = \frac{p_{xy}(x_i^*, y_1^*)}{p_X(x_i^*)}$$

where p_{xy} indicates the distribution of the joint frequency of X and Y and p_X the distribution of the marginal frequency (unidimensional) of X. Similarly, we can get k frequency distributions of the X conditioned on the k levels of Y.

Statistical software makes it easy to create and analyse contingency tables. Consider a 2×2 table where X is the binary variable Npurchases (number of purchases) and $Y =$ South (referring to the geographic area where the customer comes from); we will look at this in more detail in Chapter 10. The output

Table 2.9 Example of a two-way
contingency table: NPURCHASES (rows)
by SOUTH (columns).

	0,	1,	Total
0 ,	1102 ,	343 ,	1445
	, 44.96 ,	13.99 ,	58.96
	, 76.26 ,	23.74 ,	
	, 57.40 ,	64.60 ,	
1 ,	818 ,	188 ,	1006
	, 33.37 ,	7.67 ,	41.04
	, 81.31 ,	18.69 ,	
	, 42.60 ,	35.40 ,	
Total	1920	531	2451
	78.34	21.66	100.00

in Table 2.9 shows the following four pieces of information, for each of the
four possible levels for X and Y: (a) absolute frequency of the pair; (b) relative
frequency of the pair; (c) conditional frequency of $X = x$, conditionally on the
Y row; (d) conditional frequency of $Y = y$, conditionally on the X column.

2.5   Transformation of the data

The transformation of the data matrix into univariate and multivariate frequency
distributions is not the only possible transformation. Other transformations can
also be very important to simplify the statistical analysis and/or the interpretation
of results. For example when the p variables of the data matrix are expressed
in different measurement units, it is a good idea to put all the variables into the
same measurement unit so that the different measurement scales do not affect
the results. This can be done using a linear transformation that standardises the
variables, taking away the average of each one and dividing it by the square root
of its variance. This produces a variable with a zero average and a unit variance.
There are other particularly interesting data transformations, such as the non-
linear Box–Cox transformation. The reader can find more on this in other books,
such as Han and Kamber (2001).

The transformation of data is also a way of solving problems with data quality,
perhaps because items are missing or because there are anomalous values, known
as outliers. There are two main ways to deal with missing data: (a) remove it,
(b) substitute it using the remaining data. Identifying anomalous values is often
a motivation for data mining in the first place. The discovery of anomalous
values requires a formal statistical analysis; an anomalous value can seldom

be eliminated as its existence often provides important information about the descriptive or predictive model connected to the data under examination. For example, in the analysis of fraud detections, perhaps related to telephone calls or credit cards, the aim is to identify suspicious behaviour. Han and Kamber (2001) provide more information on data quality and its problems.

2.6 Other data structures

Some data mining applications may require a thematic database not expressible in terms of the data matrix we have considered up to now. For example, there are often other aspects to be considered such as the time and space in which the data is collected. Often in this kind of application the data is aggregated or divided (e.g. into periods or regions); for more on this topic see Diggle, Liang and Zeger (1994).

The most important case refers to longitudinal data, for example, the surveys in n companies of the p budget variables in q successive years, or surveys of socio-economic indicators for the regions in a periodic (e.g. decennial) census. In this case there will be a three-way matrix which could be described by three dimensions, concerning n statistical units, p statistical variables and q times. Another important case is data related to different geographic areas. Here too there is a three-way matrix with space as the third dimension, for example, the sales of a company in different regions or the satellite surveys of the environmental characteristics of different regions. In both these cases, data mining should be accompanied by specific methods from time series analysis (Chatfield, 1996) or from spatial data analysis (Cressie, 1991).

Developments in the information society have meant that data is now wider-ranging and increasingly complex; it is not structured and that makes it difficult to represent in the form of data matrices (even in extended forms as in the previous cases). Three important examples are text data, web data and multimedia data. Text databases consist of a mass of text documents usually connected by logical relations. Web data is contained in log files that describe what each visitor to a website does during his interaction with the site. Multimedia data can be made up of texts, images, sounds and other forms of audio-visual information that are typically downloaded from the internet and that describe an interaction with the website more complex than the previous example. This type of data analysis creates a more complex situation. The first difficulty concerns the organisation of the data; that is an important and very modern topic of research (e.g. Han and Kamber, 2001). There are still very few statistical applications for analysing this data. Chapter 8 tries to provide a statistical contribution to the analysis of these important problems; it shows how an appropriate analysis of the web data contained in the log file can give us important data mining results about access to websites.

Another important type of complex data structure arises from the integration of different databases. In the modern applications of data mining it is often necessary to combine data that comes from different sources of data; one example is the integration of official statistics from the European Statistics Office, Eurostat. Up to now this data fusion problem has been discussed mainly from a computational viewpoint (Han and Kamber, 2001).

Some data is now observable in continuous time rather than discrete time. In this case the observations for each variable on each unit are more like a function than a point value. Important examples include monitoring the presence of polluting atmospheric agents over time and surveys on the quotation of various financial shares. These are examples of continuous time stochastic processes (Hoel, Port and Stone, 1972).

2.7   Further reading

This chapter introduced the organisation and structure of databases for data mining. The most important idea is that the planning and creation of the database cannot be ignored. They are crucial to obtaining results that can be used in the subsequent phases of the analysis. I see data mining as part of a complete process of design, collection and data analysis with the aim of obtaining useful results for companies in the sphere of business intelligence. Database creation and data analysis are closely connected.

The chapter started with a description of the various ways we can structure databases, with particular reference to the data warehouse, the data webhouse and the data mart. For more details on these topic, Han and Kamber (2001) take a computational viewpoint and Berry and Linoff (1997, 2000) take a business-oriented viewpoint.

The fundamental themes from descriptive statistics are measurement scales and data classification. This leads to an important taxonomy of the statistical variables that is the basis of my operational distinction of data mining methods. Next comes the data matrix. The data matrix is a very important tool in data mining that allows us to define the objectives of the subsequent analysis according to the formal language of statistics. For an introduction to these concepts see for instance Hand *et al.* (2001).

The chapter introduced some operations on the data matrix. These operations may be essential or they may be just a good idea. Examples are binarisation, the calculation of frequency distributions, variable transformations, and the treatment of anomalous or missing data. Hand *et al.* (2001) take a statistical viewpoint and Han and Kamber (2001) take a computational viewpoint. Finally, we briefly touched on the description of complex data structures; for more details consult the previous two books.

CHAPTER 3

Exploratory data analysis

In a quality statistical data analysis the initial step has to be exploratory. This is particularly true of applied data mining, which essentially consists of searching for relationships in the data at hand, not known a priori. Exploratory data analysis has to take the available information organised as explained in Chapter 2, then analyse it, to summarise the whole data set. This is usually carried out through potentially computationally intensive graphical representations and statistical summary measures, relevant for the aims of the analysis.

Exploratory data analysis could seem equivalent to data mining itself, but there are two main differences. From the statistical viewpoint, exploratory data analysis essentially uses descriptive statistical techniques, whereas data mining can use descriptive and inferential methods; inferential methods are based on probabilistic techniques. There is a considerable difference between the purpose of data mining and exploratory analysis. The prevailing purpose of an exploratory analysis is to describe the structure and the relationships present in the data, for eventual use in a statistical model. The purpose of a data mining analysis is the direct production of decision rules based on the structures and models that describe the data. This implies, for example, a considerable difference in the use of concurrent techniques. An exploratory analysis is often composed of several exploratory techniques, each one capturing different and potentially noteworthy aspects of the data. In data mining, the various techniques are evaluated and compared in order to choose one that could subsequently be implemented as a decision rule. Coppi (2002) discusses the differences between exploratory data analysis and data mining.

This chapter takes an operational approach to exploratory data analysis. It begins with univariate exploratory analysis – examining the variables one at a time. Even though the observed data is multidimensional and we will eventually need to consider the interrelationships between the variables, we can gain a lot of insight from examining each variable on its own. Next comes bivariate analysis. At this stage, the treatment of bivariate and multivariate analysis will use quantitative variables exclusively.

This is followed by multivariate exploratory analysis of qualitative data. In particular, we will compare some of the numerous summary measures in the statistical literature. It is difficult to analyse data with many dimensions, so the

Applied Data Mining. Paolo Giudici
© 2003 John Wiley & Sons, Ltd   ISBNs: 0-470-84679-8 (Paper); 0-470-84678-X (Cloth)

final section looks at principal component analysis (PCA), a popular method for reducing dimensionality.

3.1   Univariate exploratory analysis

Analysis of the individual variables is an important step in preliminary data analysis. It can gather important information for later multivariate analysis and modelling. The main instruments of exploratory univariate analysis are univariate graphical displays and a series of summary indexes. Graphical displays differ according to the type of data. Bar charts and pie diagrams are commonly used to represent qualitative nominal data. The horizontal axis, or x-axis, of the bar chart indicates the variable's categories, and the vertical axis, or y-axis, indicates the absolute or relative frequencies of a given level of the variable. The order of the variables along the horizontal axis generally has no significance. Pie diagrams divide the pie into wedges where each wedge's area is proportional to the relative frequency of the variable level it represents. Frequency diagrams are typically used to represent ordinal qualitative and discrete quantitative variables. They are simply bar charts where the order in which the variables are inserted on the horizontal axis must correspond to the numeric order of the levels.

To obtain a frequency distribution for continuous quantitative variables, first reclassify or discretise the variables into class intervals. Begin by establishing the width of each interval. Unless there are special reasons for doing otherwise, the convention is to adopt intervals with constant width or intervals with different widths but with the same frequency (equifrequent). This may lead to some loss of information, since it is assumed that the variable distributes in a uniform way within each class. However, reclassification makes it possible to obtain a summary that can reveal interesting patterns. The graphical representation of the continuous variables, reclassified into class intervals, is obtained through a histogram. To construct a histogram, the chosen intervals are positioned along the x-axis. A rectangle with area equal to the (relative) frequency of the same class is then built on every interval. The height of these rectangles represent the frequency density, indicated through an analytic function $f(x)$, called the density function. In exploratory data analysis the density function assumes a constant value over each interval, corresponding to the height of the bar in the histogram. The density function can also be used to specify a continuous probability model; in this case $f(x)$ will be a continuous function.

The second part of the text has numerous graphical representations similar to those describe here. Using quantitative variables, Figure 3.1 shows an example of a frequency distribution and a histogram. They show, respectively, the distribution of the variables 'number of components of a family in a region' and 'net returns, in thousands of €, of a set of enterprises'.

So far we have seen how it is possible to graphically represent a univariate distribution. However, sometimes we need to further summarise all of the observations. Therefore it is useful to construct statistical indexes that are well suited to summarising the important aspects of the observations under consideration.

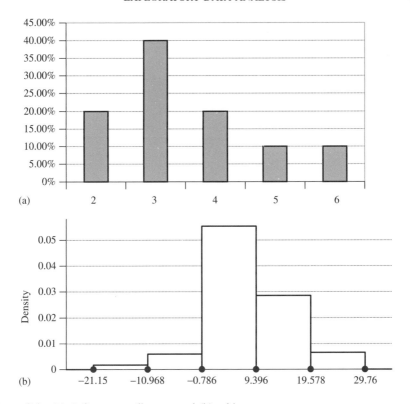

Figure 3.1   (a) A frequency diagram and (b) a histogram.

We now examine the main unidimensional or univariate statistical indexes; they can be categorised as indexes of location, variability, heterogeneity, concentration, asymmetry and kurtosis. The exposition is brief and elementary; refer to the relevant textbooks for detailed methods.

3.1.1 Measures of location

The most commonly used measure of location is the mean, computable only for quantitative variables. Given a set $x_1, x_2, \ldots, x_N$ of N observations, the arithmetic mean (the mean for short) is given by

$$\bar{x} = \frac{x_1 + x_2 + \cdots + x_N}{N} = \sum \frac{x_i}{N}$$

In calculating the arithmetic mean, the very large observations can counterbalance and even overpower the smallest ones. Since all observations are used in the calculation, any value or set of values can considerably affect the computed mean value. In financial data, where extreme outliers are common, this 'overpowering' happens often and robust alternatives to the mean are probably preferable as measures of location.

The previous expression of the arithmetic mean is to be calculated on the data matrix. When univariate data is classified in terms of a frequency distribution, the arithmetic mean can also be calculated directly on the frequency distribution, leading to the same result, indeed saving computer time. When calculated on the frequency distribution, the arithmetic mean can be expressed as

$$\bar{x} = \sum_i x_i^* p_i$$

This is known as the weighted arithmetic mean, where the x_i^* indicate the distinct levels that the variable can take and p_i is the relative frequency of each of those levels.

The arithmetic mean has some important properties:

- The sum of the deviations from the mean is zero: $\sum (x_i - \bar{x}) = 0$.
- The arithmetic mean is the constant that minimises the sum of the squares of the deviations of each observation from the constant itself: $\min_a \sum (x_i - a)^2 = \bar{x}$.
- The arithmetic mean is a linear operator: $\dfrac{1}{N} \sum (a + bx_i) = a + b\bar{x}$.

A second simple index of position is the modal value or mode. The mode is a measure of location computable for all kinds of variables, including the qualitative nominal ones. For qualitative or discrete quantitative characters, the mode is the level associated with the greatest frequency. To estimate the mode of a continuous variable, we generally discretise the data intervals as we did for the histogram and compute the mode as the interval with the maximum density (corresponding to the maximum height of the histogram). To obtain a unique mode, the convention is to use the middle value of the mode's interval.

A third important measure of position is the median. In an ordered sequence of data the median is the value for which half the observations are greater and half are less. It divides the frequency distribution into two parts with equal area. The median is computable for quantitative variables and ordinal qualitative variables. Given N observations in non-decreasing order, the median is obtained as follows:

- If N is odd, the median is the observation which occupies the position $(N + 1)/2$.
- If N is even, the median is the mean of the observations that occupy positions $N/2$ and $N/2 + 1$.

The median remains unchanged if the smallest and largest observations are substituted with any other value that is still lower (or greater) than the median. For this reason, unlike the mean, anomalous or extreme values do not influence the median assessment of the distribution's location.

As a generalisation of the median, one can consider the values that subdivide the frequency distribution into parts having predetermined frequencies or percentages. Such values are called quantiles or percentiles. Of particular interest are the quartiles; these correspond to the values which divide the distribution into four equal parts. More precisely, the quartiles q_1, q_2, q_3, the first, second and third quartile, are such that the overall relative frequency with which we observe values less than q_1 is 0.25, less than q_2 is 0.5 and less than q_3 is 0.75. Note that q_2 coincides with the median.

3.1.2 Measures of variability

It is usually interesting to study the dispersion or variability of a distribution. A simple indicator of variability is the difference between the maximum observed value and the minimum observed value of a certain variable, known as the range. Another index is constructed by taking the difference between the third quartile and the first quartile, the interquartile range (IQR). The range is highly sensitive to extreme observations, but the IQR is a robust measure of spread for the same reason the median is a robust measure of location. Range and IQR are not used very often. The measure of variability most commonly used for quantitative data is the variance. Given a set $x_1, x_2, \ldots, x_N$ of N quantitative observations of a variable X, and indicating with $\bar{x}$ their arithmetic mean, the variance is defined by

$$\sigma^2(X) = \frac{1}{N} \sum (x_i - \bar{x})^2$$

the average squared deviation from the mean. When calculated on a sample rather then the whole population it is also denoted by s^2; then using $N - 1$ in the denominator instead of N makes s^2 an unbiased estimate of the population variance (Section 5.1). When all the observations have the same value then the variance is zero. Unlike the mean, the variance is not a linear operator. It holds that $\text{Var}(a + bX) = b^2 \text{Var}(X)$.

The variance squares the units in which X is measured. That is, if X measures a distance in metres, the variance will be in square metres. In practice it is more convenient to preserve the original units for the measure of spread; that is why the square root of the variance, known as the standard deviation, is often reported. Furthermore, to facilitate comparisons between different distributions, the coefficient of variation (CV) is often used. CV equals the standard deviation divided by the absolute value of the arithmetic mean of the distribution (CV is defined only when the mean is non-zero); it is a unitless measure of spread.

3.1.3 Measures of heterogeneity

The measures in the previous section cannot be computed for qualitative data, but we can still measure dispersion by using the heterogeneity of the observed distribution. Consider the general representation of the frequency distribution of

Table 3.1 Frequency distribution for a
qualitative variable.

Modality	Relative frequencies
x_1^*	p_1
x_2^*	p_2
$\vdots$	$\vdots$
x_k^*	p_k

a qualitative variable with k levels (Table 3.1). In practice it is possible to have
two extreme situations between which the observed distribution will lie:

- Null heterogeneity is when all the observations have X equal to the same
  level; that is, $p_i = 1$ for a certain i and $p_i = 0$ for the other $k-1$ levels.
- Maximum heterogeneity is when the observations are uniformly distributed
  among the k levels; that is, $p_i = 1/k$ for all $i = 1, \ldots, k$.

A heterogeneity index will have to attain its minimum in the first situation and
its maximum in the second one. We now introduce two indexes that satisfy
such conditions.

The Gini index of heterogeneity is defined by

$$G = 1 - \sum_{i=1}^{k} p_i^2$$

It can be easily verified that the Gini index is equal to 0 in the case of perfect
homogeneity and equal to $1-1/k$ in the case of maximum heterogeneity. To
obtain a 'normalised' index, which takes values in the interval [0,1], the Gini
index can be rescaled by its maximum value, giving the following relative index
of heterogeneity:

$$G' = \frac{G}{(k-1)/k}$$

The second index of heterogeneity is the entropy, defined by

$$E = -\sum_{i=1}^{k} p_i \log p_i$$

This index equals 0 in the case of perfect homogeneity and $\log k$ in the case of
maximum heterogeneity. To obtain a 'normalised' index, which assumes values

in the interval [0,1], we can rescale E by its maximum value, obtaining the following relative index of heterogeneity:

$$E' = \frac{E}{\log k}$$

3.1.4 Measures of concentration

Concentration is very much related to heterogeneity. In fact, a frequency distribution is said to be maximally concentrated when it has null heterogeneity and minimally concentrated when it has maximal heterogeneity. It is interesting to examine intermediate situations, where the two concepts find a different interpretation. In particular, the concept of concentration applies to variables measuring transferable goods (quantitative and ordinal qualitative). The classical example is the distribution of a fixed amount of income among N individuals; we shall use this as a running example.

Consider N non-negative quantities measuring a transferable characteristic placed in non-decreasing order:

$$0 \leq x_1 \leq \cdots \leq x_N$$

The aim is to understand the concentration of the characteristic among the N quantities, corresponding to different observations. Let $N\bar{x} = \sum x_i$, the total available amount, where $\bar{x}$ is the arithmetic mean. Two extreme situations can arise:

- $x_1 = x_2 = \cdots = x_N = \bar{x}$, corresponding to minimum concentration (equal income for the running example).
- $x_1 = x_2 = \cdots = x_{N-1} = 0, x_N = N\bar{x}$, corresponding to maximum concentration (only one unit gets all income).

In general, we want to evaluate the degree of concentration, which usually lies between these two extremes. To do this, we are going to build a measure of the concentration. Define

$$F_i = \frac{i}{N} \text{ for } i = 1, \ldots, N$$

$$Q_i = \frac{x_1 + x_2 + \cdots + x_i}{N\bar{x}} = \frac{\sum\limits_{j=1}^{i} x_j}{N\bar{x}}, \text{ for } i = 1, \ldots, N$$

For each i, F_i is the cumulative percentage of considered units, up to the ith unit and Q_i is the cumulative percentage of the characteristic that belongs to the same first i units. It can be shown that:

$$0 \leq F_i \leq 1; \ 0 \leq Q_i \leq 1$$

$$Q_i \leq F_i$$

$$F_N = Q_N = 1$$

Let $F_0 = Q_0 = 0$ and consider the $N+1$ pairs of coordinates $(0,0)$, $(F_1, Q_1), \ldots, (F_{N-1}, Q_{N-1})$, $(1,1)$. If we plot these points in the plane and join them with line segments, we obtain a piecewise linear curve called the concentration curve.

To illustrate the concept, Table 3.2 contains the ordered income of seven individuals and the calculations needed to obtain the concentration curve. Figure 3.2 shows the concentration curve obtained from the data. It also includes the $45°$ line corresponding to minimal concentration. Notice how the observed situation departs from the line of minimal concentration, and from the case of maximum concentration, described by a curve almost coinciding with the x-axis, at least until the $(N-1)$th point.

Table 3.2 Construction of the concentration curve.

Income	F_i	Q_i
	0	0
11	1/7	11/256
15	2/7	26/256
20	3/7	46/256
30	4/7	76/256
50	5/7	126/256
60	6/7	186/256
70	1	1

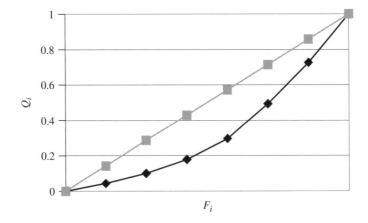

Figure 3.2 Representation of the concentration curve.

A summary index of concentration is the Gini concentration index, based on the differences $F_i - Q_i$. There are three points to note:

- For minimum concentration, $F_i - Q_i = 0, i = 1, 2, \ldots, N$.
- For maximum concentration, $F_i - Q_i = F_i, i = 1, 2, \ldots, N - 1$ and $F_N - Q_N = 0$.
- In general, $0 < F_i - Q_i < F_i$, $i = 1, 2, \ldots, N - 1$, with the differences increasing as maximum concentration is approached.

The concentration index is defined by the ratio between the quantity $\sum_{i=1}^{N-1}$ $(F_i - Q_i)$ and its maximum value, equal to $\sum_{i=1}^{N-1} F_i$. The complete expression of the index is therefore

$$R = \frac{\sum_{i=1}^{N-1} (F_i - Q_i)}{\sum_{i=1}^{N-1} F_i}$$

The Gini concentration coefficient, R, equals 0 for minimum concentration and 1 for maximum concentration. For the data in Table 3.2 it turns out that R is equal to 0.387, indicating a moderate level of concentration.

3.1.5   Measures of asymmetry

To obtain an indication of the asymmetry of a distribution it may be sufficient to compare the mean and the median. If these measures are almost the same, the data tends to be distributed in a symmetric way. If the mean exceeds the median, the data can be described as skewed to the right (positive asymmetry); if the median exceeds the mean, the data can be described as skewed to the left (negative asymmetry). Graphs of the data using bar charts or histograms are useful for investigating the form of the data distribution. For example, Figure 3.3 shows histograms for a right-skewed distribution, a symmetric distribution and a left-skewed distribution.

A further graphical tool is the boxplot. The boxplot bases uses the median (Me), the first and third quartile (Q1 and Q3) and the interquartile range (IQR). Figure 3.4 shows an example. Here the first quartile and the third quartile have been marked with Q1 and Q3, and the lower and upper limits of the figure, T1 and T2, are defined as follows:

$$T1 = \max(\text{minimum value observed, } Q1 - 1.5 \times \text{IQR})$$

$$T2 = \min(\text{maximum value observed, } Q3 + 1.5 \times \text{IQR})$$

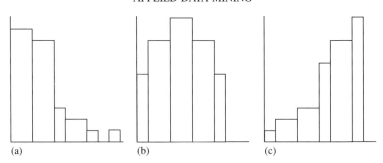

Figure 3.3   Histograms describing symmetric and asymmetric distributions: (a) mean > median, (b) mean = median, (c) mean < median.

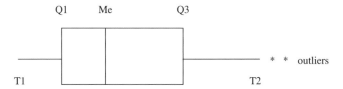

Figure 3.4   A boxplot.

The boxplot permits us to identify the asymmetry of the considered distribution. If the distribution were symmetric, the median would be equidistant from Q1 and Q3; otherwise the distribution is skewed. For example, when the distance between Q3 and the median is greater than the distance between Q1 and the median, the distribution is skewed to the right. The boxplot also indicates the presence of anomalous observations, or outliers. Observations smaller than T1 or greater than T2 can be seen as outliers, at least on an exploratory basis. Figure 3.4 indicates that the median is closer to the first quartile than the third quartile, so the distribution seems skewed to the right. Moreover, some anomalous observations are present at the right tail of the distribution.

Let us construct a summary statistical index that can measure a distribution's degree of asymmetry. The proposed index is based on calculating

$$\mu_3 = \frac{\sum (x_i - \overline{x})^3}{N}$$

known as the third central moment of the distribution. The asymmetry index is then defined by

$$\gamma = \frac{\mu_3}{\sigma^3}$$

where σ is the standard deviation. From its definition, the asymmetry index is calculable only for quantitative variables. It can assume every real value (i.e. it is not normalised). Here are three particular cases:

- If the distribution is symmetric, $\gamma = 0$.
- If the distribution is left asymmetric, $\gamma < 0$.
- If the distribution is right asymmetric, $\gamma > 0$.

3.1.6 Measures of kurtosis

Continuous data can be represented using a histogram. The form of the histogram gives information about the data. It is also possible to approximate, or even to interpolate, a histogram with a density function of a continuous type. In particular, when the histogram has a very large number of classes and each class is relatively narrow, the histogram can be approximated using a normal or Gaussian density function, which has the shape of a bell (Figure 3.5).

In Figure 3.5 the x-axis represents the observed values and the y-axis represents the values corresponding to the density function. The normal distribution is an important theoretical model frequently used in inferential statistical analysis (Section 5.1). Therefore it is reasonable to construct a statistical index that measures the 'distance' of the observed distribution from the theoretical situation corresponding to perfect normality. The index of kurtosis is a simple index that allows us to check whether the examined data follows a normal distribution:

$$\beta = \frac{\mu_4}{\mu_2^2} \text{ where } \mu_4 = \frac{\sum (x_i - \overline{x})^4}{N} \text{ and } \mu_2 = \frac{\sum (x_i - \overline{x})^2}{N}$$

This index is calculable only for quantitative variables and it can assume every real positive value. Here are three particular cases:

- If the variable is perfectly normal, $\beta = 3$.

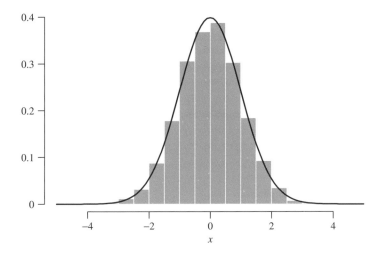

Figure 3.5   Normal approximation to the histogram.

- If $\beta < 3$ the distribution is called hyponormal (thinner with respect to the normal distribution having the same variance, so there is a lower frequency for values very distant from the mean).
- If $\beta > 3$ the distribution is called hypernormal (fatter with respect to the normal distribution, so there is a greater frequency for values very distant from the mean).

There are other graphical tools useful for checking whether the examined data can be approximated using a normal distribution. The most common one is the so-called 'quantile-quantile' plot, often abbreviated to qq-plot. This is a graph in which the observed quantiles from the observed data are compared with the theoretical quantiles that would be obtained if the data came from a true normal distribution. The graph is a set of points on a plane. The closer they come to the 45° line passing through the origin, the more closely the observed data matches data from a true normal distribution. Consider the qq-plots in Figure 3.6 they demonstrate some typical situations that occur in actual data analysis.

With most popular statistical software it is easy to obtain the indexes mentioned in this section, plus others too. Table 3.3 shows an example of a typical

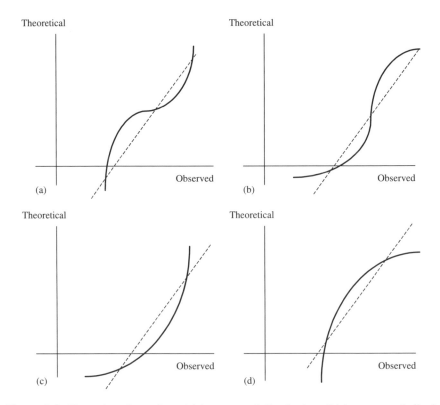

Figure 3.6 Examples of qq-plots: (a) hyponormal distribution, (b) hypernormal distribution, (c) left asymmetric distribution, (d) right asymmetric distribution.

Table 3.3 Example of software output for univariate analysis: the variable is the extra return of an investment fund.

Moments				Quantiles			
N	120	Sum Wgts	120	100%Max	2029	99%	1454
Mean	150.2833	Sum	18034	75%Q3	427	95%	861
Std Dev	483.864	Variance	234124.3	50%Med	174.5	90%	643.5
Skewness	0.298983	Kurtosis	2.044782	25%Q1	-141	10%	-445.5
CV	321.9678	Range	3360	0%Min	-1331	5%	-658.5
Q3-Q1	568	Mode	186	1%	-924		

	Extremes		
Lowest	Obs	Highest	Obs
-1331(	71)	1131(	31)
-924(	54)	1216(	103)
-843(	19)	1271(	67)
-820(	21)	1454(	81)
-754(	50)	2029(	30)

Missing Value   .

Count   140

% Count/Nobs   53.85

software output for this purpose, obtained from PROC UNIVARIATE of SAS. Besides the main measures of location, it gives the quantiles as well as the minimum and the maximum observed values. The kurtosis index calculated by SAS actually corresponds to $\beta - 3$.

3.2 Bivariate exploratory analysis

The relationship between two variables can be graphically represented using a scatterplot. Figure 3.7 shows the relationship between the observed values in two performance indicators, return on investment (ROI) and return on equity (ROE), for a set of business enterprises in the computer sector. There is a noticeable increasing trend in the relationship between the two variables. Both variables in Figure 3.7 are quantitative and continuous, but a scatterplot can be drawn for all kinds of variables.

A real data set usually contains more than two variables, but it is still possible to extract interesting information from the analysis of every possible bivariate scatterplot between all pairs of the variables. We can create a scatterplot matrix in which every element corresponds to the scatterplot of the two corresponding variables indicated by the row and the column. Figure 3.8 is an example of a scatterplot matrix for real data on the weekly returns of an investment fund made up of international shares and a series of worldwide financial indexes. The period of observation for all the variables starts on 4 October 1994 and ends on 4 October 1999, for a total of 262 working days. Notice that the variable REND shows an increasing relationship with all financial indexes and, in particular, with

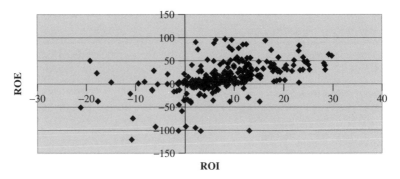

Figure 3.7   Example of a scatterplot diagram.

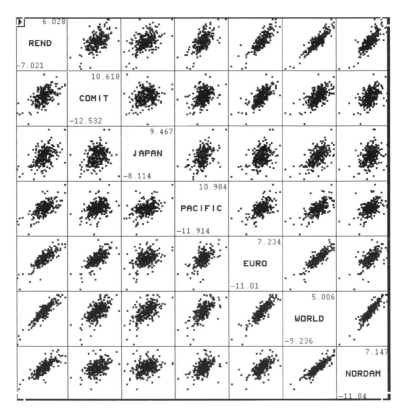

Figure 3.8   Example of a scatterplot matrix.

the EURO, WORLD and NORDAM indexes. The squares containing the variable names also contain the minimum and maximum value observed for that variable.

It is useful to develop bivariate statistical indexes that further summarise the frequency distribution, improving the interpretation of data, even though we may lose some information about the distribution. In the bivariate case, and more generally in the multivariate case, these indexes permit us to summarise the distribution of each data variable, but also to learn about the relationship between the variables (corresponding to the columns of the data matrix). The rest of this section focuses on quantitative variables, for which summary indexes are more easily formulated, typically by working directly with the data matrix. Section 3.4 explains how to develop summary indexes that describe the relationship between qualitative variables.

Concordance is the tendency of observing high (low) values of a variable together with high (low) values of the other. Discordance is the tendency of observing low (high) values of a variable together with high (low) values of the other. For measuring concordance, the most common summary measure is the covariance, defined as

$$\text{Cov}(X, Y) = \frac{1}{N} \sum_{i=1}^{N} [x_i - \mu(X)][y_i - \mu(Y)]$$

where $\mu(X)$ is the mean of variable X and $\mu(Y)$ is the mean of variable Y. The covariance takes positive values if the variables are concordant and negative values if they are discordant. With reference to the scatterplot representation, setting the point $(\mu(X), \mu(Y))$ as the origin, $\text{Cov}(X, Y)$ tends to be positive when most of the observations are in the upper right-hand and lower left-hand quadrants. Conversely, it tends to be negative when most of the observations are in the lower right-hand and upper left-hand quadrants.

Notice that the covariance is directly calculable from the data matrix. In fact, since there is a covariance for each pair of variables, this calculation gives rise to a new data matrix, called the variance–covariance matrix. In this matrix the rows and columns correspond to the available variables. The main diagonal contains the variances and the cells outside the main diagonal contain the covariances between each pair of variables. Since $\text{Cov}(X_j, X_i) = \text{Cov}(X_i, X_j)$, the resulting matrix will be symmetric (Table 3.4).

Table 3.4 The variance–covariance matrix.

	X_1	$\cdots$	X_j	$\cdots$	X_h
X_1	Var(X_1)	$\cdots$	Cov(X_1, X_j)	$\cdots$	Cov(X_1, X_h)
$\vdots$	$\vdots$	$\vdots$	$\vdots$	$\vdots$	$\vdots$
X_j	Cov(X_j, X_1)	$\cdots$	Var(X_j)	$\cdots$	$\cdots$
$\vdots$	$\vdots$	$\vdots$	$\vdots$	$\vdots$	$\vdots$
X_h	Cov(X_h, X_1)	$\cdots$	$\cdots$	$\cdots$	Var(X_h)

The covariance is an absolute index; that is, it can identify the presence of a relationship between two quantities but it says little about the degree of this relationship. In other words, to use the covariance as an exploratory index, it need to be normalised, making it a relative index. The maximum value that $Cov(X, Y)$ can assume is $\sigma_x\sigma_y$, the product of the two standard deviations of the variables. The minimum value that $Cov(X, Y)$ can assume is $-\sigma_x\sigma_y$. Furthermore, $Cov(X, Y)$ assumes its maximum value when the observed data points lie on a line with positive slope; it assumes its minimum value when the observed data points lie on a line with negative slope. In light of this, we define the (linear) correlation coefficient between two variables X and Y as

$$r(X, Y) = \frac{Cov(X, Y)}{\sigma(X)\sigma(Y)}$$

The correlation coefficient $r(X, Y)$ has the following properties:

- $r(X, Y)$ takes the value 1 when all the points corresponding to the joint observations are positioned on a line with positive slope, and it takes the value -1 when all the points are positioned on a line with negative slope. That is why r is known as the *linear* correlation coefficient.
- When $r(X, Y) = 0$ the two variables are not linked by any type of linear relationship; that is, X and Y are uncorrelated.
- In general, $-1 \leq r(X, Y) \leq 1$.

As for the covariance, it is possible to calculate all pairwise correlations directly from the data matrix, thus obtaining a correlation matrix. The structure of such a matrix is shown in Table 3.5. For the variables plotted in Figure 3.7 the correlation matrix is as in Table 3.6. Table 3.6 takes the 'visual' conclusions of Figure 3.7 and makes them stronger and more precise. In fact, the variable REND is strongly positively correlated with EURO, WORLD and NORDAM. In general, there are many variables exhibiting strong correlation.

Interpreting the magnitude of the linear correlation coefficient is not particularly easy. It is not clear how to distinguish the 'high' values from the 'low'

Table 3.5 The correlation matrix.

	X_1	...	X_j	...	X_h
X_1	1	...	$Cor(X_1, X_j)$	...	$Cor(X_1, X_h)$
⋮	⋮	⋮	⋮	⋮	⋮
X_j	$Cor(X_j, X_1)$	...	1	...	...
⋮	⋮	⋮	⋮	⋮	⋮
X_h	$Cor(X_h, X_1)$	...	...	...	1

Table 3.6   Example of a correlation matrix.

Correlation Matrix

	REND	COMIT	JAPAN	PACIFIC	EURO	WORLD	NORDAM
REND	1.0000	0.5576	0.4849	0.6324	0.8230	0.8982	0.8035
COMIT	0.5576	1.0000	0.2564	0.3777	0.7076	0.6065	0.4630
JAPAN	0.4849	0.2564	1.0000	0.4591	0.4315	0.5925	0.3375
PACIFI	0.6324	0.3777	0.4591	1.0000	0.6004	0.6671	0.4925
EURO	0.8230	0.7076	0.4315	0.6004	1.0000	0.8710	0.6613
WORLD	0.8982	0.6065	0.5925	0.6671	0.8710	1.0000	0.9008
NORDAM	0.8035	0.4630	0.3375	0.4925	0.6613	0.9008	1.0000

values of the coefficient, in absolute terms, so that we can distinguish the important correlations from the irrelevant. Section 5.3 considers a model-based solution to this problem when examining statistical hypothesis testing in the context of the normal linear model. But to do that we need to assume the pair of variables have a bivariate Gaussian distribution.

From an exploratory viewpoint, it would be convenient to have a threshold rule to inform us when there is substantial information in the data to reject the hypothesis that the correlation coefficient is zero. Assuming the observed sample comes from a bivariate normal distribution (Section 5.3), we can use a rule of the following type: Reject the hypothesis that the correlation coefficient is null when

$$\left| \frac{r(X, Y)}{\sqrt{1 - r^2(X, Y)}} \sqrt{n - 2} \right| > t_{\alpha/2}$$

where $t_{\alpha/2}$ is the $(1 - \alpha/2)$ percentile of a Student's t distribution with $n - 2$ degrees of freedom, corresponding to the number of observations minus 2 (Section 5.1). For example, for a large sample and a significance level of $\alpha = 5\%$ (which sets the probability of incorrectly rejecting a null correlation), the threshold is $t_{0.025} = 1.96$. The previous inequality asserts that we should conclude that the correlation between two variables is 'significantly' different from zero when the left-hand side is greater than $t_{\alpha/2}$. For example, applying the previous rule to Table 3.6, with $t_{\alpha/2} = 1.96$, it turns out that all the observed correlations are significantly different from zero.

3.3   Multivariate exploratory analysis of quantitative data

Matrix notation allows us to express multivariate measures more compactly. We assume that the data matrix is entirely composed of quantitative variables; Section 3.4 deals with qualitative variables. Let $\mathbf{X}$ be a data matrix with n rows and p columns. The main summary measures can be expressed directly in terms of matrix operations on $\mathbf{X}$. For example, the arithmetic mean of the variables, described by a p-dimensional vector $\overline{X}$, can be obtained directly from the data matrix as

$$\overline{X} = \frac{1}{n} \mathbf{1X}$$

where **1** indicates a (row) vector of length n with all the elements equal to 1. As we have seen in Section 2.5, it is often a good idea to standardise the variables in **X**. To achieve this aim, we first need to subtract the mean from each variable. The matrix containing the deviations from each variable's mean is

$$\tilde{\mathbf{X}} = \mathbf{X} - \frac{1}{n}\mathbf{JX}$$

where **J** is an $n \times n$ matrix with all the elements equal to 1.

Consider now the variance–covariance matrix, denoted by **S**. **S** is a $p \times p$ square matrix containing the variance of each variable on the main diagonal. The off-diagonal elements contain the $p(p-1)/2$ covariances between all the pairs of the p considered variables. In matrix notation we can write

$$\mathbf{S} = \frac{1}{n}\tilde{\mathbf{X}}'\tilde{\mathbf{X}}$$

where $\tilde{\mathbf{X}}'$ represents the transpose of $\tilde{\mathbf{X}}$. The (i, j) element of the matrix is

$$\mathbf{S}_{i,j} = \frac{1}{n}\sum_{\ell=1}^{n}(x_{\ell i} - \overline{x}_i)(x_{\ell j} - \overline{x}_j)$$

S is symmetric and positive definite, meaning that for any non-zero vector x, $x'\mathbf{S}x > 0$.

It can be appropriate, for example in a comparisons between different databases, to summarise the whole variance–covariance matrix with a real number that expresses the 'overall variability' of the system. This can be done usually through two alternative measures. The trace, denoted by tr, is the sum of the elements on the main diagonal of **S**, the variances of the variables:

$$\mathrm{tr}(\mathbf{S}) = \sum_{s=1}^{p}\sigma_s^2$$

It can be shown that the trace of **S** is equal to the sum of the eigenvalues of the matrix itself:

$$\mathrm{tr}(\mathbf{S}) = \sum_{s=1}^{p}\lambda_s$$

A second measure of overall variability is defined by the determinant of **S** and is often called the Wilks generalised variance:

$$W = |S|$$

We have seen how to transform the variance–covariance matrix to the correlation matrix so that we can interpret the relationships more easily. The correlation matrix, **R**, is computable as

$$\mathbf{R} = \frac{1}{n}\mathbf{Z}'\mathbf{Z}$$

where $\mathbf{Z} = \tilde{\mathbf{X}}\mathbf{F}$ is a matrix containing the standardised variables (Section 2.5) and $\mathbf{F}$ is a $p \times p$ matrix that has diagonal elements equal to the reciprocal of the standard deviations of the variables:

$$\mathbf{F} = [\text{diag}(s_{11}, \ldots, s_{pp})]^{-1}$$

Although the correlation matrix is very informative on the presence of statistical (linear) relationships between the considered variables, in reality it calculates them marginally for every pair of variables, without including the influence of the remaining variables.

To filter out spurious effects induced by other variables, a useful tool is the partial correlation. The partial correlation measures the linear relationship between two variables with the others held fixed. Let $r_{ij|\text{REST}}$ be the partial correlation observed between the variables X_i and X_j, given *all* the remaining variables, and let $\mathbf{K} = \mathbf{R}^{-1}$, the inverse of the correlation matrix. To calculate the partial correlation, it can be shown that

$$r_{ij|\text{REST}} = \frac{-k_{ij}}{[k_{ii}k_{jj}]^{1/2}}$$

where k_{ii}, k_{jj} and k_{ij} are the elements at positions (i, i), (j, j) and (i, j) in matrix $\mathbf{K}$. The importance of reasoning in terms of partial correlations is particularly evident in databases characterised by strong collinearities between the variables. For example, in an analysis developed on the correlation structure between daily performances of 12 sector indexes of the American stock market in the period 4/1/1999 to 29/2/2000, I have computed the marginal correlations between the NASDAQ100 index and the COMPUTER and BIOTECH sector indexes, obtaining 0.99 and 0.94 respectively. However, the corresponding partial correlations are smaller, 0.45 and 0.13 respectively. This occurs because there is strong correlation among all the considered indexes, therefore the marginal correlations tend also to reflect the spurious correlation between two variables induced by the others. The BIOTECH index has a smaller weight than the COMPUTER index in the NASDAQ100 index, in particular, as the partial correlation for the BIOTECH index is much lower.

3.4 Multivariate exploratory analysis of qualitative data

So far we have used covariance and correlation as our main measures of statistical relationships between quantitative variables. With ordinal qualitative variables, it is possible to extend the notion of covariance and correlation to the ranks of the observations. The correlation between the variable ranks is known as the Spearman correlation coefficient. Table 3.7 shows how to express the ranks of two ordinal qualitative variables that describe the quality and the menu of four different restaurants. The Spearman correlation of the data in Table 3.7 is zero, therefore the ranks of the two variables are not correlated.

Table 3.7 Ranking of ordinal variables.

Variable A	Variable B	Ranks of variable A	Ranks of variable B
High	Simple	3	1
Medium	Intermediate	2	2
Medium	Elaborated	2	3
Low	Simple	1	1

More generally, transforming the levels of the ordinal qualitative variables into the corresponding ranks allows most of the analysis applicable to quantitative data to be extended to the ordinal qualitative case. This can also include principal component analysis (Section 3.5). However, if the data matrix contains qualitative data at the nominal level (not binary, otherwise they could be considered quantitative, as in Section 2.3), the notion of covariance and correlation cannot be used. The rest of this section considers summary measures for the intensity of the relationships between qualitative variables of any kind. These measures are known as association indexes. These indexes can sometimes be applied to discrete quantitative variables, but with a loss of explanatory power.

In the examination of qualitative variables, a fundamental part is played by the frequencies for the levels of the variables. Therefore we begin with the contingency table introduced in Section 2.4. Unlike Section 2.4, qualitative data are often available directly in the form of a contingency table, without needing to access the original data matrix. To emphasise this difference, we now introduce a slightly different notation which we shall use throughout. Given a qualitative character X which assumes the levels $X_1, \ldots, X_I$, collected in a population (or sample) of n units, the absolute frequency of level X_i ($i = 1, \ldots, I$) is the number of times the variable X is observed having value X_i. Denote this absolute frequency by n_i. Table 3.8 presents a theoretical two-way contingency table to introduce the notation used in this Section. In Table 3.8 n_{ij}

Table 3.8 Theoretical two-way contingency table.

Y X	$Y_1 \ldots Y_j \ldots Y_J$	Total
X_1	$n_{11} \ldots n_{1j} \ldots n_{1J}$	n_{1+}
$\vdots$	$\vdots \quad \vdots \quad \vdots$	$\vdots$
X_i	$n_{i1} \ldots n_{ij} \ldots n_{iJ}$	n_{i+}
$\vdots$	$\vdots \quad \vdots \quad \vdots$	$\vdots$
X_I	$n_{I1} \ldots n_{Ij} \ldots n_{IJ}$	n_{I+}
Total	$n_{+1} \ldots n_{+j} \ldots n_{+J}$	n

indicates the frequency associated with the pair of levels $(X_i, Y_j), i = 1, 2, \ldots, I$; $j = 1, 2, \ldots, J$, of the variables X and Y. The n_{ij} are also called cell frequencies.

- $n_{i+} = \sum_{j=1}^{J} n_{ij}$ is the marginal frequency of the ith row of the table; it represents the total number of observations which assume the ith level of X $(i = 1, 2, \ldots, I)$.
- $n_{+j} = \sum_{i=1}^{I} n_{ij}$ is the marginal frequency of the jth column of the table; it denotes the total number of observations which assume the jth level of $Y(j = 1, 2, \ldots, J)$.

For the frequencies in the table, we can write the following marginalisation relationship:

$$\sum_{i=1}^{I} n_{i+} = \sum_{j=1}^{J} n_{+j} = \sum_{i=1}^{I} \sum_{j=1}^{J} n_{ij} = n$$

From an $n \times p$ data matrix, it is possible to construct $p(p - 1)/2$ two-way contingency tables, corresponding to all possible qualitative variable pairs. However, it is usually reasonable to limit ourselves to obtaining only those that correspond to interesting 'intersections' between the variables, those for which the joint distribution may be important and a useful complement to the univariate frequency distribution.

3.4.1 Independence and association

To develop descriptive indexes of the relationship between qualitative variables, we need the concept of statistical independence. Two variables, X and Y, are said to be independent, with reference to n observations, if they adhere to the following conditions:

$$\frac{n_{i1}}{n_{+1}} = \cdots = \frac{n_{iJ}}{n_{+J}} = \frac{n_{i+}}{n} \qquad \forall i = 1, 2, \ldots, I$$

or, equivalently,

$$\frac{n_{1j}}{n_{1+}} = \cdots = \frac{n_{Ij}}{n_{I+}} = \frac{n_{+j}}{n} \qquad \forall j = 1, 2, \ldots, J$$

If this occurs it means that, with reference to the first equation, the (bivariate) analysis of the variables does not give any additional information about X beyond the univariate analysis of the variable X itself, and similarly for Y in the second equation. It will be said in this case that Y and X are statistically independent. From the definition, notice that statistical independence is a symmetric concept in the two variables; in other words, if X is independent of Y, then Y is independent of X. The previous conditions can be equivalently, and more conveniently, expressed as a function of the marginal frequencies n_{i+} and n_{+j}. Then X and Y

are independent if

$$n_{ij} = \frac{n_{i+}n_{+j}}{n} \quad \forall i = 1, 2, \ldots, I; \quad \forall j = 1, 2, \ldots, J$$

In terms of relative frequencies, this is equivalent to

$$p_{XY}(x_i, y_j) = p_X(x_i)p_Y(y_j)$$

for every i and for every j. When working with real data, the statistical independence condition is almost never satisfied exactly. Consequently, observed data will often show some degree of interdependence between the variables.

The statistical independence notion applies to qualitative and quantitative variables. A measure of interdependence operates differently for qualitative variables than for quantitative variables. For quantitative variables, it is possible to calculate summary measures (called correlation measures) that work both on the levels and the frequencies. For qualitative variables, the summary measures (called association measures) can use only the frequencies, because the levels are not metric.

For quantitative variables, an important relationship holds between statistical independence and the absence of correlation. If two variables, X and Y, are statistically independent, then $\text{cov}(X,Y) = 0$ and $r(X, Y) = 0$. The converse is not necessarily true, in the sense that two variables can be such that $r(x, y) = 0$, even though they are not independent. In other words, the absence of correlation does not imply statistical independence. An exception occurs when the variables X and Y are jointly distributed according to a normal multivariate distribution (Section 5.1). Then the two concepts are equivalent. The greater difficulty of using association measures compared with correlation measures lies in the fact that there are so many indexes available in the statistical literature. Here we examine three different classes: distance measures, dependency measures and model-based measures.

3.4.2 Distance measures

Independence between two variables, X and Y, holds when

$$n_{ij} = \frac{n_{i+}n_{+j}}{n} \quad \forall i = 1, 2, \ldots, I; \quad \forall j = 1, 2, \ldots, J$$

for all joint frequencies of the contingency table. A first approach to the summary of an association can therefore be based on calculating a 'global' measure of disagreement between the frequencies actually observed (n_{ij}) and those expected in the hypothesis of independence between the two variables ($n_{i+}n_{+j}/n$). The original statistic proposed by Karl Pearson is the most widely used measure for verifying the hypothesis of independence between X and Y. In the general case, it is defined by

$$X^2 = \sum_{i=1}^{I} \sum_{j=1}^{J} \frac{(n_{ij} - n_{ij}^*)^2}{n_{ij}^*}$$

where
$$n_{ij}^* = \frac{n_{i+}n_{+j}}{n} \quad i = 1, 2, \ldots, I; j = 1, 2, \ldots, J$$

Note that $X^2 = 0$ if the variables X and Y are independent. In that case the factors in the numerator are all zero. The statistic X^2 can be written in the equivalent form

$$X^2 = n \left[\sum_{i=1}^{I} \sum_{j=1}^{J} \frac{n_{ij}^2}{n_{i+}n_{+j}} - 1 \right]$$

which emphasises the dependence of the statistic on the number of observations, n. This reveals a serious inconvenience – the value of X^2 is an increasing function of the sample size n.

To overcome such inconvenience, some alternative measures have been proposed, all functions of the previous statistic. Here is one of them:

$$\phi^2 = \frac{X^2}{n} = \sum_{i=1}^{I} \sum_{j=1}^{J} \frac{n_{ij}^2}{n_{i+}n_{+j}} - 1$$

This index is usually called the mean contingency, and the square root of ϕ^2 is called the phi coefficient. For 2×2 contingency tables, representing binary variables, ϕ^2 is normalised as it takes values between 0 and 1, and it can be shown that

$$\phi^2 = \frac{\text{Cov}^2(X, Y)}{\text{Var}(X)\text{Var}(Y)}$$

Therefore in the case of 2×2 tables, ϕ^2 is equivalent to the squared linear correlation coefficient. For contingency tables bigger than 2×2, ϕ^2 is not normalised. To obtain a normalised index, useful for comparison, use a different modification of X^2 called the Cramer index. Following an approach quite common in descriptive statistic, the Cramer index is obtained by dividing the ϕ^2 statistic by the maximum value it can assume, for the structure of the given contingency table. Since such maximum is the minimum between the values $I - 1$ and $J - 1$, with I and J respectively the number of rows and columns of the contingency table, the Cramer index is equal to

$$V^2 = \frac{X^2}{n \min[(I - 1), (J - 1)]}$$

It can be shown that $0 \leq V^2 \leq 1$ for any $I \times J$ contingency table, and $V^2 = 0$ if and only if X and Y are independent. On the other hand, $V^2 = 1$ for maximum dependency between the two variables. Then three situations can be distinguished, referring without loss of generality to Table 3.8:

a) There is maximum dependency of Y on X when in every row of the table there is only one non-zero frequency. This happens if to each level of X

there, corresponds one and only one level of Y. This condition occurs when $V^2 = 1$ and $I \geq J$.

b) There is maximum dependency of X on Y if in every column of the table there is only one non-null frequency. This means that to each level of Y there corresponds one and only one level of X. This condition occurs when $V^2 = 1$ and $J \geq I$.

c) If the two previous conditions are simultaneously satisfied, i.e. if $I = J$ when $V^2 = 1$, the two variables are maximally interdependent.

We have referred to the case of two-way contingency tables, involving two variables, with an arbitrary number of levels. However, the measures presented here can easily be applied to multiway tables, extending the number of summands in the definition of X^2 to account for all table cells.

The association indexes based on the Pearson statistic X^2 measure the distance of the relationship between X and Y from the situation of independence. They refer to a generic notion of association, in the sense that they measure exclusively the distance from the independence situation, without giving information on the nature of that distance. On the other hand, these indexes are rather general, as they can be applied in the same fashion to all kinds of contingency table. Furthermore, as we shall see in Section 5.4, the statistic X^2 has an asymptotic probabilistic (theoretical) distribution, so it can also be used to assess an inferential threshold to evaluate inductively whether the examined variables are significantly dependent. Table 3.9 shows an example of calculating two X^2-based measures. Several more applications are given in the second half of the book.

3.4.3 Dependency measures

The association measures seen so far are all functions of the X^2 statistics, so they are hardly interpretable in most real applications. This important aspect has been underlined by Goodman and Kruskal (1979), who have proposed an alternative

Table 3.9 Comparison of association measures.

Variable	X^2	V^2	$U_{Y|X}$
Sales variation	235.0549	0.2096	0.0759
Real estates	116.7520	0.1477	0.0514
Age of company	107.1921	0.1415	0.0420
Region of activity	99.8815	0.1366	0.0376
Number of employees	68.3589	0.1130	0.0335
Sector of activity	41.3668	0.0879	0.0187
Sales	23.3355	0.0660	0.0122
Revenues	21.8297	0.0639	0.0123
Age of owner	6.9214	0.0360	0.0032
Legal nature	4.7813	0.0299	0.0034
Leadership persistence	4.742	0.0298	0.0021
Type of activity	0.5013	−0.0097	0.0002

approach to measuring the association in a contingency table. The set-up followed by Goodman and Kruskal is based on defining indexes for the specific context under investigation. In other words, the indexes are characterised by an operational meaning that defines the nature of the dependency between the available variables.

Suppose that, in a two-way contingency table, Y is the 'dependent' variable and X is the 'explanatory' variable. It may be interesting to evaluate if, for a generic observation, knowledge of the X level is able to reduce uncertainty about the corresponding category of Y. The degree of uncertainty in the level of a qualitative character is usually expressed using a heterogeneity index (Section 3.1).

Let $\delta(Y)$ indicate a heterogeneity measure for the marginal distribution of Y, indicated by the vector of marginal relative frequencies, $\{f_{+1}, f_{+2}, \ldots, f_{+J}\}$. Similarly, let $\delta(Y|i)$ be the same measure calculated on the conditional distribution of Y to the ith row of the variable X of the contingency table, $\{f_{1|i}, f_{2|i}, \ldots, f_{J|i}\}$ see Section 2.4. An association index based on the 'proportional reduction in the heterogeneity', or error proportional reduction index (EPR), can then be calculated as follows (Agresti, 1990):

$$\text{EPR} = \frac{\delta(Y) - M[\delta(Y|X)]}{\delta(Y)}$$

where $M[\delta(Y|X)]$ indicates the mean heterogeneity calculated with respect to the distribution of X, namely

$$M[\delta(Y|X)] = \sum_i f_{i+}\delta(Y|i)$$

where

$$f_{i+} = n_{i+}/n \quad (i = 1, 2, \ldots, I)$$

This index measures the proportion of heterogeneity of Y (calculated through δ) that can be 'explained' by the relationship with X. Remarkably, its structure is analogous to that of the squared linear correlation coefficient (Section 4.3.3). By choosing δ appropriately, different association measures can be obtained. Usually the choice is between the Gini index and the entropy index. Using the Gini index in the EPR expression, we obtain the so-called concentration coefficient, $\tau_{Y|X}$:

$$\tau_{Y|X} = \frac{\sum\sum f_{ij}^2/f_{i+} - \sum f_{+j}^2}{1 - \sum_j f_{+j}^2}$$

Using the entropy index in the ERP expression, we obtain the so-called uncertainty coefficient, $U_{Y|X}$:

$$U_{Y|X} = -\frac{\sum_i \sum_j f_{ij} \log(f_{ij}/f_{i+} \cdot f_{+j})}{\sum_j f_{+j} \log f_{+j}}$$

In the case of null frequencies it is conventional to set $\log 0 = 0$. Both $\tau_{Y|X}$ and $U_{Y|X}$ take values in the interval [0,1]. In particular, we can show that

$$\tau_{Y|X} = U_{Y|X} \text{ if and only if the variables are independent}$$

$$\tau_{Y|X} = U_{Y|X} = 1 \text{ if and only if } Y \text{ has maximum dependence on } X$$

The indexes have a simple operational interpretation regarding specific aspects of the dependence link between the variables. In particular, both $\tau_{Y|X}$ and $U_{Y|X}$ represent alternative quantifications of the reduction of the Y heterogeneity that can be explained through the dependence of Y on X. From this viewpoint they are rather specific in comparison to the distance measures of association. On the other hand, they are less general than the distance measures. Their application requires us to identify a causal link from one variable (explanatory) to the other (dependent), whereas the X^2-based indexes are asymmetric. Furthermore, they cannot easily be extended to contingency tables with more than two ways, for obtaining an inferential threshold.

Table 3.9 is an actual comparison between the distance measures and the uncertainty coefficient $U_{Y|X}$. It is based on data collected for a credit-scoring problem (Chapter 11). The objective of the analysis is to explore which of the explanatory variables described in the table (all qualitative or discrete quantitative) are most associated with the binary response variable. The response variable describes whether or not each of the 7134 business enterprises examined is creditworthy. Note that the distance measures (X^2 and Cramer's V^2) are more variable and seem generally to indicate a higher degree of association. This is due to the more generic type of associations that they detect. The uncertainty coefficient is more informative. For instance, it can be said that the variable 'sales variation' reduces the degree of uncertainty on the reliability by 7.6%. On the other hand, X^2 can be easily compared to the inferential threshold that can be associated with it. For instance, with a given level of significance, only the first eight variables are significantly associated with creditworthiness.

3.4.4 Model-based measures

We can examine those association measures that do not depend on the marginal distributions of the variables. None of the previous measures satisfy this requirement. We now consider a class of easily interpretable indexes that do not depend on the marginal distributions. These measures are based on probabilistic models and therefore allow an inferential treatment (Sections 5.4 and 5.5). For ease of notation, we shall assume a probabilistic model in which cell relative frequencies are replaced by cell probabilities. The cell probabilities can be interpreted as relative frequencies when the sample size tends to infinity, therefore they have the same properties as the relative frequencies.

Consider a 2×2 contingency table, relative to the variables X and Y, respectively associated with the rows ($X = 0,1$) and columns ($Y = 0,1$) of the table. Let $\pi_{11}, \pi_{00}, \pi_{10}$ and π_{01} indicate the probabilities that one observation is classified in one of the four cells of the table. The odds ratio is a measure of association that constitutes a fundamental parameter in the statistical models for the analysis of qualitative data. Let $\pi_{1|1}$ and $\pi_{0|1}$ indicate the conditional probabilities of having a 1 (a success) and a 0 (a failure) in row 1; let $\pi_{1|0}$ and $\pi_{0|0}$ be, the same probabilities for row 0. The odds of success for row 1 are defined by

$$\text{odds}_1 = \frac{\pi_{1|1}}{\pi_{0|1}} = \frac{P(Y = 1 | X = 1)}{P(Y = 0 | X = 1)}$$

The odds of success for row 0 are defined by

$$\text{odds}_0 = \frac{\pi_{1|0}}{\pi_{0|0}} = \frac{P(Y = 1 | X = 0)}{P(Y = 0 | X = 0)}$$

The odds are always a non-negative quantity, with a value greater than 1 when a success (level 1) is more probable than a failure (level 0), that is when $P(Y = 1 | X = 1) > P(Y = 0 | X = 1)$. For example, if the odds equal 4, this means that a success is four times more probable than a failure. In other words, it is expected to observe four successes for every failure. Instead odds $= 1/4 = 0.25$ means that a failure is four times more probable than a success; it is therefore expected to observe a success for every four failures.

The ratio between the two previous odds is the odds ratio:

$$\theta = \frac{\text{odds}_1}{\text{odds}_0} = \frac{\pi_{1|1}/\pi_{0|1}}{\pi_{1|0}/\pi_{0|0}}$$

From the definition of the odds, and using the definition of joint probability, it can easily be shown that:

$$\theta = \frac{\pi_{11}\pi_{00}}{\pi_{10}\pi_{01}}$$

This expression shows that the odds ratio is a cross product ratio, the product of probabilities on the main diagonal to the product of the probabilities on the secondary diagonal of a contingency table. In the actual computation of the odds ratio, the probabilities will be replaced with the observed frequencies, leading to the following expression:

$$\theta_{ij} = \frac{n_{11}n_{00}}{n_{10}n_{01}}$$

Here are three properties of the odds ratio:

- The odds ratio can be equal to any non-negative number; that is, it can take values in the interval $[0, +\infty)$.
- When X and Y are independent $\pi_{1|1} = \pi_{1|0}$, so that $\text{odds}_1 = \text{odds}_0$ and $\theta = 1$. On the other hand, depending on whether the odds ratio is greater or less than 1, it is possible to evaluate the sign of the association:

- For $\theta > 1$ there is a positive association, since the odds of success are greater in row 1 than in row 0.
- For $0 < \theta < 1$ there is a negative association, since the odds of success are greater in row 0 that in row 1.

• When the order of the rows or the order of the columns is reversed, the new value of θ is the reciprocal of the original value. The odds ratio does not change value when the orientation of the table is reversed so that the rows become columns and the columns become rows. This means that the odds ratio deals with the variables in a symmetrical way, so it is not necessary to identify a variable as dependent and the other as explanatory.

The odds ratio can be used as an exploratory tool aimed at building a probabilistic model, similar to the linear correlation coefficient. In particular, we can construct a decision rule that allows us to establish whether a certain observed value of the odds ratio indicates a significant association between the corresponding variables. In that sense it is possible to derive a confidence interval, as done for the correlation coefficient. The interval says that an association is significant when

$$\left| \log \theta_{ij} \right| > z_{\alpha/2} \sqrt{\sum_{ij} \frac{1}{\sqrt{n_{ij}}}}$$

where $z_{\alpha/2}$ is the $(1 - \alpha/2)$ percentile of a standard normal distribution. For instance, when $\alpha = 5\%$ then $z_{\alpha/2} = 1.96$. The confidence interval used in this case is only approximate; the accuracy of the approximation improves with the sample size.

Table 3.10 shows data on whether different visitors see the group pages catalog (C) and windows (W), from the database described in Chapter 8. From Table 3.10 we have that

$$\text{odds}_1 = \frac{P(C = 1|W = 1)}{P(C = 0|W = 1)} = \frac{0.1796}{0.1295} = 1.387$$

$$\text{odds}_0 = \frac{P(C = 1|W = 0)}{P(C = 0|W = 0)} = \frac{0.2738}{0.4171} = 0.656$$

Therefore, when W is visited ($W = 1$) it is more likely that C also is visited ($C = 1$). When W is not visited ($W = 0$) then, C is not visited much ($C = 0$).

Table 3.10 Observed contingency table between catalog and windows pages.

W	$W = 0$	$W = 1$
$C = 0$	0.4171	0.1295
$C = 1$	0.2738	0.1796

The odds ratio turns out to be $\theta = 2.114$, reflecting a positive (and significant) association between the two variables.

So far we have defined the odds ratio for 2×2 contingency tables. But the odds ratios can be calculated in the same fashion for larger contingency tables. The odds ratio for $I \times J$ tables can be defined with reference to each of the

$$\binom{I}{2} = I(I-2)/2$$

pairs of rows in combination with each of the

$$\binom{J}{2} = J(J-2)/2$$

pairs of columns. There are $\binom{I}{2}\binom{J}{2}$ odds ratios of this type. Evidently, the number of odds ratios becomes enormous, and it is wise to choose parsimonious representations. It may be useful to employ graphical representations of the odds ratio. For example, wanting to investigate the dependence of a dichotomous response variable from an explanatory variable with J levels, it can be effective to graphically represent the J odds ratios that are obtained by crossing the response variable with J binary variables describing the presence or absence of each level of the explanatory variable.

3.5   Reduction of dimensionality

Multivariate analysis can often be made easier by reducing the dimensionality of the problem, expressed by the number of variables present. For example, it is impossible to visualise graphs for a dimension greater than 3. The technique that is typically used is the linear operation known as principal component transformation. This technique can be used only for quantitative variables and, possibly for binary variables. But in practice it is often also applied to labelled qualitative data for exploratory purposes. The method is an important starting point for studying all dimensionality reduction techniques.

The idea is to transform p statistical variables (usually correlated) in terms of $k < p$ uncorrelated linear combinations, organised according to the explained variability. Consider a matrix of data $\mathbf{X}$ with n rows and p columns. The starting point of the analysis is the variance–covariance matrix, $\mathbf{S} = \frac{1}{n}\tilde{\mathbf{X}}'\tilde{\mathbf{X}}$ (Section 3.3). To simplify the notation, in the rest of this section it will be assumed that the observations are already expressed as deviations from the mean and therefore $\mathbf{X} = \tilde{\mathbf{X}}$.

Whenever the variables are expressed according to different measurement scales, it is best to standardise all the variables before calculating $\mathbf{S}$. Alternatively, it is sufficient to substitute $\mathbf{S}$ with the correlation matrix $\mathbf{R}$, since $\mathbf{R} = \frac{1}{n}\mathbf{Z}'\mathbf{Z}$. In any case, it is assumed that both $\mathbf{S}$ and $\mathbf{R}$ are of full rank; this implies that none of the considered variables is a perfect linear function of the others (or a linear combination of them). The computational algorithm for principal components can be described in an iterative way.

Definition. The *first principal component* of the data matrix $\mathbf{X}$ is a vector described by the following linear combination of the variables:

$$\begin{pmatrix} Y_{11} \\ \vdots \\ Y_{n1} \end{pmatrix} = a_{11} \begin{pmatrix} x_{11} \\ \vdots \\ x_{n1} \end{pmatrix} + a_{21} \begin{pmatrix} x_{12} \\ \vdots \\ x_{n2} \end{pmatrix} + \cdots + a_{p1} \begin{pmatrix} x_{1p} \\ \vdots \\ x_{np} \end{pmatrix}$$

that is, in matrix terms

$$Y_1 = \sum_{j=1}^{p} a_{j1} X_j = \mathbf{X} a_1$$

Furthermore, in the previous expression, the vector of the coefficients (also called weights) $a_1 = (a_{11}, a_{21}, \ldots, a_{p1})'$ is chosen to maximise the variance of the variable Y_1. To obtain a unique solution it is required that the weights are normalised, constraining the sum of their squares to be 1. Therefore, the first principal component is determined by the vector of weights a_1 such that max $\text{Var}(Y_1) = \max(a_1, \mathbf{S}a_1)$, under the constraint $a_1'a_1 = 1$, which normalises the vector.

The solution of the previous problem is obtained using Lagrange multipliers. It can be shown that, in order to maximise the variance of Y_1, the weights can be chosen to be the eigenvector corresponding to the largest eigenvalue of the variance–covariance matrix $\mathbf{S}$. The details can be found in a text such as Mardia, Kent and Bibby (1979).

Definition. The second principal component of the data matrix $\mathbf{X}$ is the linear combination

$$\begin{pmatrix} Y_{12} \\ \vdots \\ Y_{n2} \end{pmatrix} = a_{12} \begin{pmatrix} X_{11} \\ \vdots \\ X_{n1} \end{pmatrix} + a_{22} \begin{pmatrix} X_{12} \\ \vdots \\ X_{n2} \end{pmatrix} + \cdots + a_{p2} \begin{pmatrix} X_{1p} \\ \vdots \\ X_{np} \end{pmatrix}$$

that is, in matrix terms

$$Y_2 = \sum_{j=1}^{p} a_{j2} X_j = \mathbf{X} a_2$$

where the vector of the coefficients $a_2 = (a_{12}, a_{22}, \ldots, a_{p2})'$ is chosen in such a way that max $\text{Var}(Y_2) = \max(a_2'\mathbf{S}a_2)$, under the constraints $(a_2'a_2) = 1$ and $a_2'a_1 = 0$. Note the second constraint, which requires a_1, and a_2 to be orthogonal. This means the first and second components will be uncorrelated. The expression for the second principal component can be obtained using Lagrange multipliers, and a_2 is the eigenvector (normalised and orthogonal to a_1) corresponding to the second largest eigenvalue of $\mathbf{S}$.

This process can be used recursively for the definition of the kth component, with k less than the number of variables p. In general, the vth principal component, for $v = 1, \ldots, k$ is the linear combination

$$Y_v = \sum_{j=1}^{p} a_{jv} X_j = X a_v$$

in which the vector of the coefficients a_v is the eigenvector of S corresponding to the vth largest eigenvalue. This eigenvector is normalised and orthogonal to all the previous eigenvectors.

3.5.1 Interpretation of the principal components

The main difficulty with principal components is their interpretation. This is because each principal component is a linear combination of all the available variables, hence they do not have a clear measurement scale. To facilitate their interpretation, we will now introduce the concepts of absolute and relative importance of the principal components. To solve the maximisation problem that leads to the principal components, it can be shown that $S a_v = \lambda_v a_v$. Therefore the variance of the vth principal component corresponds the vth eigenvalue of the data matrix:

$$\text{Var}(Y_v) = \text{Var}(X a_v) = a_v' S a_v = \lambda_v$$

And the covariance between the principal components satisfies

$$\text{Cov}(Y_i, Y_j) = \text{Cov}(X a_i, X a_j) = a_i' S a_j = a_i' \lambda_j a_j = 0$$

because a_i and a_j are assumed to be orthogonal. This implies that the principal components are uncorrelated.

The variance–covariance matrix between them is thus expressed by the following diagonal matrix:

$$\text{Var}(Y) = \begin{bmatrix} \lambda_1 & & 0 \\ & \ddots & \\ 0 & & \lambda_k \end{bmatrix}$$

Consequently, the following ratio expresses the proportion of variability that is 'maintained' in the transformation from the original p variables to $k < p$ principal components:

$$\frac{\text{tr}(\text{Var } Y)}{\text{tr}(\text{Var } X)} = \sum_{i=1}^{k} \lambda_i / \sum_{i=1}^{p} \lambda_i$$

This equation expresses a cumulative measure of the quota of variability (and therefore of the statistical information) 'reproduced' by the first k components, with respect to the overall variability present in the original data matrix, as measured by the trace of the variance–covariance matrix. Therefore it can be used as a measure of absolute importance of the chosen k principal components, in terms of 'quantity of information' maintained by passing from p variables to k components.

We now examine the relative importance of each principal component (with respect to the single original variables). To achieve this we first obtain the general expression of the linear correlation between a principal component and an original variable. It holds that

$$\text{Cov}(Y_j, X) = \text{Cov}(\mathbf{X}a_j, X) = \mathbf{S}a_j = \lambda_j a_j$$

and therefore $\text{Cov}(Y_j, X_i) = \lambda_j a_{ij}$. Furthermore, writing s_i^2 for $\text{Var}(X_i)$ and recalling that $\text{Var}(Y_v) = \lambda_v$, we have that

$$\text{Corr}(Y_j, X_i) = \frac{\sqrt{\lambda_j} a_{ji}}{s_i}$$

Notice that the algebraic sign and the value of the coefficient a_{ij}, also called the loading, determine the sign and the strength of the correlation between the jth principal component and the ith original variable. It also follows that the portion of variability of an original variable, say X_i, explained by k principal components can be described by the following expression:

$$\sum_{j=1}^{k} \text{Corr}^2(Y_j, X_i) = (\lambda_1 a_{1i}^2 + \cdots + \lambda_k a_{ki}^2)/s_i^2$$

which describes the quota of variability (information) of each explanatory variable that is maintained in passing from the original variables to the principal components. This permits us to interpret each principal component by referring it mainly to the variables with which it is strongly correlated (in absolute value). Here are three concluding remarks on principal component analysis:

- The method of principal components permits us to reduce the complexity of a data matrix, in terms of number of variables, passing from a data matrix $\mathbf{X}_{n \cdot p}$ to a matrix with a lower number of columns, according to the transformation $\mathbf{Y}_{n \cdot k} = \mathbf{X}_{n \cdot p} \mathbf{A}_{p \cdot k}$, where $\mathbf{A}_{p \cdot k}$ is the matrix that is obtained by stacking columnwise the eigenvectors corresponding to the principal components. The resulting transformed observations are usually called principal component scores and 'reproduce' the data matrix in a space of a lower dimension.
- The principal components can be calculated by extracting the eigenvalues and the corresponding eigenvectors from the correlation matrix $\mathbf{R}$ instead of from the variance–covariance matrix $\mathbf{S}$. The principal components obtained from $\mathbf{R}$ are not the same as those obtained from $\mathbf{S}$. In order to choose which matrix to start from, in general use $\mathbf{R}$ when the variables are expressed in

different measurement scales. Note also that, using **R**, the interpretation of the importance of components is simpler. In fact, since $\text{tr}(\mathbf{R}) = p$, the degree of absolute importance of k components is given by

$$\frac{\text{tr}(\text{Var } Y)}{\text{tr}(\text{Var } X)} = \frac{1}{p} \sum_{i=1}^{k} \lambda_i$$

and the degree of relative importance of a principal component, with respect to a variable, is

$$\text{Corr}(Y_j, X_i) = \sqrt{\lambda_i} a_{ji}$$

- How many principal components should we choose? That is, how many columns are needed in the transformed matrix of scores? This is a critical point, for which there are different empirical criteria. For example, it is possible to proceed until the absolute degree of importance of the considered components passes a certain threshold thought to be reasonable, such as 50%. Or if **R** has been used, it is possible to choose all the principal components with corresponding eigenvalues greater than 1; because the overall variance is equal to p, the average variance should be at least equal to 1. A useful graphical instrument is the so-called 'scree plot', which plots on the x-axis the index of the component (1, 2, 3, ..., k), and on the y-axis, the corresponding eigenvalue. An empirical rule suggests choosing the number of components to be the value corresponding to the point where there is a significant 'fall' in the y-axis.

As alternatives to the empirical criteria presented, there are inferential types that require the assumption of a specific probabilistic model; for more details see Mardia, Kent and Bibby (1979).

3.5.2 Application of the principal components

We now apply the method of principal components to the data in Figure 3.8. More precisely, the objective of the analysis is to determine a compound index, a function of the five available financial indexes EURO, NORDAM, JAPAN, PACIFIC and COMIT, that can eventually substitute the aggregate WORLD index as a predictor of the considered investment fund return. Therefore the starting data matrix contains 262 rows and 5 columns.

In Section 3.2 we looked at the scatterplot matrix and the correlation matrix for this data. We need both matrices before we can apply the method of principal components. In fact, the methodology will typically be efficient only in presence of a certain degree of correlation (collinearity) between the variables; otherwise the principal components will eventually reproduce the original variables. Indeed, in the limiting case where the original variables are mutually uncorrelated, the principal components will coincide with them. In this example there is high collinearity between the variables, and this justifies using the method.

Having determined that the method is appropriate, we need to choose the number of components. Table 3.11 shows part of the output from SAS `Proc`

Table 3.11   Absolute importance of the principal components.

▶	Eigenvalues (CORR)			
Component	Eigenvalue	Difference	Proportion	Cumulative
PCR1	2.9507	2.1271	0.5901	0.5901
PCR2	0.8236	0.2741	0.1647	0.7549
PCR3	0.5495	0.0814	0.1099	0.8648
PCR4	0.4681	0.2600	0.0936	0.9584
PCR5	0.2081	.	0.0416	1.0000

Table 3.12   Relative importance of the principal components.

▶	Eigenvectors (CORR)				
Variable	PCR1	PCR2	PCR3	PCR4	PCR5
COMIT	0.4329	-0.5258	0.5450	-0.1568	0.4632
JAPAN	0.3574	0.7474	0.4642	0.3050	0.0714
PACIFIC	0.4455	0.3139	-0.4197	-0.6986	0.1973
EURO	0.5278	-0.2057	0.0710	-0.0302	-0.8205
NORDAM	0.4560	-0.1552	-0.5535	0.6272	0.2612

▶	Pattern Matrix (CORR)				
Variable	PCR1	PCR2	PCR3	PCR4	PCR5
COMIT	0.7436	-0.4772	0.4040	-0.1073	0.2113
JAPAN	0.6139	0.6783	0.3441	0.2087	0.0326
PACIFIC	0.7652	0.2849	-0.3111	-0.4779	0.0900
EURO	0.9066	-0.1867	0.0526	-0.0207	-0.3743
NORDAM	0.7832	-0.1409	-0.4103	0.4291	0.1192

`Princomp` used on the available data matrix. The contribution of the first principal component is around 59%, the contribution of the first two components together is around 75%, and so on. Therefore there is a big gap in passing from one to two components. It seems reasonable to choose only one principal component, even though this leads to a loss of around 40% of the overall variability. This decision is further enforced by the objective of the analysis – to obtain *one* composite index of the financial markets, to be used as a financial benchmark. To interpret the chosen component, we look at the relative importance of the components (Table 3.12).

The table reports the weight coefficients (loadings) relative to each of the five principal components that can be extracted from the data matrix, corresponding to the eigenvector of the variance–covariance matrix. Secondly, it presents the correlation coefficient of each component with the original variable, which represents the degree of relative importance of each component. It turns out that the first principal component is linked to all indexes and particularly with the EURO index.

3.6   Further reading

Exploratory data analysis has developed as an autonomous field of statistics, in parallel with the development of computing resources. It is possible to date the initial developments in the field to the publication of texts by Benzecri (1973) and Tukey (1977).

Univariate exploratory analysis is often fundamental to understanding what might be discovered during a data mining analysis. It often reveals problems with data quality, such as missing items and anomalous values. But most real problems are multivariate. Given the difficulty of visualising multidimensional graphical representations, many analyses concentrate on bivariate exploratory analysis, and on how the relationships found in a bivariate analysis can modify themselves, conditioning the analysis on the other variables. We looked at how to calculate the partial correlation for quantitative variables. Similar calculations can be performed on qualitative variables, for example, comparing the marginal odds ratios with those calculated conditionally on the levels of the remaining variables. This leads to a phenomenon known as Simpson's paradox (e.g. Agresti, 1990), for which a certain observed marginal association can completely change direction when conditioning the odds ratio on the level of additional variables.

We focused on some important matrix representations that allow simpler notation and easier analysis when implemented using a computer program. Searle (1982) covers matrix calculations in statistics. Multidimensional exploratory data analysis is a developing field of statistics, incorporating developments in computer science. Substantial advances may well come from this research in the near future. For a review of some of these developments, particularly multidimensional graphics, consult Hand, Mannila and Smyth (2001).

We introduced multidimensional analysis of qualitative data, trying to systematise the argument from an applied viewpoint. This too is a developing field and the existence of so many indexes suggests that the arguments have yet to be consolidated. We put the available indexes into three principal classes: distance measures, dependence measures and model-based indexes. Distance measures are applicable to any contingency tables, for dimension and number of levels, but the results they produce are only moderately informative. Dependence measures give precise information on the type of dependence among the variables being examined, but they are hardly applicable to contingency table of dimension greater than 2. Model-based indexes are a possible compromise. They are sufficiently broad and they offer a good amount of information. An extra advantage is that they relate to the most important statistical models for analysing qualitative data: logistic and log-linear regression models (Chapter 5). For an introduction to descriptive analysis of qualitative data, consult Agresti (1990).

An alternative approach to multidimensional visualisation of the data is reduction to spaces of lower dimension. The loss of information and the difficulty of interpreting the reduced information may be compensated by greater usability of the results. The classical technique is principal component analysis. We looked at how it works, but for greater detail on the formal aspects consult Mardia, Kent and Bibby (1979). The method of principal components is used for more than exploratory data analysis; it underpins an important modelling technique known as (confirmatory) factor analysis, widely adopted in the social sciences. Assuming a probabilistic model, usually Gaussian, it decomposes the variance–covariance matrix into two parts: one part is common to all the variables and corresponds to the presence of underlying latent variables (variables that are unobserved or not measurable) and the other part is specific to each variable. In this framework, the chosen principal components identify the latent variables and are interpreted accordingly. Rotation of the components (latent factors) is a way of modifying the weight coefficients to improve their interpretability. For further details on factor analysis consult Bollen (1989).

Principal component analysis is probably the simplest way to accomplish data reduction as it is based on linear transformations. Essentially, the obtained scores transform the original data into linear projections on the reduced space, minimising the Euclidean distance between the coordinates in the original space and the transformed data. Other types of transformation include wavelet methods, based on Fourier transforms, as well as the methods of projection pursuit, which look for the best directions of projection on a reduced space. Both techniques are covered in Hand, Mannila and Smyth (2001) and Hastie, Tibshirani and Friedman (2001). There are also methodologies for reducing the dimensionality of qualitative data. For every row of a contingency table with two dimensions, correspondence analysis produces a graphical row profile, corresponding to the conditional frequency distribution of the row. It produces a similar profile for every column. Dimensionality reduction is then performed by projecting these profiles in a space of lower dimension that reproduces the most likely of the original dispersion, which is related to the X^2 statistic. Correspondence analysis can also be applied to contingency tables of arbitrary dimension (represented using the Burt matrix). Greenacre (1983) provides an introduction to correspondence analysis.

CHAPTER 4

Computational data mining

This chapter and the next will examine the main data mining methodologies. This chapter contains methodologies which do not necessarily require formulation in terms of a probabilistic model. In fact, many of these methodologies were invented and developed in the field of computer science rather than in statistics. Recently, however, statisticians have also made use of these methodologies because of their proven usefulness in solving data mining problems.

The methodologies in Chapter 5 adopt a probabilistic model that describes the generating mechanism of the observed data. The introduction of such a framework allows more subtle information to be extracted from the data; on the other hand, it requires more sophisticated background knowledge. Most of the methodologies that will be presented in this group were invented and developed within the field of statistics. However, they have been taken up by computer scientists working with data mining, thanks to their greater accuracy.

Because of their main origin in computer science, the methods presented in this chapter will be called 'computational methods for data mining', and those in the following chapter will be called 'statistical models for data mining'. The distinction is not rigid; the methodologies discussed in this chapter are also statistical in nature since they deal with the analysis of statistical data. Often they are accompanied by the formulation of a probabilistic model. Some of them, like linear regression and logistic regression, were actually invented and developed in statistics. Likewise, the methodologies discussed in the next chapter are often closely related to computational aspects in the sense that the same properties of the methods can sometimes be verified only with the help of computational analysis.

Broadly speaking, both computer scientists and statisticians have been working on data mining methodologies but emphasising different aspects: computer scientists have been more concerned with algorithmic aspects and computational efficiency of the procedure, whereas statisticians have studied mathematical foundations and statistical properties. We will be more concerned with the second aspects, and on the applications of the methods. By dividing the methodologies into two chapters, I have introduced data mining ideas in two stages: an introductory stage (this chapter) and a more advanced stage (next chapter).

Applied Data Mining.   Paolo Giudici
© 2003 John Wiley & Sons, Ltd   ISBNs: 0-470-84679-8 (Paper); 0-470-84678-X (Cloth)

Section 4.1 deals with the important concepts of proximity and distance between statistical observations, concepts that are basic to many of the methodologies developed in the chapter. Section 4.2 deals with clustering methods, aimed at classifying observations into homogeneous groups. Clustering is probably the most well-known descriptive data mining method. In the section we will examine non-probabilistic clustering methods, leaving probabilistic clustering ideas to Section 5.2. Linear regression is the most important prediction method for continuous variables; Section 4.3 examines it from a non-probabilistic viewpoint. Probabilistic aspects will be considered when dealing with the linear model in Section 5.3. Logistic regression is the main prediction method for qualitative variables; Section 4.4 examines it from a non-probabilistic viewpoint. Section 5.4 will deal with the full probabilistic logistic regression model.

Another important predictive methodology is represented by tree models, described in Section 4.5, which can be used for regression and clustering purposes. There is a fundamental difference between cluster analysis, on one hand, and logistic regression and tree models, on the other hand. In logistic regression and tree models, the clustering is supervised – it is measured against a reference variable (target or response) whose levels are known. In cluster analysis the clustering is unsupervised – there are no reference variables. The clustering analysis determines the nature and the number of groups and allocates the observations within them. Section 4.6 deals with neural networks. It examines two main types of network: the multilayer perceptron, which can be used for predictive purposes, in a supervised manner; and the Kohonen networks (also known as self-organising maps), which are clustering methods useful for unsupervised learning. Section 4.7 deals with another important predictive methodology, based on the rather flexible class of nearest-neighbour methods, sometimes called memory-based reasoning models. Section 4.8 deals with the two most important local data mining methods: association and sequence rules, which are concerned with relationships between variables, and retrieval by content, which is concerned with relationships between observations. Finally, Section 4.9 contains a brief overview of recent computational methods and gives some pointers to the literature.

4.1 Measures of distance

Often in this chapter, we will discuss the methods suitable for classifying and grouping observations in homogeneous groups. In other words, we will consider the relationships between the rows of the data matrix which correspond to observations. In order to compare observations, we need to introduce the idea of a distance measure, or proximity, among them. The indexes of proximity between pairs of observations furnish indispensable preliminary information for identifying homogeneous groups. More precisely, an index of proximity between any two observations x_i and x_j can be defined as a function of the corresponding row vectors in the data matrix:

$$IP_{ij} = f(x_i^{'}, x_j^{'}) \qquad i, j = 1, 2, \ldots, n$$

We will use an example from Chapter 8 as a running example in this chapter. We have $n = 22\,527$ visitors to a website and $p = 35$ dichotomous variables that define the behaviour of each visitor. In this case a proximity index will be a function of two 35-dimensional row vectors. Knowledge of the proximity indexes for every pair of visitors allows us to individualize those among them that are more similar, or at least the less different ones, with the purpose of constituting some groups as the most possible homogeneous among them.

When the considered variables are quantitative, the proximity indexes are typically known as distances. If the variables are qualitative, the distance between the observations can be measured by indexes of similarity. If the data are contained in a contingency table, the chi-squared distance can also be employed. There are also indexes of proximity that can be used on a mixture of qualitative and quantitative variables. We will examine the Euclidean distance for quantitative variables and some indexes of similarity for qualitative variables.

4.1.1 Euclidean distance

Consider a data matrix containing only quantitative (or binary) variables. If x and y are rows from the data matrix then a function $d(x, y)$ is said to be a distance between two observations if it satisfies the following properties:

- *Non-negativity:* $d(x, y) \geq 0$ for all x and y
- *Identity:* $d(x, y) = 0 \Leftrightarrow x = y$ for all x and y
- *Symmetry:* $d(x, y) = d(y, x)$ for all x and y
- *Triangle inequality:* $d(x, y) \leq d(x, z) + d(y, z)$ for all x, y and z

To achieve a grouping of all observations, the distance is usually considered between all observations present in the data matrix. All such distances can be represented in a matrix of distances. A distance matrix can be represented in the following way:

$$
\Delta = \begin{pmatrix}
0 & \dots & d_{1i} & \dots & d_{1n} \\
\vdots & \ddots & \vdots & & \vdots \\
d_{i1} & \dots & 0 & \dots & d_{in} \\
\vdots & & \vdots & \ddots & \vdots \\
d_{n1} & \dots & d_{ni} & \dots & 0
\end{pmatrix}
$$

where the generic element d_{ij} is a measure of distance between the row vectors x_i and x_j. The Euclidean distance is the most used distance measure. It is defined, for any two units indexed by i and j, as the square root of the difference between the corresponding vectors, in the p-dimensional Euclidean space:

$$
{}_2d_{ij} = d(x_i, x_j) = \left[\sum_{s=1}^{p} (x_{is} - x_{js})^2 \right]^{1/2}
$$

The Euclidean distance can be strongly influenced by a single large difference in one dimension of the values, because the square will greatly magnify that difference. Dimensions having different scales (e.g. some values measured in centimetres, others measured in metres) are often the source of these overstated differences. To overcome this limitation, the Euclidean distance is often calculated not on the original variables, but on useful transformations of them. The commonest choice is to standardise the variables (Section 2.5). After standardisation, every transformed variable contributes to the distance calculation with equal weight. When the variables are standardised, they have a zero mean and unit variance; furthermore, it can be shown that, for $i, j = 1, \ldots, p$,

$$_2d_{ij}^2 = 2(1 - r_{ij})$$

$$r_{ij} = 1 - d_{ij}^2/2$$

where r_{ij} indicates the correlation coefficient between the observations x_i and x_j. The previous relationships shows that the Euclidean distance between two observations is a function of the correlation coefficient between them.

4.1.2 Similarity measures

Given a finite set of observations $u_i \in U$, a function $S(u_i, u_j) = S_{ij}$ from $U \times U$ to $\mathbb{R}$ is called an index of similarity if it satisfies the following properties:

- *Non-negativity:* $S_{ij} \geq 0, \forall u_i, u_j \in U$
- *Normalisation:* $S_{ii} = 1, \forall u_i \in U$
- *Symmetry:* $S_{ij} = S_{ji}, \forall u i_i, u_j \in U$

Unlike distances, the indexes of similarity can be applied to all kinds of variables, including qualitative variables. They are defined with reference to the observation indexes, rather than to the corresponding row vectors, and they assume values in the closed interval [0, 1], rather than on any non-negative value, facilitating interpretation. The complement of an index of similarity is called an index of dissimilarity and represents a class of indexes of proximity wider than that of the distances. In fact, as a distance, a dissimilarity index satisfies the properties of non-negativity and symmetry. However, the property of normalisation is not equivalent to the property of identity of the distances. And, finally, dissimilarities do not have to satisfy the triangle inequality.

Indexes of similarity can be calculated, in principle, for quantitative variables. But they would be of limited use, since they would distinguish only whether two observations had, for the different variables, observed values equal or different, without saying anything about the size of the difference. From an operational viewpoint, the principal indexes of similarity make reference to data matrices containing binary variables. More general cases, with variables having more than two levels, can be brought into this framework through binarisation (Section 2.3).

Consider data regarding n visitors to a website, which has P pages. Correspondingly, there are P binary variables, which assume the value 1 if the specific

Table 4.1 Classification of the visited webpages.

Visitor B Visitor A	1	0	Total
1	$CP = 2$	$PA = 4$	6
0	$AP = 1$	$CA = 21$	22
	3	25	$P = 28$

page has been visited, or else the value 0. To demonstrate the application of similarity indexes, we now analyse only data concerning the behaviour of the first two visitors (2 of the n observations) to the website described in Chapter 8, among the $P = 28$ webpages they can visit. Table 4.1 summarises the behaviour of the two visitors, treating each page as a binary variable.

Note that, of the 28 considered pages ($P = 28$), 2 have been visited by both visitors. In other words, 2 represents the absolute frequency of contemporary occurrences (CP, for co-presence, or positive matches) for the two observations. In the lower right corner of the table there is a frequency of 21, equal to the number of pages that are visited neither by A nor by B. This frequency corresponds to contemporary absences in the two observations (CA, for co-absences or negative matches). Finally, the frequencies of 4 and 1 indicate the number of pages that only one of the two navigators visits (PA indicates presence-absence and AP absence-presence, where the first letter refers to visitor A and the second to visitor B).

The latter two frequencies denote the differential aspects between the two visitors and therefore must be treated in the same way, being symmetrical. The co-presence is aimed at determining the similarity between the two visitors, a fundamental condition because they could belong to the same group. The co-absence is less important, perhaps negligibly important for determining the similarities between the two units. In fact, the indexes of similarity developed in the statistical literature differ in how they treat the co-absence, as we now describe.

Similarity index of Russel and Rao

$$S_{ij} = \frac{CP}{p}$$

This index is a function of the co-presences and is equal to the ratio between the number of co-presences and the total number of considered binary variables, P. From Table 4.1 we have

$$S_{ij} = \frac{2}{28} \approx 0.07$$

Similarity index of Jaccard

$$S_{ij} = \frac{CP}{CP + PA + AP}$$

This index is the ratio between the number of co-presences and the total number of variables, excluding those that manifest co-absences. Note that this index is indefinite when the two visitors, or more generally the two observations, manifest only co-absences ($CA = P$). In our example we have

$$S_{ij} = \frac{2}{7} \approx 0.286$$

Similarity index of Sokal and Michener

$$S_{ij} = \frac{CP + CA}{P}$$

This represents the ratio between the number of co-presences or co-absences and the total number of variables. In our example we have

$$S_{ij} = \frac{23}{28} \approx 0.82$$

For the index of Sokal and Michener (also called the simple matching coefficient) it is simple to demonstrate that its complement to one (a dissimilarity index) corresponds to the average of the squared Euclidean distance between the two vectors of binary variables associated with the observations:

$$1 - S_{ij} = \frac{1}{P} \left({}_2d_{ij}^2 \right)$$

This relationship shows that the complement to one of the index of Sokal and Michener is a distance. In fact, it is one of the most used indexes of similarity. It is also known as the coefficient of 'simple matching' and the 'binary distance'; calling it the binary distance is a slight abuse of terminology. Chapter 12 contains a real application of the index of Sokal and Michener.

4.1.3 Multidimensional scaling

We have seen how to calculate proximities between observations, on the basis of a given data matrix, or a table derived from it. Sometimes only the proximities between observations are available, for instance in terms of a distance matrix, and it is desired to reconstruct the values of the observations. In other cases the proximities are calculated using a dissimilarity measure and it is desired to reproduce them in terms of a Euclidean distance, to obtain a representation of the observations in a two-dimensional plane. Multidimensional scaling methods are aimed at representing observations whose observed values are unknown (or not expressed numerically) in a low-dimensional Euclidean space (usually in $\mathbb{R}^2$). The representation is achieved by preserving the original distances as far as possible.

Section 3.5 explained how to use the method of principal components on a quantitative data matrix in a Euclidean space. It turns the data matrix into a lower-dimensional Euclidean projection by minimising the Euclidean distance between the original observations and the projected ones. Similarly, multidimensional scaling methods look for low-dimensional Euclidean representations of the observations, representations which minimise an appropriate distance between the original distances and the new Euclidean distances. Multidimensional scaling methods differ in how such distance is defined. The most common choice is the stress function, defined by

$$\sqrt{\sum_{i=1}^{n} \sum_{j=1}^{n} (\delta_{ij} - d_{ij})^2}$$

where δ_{ij} are the original distances (or dissimilarities) between each pair of observations, and d_{ij} are the corresponding distances between the reproduced coordinates.

Metric multidimensional scaling methods look for k real-valued n-dimensional vectors, each representing one coordinate measurement of the n observations, such that the $n \times n$ distance matrix between the observations, expressed by d_{ij}, minimises the squared stress function. Typically $k = 2$, so the results of the procedure can be conveniently represented in a scatterplot. The illustrated solution is also known as least squares scaling. A variant of least squares scaling is Sammon mapping, which minimises

$$\sqrt{\sum_{i=1}^{n} \sum_{j=1}^{n} \frac{(\delta_{ij} - d_{ij})^2}{\delta_{ij}}}$$

thereby preserving smaller distances.

When the proximities between objects are expressed by a Euclidean distance, it can be shown that the solution of the previous problem corresponds to the principal component scores that would be obtained if the data matrix were available.

It is possible to define non-metric multidimensional scaling methods, where the preserved relationship between the original and the reproduced distances is not necessarily Euclidean. Chapter 12 contains some applications of multidimensional scaling methods. For further information see Mardia, Kent and Bibby (1979).

4.2 Cluster analysis

This section is about cluster analysis and methodologies for grouping a given set of observations. Cluster analysis is the most well-known descriptive data mining method. Given a data matrix composed of n observations (rows) and p variables (columns), the objective of cluster analysis is to cluster the observations into groups that are internally homogeneous (internal cohesion) and heterogeneous from group to group (external separation). Note that the constitution of homogeneous groups of observations can be interpreted as a reduction of the dimension of the space $\mathbb{R}^n$, but not in the same way as in principal component analysis (Section 3.5). In fact, in a cluster analysis, the n observations are grouped into g subsets (with $g < n$), whereas in principal component analysis the p statistical variables are transformed into k new variables (with $k < p$). There are several ways to perform a cluster analysis. It is therefore important to have a clear understanding of how the analysis will proceed. Here are some important points to consider.

Choice of variables to be used

The choice of the variables to be used for clustering has to consider all the relevant aspects to achieve the stated objectives. Remember that using variables of little importance will inevitably worsen the results. This is a crucial problem since it will strongly condition the final result. In general, clustering can be considered satisfactory when it does not show an excessive sensitivity to small changes in the set of used variables. Before doing a cluster analysis, it is prudent to conduct accurate exploratory investigations that are able to suggest possible final configurations for the clustering. To help with visualisation and interpretation of the results, it is often appropriate to reduce the dimensionality of the data matrix, perhaps through the method of principal components.

During the exploratory phase, pay particular attention to anomalous observations that might negatively affect the analysis. Some data mining textbooks (e.g. Han and Kamber, 2001) link the methods of cluster analysis with those that search for outliers. Although there are similarities, I still maintain that one should choose cluster analysis to classify data into groups and outlier detection to search for anomalous observations.

Method of group formation

We can distinguish hierarchical and non-hierarchical methods. Hierarchical methods allow us to get a succession of groupings (called partitions or clusters) with a number of groups from n to 1, starting from the simplest, where all observations are separated, to the situation where all observations belong to a unique group. Non-hierarchical methods allow us to gather the n units directly into a number of previously defined groups.

Type of proximity index

According to the nature of the available variables, it is necessary to define a measure of proximity among the observations, to be used for calculating distances between them. If the data is predominantly quantitative, use the Euclidean distance; if the data is predominantly qualitative, use an index of similarity; if the data is available in a contingency table format, use the chi-squared distance between the levels. As shown in Section 4.1, most measures of proximity can be interpreted as distances, so we will make exclusive reference to this concept. Remember the importance of standardising the variables so that all carry the same weight in the final results.

Besides establishing a measure of proximity between observations, for hierarchical clustering methods we need to establish how to calculate the distances between groups. It is usually appropriate to use the same type of distance as the distance between observations. It remains to establish which units (or synthesis of them) to use as 'representative' of the group. This depends on the method of hierarchical clustering.

Choice of evaluation criteria

Evaluating the results of the obtained grouping means verifying that the groups are consistent with the primary objective of the cluster analysis and that they therefore satisfy the conditions of internal cohesion and external separation. Choosing the right number of groups is fundamentally important. There is a trade-off between obtaining homogeneous groups, which typically increases the number of groups, and the need to get a parsimonious representation, which reduces the number of groups. We will return to this point.

4.2.1 Hierarchical methods

Hierarchical methods of clustering allow us to get a family of partitions, each associated with the subsequent levels of grouping among the observations, calculated on the basis of the available data. The different families of partitions can be represented graphically through a tree-like structure called a tree of hierarchical clustering or a dendrogram. This structure associates to every step of the hierarchical procedure, corresponding to a fixed number of groups g, one and only one clustering of the observations in the g groups.

A hierarchical clustering tree can be represented as in Figure 4.1, where for simplicity we suppose there are only five observations available, numbered from 1 to 5. The branches of the tree describe subsequent clusterings of the observations. At the root of the tree, all the observations are contained in only one class. The branches of the tree indicate divisions of the observations into clusters. The five terminal nodes indicate the situation where each observation belongs to a separate group.

Agglomerative clustering is where the groups are formed from the branches to the root (left to right in Figure 4.1). Divise clustering is where the groups

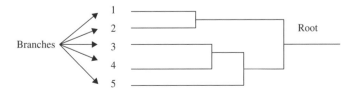

Figure 4.1 Structure of the dendrogram.

Table 4.2 Partitions corresponding to the dendrogram in Figure 4.1.

Number of clusters	Clusters
5	(1) (2) (3) (4) (5)
4	(1,2) (3) (4) (5)
3	(1,2) (3,4) (5)
2	(1,2) (3,4,5)
1	(1,2,3,4,5)

are formed from the root to the branches. Statistical software packages usually report the whole dendrogram, from the root to a number of terminal branches equal to the number of observations. It then remains to choose the optimal number of groups. This will identify the result of the cluster analysis, since in a dendrogram the choice of the number of groups g identifies a unique partition of the observations.

For example, the partitions of the five observations described by the dendrogram in Figure 4.1 can be represented as in Table 4.2.

Table 4.2 shows that the partitions described by a dendrogram are nested. This means that, in the hierarchical methods, the elements that are united (or divided) at a certain step will remain united (separated) until the end of the clustering process. Supposing we consider an agglomerative method that proceeds from 5 groups to 1 group, then units 1 and 2 are united at the second step and remain in the same group until the end of the procedure. Nesting reduces the number of partitions to compare, making the procedure computationally more efficient, but the disadvantage is not being able 'to correct' errors of clustering committed in the preceding steps. Here is an outline for an agglomerative clustering algorithm:

1. *Initialization*: given n statistical observations to classify, every element represents a group (put another way, the procedure starts with n clusters). The clusters will be identified with a number that goes from 1 to n.
2. *Selection*: the two 'nearest' clusters are selected, in terms of the distance initially fixed, for example in terms of the Euclidean distance.
3. *Updating*: the number of clusters is updated (to $n-1$) through the union, in a unique cluster, of the two groups selected in step 2. The matrix of the distances is updated, taking the two rows (and two columns) of distances between the two clusters and replacing them with only one row (and one column) of distances, 'representative' of the new group. Different clustering methods define this representation in different ways.
4. *Repetition*: steps 2 and 3 are performed $n-1$ times.
5. *End*: the procedure stops when all the elements are incorporated in a unique cluster.

We will now look at some of the different clustering methods mentioned in step 3. They will be introduced with reference to two groups, C_1 and C_2. Some methods require only the distance matrix and some require the distance matrix plus the original data matrix. These examples require only the distance matrix:

- *Single linkage*: the distance between two groups is defined as the minimum of the $n_1 n_2$ distances between each observation of group C_1 and each observation of group C_2:

$$d(C_1, C_2) = \min(d_{rs}) \text{ with } r \in C_1, s \in C_2$$

- *Complete linkage*: the distance between two groups is defined as the maximum of the $n_1 n_2$ distances between each observation of a group and each observation of the other group:

$$d(C_1, C_2) = \max(d_{rs}) \text{ with } r \in C_1, s \in C_2$$

- *Average linkage*: the distance between two groups is defined as the arithmetic average of the $n_1 n_2$ distances between each of the observations of a group and each of the observations of the other group:

$$d(C_1, C_2) = \frac{1}{n_1 n_2} \sum_{r=1}^{n_1} \sum_{s=1}^{n_2} d_{rs} \quad \text{with} \quad r \in C_1, s \in C_2$$

Two methods that require the data matrix as well as the distance matrix are the method of the centroid and Ward's method.

Method of the centroid
The distance between two groups C_1 and C_2, having n_l and n_2 observations respectively, is defined as the distance between the respective centroids (usually the means), $\overline{x_1}$ and $\overline{x_2}$:

$$d(C_1, C_2) = d(\overline{x}_1, \overline{x}_2)$$

To calculate the centroid of a group of observations we need the original data, and we can obtain that from the data matrix. It will be necessary to replace the distances with respect to the centroids of the two previous clusters by the distances with respect to the centroid of the new cluster. The centroid of the new cluster can be obtained from

$$\frac{\overline{x}_1 n_1 + \overline{x}_2 n_2}{n_1 + n_2}$$

Note the similarity between this method and the average linkage method: the average linkage method considers the average of the distances between the observations of each of the two groups, whereas the centroid method calculates the centroid of each group then measures the distance between the centroids.

Ward's method

In choosing the groups to be joined, Ward's method minimises an objective function using the principle that clustering aims to create groups which have maximum internal cohesion and maximum external separation.

The total deviance (T) of the p variables, corresponding to n times the trace of the variance–covariance matrix, can be divided in two parts: the deviance within the groups (W) and the deviance between the groups (B), so $T = W + B$. This is analogous to dividing the variance into two parts for linear regression (Section 4.3). In that case B is the variance explained by the regression and W is the residual variance, the variance not explained by the regression. In formal terms, given a partition into g groups then the total deviance (T) of the p variables corresponds to the sum of the deviances of the single variables, with respect to the overall mean $\bar{x}_s$, defined by

$$T = \sum_{s=1}^{p} \sum_{i=1}^{n} (x_{is} - \bar{x}_s)^2$$

The deviance within the groups (W) is given by the sum of the deviances of each group:

$$W = \sum_{k=1}^{g} W_k$$

where W_k represents the deviance of the p variables in the kth group (number n_k and centroid $\bar{x}_k = [\bar{x}_{1k}, \ldots, \bar{x}_{pk}]'$), described by the following expression:

$$W_k = \sum_{s=1}^{p} \sum_{i=1}^{n_k} (x_{is} - \bar{x}_{sk})^2$$

The deviance between the groups, (B) is given by the sum (calculated on all the variables) of the weighted deviances of the group means with respect to the corresponding general averages:

$$B = \sum_{s=1}^{p} \sum_{k=1}^{g} n_k (\bar{x}_{sk} - \bar{x}_s)^2$$

Using Ward's method, groups are joined so that the increase in W is smaller and the increase in B is larger. This achieves the greatest possible internal cohesion and external separation. Notice that it does not require preliminary calculation of the distance matrix. Ward's method can be interpreted as a variant of the centroid method, which does require the distance matrix.

How do we choose which method to apply?

In practice there is not a method that can give the most qualified result with every type of data. Experiment with the different alternatives and compare them in terms of the chosen criteria. We shall see some criteria in Section 4.2.2 and more generally in Chapter 6.

Divise clustering algorithms

The algorithms used for divisive clustering are very similar to those used for tree models (Section 4.5). In general, they are less used in routine applications, as they tend to be more computationally intensive. However, although naive implementation of divisive methods requires n^2 distance calculations on the first iteration, subsequent divisions are on much smaller cluster sizes. Also, efficient implementations do not compute all pairwise distances but only those that are reasonable candidates for being the closest together.

4.2.2   Evaluation of hierarchical methods

A hierarchical algorithm produces a family of partitions of the n initial statistical units, or better still, a succession of n clusterings of the observations, with the number of groups decreasing from n to 1. To verify that the partitions achieve the primary objective of the cluster analysis – internal cohesion and external separation – the goodness of the obtained partition should be measured at every step of the hierarchical procedure.

A first intuitive criterion for goodness of the clustering is the distance between the joined groups at every step; the process can be stopped when the distance increases abruptly. A criterion used more frequently is based on the decomposition of the total deviance of the p variables, as in Ward's method. The idea is to have a low deviance within the groups (W) and a high deviance between the groups (B). For a partition of g groups here is a synthetic index that expresses this criterion:

$$R^2 = 1 - \frac{W}{T} = \frac{B}{T}$$

Since $T = W + B$, the index $R^2 \in [0, 1]$; if the value of R^2 approaches 1, it means that the corresponding partition is optimal, since the observations belonging to the same group are very similar (low W) and the groups are well separated (high B). Correspondingly, the goodness of the clustering decreases as R^2 approaches 0.

Note that $R^2 = 0$ when there is only one group and $R^2 = 1$ when there are as many groups as observations. As the number of groups increases, the homogeneity within the groups increases (as each group contains fewer observations), and so does R^2. But this leads to a loss in the parsimony of the clustering. Therefore the maximisation of R^2 cannot be considered the only criterion for defining the optimal number of groups. Ultimately it would lead to a clustering (for which $R^2 = 1$) of n groups, each having one unit.

A common measure to accompany R^2 is the pseudo-F criterion. Let c be a certain level of the procedure, corresponding to a number of groups equal to c, and let n be the number of observations available. The pseudo-F criterion is defined as follows:

$$F_c = \frac{B/(c-1)}{W/(n-c)}$$

Generally F_c decreases with c since the deviance between groups should decrease and the deviance within groups should increase. If there is an abrupt fall, it means that very different groups are united among them. The advantage of the pseudo-F criterion is that, in analogy with what happens in the context of the normal linear model (Section 5.3), it is possible to show how to build a decision rule that allows us to establish whether to accept the fusion among the groups (null hypothesis) or to stop the procedure, choosing the less parsimonious representation (alternative hypothesis). This decision rule is specified by a confidence interval based on the F distribution, with $(c-1)$ and $(n-c)$ degrees of freedom. But in applying the decision rule, we assume that the observations follow a normal distribution, reducing the advantages of a model-free formulation, such as that adopted here.

An alternative to R^2 is the root mean square standard deviation (RMSSTD). This only considers the part of the deviance in the additional groups formed at each step of the hierarchical clustering. Considering the hth step ($h = 2, \ldots, n - 1$) of the procedure, RMSSTD is defined by the following expression:

$$\text{RMSSTD} = \sqrt{\frac{W_h}{p(n_h - 1)}}$$

where W_h is the deviance in the group constituted at step h of the procedure, n_h is its numerosity and p is the number of available variables. A strong increase of RMSSTD from one step to the next shows that the two groups being united are strongly heterogeneous and therefore it would be appropriate to stop the procedure at the earlier step.

Another index that, similar to RMSSTD, measures the 'additional' contribution of the hth step of the procedure is the so-called 'semipartial' R^2 (SPRSQ). It is defined by

$$\text{SPRSQ} = \frac{W_h - W_r - W_s}{T}$$

where h is the new group, obtained at step h as a fusion of groups r and s. T is the total deviance of the observations, while W_h, W_r and W_s are the deviance of the observations in the groups h, r and s, respectively. Put another way, SPRSQ measures the increase of the within-group deviance W obtained by joining groups r and s. An abrupt increase of SPSRQ indicates that heterogeneous groups are being united and therefore it is appropriate to stop at the previous step.

I believe that choosing one index from the 'global' indexes R^2 and pseudo-F and one index from the 'local' indexes RMSSTD and SPRSQ allows us to evaluate adequately the degree of homogeneity of the obtained groups in every step of a hierarchical clustering and therefore to choose the best partition.

Table 4.3   Output of a cluster analysis.

NCL	--Clusters Joined---		FREQ	SPRSQ	RSQ
11	CL19	CL24	13	0.0004	.998
10	CL14	CL18	42	0.0007	.997
9	CL11	CL13	85	0.0007	.996
8	CL16	CL15	635	0.0010	.995
7	CL17	CL26	150	0.0011	.994
6	CL9	CL27	925	0.0026	.991
5	CL34	CL12	248	0.0033	.988
4	CL6	CL10	967	0.0100	.978
3	CL4	CL5	1215	0.0373	.941
2	CL7	CL3	1365	0.3089	.632
1	CL2	CL8	2000	0.6320	.000

Table 4.3 gives an example of cluster analysis, obtained with Ward's method, in which the indexes R^2 and SPRSQ are indeed able to give an indication about the number of partitions to choose. A number of clusters (NCL) equal to 3 is more than satisfactory, as indicated by the row third from last, in which clusters 4 and 5 are united. In fact, the further step to unite groups 7 and 3 leads to a relevant reduction of R^2 and to an abrupt increase of SPRSQ. On the other hand, choosing NCL equal to 4 does not give noticeable improvements in R^2. Note that the cluster joined at NCL $= 3$ contains 1215 observations (FREQ).

To summarise, there is no unequivocal criterion for evaluating the methods of cluster analysis but a whole range of criteria. Their application should strike a balance between simplicity and information content.

4.2.3   Non-hierarchical methods

The non-hierarchical methods of clustering allow us to obtain one partition of the n observations in g groups ($g < n$), with g defined a priori. Unlike what happens with hierarchical methods, the procedure gives as output only one partition that satisfies determined optimality criteria, such as the attainment of the grouping that allows us to get the maximum internal cohesion for the specified number of groups. For any given value of g, according to which it is intended to classify the n observations, a non-hierarchical algorithm classifies each of the observations only on the basis of the selected criterion, usually stated by means of an objective function. In general, a non-hierarchical clustering can be summarised by the following algorithm:

1.   Choose the number of groups g and choose an initial clustering of the n statistical units in that number of groups.
2.   Evaluate the 'transfer' of each observation from the initial group to another group. The purpose is to maximise the internal cohesion of the groups. The variation in the objective function determined by the transfer is calculated and, if relevant, the transfer becomes permanent.
3.   Repeat step 2 until a stopping rule is satisfied.

Non-hierarchical algorithms are generally much faster than hierarchical ones, because they employ an interactive structure calculation, which does not require us to determine the distance matrix. The construction of non-hierarchical algorithms tends to make them more stable with respect to data variability. Furthermore non-hierarchical algorithms are suitable for large data sets where hierarchical algorithms would be too slow. Nevertheless, there can be many possible ways of dividing n observations into g non-overlapping groups, especially for real data, and it is impossible to obtain and compare all these combinations. This can make it difficult to do a global maximisation of the objective function, and non-hierarchical algorithms may produce constrained solutions, often corresponding to local maxima of the objective function.

In a non-hierarchical clustering we need to begin by defining the number of the groups. This is usually done by conducting the analysis with different values of g (and different algorithm initialisations) and determining the best solution by comparing appropriate indexes for the goodness of the clustering (such as R^2 or the pseudo-F index).

The most used method of non-hierarchical clustering is the k-means method, where k indicates the number of groups established a priori (g in this section). The k-means algorithm performs a clustering of the n starting elements, in g distinct groups (with g previously fixed), according to the following operational flow:

1. *Initialisation*: having determined the number of groups, g points, called seeds, are defined in the p-dimensional space. The seeds constitute the centroids (measures of position, usually means) of the clusters in the initial partition. There should be sufficient distance between them to improve the properties of convergence of the algorithm. For example, to space the centroids adequately in $\mathbb{R}^p$, the SAS software uses the procedure Fast-clust to perform a preliminary analysis of the data; it selects g observations (seeds) whose reciprocal distance is greater than a predefined threshold, and greater than the distance between them and the observations. Once the seeds are defined, an initial partition of the observations is built, allocating each observation to the group whose centroid is closer.
2. *Transfer evaluation*: the distance of each observation from the centroids of the g groups is calculated. The distance between an observations and the centroid of the group to which it has been assigned has to be a minimum; if it is not a minimum, the observations will be moved to the cluster whose centroid is closest. The centroids of the old group and the new group are then recalculated.
3. *Repetition*: We repeat step 2 until we reach a suitable stabilisation of the groups.

To calculate the distance between the observations and the centroids of the groups, the k-means algorithm employs the Euclidean distance: at the tth iteration, the distance between the ith observation and the centroid of group l (with $i = 1, 2, \ldots, n$

and $l = 1, 2, \ldots, g$) will be equal to

$$d(x_i, \overline{x}_l^{(t)}) = \sqrt{\sum_{s=1}^{p} (x_{is} - \overline{x}_{sl}^{(t)})^2}$$

where $\overline{x}_l^{(t)} = [\overline{x}_{1l}^{(t)}, \ldots, \overline{x}_{pl}^{(t)}]'$ is the centroid of group l calculated at the tth iteration. This shows that the k-means method searches for the partition of the n observations in g groups (with g fixed in advance) that satisfies a criterion of internal cohesion based on the minimisation of the within-group deviance W, therefore the goodness of the obtained partition can be evaluated by calculating the index R^2 of the pseudo-F statistic. A disadvantage of the k-means method is the possibility of obtaining distorted results when there are outliers in the data. Then the non-anomalous units will tend to be classified into very few groups, but the outliers will tend to be put in very small groups on their own. This can create so-called 'elephant clusters' – clusters too big and containing most of the observations. Chapter 9 looks at an application of the k-means clustering method.

4.3 Linear regression

In Chapter 3, dealing with correlation and association between statistical variables, the variables were treated in a symmetric way. We now consider the common situation where we wish to deal with the variables in a non-symmetric way, to derive a predictive model for one (or more) response variables, on the basis of one (or more) of the others. This section focuses on quantitative response variables and the next section focuses on qualitative response variables. Chapter 1 introduced the distinction between descriptive, predictive and local data mining methods. Linear regression is a predictive data mining method.

We will initially suppose that only two variables are available. Later we will consider the multivariate case.

4.3.1 Bivariate linear regression

In many applications it is interesting to evaluate whether one variable, called the dependent variable or the response, can be caused, explained and therefore predicted as a function of another, called the independent variable, the explanatory variable, the covariate or the feature. We will use Y for the dependent (or response) variable and X for the independent (or explanatory) variable. The simplest statistical model that can describe Y as a function of X is linear regression. The linear regression model specifies a noisy linear relationship between variables Y and X, and for each paired observation (x_i, y_i) this can be expressed by the so-called regression function:

$$y_i = a + bx_i + e_i \quad (i = 1, 2, \ldots, n)$$

where a is the intercept of the regression function, b is the slope coefficient of the regression function, also called the regression coefficient, and e_i is the random error of the regression function, relative to the ith observation.

Note that the regression function has two main parts: the regression line and the error term. The regression line can be built empirically, starting from the matrix of available data. The error term describes how well the regression line approximates the observed response variable. From an exploratory view point, determination of the regression line can be described as a problem of fitting a straight line to the observed dispersion diagram. The regression line is the linear function

$$\hat{y}_i = a + bx_i \quad (i = 1, 2, \ldots, n)$$

where $\hat{y}_i$ indicates the fitted ith value of the dependent variable, calculated on the basis of the ith value of the explanatory variable x_i. Having defined the regression line, it follows that the error term e_i in the expression of the regression function represents, for each observation y_i, the residual, namely the difference between the observed response values y_i, and the corresponding values fitted with the regression line, $\hat{y}_i$:

$$e_i = y_i - \hat{y}_i$$

Each residual can be interpreted as the part of the corresponding value that is not explained by the linear relationship with the explanatory variable. What we have just described can be represented graphically as in Figure 4.2. To obtain the analytic expression of the regression line it is sufficient to calculate the parameters a and b on the basis of the available data. The method of least squares is often used for this. It chooses the straight line that minimises the sum of the squares

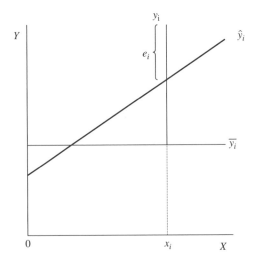

Figure 4.2   Representation of the regression line.

of the errors of the fit (SSE), defined by

$$\text{SSE} = \sum_{i=1}^{n} e_i^2 = \sum_{i=1}^{n} (y_i - \hat{y}_i)^2 = \sum_{i=1}^{n} (y_i - a - bx_i)^2$$

To find the minimum of SSE we need to take the first partial derivatives of the SSE function with respect to a and b then equate them to zero. Since the sum of the squares of the errors is a quadratic function, if an extremal point exists then it is a minimum. Therefore the parameters of the regression line are found by solving the following system of equations, called normal equations:

$$\frac{\partial \sum (y_i - a - bx_i)^2}{\partial a} = -2 \sum_i (y_i - a - bx_i) = 0$$

$$\frac{\partial \sum (y_i - a - bx_i)^2}{\partial b} = -2 \sum_i x_i (y_i - a - bx_i) = 0$$

From the first equation we obtain

$$a = \sum \frac{y_i}{n} - b \sum \frac{x_i}{n} = \mu_Y - b\mu_X$$

Substituting it into the second equation and simplifying, we obtain

$$b = \left(\frac{\sum x_i y_i / n - \sum y_i \sum x_i / n^2}{\sum x_i^2 / n - (\sum x_i / n)^2} \right) = \frac{\text{Cov}(X, Y)}{\text{Var}(X)} = r(X, Y) \frac{\sigma_Y}{\sigma_X}$$

where μ_Y and μ_X are the means, σ_Y and σ_X the standard deviations of the variables Y and X, and $r(X, Y)$ is the correlation coefficient between X and Y.

Regression is a simple and powerful predictive tool. To use it in real situations, it is only necessary to calculate the parameters of the regression line, according to the previous formulae, on the basis of the available data. Then a value for Y is predicted simply by substituting a value for X into the equation of the regression line. The predictive ability of the regression line is a function of the goodness of fit of the regression line, which is very seldom perfect.

If the variables were both standardised, with zero mean and unit variance, then $a = 0$ and $b = r(X, Y)$. Then $y_i = r(X, Y) x_i$ and the regression line of X, as a function of Y, is simply obtained by inverting the linear relation between Y and X. Even though not generally true, this particular case shows the link between a symmetric analysis of the relationships between variables (described by the linear correlation coefficient) and an asymmetric analysis (described by the regression coefficient b).

Here is a simple regression model for the real data introduced in Section 3.2, on the weekly returns of an investment fund. The considered period goes from 4th October 1994 to 4th October 1999. The objective of the analysis is to study the dependence of the returns on the weekly variations of a stock market index

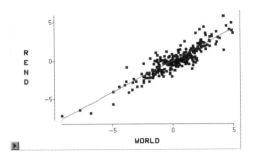

Figure 4.3 Example of a regression line fit.

typically used as benchmark (predictor) of the returns themselves; the index is named MSCI WORLD.

Figure 4.3 shows the behaviour of a simple regression model for this data, along with the scatterplot matrix. The intercept parameter a has been set to zero before adapting the model. This was done to obtain a fitted model that would be the closest possible to the theoretical financial model known as the capital asset pricing model (CAPM). The slope parameter of the regression line in Figure 4.3 is calculated on the basis of the data, according to the formula presented earlier, from which it turns out that $b = 0.8331$. Therefore the regression line can be analytically described by the following equation:

$$REND = 0.8331 \ WORLD$$

where REND is the response variable and WORLD is the explanatory variable. The main utility of this model is in prediction; for example, on the basis of the fitted model, we can forecast that if the WORLD index increases by 10% in a week, the fund returns will increase by 8.331%.

4.3.2 Properties of the residuals

We will now look at some important properties of the regression residuals that will permit us to draw some operational conclusions for the diagnostic phase of the model. We will also see an important geometric interpretation of the regression line, an interpretation we can use in the multivariate case. From the first normal equation we have that

$$\sum_{i=1}^{n} e_i = \sum_{i=1}^{n} (y_i - \hat{y}_i) = 0$$

which shows that the sum of the residuals is null. If in the regression line we set $b = 0$, the arithmetic mean is obtained as a particular linear fit of the dispersion diagram. Such a fit predicts Y with a constant function, ignoring the information provided by X. This property of the regression line coincides, in this particular case, to one of the properties of the arithmetic mean.

From the second normal equation we have that

$$\sum_{i=1}^{n} e_i x_i = \sum_{i=1}^{n} (y_i - \hat{y}_i) x_i = 0$$

This shows that the residuals are uncorrelated with the explanatory variable. It can also be shown that

$$\sum_{i=1}^{n} e_i \hat{y}_i = \sum e_i (a + bx_i) = a \sum e_i + b \sum e_i x_i = 0$$

and therefore the residuals are uncorrelated with the fitted Y values.

To investigate the goodness of fit of the regression line, these properties of the residuals suggest that we plot the residuals against the explanatory variable and that we plot the residuals against the fitted values. Both should show a null correlation in mean, and it is interesting to see whether this null correlation is uniform for all the considered observations or whether it arises from compensation of underfit (i.e. the fitted values are smaller than the observed values) and overfit (i.e. the fitted values are greater than the observed values). Compensation of underfit or overfit reduces the validity of the fit. Figure 4.3 shows a uniform distribution of the residuals. There is a slight difference in behaviour between the central part of the regression line, where the variability of the residuals is much larger than in the remaining part. But this difference does not undermine the excellent fit of the regression line to the data.

The following geometric interpretation is developed for the bivariate case but it can also be extended to the multivariate case. The columns of the data matrix are vectors of dimension n. Therefore they can be thought of as belonging to a linear space. If the variables are quantitative, this space will be the Euclidean space $\mathbb{R}^n$. In the bivariate case under examination in $\mathbb{R}^n$ there will be the vectors $\boldsymbol{y}$, $\boldsymbol{x}$ and also $\boldsymbol{\mu} = (1, \ldots, 1)'$, the column vector needed to obtain the arithmetic means of Y and of X. In geometric terms, the regression line is a linear combination of two vectors, $\hat{\boldsymbol{y}} = a\boldsymbol{\mu} + b\boldsymbol{x}$, determinated by two parameters a and b. Therefore it identifies a linear subspace (hyperplane) of $\mathbb{R}^n$ of dimension 2. In general, if we consider k explanatory variables, we obtain a linear subspace of dimension $k + 1$.

To determine a and b we apply the method of least squares. In geometric terms, we determine a vector in $\mathbb{R}^n$ that minimises the Euclidean distance between the observed vector $\boldsymbol{y}$ in the space $\mathbb{R}^n$ and the estimated vector $\hat{\boldsymbol{y}}$ belonging to the subspace of dimension $k = 2$ in $\mathbb{R}^n$. The square of this distance is given by

$$d^2(\boldsymbol{y}, \hat{\boldsymbol{y}}) = \sum (y_i - \hat{y}_i)^2$$

The least squares method minimises the above distance by setting $\hat{\boldsymbol{y}}$ equal to the projection of the vector $\boldsymbol{y}$ on the subspace of dimension 2. The properties of the residuals help us to comprehend the meaning of this projection. The projection $\hat{\boldsymbol{y}}$ is orthogonal to the vector of the residuals $\boldsymbol{e}$ (third property). The residuals are orthogonal to x (second property) and to μ (first property). We can therefore conclude that the least squares method defines a right-angled triangle, having y as the hypotenuse and $\hat{y}$ and e as the other two sides.

A least squares principle also forms the basis of principal component analysis (Section 3.5); the difference is that in linear regression the distance to be minimised is measured with respect to the response variable only, whereas in principal component analysis it is measured in terms of all variables. We expand on these ideas in the next section, on goodness of fit, but first let us see how to interpret the arithmetic mean in geometric terms. The arithmetic mean is definable as the constant quantity, a, that minimises the expression

$$d^2(y, a) = \sum (y_i - a)^2$$

which represents the distance between y in $\mathbb{R}^n$ and a constant, a, belonging to the subspace of the real numbers of dimension 1 in $\mathbb{R}^n$. Therefore the arithmetic mean is also a solution of the least squares method – it is the projection $\hat{y}$ of the vector of the observations y in the subspace $\mathbb{R}$.

4.3.3 Goodness of fit

The regression line represents a linear fit of the dispersion diagram and therefore involves a degree of approximation. We want to measure the accuracy of that approximation. An important judgement criterion is based on a decomposition of the variance of the dependent variable. Recall that the variance is a measure of variability, and variability in statistics means 'information'. By applying Pythagoras' theorem to the right-angled triangle in Section 4.3.2, we obtain

$$\sum (y_i - \overline{y})^2 = \sum (\hat{y}_i - \overline{y})^2 + \sum (y_i - \hat{y}_i)^2$$

This identity establishes that the total sum of squares (SST), on the left, equals the sum of squares explained by the regression (SSR) plus the sum of squares of the errors (SSE). It can also be written like this:

$$SST = SSR + SSE$$

These three quantities are called deviances; if we divide them by the number of observations n, and indicate statistical variables using the corresponding capital letters, we obtain

$$Var(Y) = Var(\hat{Y}) + Var(E)$$

We have decomposed the variance of the response variable into two components: the variance 'explained' by the regression line, and the 'residual' variance. This leads to our main index for goodness of fit of the regression line; it is the index of determination R^2, defined by

$$R^2 = \frac{Var(\hat{Y})}{Var(Y)} = 1 - \frac{Var(E)}{Var(Y)}$$

The coefficient R^2 is equivalent to the square of the linear correlation coefficient, so it takes values between 0 and 1. It is equal to 0 when the regression line is constant ($Y = \overline{y}$, i.e. $b = 0$); it is equal to 1 when the fit is perfect (the residuals are all null). In general, a high value of R^2 indicates that the dependent variable Y can be well predicted by a linear function of X. The R^2 coefficient of cluster analysis can be derived in exactly the same way by substituting the group means for the fitted line. From the definition of R^2, notice that $\text{Var}(E) = \text{Var}(Y)(1 - R^2)$. This relationship shows how the error in predicting Y reduces from $\text{Var}(Y)$, when the predictor is $Y = \overline{y}$, to $\text{Var}(E)$, when the predictor is $\hat{y}_i = a + bx_i$. Notice that the linear predictor is at least as good as the mean predictor and its superiority increases with $R^2 = r^2(X, Y)$.

Figure 4.3 has R^2 equal to 0.81. This indicates a good fit of the regression line to the data. For the time being, we cannot establish a threshold value for R^2, above which we can say that the regression is valid, and vice versa. We can do this if we assume a normal linear model, as in Section 5.3.

R^2 is only a summary index. Sometimes it is appropriate to augment it with diagnostic graphical measures, which permit us to understand where the regression line approximates the observed data well and where the approximation is poorer. Most of these tools plot the residuals and see what they look like. If the linear regression model is valid, the Y points should be distributed around the fitted line in a random way, without showing obvious trends.

It may be a good starting point to examine the plot of the residuals against the fitted values of the response variable. If the plot indicates a difficult fit, look at the plot of the residuals with respect to the explanatory variable and try to see where the explanatory variable is above or below the fit. Figure 4.4 is a diagnostic plot of the residuals (R_REND) against the fitted values (P_REND) for the financial data in Figure 4.3. The diagnostic confirms a good fit of the regression line. Determination of the regression line can be strongly influenced by the presence of anomalous values, or outliers. This is because the calculation of the parameters is fundamentally based on determining mean measures, so it is sensitive to the presence of extreme values. Before fitting a regression model, it is wise to conduct accurate exploratory analysis to identify anomalous observations. Plotting the residuals against the fitted values can support the univariate analysis of Section 3.1 in locating such outliers.

4.3.4 Multiple linear regression

We now consider a more general (and realistic) situation, in which there is more than one explanatory variable. Suppose that all variables contained in the data matrix are explanatory, except for the variable chosen as response variable. Let k be the number of such explanatory variables. The multiple linear regression is defined by the following relationship, for $i = 1, 2, \ldots, n$:

$$y_i = a + b_1 x_{i1} + b_2 x_{i2} + \cdots + b_k x_{ik} + e_i$$

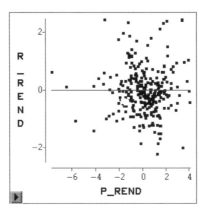

Figure 4.4 Diagnostic of a regression model.

or, equivalently, in more compact matrix terms:

$$Y = Xb + E$$

where, for all the n considered observations, Y is a column vector with n rows containing the values of the response variable; X is a matrix with n rows and $k + 1$ columns containing for each column the values of the explanatory variables for the n observations, plus a column (to refer to the intercept) containing n values equal to 1; b is a vector with $k + 1$ rows containing all the model parameters to be estimated on the basis of the data: the intercept and the k slope coefficients relative to each explanatory variable. Finally E is a column vector of length n containing the error terms. In the bivariate case the regression model was represented by a line, now it corresponds to a $(k + 1)$-dimensional plane, called the regression plane. This plane is defined by the equation

$$\hat{y}_i = a + b_1 x_{i1} + b_2 x_{i2} + \cdots + b_k x_{ik}$$

To determine the fitted plane it is necessary to estimate the vector of the parameters $(a, b_1, \ldots, b_k)$ on the basis of the available data. Using the least squares optimality criterion, as before, the b parameters will be obtained by minimising the square of the Euclidean distance:

$$d^2(y, \hat{y}) = \sum_{i=1}^{n} (y_i - \hat{y}_i)^2$$

We can obtain a solution in a similar way to bivariate regression; in matrix terms it is given by $\hat{Y} = X\beta$ where

$$\beta (X'X)^{-1} X'Y$$

Therefore the optimal fitted plane is defined by

$$\hat{Y} = \mathbf{X}(\mathbf{X}'\mathbf{X})^{-1}\mathbf{X}'Y = \mathbf{H}Y$$

In geometric terms this establishes that the optimal plane is obtained as the projection of the observed vector $y \in \mathbb{R}^n$ on to the $(k + 1)$-dimensional hyperplane. Here the projection operator is the matrix $\mathbf{H}$; in bivariate regression with $a = 0$ the projection operator is b. In fact, for $k = 1$ the two parameters in $\boldsymbol{\beta}$ coincide with parameters a and b in the bivariate case. The properties of the residuals we obtained for the bivariate case can be extended to the multivariate case.

We now apply multiple regression to the investment fund data we have been investigating. We assume a multifactorial model, in conformity with the theory of the arbitrage pricing theory (APT) model. Instead of considering the WORLD index as a unique explanatory variable, we use five indexes relative to specific geographic areas – JAPAN, PACIFIC, EURO, NORDAM, COMIT – as the explanatory variables of the fund return (REND). Table 4.4 summarises the outcome. Notice that the indexes EURO and NORDAM have the strongest effect on the fund return, giving estimated values for the slope regression coefficients that are noticeably greater than the other indexes. For goodness of fit we can still use the variance decomposition identity we obtained for bivariate regression:

$$\mathrm{Var}(Y) = \mathrm{Var}(\hat{Y}) + \mathrm{Var}(E)$$

with $\hat{Y}$ now indicating the regression plane fit. This permits us to define the coefficient of multiple determination as a summary index for the plane's goodness of fit:

$$R^2 = \frac{\mathrm{Var}(\hat{Y})}{\mathrm{Var}(Y)} = 1 - \frac{\mathrm{Var}(E)}{\mathrm{Var}(Y)}$$

The terminology reflects the fact that the plane's goodness of fit depends on the joint effect of the explanatory variables on the response variable. In bivariate regression R^2 is simply the square of the linear correlation coefficient of the

Table 4.4 Least squares estimates from a multiple regression model.

Variable	Parameter estimate
INTERCEPT	−0.0077
COMIT	−0.0145
JAPAN	0.0716
PACIFIC	0.0814
EURO	0.3530
NORDAM	0.3535

response variable with the single explanatory variable; in multivariate regression the relationship is not so straightforward, due to the presence of more than one explanatory variable. An important aim of multivariate regression is to understand not only the absolute contribution of the fitted plane to explaining the variability of Y, as expressed by R^2, but also to determine the partial contribution of each explanatory variable. We now examine in greater detail the variance decomposition identity. It can be demonstrated that

$$\text{Var}(Y) = \sum_{j=1}^{k} b_j \, \text{Cov}(X_j, Y) + \text{Var}(E)$$

But in general

$$b_j \neq \frac{\text{Cov}(X_j, Y)}{\text{Var}(X_i)}$$

If the previous equation were true we would obtain

$$\text{Var}(Y) = \sum_{j=1}^{k} \text{Var}(Y) \, r^2(X_j, Y) + \text{Var}(E)$$

Therefore

$$\text{Var}(\hat{Y}) = \text{Var}(\hat{Y}_1) + \text{Var}(\hat{Y}_2) + \cdots + \text{Var}(\hat{Y}_k)$$

so that

$$R^2 = \sum_{j=1}^{k} r_{Y,X_j}^2$$

The variance of Y explained by the fitting plane would be equal to the sum of the variance of Y explained by each of the fitting lines, built separately for each of the explanatory variables.

However, this situation occurs only when the explanatory variables are uncorrelated. For example, if the explanatory variables are principal components, obtained using the method in Section 3.5. In general it can be shown that the overall contribution of the fitted plane depends on the single contributions through the following recursive relationship:

$$R^2 = \sum_{j=1}^{k} r_{Y,X_j|X_{i<j}}^2 \, (1 - R_{Y,X_1,\ldots,X_{j-1}}^2)$$

where $R_{Y,X_1,\ldots,X_{j-1}}^2$ indicates the coefficient of multiple correlation between Y and the fitted plane determined by the explanatory variables $X_1, \ldots, X_{j-1}$ and $r_{Y,X_j|X_{i<j}}$ indicates the coefficient of partial correlation between Y and X_j, conditional on the 'previous' variables $X_1, \ldots, X_{j-1}$. To clarify how this works in

practice, consider the case of two explanatory variables ($k = 2$). Fitting first X_1 and then X_2, we get

$$R^2 = r^2_{Y,X_1} + r^2_{Y,X_2|X_1}(1 - R^2_{Y,X_1})$$

The term in parentheses takes the amount of variance not explained by the regression (of Y on X_1) and reduces it by a fraction equal to the square of the partial correlation coefficient between itself and the response variable, conditional on the variable X_1 already being present.

To summarise, a single explanatory variable, say X_j, makes an additive contribution to the fitting plane, therefore R^2 increases as the number of variables increases. However, the increase is not necessarily equal to r^2_{Y,X_j}. This occurs only in the uncorrelated case. In general, it can be smaller or greater according to the degree of correlation of the response variable with those already present, and of the latter with X_j.

When the explanatory variables are correlated, the coefficient of regression estimated for a certain variable can change its sign and magnitude according to the order with which the explanatory variables are inserted in the fitted plane. This can be easily verified with a real application and it emphasises the importance of ordering the explanatory variables. Software packages order the variables according to their predictive capacity, obtained from an exploratory analysis. They might order the variables according to the absolute value of the linear correlation coefficient $r(X, Y)$.

Note the importance of the partial correlation coefficient in explaining an extra variable's contribution to the fitted plane. Consider a fitted plane with k explanatory variables. Suppose we want to add a $(k + 1)$th explanatory variable. The contribution of this variable will be the increase in the variance explained by the plane, from $\text{Var}(\hat{Y}_k)$ to $\text{Var}(\hat{Y}_{k+1})$. This contribution can be measured by the difference

$$\text{Var}(\hat{Y}_{k+1}) - \text{Var}(\hat{Y}_k).$$

The square of the coefficient of partial correlation relates this additional contribution to the variance not explained by the fitted plane $\hat{Y}_k$:

$$r^2_{Y,X_{k+1}|X_1,...,X_k} = \frac{\text{Var}(\hat{Y}_{k+1}) - \text{Var}(\hat{Y}_k)}{\text{Var}(Y) - \text{Var}(\hat{Y}_k)}$$

In our financial example the model with the five explanatory variables has a coefficient of multiple determination equal to 0.8191. Among the five considered explanatory variables, the COMIT variable has a coefficient of partial correlation with the response variable, given all the other explanatory variables, equal to about 0.0003. This suggests the possible elimination of the COMIT variable, as it appears substantially irrelevant after having inserted the other explanatory variables. In fact, the coefficient of multiple determination relative to the fit of a model that explains the return as a function of the other four explanatory variables is equal to 0.8189, only slightly inferior to 0.8191.

4.4 Logistic regression

Section 4.3 considered a predictive model for a quantitative response variable; this section considers a predictive model for a qualitative response variable. A qualitative response problem can often be decomposed into binary response problems (e.g. Agresti, 1990). The building block of most qualitative response models is the logistic regression model, one of the most important predictive data mining methods. Let y_i $(i = 1, 2, \ldots, n)$ be the observed values of a binary response variable, which can take only the values 0 or 1. The level 1 usually represents the occurrence of an event of interest, often called a 'success'. A logistic regression model is defined in terms of fitted values to be interpreted as probabilities (Section 5.1) that the event occurs in different subpopulations:

$$\pi_i = P(Y_i = 1), \quad \text{for } i = 1, 2, \ldots, n$$

More precisely, a logistic regression model specifies that an appropriate function of the fitted probability of the event is a linear function of the observed values of the available explanatory variables. Here is an example:

$$\log\left[\frac{\pi_i}{1 - \pi_i}\right] = a + b_1 x_{i1} + b_2 x_{i2} + \cdots + b_k x_{ik}$$

The left-hand side defines the logit function of the fitted probability, logit(π_i), as the logarithm of the odds for the event, namely the natural logarithm of the ratio between the probability of occurrence (success) and the probability of non-occurrence (failure):

$$\text{logit}(\pi_i) = \log\left[\frac{\pi_i}{1 - \pi_i}\right]$$

Once π_i is calculated, on the basis of the data, a fitted value for each binary observation $\hat{y}_i$ can be obtained, introducing a threshold value of π_i above which $\hat{y}_i = 1$ and below which $\hat{y}_i = 0$. The resulting fit will seldom be perfect, so there will be a fitting error that will have to be kept as low as possible. Unlike linear regression, the observed response values cannot be decomposed additively as the sum of a fitted value and an error term.

The choice of the logit function to describe the function that links π_i to the linear combination of the explanatory variables, is motivated by the fact that with this choice the probability tends towards 0 and 1 gradually. And these limits are never exceeded, guaranteeing that π_i is a valid probability. A linear regression model would be inappropriate to predict a binary response variable, simply because a linear function is unlimited, so the model could predict values for the response variable outside the interval [0,1], which would be meaningless. But other types of link are possible, as will be seen in Section 5.4.

4.4.1 Interpretation of logistic regression

The logit function implies that the dependence of π_i on the explanatory variables is described by a sigmoid or S-shaped curve. By inverting the definition of the logit function, we obtain

$$\pi_i = \frac{\exp(a + b_1 x_{i1} + b_2 x_{i2} + \cdots + b_k x_{ik})}{1 + \exp(a + b_1 x_{i1} + b_2 x_{i2} + \cdots + b_k x_{ik})}$$

This relationship corresponds to the function known as a 'logistic curve', often employed for diffusion problems, including the launch of a new product or the diffusion of a reserved piece of information. These applications often concern the simple case of only one explanatory variable, corresponding to a bivariate logistic regression model:

$$\pi_i = \frac{e^{a + b_1 x_{i1}}}{1 + e^{a + b_1 x_{i1}}}$$

Here the value of the success probability varies according to the observed values of the unique explanatory variable. This simplified case is useful to visualise the behaviour of the logistic curve, and to make two more remarks about interpretation. Figure 4.5 shows the graph of the logistic function that links the probability of success π_i to the possible values of the explanatory variable x_i, corresponding to two different signs of the coefficient β. We have assumed the more general setting, in which the explanatory variable is continuous and therefore the success probability can be indicated as $\pi(x)$. For discrete or qualitative explanatory variables the results will be a particular case of what I am about to describe. Notice

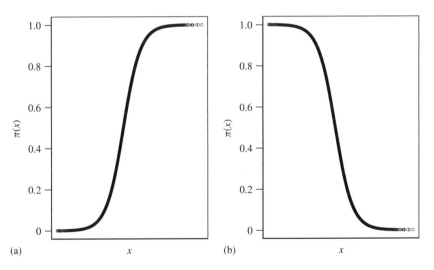

Figure 4.5 The logistic function.

that the parameter β determines the rate of growth or increase of the curve; the sign of β indicates whether the curve increases or decreases and the magnitude of β determines the rate of that increase or decrease:

- When $\beta > 0$ then (x) increases as x increases.
- When $\beta < 0$ then $\pi(x)$ decreases as x increases.

Furthermore, for $\beta \to 0$ the curve tends to become a horizontal straight line. In particular, when $\beta = 0$, Y is independent of X.

Although the probability of success is a logistic function and therefore not linear in the explanatory variables, the logarithm of the odds is a linear function of the explanatory variables:

$$\log\left(\frac{\pi(x)}{1 - \pi(x)}\right) = \alpha + \beta x$$

Positive log-odds favour $Y = 1$ whereas negative log-odds favour $Y = 0$. The log-odds expression establishes that the logit increases by β units for a unit increase in x. It could be used during the exploratory phase to evaluate the linearity of the observed logit. A good linear fit of the explanatory variable with respect to the observed logit will encourage us to apply the logistic regression model. The concept of odds was introduced in Section 3.4. For the logistic regression model, the odds of success can be expressed by

$$\frac{\pi(x)}{1 - \pi(x)} = e^{\alpha + \beta x} = e^{\alpha}(e^{\beta})^x$$

This exponential relationship offers a useful interpretation of the parameter β: a unit increase in x multiplies the odds by a factor e^{β}. In other words, the odds at level $x + 1$ equal the odds at level x multiplied by e^{β}. When $\beta = 0$ we obtain $e^{\beta} = 1$, therefore the odds do not depend on X.

What about the fitting algorithm, the properties of the residuals, and goodness of fit indexes? These concepts can be introduced by interpreting logistic regression as a linear regression model for appropriate transformation of the variables. They are examined as part of the broader field of generalised linear models (Section 5.4), which should make them easier to understand. I have waited until Section 5.4 to give a real application of the model.

4.4.2 Discriminant analysis

Linear regression and logistic regression models are essentially scoring models – they assign a numerical score to each value to be predicted. These scores can be used to estimate the probability that the response variable assumes a predetermined set of values or levels (e.g. all positive values if the response is continuous or a level if it is binary). Scores can then be used to classify the observations into disjoint classes. This is particularly useful for classifying new observations not already present in the database. This objective is more natural for logistic regression models, where predicted scores can be converted in binary values, thus classifying observations in two classes: those predicted to be 0 and those predicted to be 1. To do this, we need a threshold or cut-off rule. This type of predictive classification rule is studied by the classical theory of discriminant analysis. We will consider the simple and common case in which each observation is to be classified using a binary response: it is either in class 0 or in class 1. The more general case is similar, but more complex to illustrate.

The choice between the two classes is usually based on a probabilistic criterion: choose the class with the highest probability of occurrence, on the basis of the observed data. This rationale, which is optimal when equal misclassification costs are assumed (Section 5.1), leads to an odds-based rule that allows us to assign an observation to class 1 (rather than class 0) when the odds in favour of class 1 are greater than 1, and vice versa. Logistic regression can be expressed as a linear function of log-odds, therefore a discriminant rule can be expressed in linear terms, by assigning the ith observations to class 1 if

$$a + b_1 x_{i1} + b_2 x_{i2} + \cdots + b_k x_{ik} > 0$$

With a single predictor variable, the rule simplifies to

$$a + b x_i > 0$$

This rule is known as the logistic discriminant rule; it can be extended to qualitative response variables with more than two classes.

An alternative to logistic regression is linear discriminant analysis, also known as Fisher's rule. It is based on the assumption that, for each given class of the response variable, the explanatory variables are distributed as a multivariate normal distribution (Section 5.1) with a common variance–covariance matrix. Then it is also possible to obtain a rule in linear terms. For a single predictor, the rule assigns observation i to class 1 if

$$\log \frac{n_1}{n_0} - \frac{(\overline{x}_1 - \overline{x}_0)^2}{2s^2} + \frac{x_i(\overline{x}_1 - \overline{x}_0)}{s^2} > 0$$

where n_1 and n_0 are the number of observations in classes 1 and 0; $\overline{x}_1$ and $\overline{x}_0$ are the observed means of the predictor X in the two classes, 1 and 0; s^2 is the variance of X for all the observations. Both Fisher's rule and the logistic discriminant rule can be expressed in linear terms, but the logistic rule is simpler to apply and interpret and it does not require any probabilistic assumptions. Fisher's rule is more explicit than the logistic discriminant rule. By assuming a normal distribution, we can add more information to the rule, such as an assessment of its sampling variability. We shall return to discriminant analysis in Section 5.1.

4.5 Tree models

While linear and logistic regression methods produce a score and then possibly a classification according to a discriminant rule, tree models begin by producing a classification of observations into groups and then obtain a score for each group. Tree models are usually divided into regression trees, when the response variable is continuous, and classification trees, when the response variable is quantitative discrete or qualitative (categorical, for short). However, as most concepts apply equally well to both, here we do not distinguish between them, unless otherwise specified. Tree models can be defined as a recursive procedure, through which a set of n statistical units are progressively divided into groups, according to a division rule that aims to maximise a homogeneity or purity measure of the response variable in each of the obtained groups. At each step of the procedure, a division rule is specified by the choice of an explanatory variable to split and the choice of a splitting rule for such variable, which establishes how to partition the observations.

The main result of a tree model is a final partition of the observations. To achieve this it is necessary to specify stopping criteria for the division process. Suppose that a final partition has been reached, consisting of g groups ($g < n$). Then for any given observation response variable observation y_i, a regression tree produces a fitted value $\hat{y}_i$ that is equal to the mean response value of the group to which the observation i belongs. Let m be such a group; formally we have that

$$\hat{y}_i = \frac{1}{n_m} \sum_{l=1}^{n_m} y_{lm}$$

For a classification tree, fitted values are given in terms of fitted probabilities of affiliation to a single group. If only two classes are possible (binary classification), the fitted success probability is therefore

$$\pi_i = \frac{1}{n_m} \sum_{l=1}^{n_m} y_{lm}$$

where the observations y_{lm} can take the value 0 or 1, therefore the fitted probability corresponds to the observed proportion of successes in group m. Notice that $\hat{y}_i$ and π_i are constant for all the observations in the group.

The output of the analysis is usually represented using a tree; it looks very similar to the dendrogram produced by hierarchical clustering (Section 4.2). This implies that the partition performed at a certain level is influenced by the previous choices. Figure 4.6 shows a classification tree for a credit scoring application described in Chapter 11. For this problem the response variable is binary, and for the time being we use a 1 to indicate the event corresponding to the consumer not being reliable (bad). In Chapter 11 we will follow the opposite convention,

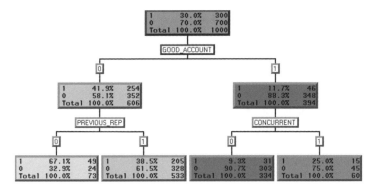

Figure 4.6 Example of a decision tree.

where 1 indicates the 'good' customers. The choice is irrelevant for the final results, but it affects how the model is interpreted.

Figure 4.6 describes the typical output of a tree model analysis. The analysis proceeds in a divisive way. On top of the figure there is the root node of the tree model, which contains all the 1000 available observations; 70% are credit reliable (good) and 30% are credit unreliable (bad). In the first step of the procedure, the consumers are divided into two groups, according to the levels of the variable 'Good Account', estimated to be the most discriminatory. In the group on the right are the 394 consumers with a good account (Good Account = 1), of which about 88% are credit reliable; in the group on the left are the 606 consumers with a bad account (Good Account = 0), of which about 58% are credit reliable. Subsequently, the bad accounts group is further split according to the variable 'Previous Repayments' and the good accounts group is separated according to the variable 'Concurrent' (debts). The tree stops at these levels, so there are four terminal nodes (groups not further divisible).

The terminal nodes of a tree are often called the 'leaves'. The leaves contain the main information conveyed by a tree model analysis; in this example they partition the observations into four groups, ordered by the fitted probability of credit unreliability (response variable): 9.3%, 25%, 38.5% and 67.1%. These fitted probabilities can be compared with those that could be obtained from a logistic regression model.

We can now classify new observations, for which the levels of the response variable are unknown. In Figure 4.6 we can do this by locating such observations in one of the four classes corresponding to the terminal branches, according to the levels assumed by the explanatory variables Good Account, Previous Repayments, and Concurrent, and following the described rules. For example, a consumer with level 0 of the variable Good Account and level 0 of the variable Previous Repayments will be classified as credit unreliable, since the corresponding terminal node (the leftmost leaf) has a very high probability of unreliability (equal to 67.1%). A consumer with level 1 of Good Account and level 0 of Concurrent will be classified as credit reliable, as they have a very low probability of unreliability (9.3%).

For classification trees, a discriminant rule can be derived at each leaf of the tree. A commonly used rule is to classify all observations belonging to a terminal node in the class corresponding to the most frequent level (mode). This corresponds to the so-called 'majority rule'. Other 'voting' schemes are also possible but, in the absence of other considerations, this rule is the most reasonable. Therefore each of the leaves points out a clear allocation rule of the observations, which is read by going through the path that connects the initial node to each of them. Every path in a tree model thus represents a classification rule. Compared with discriminant models, tree models produce rules that are less explicit analytically but easier to understand graphically.

Tree models can be considered as non-parametric predictive models (Section 5.2), since they do not require assumptions about the probability distribution of the response variable. In fact, this flexibility means that tree models are generally applicable, whatever the nature of the dependent variable and the explanatory variables. But this greater flexibility may have disadvantages, for instance, a higher demand of computational resources. Furthermore, their sequential nature and their algorithmic complexity can make them dependent on the observed data, and even a small change might alter the structure of the tree. It is difficult to take a tree structure designed for one context and generalize it to other contexts.

Despite their graphical similarities, there are important differences between hierarchical cluster analysis and classification trees. Classification trees are predictive rather than descriptive. Cluster analysis performs an unsupervised classification of the observations on the basis of all available variables, whereas classification trees perform a classification of the observations on the basis of all explanatory variables and supervised by the presence of the response (target) variable. A second important difference concerns the partition rule. In classification trees the segmentation is typically carried out using only one explanatory variable at a time (the maximally predictive explanatory variable), whereas in hierarchical clustering the divisive (or agglomerative) rule between groups is established on the basis of considerations on the distance between them, calculated using all the available variables.

We now describe in more detail the operational choices that have to be made before fitting a tree model to the data. It is appropriate to start with an accurate preliminary exploratory analysis. First, it is necessary to verify that the sample size is sufficiently large. This is because subsequent partitions will have fewer observations, for which the fitted values may have a lot of variance. Second, it is prudent to conduct accurate exploratory analysis on the response variable, especially to identify possible anomalous observations that could severely distort the results of the analysis. Pay particular attention to the shape of the response variable's distribution. For example, if the distribution is strongly asymmetrical, the procedure may lead to isolated groups with few observations from the tail of the distribution. Furthermore, when the dependent variable is qualitative, ideally the number of levels should not be too large. Large numbers of levels should be reduced to improve the stability of the tree and to achieve improved predictive performance.

After the preprocessing stage, choose an appropriate tree model algorithm, paying attention to how it performs. The two main aspects are the division criteria and the methods employed to reduce the dimension of the tree. The most used algorithm in the statistical community is the CART algorithm (Breiman *et al.*, 1984), which stands for 'classification and regression trees'. Other algorithms include CHAID (Kass, 1980), C4.5 and its later version, C5.0 (Quinlan, 1993). C4.5 and C5.0 are widely used by computer scientists. The first versions of C4.5 and C5.0 were limited to categorical predictors, but the most recent versions are similar to CART. We now look at two key aspects of the CART algorithm: division criteria and pruning, employed to reduce the complexity of a tree.

4.5.1 Division criteria

The main distinctive element of a tree model is how the division rule is chosen for the units belonging to a group, corresponding to a node of the tree. Choosing a division rule means choosing a predictor from those available, and choosing the best partition of its levels. The choice is generally made using a goodness measure of the corresponding division rule. This allows us to determine, at each stage of the procedure, the rule that maximises the goodness measure. A goodness measure $\Phi(t)$ is a measure of the performance gain in subdividing a (parent) node t according to a segmentation in a number of (child) nodes. Let t_r, $r = 1, \ldots, s$, indicate the child groups generated by the segmentation ($s = 2$ for a binary segmentation) and let p_r indicate the proportion of observations, among those in t, that are allocated to each child node, with $\sum p_r = 1$. The criterion function is usually expressed as

$$\Phi(s, t) = I(t) - \sum_{r=1}^{s} I(t_r) p_r$$

where the symbol I indicates an impurity function. High values of the criterion function imply that the chosen partition is a good one. The concept of impurity refers to a measure of variability of the response values of the observations. In a regression tree, a node will be pure if it has null variance (all observations are equal) and impure if the variance of the observations is high. More precisely, for a regression tree, the impurity at node m can be defined by

$$I_V(m) = \frac{\sum_{l=1}^{n_m} (y_{lm} - \hat{y}_m)^2}{n_m}$$

where $\hat{y}_m$ indicates the fitted mean value for group m. For regression trees impurity corresponds to the variance; for classification trees alternative measures should be considered. Here are the usual choices.

Misclassification impurity

$$I_M(m) = \frac{\sum_{l=1}^{n_m} 1(y_{lm}, y_k)}{n_m} = 1 - \pi_k$$

where y_k is the modal category of the node, with fitted probability π_k; the function $1()$ indicates the indicator function, which takes the value 1 if $y_{lm} = y_k$ and 0 otherwise.

Gini impurity

$$I_G(m) = 1 - \sum_{i=1}^{k(m)} \pi_i^2$$

where π_i are the fitted probabilities of the levels present in node m, which are at most $k(m)$.

Entropy impurity

$$I_E(m) = -\sum_{i=1}^{k(m)} \pi_i \log \pi_i$$

with π_i as above. Notice that the entropy impurity and the Gini impurity correspond to the application of the heterogeneity indexes (Section 3.1) to the observations in node m. Compared to the misclassification impurity, both are more sensitive to changes in the fitted probabilities; they decrease faster than the misclassification rate as the tree grows. Therefore, to obtain a parsimonious tree, choose the misclassification impurity.

Tree assessments
Besides giving a useful split criterion, an impurity measure can be used to give an overall assessment of a tree. Let $N(T)$ be the number of leaves (terminal nodes) of a tree T. The total impurity of T is obtained as

$$I(T) = \sum_{m=1}^{N(T)} I(t_m) p_m$$

where p_m are the observed proportions of observations in the final classification. In particular, the misclassification impurity constitutes a very important assessment of the goodness of fit of a classification tree. Even when the number of leaves coincides with the number of levels of the response variable, it need not to be that all the observations classified in the same node actually have the same level of the response variable. The percentage of misclassifications, or the percentage of observations classified with a level different from the observed value, is also called misclassification error or misclassification rate; it is another important overall assessment of a classification tree.

The impurity measure used by CHAID is the distance between the observed and the expected frequencies; the expected frequencies are calculated using the hypotheses for homogeneity for the observations in the considered node. This split criterion function is the Pearson X^2 index. If the decrease in X^2 is significant (i.e. the p-value is lower than a prespecified level α) then a node is split, otherwise it remains unsplit and becomes a leaf.

4.5.2 Pruning

In the absence of a stopping criterion, a tree model could grow until each node contains identical observations in terms of values or levels of the dependent variable. This obviously does not constitute a parsimonious segmentation. Therefore it is necessary to stop the growth of the tree at a reasonable dimension. The ideal final tree configuration is both parsimonious and accurate. The first property implies that the tree has a small number of leaves, so that the predictive rule can be easily interpreted. The second property implies a large number of leaves that are maximally pure. The final choice is bound to be a compromise between the two opposing strategies. Some tree algorithms use stopping rules based on thresholds on the number of the leaves, or on the maximum number of steps in the process. Other algorithms introduce probabilistic assumptions on the variables, allowing us to use suitable statistical tests. In the absence of probabilistic assumptions, the growth is stopped when the decrease in impurity is too small. The results of a tree model can be very sensitive to the choice of a stopping rule.

The CART method uses a strategy somewhat different from the stepwise stopping criteria; it is based on the concept of pruning. First the tree is built to its greatest size. This might be the tree with the greatest number of leaves, or the tree in which every node contains only one observation or observations all with the same outcome value or level. Then the tree is 'trimmed' or 'pruned' according to a cost-complexity criterion. Let T_0 indicate the tree of greatest size and let T indicate, in general, a tree. From any tree a subtree can be obtained by collapsing any number of its internal (non-terminal) nodes. The idea of pruning is to find a subtree of T_0 in an optimal way, the one that minimises a loss function. The loss function implemented in the CART algorithm depends on the total impurity of the tree T and the tree complexity:

$$C_\alpha(T) = I(T) + \alpha N(T)$$

where, for a tree T, $I(T)$ is the total impurity function calculated at the leaves, and $N(T)$ is the number of leaves; with α a constant that penalises complexity linearly. In a regression tree the impurity is a variance, so the total impurity can be determined as

$$I(T) = \sum_{m=1}^{N(T)} I_V(m) n_m$$

We have seen how impurity can be calculated for classification trees. Although any of the three impurity measures can be used, the misclassification impurity is usually chosen in practice. Notice that the minimisation of the loss function leads to a compromise between choosing a complex model (low impurity but high complexity cost) and choosing a simple model (high impurity but low complexity cost). The choice depends on the chosen value of α. For each α it can be shown that there is a unique subtree of T_0 which minimises $C_\alpha(T)$.

A possible criticism of this loss function is that the performance of each tree configuration is evaluated with the same data used for building the classification rules, which can lead to optimistic estimates of the impurity. This is particularly true for large trees, due to the phenomenon we have already seen for regression models: the goodness of fit to the data increases with the complexity, here represented by the number of leaves. An alternative pruning criterion is based on the predictive misclassification errors, according to a technique known as cross-validation (Section 6.4). The idea is to split the available data set, use one part to train the model (i.e. to build a tree configuration), and use the second part to validate the model (i.e. to compare observed and predicted values for the response variable), thereby measuring the impurity in an unbiased fashion. The loss function is thus evaluated by measuring the complexity of the model fitted on the training data set, whose misclassification errors are measured on the validation data set.

To further explain the fundamental difference between training and validation error, Figure 4.7 takes a classification tree and illustrates the typical behaviour of the misclassification errors on the training and validation data sets, as functions of model complexity. $I(T)$ is always decreasing on the training data. $I(T)$ is non-monotone on the validation data; it usually follows the behaviour described in the figure, which allows us to choose the optimal number of leaves as the value of $N(T)$ such that $I(T)$ is minimum. For simplicity, Figure 4.7 takes $\alpha = 0$. When greater values for the complexity penalty are specified, the optimal number of nodes decreases, reflecting aversion towards complexity.

The misclassification rate is not the only possible performance measure to use during pruning. Since the costs of misclassification can vary from one class

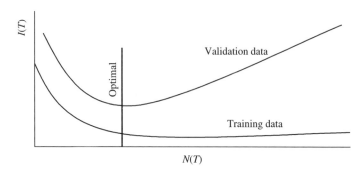

Figure 4.7　Misclassification rates.

to another, the misclassification impurity could be replaced by a simple cost function that multiplies the misclassification impurity by the costs attached to the consequence of such errors. This is further discussed in Section 6.5.

The CHAID algorithm uses chi-squared testing to produce an implicit stopping criterion based on testing the significance of the homogeneity hypothesis; the hypothesis is rejected for large values of χ^2. If homogeneity is rejected for a certain node, then splitting continues, otherwise the node becomes terminal. Unlike the CART algorithm, CHAID prefers to stop the growth of the tree through a stopping criterion based on the significance of the chi-squared test, rather than through a pruning mechanism.

4.6   Neural networks

Neural networks, can be used for many purposes, notably descriptive and predictive data mining. They were originally developed in the field of machine learning to try to imitate the neurophysiology of the human brain through the combination of simple computational elements (neurons) in a highly interconnected system. They have become an important data mining method. However, the neural networks developed since the 1980s have only recently received attention from statisticians (e.g. Bishop, 1995; Ripley, 1996). Despite controversies over the real 'intelligence' of neural networks, there is no doubt they have now become useful statistical models. In particular, they show a notable ability to fit observed data, especially with high-dimensional databases, and data sets characterised by incomplete information, errors or inaccuracies. We will treat neural networks as a methodology for data analysis; we will recall the neurobiological model only to illustrate the fundamental principles.

A neural network is composed of a set of elementary computational units, called neurons, connected together through weighted connections. These units are organised in layers so that every neuron in a layer is exclusively connected to the neurons of the preceding layer and the subsequent layer. Every neuron, also called a node, represents an autonomous computational unit and receives inputs as a series of signals that dictate its activation. Following activation, every neuron produces an output signal. All the input signals reach the neuron simultaneously, so the neuron receives more than one input signal, but it produces only one output signal. Every input signal is associated with a connection weight. The weight determines the relative importance the input signal can have in producing the final impulse transmitted by the neuron. The connections can be exciting, inhibiting or null according to whether the corresponding weights are respectively positive, negative or null. The weights are adaptive coefficients that, in analogy with the biological model, are modified in response to the various signals that travel on the network according to a suitable learning algorithm. A threshold value, called bias, is usually introduced. Bias is similar to an intercept in a regression model.

In more formal terms, a generic neuron j, with a threshold θ_j, receives n input signals $x = [x_1, x_2, \ldots, x_n]$ from the units to which it is connected in

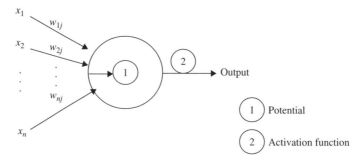

Figure 4.8 Representation of the activity of a neuron in a neural network.

the previous layer. Each signal is attached with an importance weight $w_j = [w_{1j}, w_{2j}, \ldots, w_{nj}]$.

The same neuron elaborates the input signals, their importance weights and the threshold value through something called a combination function. The combination function produces a value called potential, or net input. An activation function transforms the potential into an output signal. Figure 4.8 schematically represents the activity of a neuron. The combination function is usually linear, therefore the potential is a weighted sum of the input values multiplied by the weights of the respective connections. This sum is compared with the value of the threshold. The potential of neuron j is defined by the following linear combination:

$$P_j = \sum_{i=1}^{n} (x_i w_{ij} - \theta_j)$$

To simplify the expression for potential, the bias term can be absorbed by adding a further input with constant value $x_0 = 1$, connected to the neuron j through a weight $w_{0j} = -\theta_j$:

$$P_j = \sum_{i=0}^{n} (x_i w_{ij})$$

Now consider the output signal. The output of the jth neuron, y_j, is obtained by applying the activation function to potential P_j:

$$y_j = f(\boldsymbol{x}, \boldsymbol{w}_j) = f(P_j) = f\left(\sum_{i=0}^{n} x_i w_{ij}\right)$$

The quantities in bold italics are vectors. In defining a neural network model, the activation function is typically one of the elements to specify. Three types are commonly employed: linear, stepwise and sigmoidal. A linear activation function is defined by

$$f(P_j) = \alpha + \beta P_j$$

where P_j is defined on the set of real numbers, and α and β are real constants; $\alpha = 0$ and $\beta = 1$ is a particular case called the identity function, usually employed when the model requires the output of a neuron to be exactly equal to its level of activation (potential). Notice the strong similarity between the linear activation function and the expression for a the regression line (Section 4.3). In fact, a regression model can be seen as a simple type of neural network.

A stepwise activation function is defined by

$$f(P_j) = \begin{cases} \alpha & P_j \geq \theta_j \\ \beta & P_j < \theta_j \end{cases}$$

The activation function can assume only two values according to whether or not the potential exceeds the threshold θ_j. For $\alpha = 1$, $\beta = 0$ and $\theta_j = 0$ we obtain the so-called sign activation function, which takes value 0 if the potential is negative and value $+1$ if the potential is positive.

Sigmoidal, or S-shaped, activation functions are probably the most used. They produce only positive output; the domain of the function is the interval [0, 1]. They are widely used because they are non-linear and also because they are easily differentiable and understandable. A sigmoidal activation function is defined by

$$f(P_j) = \frac{1}{1 + e^{-\alpha P_j}}$$

where α is a positive parameter that regulates the slope of the function.

Another type of activation function, the softmax function, is typically used to normalise the output of different but related nodes. Consider g such nodes, and let their outputs be v_j, $j = 1, \ldots, g$. The softmax function normalises the v_j so they sum to 1:

$$\text{softmax}(v_j) = \frac{\exp(v_j)}{\sum\limits_{h=1}^{g} \exp(v_h)} \qquad (j = 1, \ldots, g)$$

The softmax function is used in supervised classification problems, where the response variable can take g alternative levels.

4.6.1 Architecture of a neural network

The neurons of a neural network are organised in layers. These layers can be of three types: input, output or hidden. The input layer receives information only from the external environment; each neuron in it usually corresponds to an explanatory variable. The input layer does not perform any calculation; it transmits information to the next level. The output layer produces the final results, which are sent by the network to the outside of the system. Each of its neurons corresponds to a response variable. In a neural network there are generally two or more response variables. Between the output layer and the input layer there can be one or more intermediate layers, called hidden layers because they are not directly in contact with the external environment. These layers are exclusively for analysis; their function is to take the relationship between the input variables and the output variables and adapt it more closely to the data. In the literature there is no standard convention for calculating the number of layers in a neural network. Some authors count all the layers of neurons and others count the number of layers of weighted neurons. I will use the weighted neurons and count the number of layers that are to be learnt from the data. The 'architecture' of a neural network refers to the network's organisation: the number of layers, the number of units (neurons) belonging to each layer, and the manner in which the units are connected. Network architecture can be represented using a graph, hence people often use the term 'network topology' instead of 'network architecture'. Four main characteristics are used to classify network topology:

- Degree of differentiation of the input and output layer
- Number of layers
- Direction of flow for the computation
- Type of connections

The simplest topology is called autoassociative; it has a single layer of intra-connected neurons. The input units coincide with the output units; there is no differentiation. We will not consider this type of network, as it has no statistical interest. Networks with a single-layer of weighted neurons are known as single-layer perceptrons. They have n input units $(x_1, \ldots, x_n)$ connected to a layer of p output units $(y_1, \ldots, y_p)$ through a system of weights. The weights can be represented in matrix form:

$$
\begin{bmatrix}
w_{11} & \cdots & w_{1j} & \cdots & w_{1p} \\
\vdots & \vdots & \vdots & \vdots & \vdots \\
w_{i1} & \cdots & w_{ij} & \cdots & w_{ip} \\
\vdots & \vdots & \vdots & \vdots & \vdots \\
w_{n1} & \cdots & w_{nj} & \cdots & w_{np}
\end{bmatrix}
$$

for $i = 1, \ldots, n$; $j = 1, \ldots, p$. The generic weight w_{ij} represents the weight of the connection between the ith neuron of the input layer and the jth neuron of the output layer.

Neural networks with more than one layer of weighted neurons, which contain one or more hidden layers, are called multilayer perceptrons, and we will concentrate on these. A two-layer network has one hidden layer; there are n neurons in the input layer, h in the hidden layer and p in the output layer. Weights w_{ik} $(i = 1, \ldots, n; k = 1, \ldots, h)$ connect the input layer nodes with the hidden layer nodes; weights z_{kj} $(k = 1, \ldots, h; j = 1, \ldots, p)$ connect the hidden layer nodes with the output layer nodes. The neurons of the hidden layer receive information from the input layer, weighted by the weights w_{ik}, and produce outputs $h_k = f(\mathbf{x}, \mathbf{w}_k)$, where f is the activation function of the units in the hidden layer. The neurons of the output layer receive the outputs from the hidden layer, weighted by the weights z_{kj}, and produce the final network outputs $y_j = g(\boldsymbol{h}, z_j)$. The output of neuron j in the output layer is

$$y_j = g\left(\sum_k h_k z_{kj}\right) = g\left(\sum_k z_{kj} f\left(\sum_i x_i w_{ik}\right)\right)$$

This equation shows that the output values of a neural network are determined recursively and typically in a non-linear way.

Different information flows lead to different types of network. In feedforward networks the information moves in only one direction, from one layer to the next, and there are no return cycles. In feedback networks it is possible that information returns to previous layers. If each unit of a layer is connected to all the units of the next layer, the network is described as totally interconnected; if each unit is connected to every unit of every layer, the network is described as totally connected.

Networks can also be classified into three types according to their connection weightings: networks with fixed weights, supervised networks and unsupervised networks. We shall not consider networks with fixed weights as they cannot learn from the data and they do not offer a statistical model. Supervised networks use a supervising variable, a concept introduced in Section 4.5. With a supervised network, there can be information about the value of a response variable corresponding to the values of the explanatory variables; this information can be used to learn the weights of the neural network model. The response variable behaves as a supervisor for the problem. When this information is not available, the learning of the weights is exclusively based on the explanatory variables and there is no supervisor. Here is the same idea expressed more formally:

- *Supervised learning*: assume that each observation is described by a pair of vectors $(\boldsymbol{x}_i, \boldsymbol{t}_i)$ representing the explanatory and response variables, respectively. Let $D = \{(\boldsymbol{x}_1, \boldsymbol{t}_1), \ldots, (\boldsymbol{x}_n, \boldsymbol{t}_n)\}$ represent the set of all available observations. The problem is to determine a neural network $y_i = f(\boldsymbol{x}_i)$, $i = 1, \ldots, n$, such that the sum of the distances $d(y_i, \boldsymbol{t}_i)$ is minimum. Notice the analogy with linear regression models.
- *Unsupervised learning*: each observation is described by only one vector, with all available variables, $D = \{\boldsymbol{x}_1, \ldots, \boldsymbol{x}_n\}$. The problem is the partitioning of the set D into subsets such that the vectors $\boldsymbol{x}_i$, belonging to the same subset are 'close' in comparison to a fixed measure of distance. This is basically a classification problem.

We will now examine the multilayer perceptron, an example of a supervised network, and the Kohonen network, an example of an unsupervised network.

4.6.2 The multilayer perceptron

The multilayer perceptron is the most used architecture for predictive data mining. It is a feedforward network with possibly several hidden layers, one input layer and one output layer, totally interconnected. It can be considered as a highly non-linear generalisation of the linear regression model when the output variables are quantitative, or of the logistic regression model when the output variables are qualitative.

Preliminary analysis
Multilayer perceptrons, and neural networks in general, are often used inefficiently on real data because no preliminary considerations are applied. Although neural networks are powerful computational tools for data analysis, they also require exploratory analysis (Chapter 3).

Coding of the variables
The variables used in a neural network can be classified by type – qualitative or quantitative – and by their role in the network – input or output. Input and output in neural networks correspond to explanatory and response in statistical methods. In a neural network, quantitative variables are represented by one neuron. The qualitative variables, both explanatory and responses, are represented in a binary way using several neurons for every variable; the number of neurons equals, the number of levels of the variable (Section 2.3). In practice the number of neurons to represent a variable need not be exactly equal to the number of its levels. It is advisable to eliminate one level, and therefore one neuron, since the value of that neuron will be completely determined by the others.

Transformation of the variables
Once the variables are coded, a preliminary descriptive analysis may underline the need for some kind of transformation, perhaps to standardise the input variables to weight them in a proper way. Standardisation of the response variable is not strictly necessary. If a network has been trained with transformed input or output, when it is used for prediction, the outputs must be mapped on to the original scale.

Reduction in the dimensionality of the input variables
One of the most important forms of preprocessing is reduction in the dimensionality of the input variables. The simplest approach is to eliminate a subset of the original inputs. Other approaches create linear or non-linear combinations of the original variables to represent the input for the network. Principal component methods can be usefully employed here (Section 3.5).

Choice of the architecture
The architecture of a neural network can have a fundamental impact on real data. Nowadays, many neural networks optimise their architecture as part of the learning process. Network architectures are rarely compared using the classical methods of Chapter 5; this is because a neural network does not need an underlying probabilistic model and seldom has one. Even when there is an underlying probabilistic model, it is often very difficult to draw the distribution of the statistical test functions. Instead it is possible to make comparison based

on the predictive performances of the alternative structures; an example is the cross-validation method (Chapter 6).

Learning of the weights

Learning the weights in multilayer perceptrons appears to introduce no particular problems. Having specified an architecture for the network, the weights are estimated on the basis of the data, as if they were parameters of a (complex) regression model. But in practice there are at least two aspects to consider:

- The error function between the observed values and the fitted values could be a classical distance function, such as the Euclidean distance or the misclassification error, or it could be depend in a probabilistic way on the conditional distribution of the output variable with respect to the inputs.
- The optimisation algorithm needs to be a computationally efficient method to obtain estimates of the weights by minimising of the error function.

The error functions usually employed for multilayer perceptrons are based on the maximum likelihood principle (Section 5.1). For a given training data set $D = \{(x_1, t_1), \ldots, (x_n, t_n)\}$, this requires us to minimise the entropy error function:

$$E(w) = -\sum_{i=1}^{n} \log p(t_i | x_i; w)$$

where $p(t_i | x_i; w)$ is the distribution of the response variable, conditional on the input values and the weighting function. For more details see Bishop (1995). We will now look at the form of the error function for the two principal applications of the multilayer perceptron: predicting a continuous response (predictive regression) and predicting a qualitative response (predictive classification).

Error functions for predictive regression

Every component $t_{i,k}$ of the response vector t_i is assumed to be the sum of a deterministic component and an error term, similar to linear regression:

$$t_{i,k} = y_{i,k} + \varepsilon_{i,k} \qquad (k = 1, \ldots, q)$$

where $y_{i,k}$ is the kth component of the output vector y_i. To obtain more information from a neural network for this problem it can be assumed that the error terms are normally distributed, similar to the normal linear model (Section 5.3).

Since the objective of statistical learning is to minimise the error function in terms of the weights, we can omit everything that does not depend on the weights. Then we obtain

$$E(w) = \sum_{i=1}^{n} \sum_{k=1}^{q} (t_{i,k} - y_{i,k})^2$$

This expression can be minimised using a least squares procedure (Section 4.3). In fact, linear regression can be seen as a neural network model without hidden layers and with a linear activation function.

Error functions for predictive classification
Multilayer perceptrons can also be employed for solving classification problems. Then it is used to estimate the probabilities of affiliation of every observation to the various groups. There is usually an output unit for each possible class, and the activation function for each output unit represents the conditional probability $P(C_k|x)$, where C_k is the kth class and x is the input vector. Output value $y_{i,k}$ represents the fitted probability that the observation i belongs to the kth group C_k. To minimise the error function with respect to the weights, we need to minimise

$$E(w) = -\sum_{i=1}^{n}\sum_{k=1}^{q}[t_{i,k}\log y_{i,k} + (1 - t_{i,k})\log(1 - y_{i,k})]$$

which represents a distance based on the entropy index of heterogeneity (Section 3.1). Notice that a particular case can be obtained for the logistic regression model.

In fact, logistic regression can be seen as a neural network model without hidden nodes and with a logistic activation function and softmax output function. In contrast to logistic regression, which produces a linear discriminant rule, a multilayer perceptron provides a non-linear discriminant rule and this cannot be given a simple analytical description.

Choice of optimisation algorithm
In general, the error function $E(w)$ of a neural network is highly non-linear in the weights, so there may be many minima that satisfy the condition $\nabla E = 0$. Consequently, it may not be possible, in general, to find a globally optimal solution, w^*. Therefore we must resort to iterative algorithms. We guess an initial estimate $w^{(0)}$ then produce a sequence of points $w^{(s)}$, $s = 1, 2, \ldots$ that converge to a certain value $\hat{w}$. Here are the steps in more detail:

1. Choose a direction $d^{(s)}$ for the search.
2. Choose a width (or momentum) $\alpha^{(s)}$ and set $w^{(s+1)} = w^{(s)} + \alpha^{(s)}d^{(s)}$.
3. If a certain criterion of convergence is verified then set $\hat{w} = w^{(s+1)}$, otherwise set $s = s + 1$ and return to step 1.

Iterative methods guarantee convergence towards minimum points for which $\nabla E = 0$. Different algorithms have different ways of changing the vector of weights $\Delta w^{(s)} = \alpha^{(s)}d^{(s)}$. A potential problem for most of them is getting stuck in a local minimum; the choice of the initial weights determines the minimum to which the algorithm will converge. It is extremely important to choose the weights carefully to obtain a valid fit and a good convergence rate. The momentum parameter also needs to be chosen carefully. If it is too small, the algorithm will converge too slowly; if it is too large, the algorithm will oscillate in an unstable way and may never converge.

One last choice for the analyst is when to interrupt the learning algorithm. Here are some possibilities: stop after a defined number of iterations; stop after a defined amount of computer time (CPU usage); stop when the error function falls below a preset value; stop when the difference between two consecutive values of the error function is less than a preset value; stop when the error of classification or forecast, measured on an appropriate validation data set, starts to grow (early stopping), similar to tree pruning (Section 4.5). For more details see Bishop (1995). It is not possible to establish in general which is the best algorithm; performance varies from problem to problem.

Generalisation and prediction
The objective of training a neural network with data, to determine its weights on the basis of the available data set, is not to find an exact representation of the training data, but to build a model that can be generalised or that allows us to obtain valid classifications and predictions when fed with new data. Similar to tree models, the performance of a supervised neural network can be evaluated with reference to a training data set or validation data set. If the network is very complex and the training is carried out for a large number of iterations, the network can perfectly classify or predict the data in the training set. This could be desirable when the training sample represents a 'perfect' image of the population from which it has been drawn, but it is counterproductive in real applications since it implies reduced predictive capacities on a new data set. This phenomenon is known as overfitting. To illustrate the problem, consider only two observations for an input variable and an output variable. A straight line adapts perfectly to the data but poorly predicts a third observation, especially if it is radically different from the previous two. A simpler model, the arithmetic average of the two output observations, will fit the two points worse but may be a reasonable predictor of a third point.

To limit the overfitting problem, it is important to control the degree of complexity of the model. A model with few parameters will involve a modest generalisation. A model that is too complex may even adapt to noise in the data set, perhaps caused by measurement errors or anomalous observations; this will lead to inaccurate generalisations. There are two main approaches to controlling a neural network's complexity. Regularisation is the addition of a penalty term to the error function. Early stopping is the introduction of stopping criteria in the iterative procedure of learning.

In regularisation, overfitting is tackled directly when the weights are estimated. More precisely, the weights are trained by minimising an error function of the following type:

$$\tilde{E}(w) = E(w) + v\Omega$$

where E is an error function, Ω describes the complexity of the network and v is a parameter that penalises for complexity. Notice again the analogies with pruning in tree models (Section 4.5). A complex network that produces a good fit to the training data will show a minimum value of E, whereas a very simple function will have low value of Ω. Therefore, what will be obtained at the end of the training procedure will be a compromise between a simple model and a good fit to the data.

A useful regularisation function is based on weight decay, which consists of taking Ω equal to the sum of the squares of the weights (including the bias) of the neural network:

$$\Omega = \frac{1}{2} \sum_i w_i^2$$

Early stopping uses the fact that the error function usually shows an initial reduction followed by an increase; the increase starts when the network begins to have problems with overfitting. Training can be stopped when the lowest prediction error is observed.

Optimality properties of multilayer perceptrons
Multilayer perceptrons have optimal properties. Researchers have shown that, given a sufficiently large number of nodes in the hidden layer, a simple neural network structure (with two layers of weights, sigmoidal activation function for the hidden nodes and identity activation function for the output nodes) is able to approximate any functional form with arbitrary accuracy. This is known as the principle of universal approximation – the rate of convergence does not depend on the dimension of the problem. If a network with only one hidden layer can approximate any functional form with arbitrary accuracy, why use any other network topology? One reason is that extra hidden layers may produce a more efficient approximation that achieves the same level of accuracy using fewer neurons and fewer weights.

Application
In the second part of the book, particularly Chapters 10, 11 and 12, there are some case studies using neural networks. But here is a simple example to illustrate the methodology. The data is a sample of 51 enterprises in the European software industry, for which a series of binary variables have been measured. Here are some of them: N (degree of incremental innovations: low/high); I (degree of radical innovations: low/high); S (relationships of the enterprise with the software suppliers: low/high); A (applicative knowledge of the employees of the enterprise: low/high); M (scientific knowledge of the employees of the enterprise: low/high); H (relationships of the enterprise with the hardware suppliers: low/high). The variable Y (revenues) is a continuous variable.

The objective of the analysis is to classify the 51 enterprises into the two groups of variable N, according to the values of the six remaining (explanatory) variables, so as to build a predictive model for the degree of incremental innovations. Since there is only one response variable and six explanatory variables, the network architecture will have one output variable and six input variables. It remains to see how many neurons to allocate to the hidden nodes. Suppose that, for parsimony, there is only one hidden node in a unique hidden layer. Finally, given the nature of the problem, a logistic activation function is chosen for the hidden layer node and an identity activation function for the output nodes. The following formula specifies the non-linear relationship for the model:

$$\text{logit}(\pi_N) = w_{08} + w_{18}m + w_{28}a + w_{38}h + w_{48}i + w_{58}s + w_{68}y$$
$$+ w_{78}\phi(w_{07} + w_{17}m + w_{27}a + w_{37}h + w_{47}i + w_{57}s + w_{67}y)$$

where the left-hand side is the logit function for $N = 1$ and ϕ is the inverse logistic function. Notice that a logistic regression model differs from this one in not having the term $w_{78}\phi()$. The process of learning the weights converges and produces the following 15 final weights:

$$\hat{\omega}_{07} = 32.76, \hat{\omega}_{17} = 9.25, \hat{\omega}_{27} = 14.72, \hat{\omega}_{37} = 3.63, \hat{\omega}_{47} = -10.65, \hat{\omega}_{57} = 10.39,$$

$$\hat{\omega}_{67} = -22.34, \hat{\omega}_{08} = 0.06, \hat{\omega}_{78} = 10.89, \hat{\omega}_{18} = -1.44, \hat{\omega}_{28} = -0.82,$$

$$\hat{\omega}_{38} = -2.18, \hat{\omega}_{48} = -0.70, \hat{\omega}_{58} = -8.34, \hat{\omega}_{68} = 0.43$$

As a simple measure of its performance, consider the number of misclassified observations. Given the limited number of observations, the model was initially trained and validated on the whole data set. Then the 51 observations were divided in a random way into 39 observations for training and 12 observations for validation by considering misclassifications of these 12 observations. Adopting the threshold rule that $N = 1$ if the estimated value of π_N is greater than 0.5, the number of misclassifications is 9 on 51 training cases and 8 on 12 validation cases. The proposed model is too adaptive. It performs well on training error but very badly on classification ability. Application of a simpler logistic regression model led to these errors: 15 out of 51 and 3 out of 12. So compared with the neural network model, the logistic regression model is not as adaptive but more predictive.

4.6.3 Kohonen networks

Self-organizing maps (SOMs), or Kohonen networks, can be employed in a descriptive data mining context, where the objective is to cluster the observations into homogeneous groups. In these models the parameters are constituted by the weights of the net (the thresholds are not present) and learning occurs in the absence of an output variable acting as supervisor. A model of this type is generally specified by a layer of input neurons and a layer of output neurons. For a given set of n observations, the n input nodes are represented by p-dimensional vectors (containing qualitative and/or quantitative variables), each of which represents one multivariate observation, whereas the output nodes are described by discrete values, each of which corresponds to a group (cluster) of the observations. The number of groups is typically unknown a priori.

The objective of Kohonen maps is to map every p-dimensional input observation to an output space represented by a spatial grid of output neurons. Adjacent output nodes will be more similar than distant output nodes. The learning technique for the weights in a Kohonen map is based on competition among the output neurons for assignment of the input vectors. For every assigned input node, a neuron of winning output is selected on the basis of the distance function in the input space.

Kohonen networks can be considered as a non-hierarchical method of cluster analysis. As non-hierarchical methods of clustering, they assign an input vector to the nearest cluster, on the basis of a predetermined distance function but they try to preserve a degree of dependence among the clusters by introducing a distance between them. Consequently, each output neuron has its own neighbourhood, expressed in terms of a distance matrix. The output neurons are characterised by a distance function between them, described using the configuration of the nodes in a unidimensional or bidimensional space. Figure 4.9 shows a two-dimensional grid of output neurons. In such a 7×7 map, each neuron is described by a square and the number on each square is the distance from the central neuron. Consider the simplest algorithm, in which the topological structure of the output nodes is constant during the learning process. Here are the basic steps:

1. *Initialisation*: having fixed the dimensions of the output grid, the weights that connect the input neurons to the output neurons are randomly initialised. Let r indicate the number of iterations of the algorithm and set $r = 0$.
2. *Selection of the winner*: for each input neuron x_j, select the winning output neuron $i*$ that minimises the Euclidean distance $\|x_j - w_i^r\|$ between the p-dimensional vector of input x_j and the p-dimensional weight vector w_i that connects the jth input neuron to the ith output neuron.
3. *Updating of the weights*: let $N(i*)$ be a neighbourhood of the winning output neuron $i*$, implicitly specified by the distance function among the output neurons. For every output neuron $i \in \{N(i*), i*\}$, the weights are updated according to the rule $w_i^{r+1} = w_i^r + \eta(x_j - w_i^r), \forall i \in \{N(i*), i*\}$; η is called the rate of learning and is specified in advance. The rule updates only the neighbours of the winning output neuron.

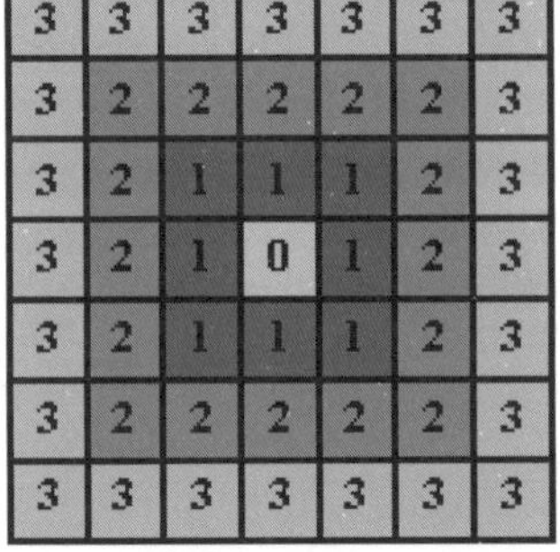

Figure 4.9 Example output grid in a Kohonen network.

4. *Normalisation of the weights*: after updating, the weights are normalised so they are consistent with the input measurement scales.

5. *Looping through*: steps 1 to 4 are repeated and the number of iterations is set to $r = r + 1$, until an appropriate stopping criterion is reached, or until a maximum number of iterations is exceeded.

This algorithm can be modified in two important ways. One way is to introduce a varying neighbourhood. After selecting the winning output neuron, its neighbourhood is recomputed along with the relevant weights. Another way is to introduce algorithms based on sensitivity to history. Then the learning algorithm, hence the cluster allocation, can be made to depend on the frequency of past allocations. This allows us to avoid phenomena that typically occur with non-hierarchical clustering, such as obtaining one enormous cluster compared to the others.

SOMs are an important methodology for descriptive data mining and they represent a valid alternative to clustering methods. They are closely related to non-hierarchical clustering algorithms, such as the k-means method. The fundamental difference between the two methodologies is that SOM algorithms introduce a topological dependence between clusters. This can be extremely important when it is fundamental to preserve the topological order among the input vectors and the clusters. This is what happens in image analysis, where it is necessary to preserve a notion of spatial correlation between the pixels of the image. Clustering methods may overcentralise, since the mutual independence of the different groups leads to only one centroid being modified, leaving the centroids of the other clusters unchanged; this means that one group gets bigger and bigger while the other groups remain relatively empty. But if the neighbourhood of every neuron is so small as to contain only one output neuron, the Kohonen maps will behave analogously to the k-means algorithm. For a practical comparison of descriptive clustering algorithms, in Chapter 9 compares Kohonen networks with the k-means non-hierarchical clustering method.

4.7 Nearest-neighbour models

Nearest-neighbour models are a flexible class of predictive data mining methods based on a combination of local models. This does not mean they are local in the sense of Section 4.8; they are still applied to the whole data set, but the statistical analysis is split into separate local analyses. The basic idea is rather simple and builds on the theory we have already elaborated. The available variables are divided into the explanatory variables (x) and the target variable (y). A sample of observations in the form (x,y) is collected to form a training data set. For this training data, a distance function is introduced between the x values of the observations. This can be used to define, for each observation, a neighbourhood formed by the observations that are closest to it, in terms of the distance between the x values. For a continuous response variable, the nearest-neighbour fitted value for each observation's response value y_i is defined by

$$\hat{y}_i = \frac{1}{k} \sum_{x_j \in N(x_i)} y_j$$

This is the arithmetic mean of all response values, whose corresponding x values are contained in the neighbourhood of x_i, $N(x_i)$. Furthermore, k is a fixed constant that specifies the number of elements to be included in each neighbourhood. The model can be easily applied to predict a future value of y, say y_0, when the values of the explanatory variables, say x_0, are known. It is required to identify, in the training data set, the k values of y belonging to the neighbourhood of the unknown y_0. This is done by taking the k explanatory variable observations in the training data set, closest to x_0. The arithmetic mean of these y values is the prediction of y_0. In contrast with linear regression, the nearest-neighbour fit is simpler, as it is an arithmetic mean. However, it is not calculated over all observation points, but on a local neighbourhood. This implies that the nearest-neighbour model fits the data more closely; on the other hand, this may lead to overfitting and difficulty with generalisation.

Nearest-neighbour methods can also be used for predictive classification. To classify an observation y, its neighbourhood is determined as before and the fitted probabilities of each category are calculated as relative frequencies in the neighbourhood. The class with the highest fitted probability is finally chosen. Like tree models, nearest-neighbour models do not require a probabilistic distribution. But whereas classification trees partition the data into exclusive classes, providing explicit predictive rules in terms of tree paths, the fitted values in nearest-neighbour models are based on overlapping sets of observations, not on explicit rules. These methods are also known as memory-based models, as they require no model to be fitted, or function to be estimated. Instead they require all observations to be maintained in memory, and when a prediction is required, they recall items from memory and calculate what is required.

Two crucial choices in nearest neighbour-methods are the distance function and the cardinality k of the neighbourhood. Distance functions are discussed in Section 4.1. The cardinality k represents the complexity of the nearest-neighbour model; the higher the value of k, the less adaptive the model. Indeed the model is often called the k-nearest-neighbour model to emphasise the importance of k. In the limit, when k is equal to the number of observations, the nearest-neighbour fitted values coincide with the sample mean. As we have seen for other models in this chapter (e.g. Sections 4.5 and 4.6), k can be chosen to balance goodness of fit with simplicity. The evaluation criteria in Chapter 6 can be used for these purposes.

Possible disadvantages of these models are that computationally they are highly intensive, especially when the data set contains many explanatory variables. In this case the neighbourhood may be formed by distant points, therefore taking their mean may not be a sensible idea. Chapter 10 contains an application of nearest-neighbour methods. Among other possible data mining applications, they are used for detecting frauds involving telephone calls, credit cards, etc. (Cortes and Pregibon, 2001). Impostors are discovered by identifying the characteristics, or footprints, of previous frauds and formulating a rule to predict future occurrences.

4.8 Local models

So far we have looked at global models, but local models are also very important. They look at selected parts of the data set (subsets of variables or subsets of observations), rather than being applied to the whole data set. Hand, Mannila and Smyth (2001) use the concept of 'pattern' rather than the concept of 'model'. Relevant examples are the association rules, developed in market basket analysis and web clickstream analysis, and the retrieval-by-content methods, developed for text mining. Another important example is searching for outliers, introduced in Chapter 3 and revisited several times in the book.

4.8.1 Association rules

Association rules were developed in the field of computer science and are often used in important applications such as market basket analysis, to measure the associations between products purchased by a particular consumer, and web clickstream analysis, to measure the associations between pages viewed sequentially by a website visitor. In general, the objective is to underline groups of items that typically occur together in a set of transactions. The data on which association rules are applied is usually in the form of a database of transactions. For each transaction (a row in the database) the database contains the list of items that occur. Note that each individual may appear more than once in the data set. In market basket analysis a transaction means a single visit to the supermarket, for which the list of purchases is recorded; in web clickstream analysis a transaction means a web session, for which the list of all visited webpages is recorded.

Rows typically have a different number of items, and this is a remarkable difference with respect to data matrices. Alternatively, the database can be converted in a binary data matrix, with transactions as rows and items as columns. Let $X_1, \ldots, X_p$ be a collection of random variables. In general, a pattern for such variables identifies a subset of all possible observations over them. A useful way to describe a pattern is through a collection of primitive patterns and a set of logical connectives that can act on them. For two variables, Age and Income, a pattern could be $\alpha = (\text{Age} < 30 \wedge \text{Income} > 100)$, where $\wedge$ is the logical operator 'AND' (intersection). Another pattern could be $\beta = (\text{Gender} = \text{male} \vee \text{Education} = \text{High})$, where $\vee$ is the logical operator 'OR' (union). The primitive patterns in the first expression are Age < 30 and Income > 100; the primitive patterns in the second expression are Gender $=$ male and Education $=$ High. A rule is a logical statement between two patterns, say α and β, written as $\alpha \rightarrow \beta$. This means that α and β occur together; in other words, if α occurs, then β also occurs. It is an expression of the type 'if condition, then result'.

Association rules consider rules between special types of pattern, called item sets. In an item set each variable is binary: it takes value 1 if a specific condition is true, otherwise it takes value 0. Let $A_1, \ldots, A_p$ indicate a collection of such binary variables, and let $j_1, \ldots, j_k$ indicate a subset of them. An item set is then defined by a pattern of the type $A = (A_{j1} = 1 \wedge, \ldots, \wedge A_{jk} = 1)$. Thus, in an item set, primitive patterns always indicate that a particular variable is true, and the logical connectives are only conjunctions (AND operators). An association rule is a statement between two item sets that can be written in the form $A \to B$, where both A and B are item sets. For simplicity, the right-hand item set is usually formed of a single primitive item, and we will do the same. Therefore an association rule will have the form $(A_{j1} = 1 \wedge, \ldots, \wedge A_{jk} = 1) \to A_{jk+1} = 1$, where we have now considered a subset containing $k + 1$ of the original p variables. More briefly, such an association rule is usually written as $(A_{j1} \wedge, \ldots, \wedge A_{jk}) \to A_{jk+1}$.

The order of an association rule usually refers to the total number of items considered, here, $k + 1$. Suppose a supermarket has a total of 100 000 available products. Each of them can correspond to a binary random variable, depending on whether or not the product is bought in each transaction. A simple association rule of order 3 would be (Milk $\wedge$ Tea) $\to$ Biscuits. We shall simply write $A \to B$ to indicate an association rule of the described type. A is the antecedent, or body of the rule, and B is the consequent, or head of the rule. Chapters 7 and 8 consider specific applications and use real variables.

Each association rule describes a particular local pattern that selects a restricted set of binary variables. In market basket analysis and web clickstream analysis, rules are relationships between variables that are binary by nature. This need not always be the case; continuous rules are also possible. Then the elements of the rules would be intervals of the real line, conventionally assigned a value of TRUE = 1. A rule of this kind is $X > 0 \to Y > 100$. Here we shall be mainly concerned with binary variables. The strength of an association rule is commonly measured using support, confidence and lift, also known as measures of a rule's 'statistical interestingness' (Hand, Mannila and Smyth, 2001).

The main problem in association rule modelling is to find, from the available database, a subset of association rules that are interesting. Interestingness can be measured according to various criteria, including subject-matter criteria and objective-driven criteria. Here we consider statistical interestingness, which is related to the observed frequency of the rules. For a given rule, say $A \to B$, let $N_{A \to B}$ be its absolute frequency (count), that is, the number of times in which this rule is observed at least once. In other words, $N_{A \to B}$ measures the number of transactions in which the rule is satisfied. This does not take into account repeated sequences (occurring more than once), and this may sometimes be a limitation, as in web clickstream analysis. The support for a rule $A \to B$ is obtained by dividing the number of transactions which satisfy the rule by the total number of transactions, N:

$$\text{support } \{A \to B\} = \frac{N_{A \to B}}{N}$$

The support of a rule is a relative frequency that indicates the proportion of transactions in which the rule is observed. When a large sample is considered, the support approximates the rule's probability of occurrence:

$$\text{support } \{A \to B\} = \text{Prob}(A \to B) = \text{Prob}(A \text{ and } B \text{ occur})$$

The support is quite a useful measure of a rule's interestingness; it is typically employed to filter out the rules that are less frequent. The confidence of the rule $A \to B$ is obtained by dividing the number of transactions which satisfy the rule by the number of transactions which contain the body of the rule, A:

$$\text{confidence } \{A \to B\} = \frac{N_{A \to B}}{N_A} = \frac{N_{A \to B}/N}{N_A/N} = \frac{\text{support}\{A \to B\}}{\text{support}\{A\}}$$

The confidence expresses a relative frequency (a probability in the limit) that indicates the proportion of times that, if a rule contains the body A, it will also contain the head B. In other words, it is the frequency (or probability) of occurrence of B, conditional on A being true. Confidence is the most used interestingness measure of an association rule; it aims to measure the strength of the relationship between two items. For instance, in market basket analysis, the higher the confidence of the association rule $A \to B$, the greater the probability that if a customer buys products in A, it will also buy product B. In web clickstream analysis, the higher the confidence of the sequence rule $A \to B$, the greater the probability that if a visitor looks at page A, it will also look at page B.

The language of conditional frequencies and conditional probabilities can be employed to give a normalised strength of the relationship between items A and B. One common measure is the lift; this takes the confidence of a rule and relates it to the support for the rule's head:

$$\text{lift}\{A \to B\} = \frac{\text{confidence}\{A \to B\}}{\text{support}\{B\}} = \frac{\text{support}\{A \to B\}}{\text{support }\{A\} \text{ support}\{B\}}$$

Notice how the lift is a ratio between the relative frequency (probability) of both items occurring together, and the relative frequency (probability) of the same event but assuming the two items are independent (Section 3.4). Therefore a lift value greater than 1 indicates there is a positive association, whereas a value less than 1 indicates there is a negative association.

These three interestingness measures can be used to search for association rule models in the data. This amounts to finding a set of rules that are statistically interesting. As the number of possible rules is very large, we need some strategies for model selection. This forward approach is to start from the simplest rules and proceed by adding items, as in the well-known Apriori algorithm (Agrawal et al., 1995). From a given set of items, the algorithm starts by selecting a subset for which the support passes a prefixed threshold t; the other items are discarded. A higher threshold will reduce the complexity of the final solution, as fewer items will be considered.

Next all pairs of items that have passed the previous selection are joined to produce item sets with two items. Item sets are discarded if their support is below the threshold t. The discarded item sets are stored as candidate association rules of order 2; the item selected in this step is the head of the rule. The procedure is repeated. At the mth step, item sets of size m are formed by taking all item sets of size $m - 1$ that have survived and joining them with all those items that have passed the first step. The item sets that do not pass the threshold are discarded and stored to form an association rule of order m; the last item joined is the head and all the previous items are the body. The procedure continues until no rule passes the threshold. The higher the number of variables, with respect to the number of observations, and the higher the threshold value, the quicker the algorithm will terminate.

Notice that the algorithm incorporates a principle of nesting: if a rule of order 2 is discarded, all rules that contain it as antecedent will also be discarded. A disadvantage of the algorithm is that rules with very high confidence or lift, but low support will not be discovered. Also the algorithm can find rules with high support, high confidence and lift close to 1 (indicating that the two item sets are approximately independent) and flag them as interesting. As the strength of an association is not measured by the support, but by the confidence (or the lift), the Apriori algorithm outputs only those rules that pass a fixed confidence threshold.

An alternative way to generate association rules is by using tree models. This can be seen as an instance of backward search, and is somewhat analogous to pruning in tree models. Indeed a tree model can be seen as a supervised generator of item sets, each corresponding to the path from the root node to a leaf. In other words, there are as many rules as the tree has leaves. As a tree gives a partition of the observations into exclusive groups, the support and confidence of each decision tree rule can be easily calculated by going through the nodes of the tree. However, the association rules that can be produced by a tree are built globally and may be too few and too long. To achieve a larger set of rules, fitted locally, each tree model can be pruned using support and confidence thresholds. The advantage of using a tree representation to build rules is that pruning is efficient because of their global modelling nature. Furthermore, they can easily deal with all kinds of variables.

The interestingness measures we have used to find rules can also be used to assess the final model (i.e. the list of rules we obtain) by combining the scores of the individual rules. Alternatively, we can use the measures of association introduced in Section 3.4 for analysing interrelationships between qualitative variables. An important difference is that whereas the measures of association refer to all possible pairs of values of the binary variables, association rules consider only the pair (1,1). For instance, as in Section 3.4, the Pearson statistic X^2 is a very general measure of association. It can be used to give an interestingness measure as well:

$$X^2\{A \rightarrow B\} = \frac{(\text{support}\{A \rightarrow B\} - \text{support }\{A\} \text{ support}\{B\})^2}{\text{support }\{A\} \text{ support}\{B\}}$$

This interestingness measure can be extended to a large number of rules and can be used to assess the departure from independence by appealing to an inferential threshold (based on the chi-squared distribution in Section 5.1). Inferential thresholds can also be derived for association rules. For instance, a large-sample confidence interval for the logarithm of the lift is given by

$$\log(\text{lift}) \pm z_{1-\alpha/2} \sqrt{\frac{1}{\text{support}\{A \to B\}} - \frac{1}{N} + \frac{1}{\text{support}\{A\}} + \frac{1}{\text{support}\{B\}}}$$

where log(lift) is the observed lift and $z_{1-\alpha/2}$ is the $1 - \alpha/2$ percentile of a normal distribution. Exponentiating this expression leads to a confidence interval for the lift. Not only does the width of the interval depend on the confidence level α, it is also directly proportional to the informational content of the rule (support$\{A \to B\}$, support $\{A\}$ and support $\{B\}$) and inversely proportional to the number of transactions N. In other words, the length of the interval, hence the uncertainty on the interestingness of the relationship, decreases as the frequency of the rule increases and in a balanced way (i.e. both the frequency of A and the frequency of B increase).

A confidence interval permits us to decide on the statistical significance of an association rule: if a value of 1 for the lift is within the confidence interval, then the rule is not significant. When more than one rule is tested in this way, the conclusions may be overly restrictive, as the tests are not truly independent. In this case it may be appropriate to increase the width of the confidence intervals and therefore reject fewer rules. To assess the validity of a set of rules, we can also use rules based on a comparison between complementary rules, such as $A \to B$ and $A \to \overline{B}$, where $\overline{B}$ is the complement of B (true when B is false, and vice versa). A simple one is the odds, seen in Section 3.4:

$$\text{odds}\{A \to B\} = \frac{\text{support}\{A \to B\}}{\text{support}\{A \to \overline{B}\}}$$

The Gini index and the entropy index can also be applied in this context as measures of heterogeneity for binary variables.

We now consider a specific type of association rule, particularly relevant for some applications. So far we have said that an association rule is simply a rule of joint occurrence between two item sets, A and B. It is possible to attach to this joint occurrence a meaning of logical precedence, so that the rule's body logically precedes the rule's head. The resulting rule is called a sequence. Association rules can be specifically calculated for sequences, by linking the transaction data set to an ordering variable. A typical way of introducing a logical precedence is through time. Sequences are not needed in market basket analysis; although products are taken off the shelf in a temporal order, this order gets lost when the products are presented at the counter. On the other hand, web clickstream data typically comes in as a log file, which preserves the temporal order in which the pages were visited. Therefore it is important to take account of the order in which the pages were visited. When sequences are considered, the meaning of support and confidence change: support can be interpreted as the number of times that A precedes B; confidence can be interpreted as the conditional probability of B, conditional on A having already occurred. We will look at this difference in Chapter 8.

A further distinction is between direct and indirect sequence rules. A sequence rule is usually indirect, in the sense there may be other elements that logically sit between the body and the head of the rule, but they are not considered. For example, if A and B are two webpages, the sequence rule $A \to B$ searches for all occurrences in which A precedes B, even if other webpages were viewed in between. To allow comparison with the results of global models, it may be interesting to consider direct sequences. A direct sequence searches only for the occurrences in which A exactly precedes B. Note the difference between association and sequence rules. Association rules produce a symmetric relationship, hence the confidence is a measure of association between the binary variables in the two item sets. Sequence rules produce an asymmetric relationship, hence the confidence is a measure of how the variable in the head depends on the variables in the body.

Association rules are probably the most well-known local method for detecting relationships between variables. They can be used to mine very large data sets, for which a global analysis may be too complex and unstable. Section 5.6 explains two related types of global model that can provide a very helpful visual representation of the association structures. These models are known as undirected graphical models (for association modelling) and probabilistic expert systems (for dependency modelling). Chapters 7 and 8 show how such global models compare with the local models presented here. Association rules per se cannot be used predictively, as there would be more than one sequence to predict a given head of a rule. Tree models can be used predictively and also provide a set of association rules.

As two chapters (7 and 8) are entirely devoted to local association models, there are no practical examples in this section. Algorithmic aspects are discussed in Hand, Mannila and Smyth (2001), which contains a comprehensive description of how to find interesting rules using the Apriori algorithm. The advantages of association rules are their extreme simplicity and interpretational capacity; their disadvantages are the lengthy computing times and analysis costs but, above all, the need for sensible pruning. Software packages produce huge numbers of rules, and without sensible pruning, it is easy to get lost in the details and lose sight of the problem.

4.8.2 Retrieval by content

Retrieval-by-content models are local methods based on identifying a query object of interest then searching the database for the k objects that are most similar to it. In association rules the local aspect is in selecting the variables; in retrieval by content the local aspect is in selecting the observations. The main problem is in finding valid measures of proximity to identify observations that are 'similar'.

Notable examples of retrieval by content are searching for information on the internet using a search engine and, more generally, the analysis of text documents, or text mining. The technique is quite broad and can also be applied to audio and video data. There are similarities with memory-based reasoning models (Section 4.7); the main differences are that retrieval by content is not aimed at predicting target variable values, and it is not based on a global assessment of distance between objects, but on distances from the query object. For more details see Hand, Mannila and Smyth (2001).

4.9 Further reading

The first section explained how to calculate a distance matrix from a data matrix. Sometimes we want to build a data matrix from a distance matrix, and one solution is the method of multidimensional scaling (e.g. Mardia, Kent and Bibby, 1979). Having applied multidimensional scaling, it is possible to represent the row vectors (statistical observations) and the column vectors (statistical variables) in a unique plot called biplot; this helps us to make interesting interpretations of the obtained scores. In general, biplots are used with tools for reducing dimensionality, such as principal component analysis and correspondence analysis. For an introduction to this important theme, see Gower and Hand (1996); in a data mining context see Hand, Mannila and Smyth (2001).

An interesting extension of cluster analysis is fuzzy classification; this allows a 'weighted' allocation of the observations to the clusters (Zadeh, 1977).

Multivariate linear regression is best dealt with using matrix notation. For an introduction to matrix algebra in statistics, see Searle (1982). The logistic regression model is for predicting categorical variables. The estimated category probabilities can then be used to classify statistical observations in groups, according to a supervised methodology. Probit models, well known in economics, are essentially the same as logistic regression models, once the logistic link is replaced by an inverse Gaussian link (e.g. Agresti, 1990).

Tree models are probably the most used data mining technique. A more detailed account can be found in advanced data mining textbooks, such as Hastie, Tibshirani and Friedman (2001) and Hand, Mannila and Smyth (2001). These texts offer a statistical treatment; a computational treatment can be found in Han and Kamber (2001). The original works on CART and CHAID are Breiman *et al.* (1984) and Kass (1980).

The literature on neural networks is vast. Neural networks are treated in all data mining textbooks, such as those previously quoted. For a classical statistical approach, consult Bishop (1995); for a Bayesian approach, consult Neal (1996). Section 4.6 considered only two principal network architectures; there was not room to consider others, such as radial basis function (RBF) networks. RBF networks have only one hidden layer and the activation function of every hidden node is a kernel density function (Section 5.2). In this way, the activation function becomes a function of the distance between the input vector and a characteristic vector of the hidden node. Hidden nodes of this type can take non-zero values only in a limited area of the space related to the input variable, as in nearest-neighbour methods. This allows a better separation of the input information and generally a faster learning speed. Support vector machines are a powerful alternative to multilayer perceptrons. The classification rules determined by multilayer perceptrons find a non-linear hyperplane separating the observations, assuming the classes are perfectly separable, but support vector machines generalise this to more complex observation spaces by allowing variable transformations to be performed. Support vector machines optimise the location of the decision boundary between classes. Research is still in progress on these methods. For more details consult Vapnik (1995, 1998). Recently researchers have developed complex statistical models that closely resemble neural networks, but with a more statistical structure. Examples are projection pursuit models, generalised additive models and MARS models (multivariate adaptive regression splines). They are reviewed in Cheng and Titterington (1994) and Hastie, Tibshirani and Friedman (2001). Nearest-neighbour models provide a rather flexible predictive algorithm using memory-based reasoning. Instead of fitting a global model, they fit a local model for the neighbourhood of the observation that is the prediction target. They are related to the descriptive methodology of kernel methods (Section 5.2).

Local model rules are still in an embryonic stage of development, at least from a statistical viewpoint. We looked at association rules, which seem ripe for a full statistical treatment. We briefly examined retrieval-by-content methods, which are expected to gain importance in the foreseeable future, especially with reference to text mining. Consult Hand, Mannila and Smyth (2001) on retrieval by content and Zanasi (2003) on text mining. I think that the statistical understanding of local models will be an important area of research. Local models can be used as an exploratory tool for a global model. Chapters 7 and 8 show how to exploit sequence and association rules to derive a similarity measure between a pair of items and then multidimensional scaling to obtain a global representation of the similarity and the degree of interrelationship between them. This is an example of a link analysis, which tries to establish logical connections among single rows of a database. These connections are similar to the concept of association; the difference is that link analysis is mainly a global analysis of the interrelations among the observations, not among the variables.

CHAPTER 5

Statistical data mining

The principal purpose of this chapter is to illustrate data mining methodologies that are supported by the presence of an underlying probabilistic model. This presence, albeit complicated in structure, allows us to derive more powerful and better interpretable results, based on the ideas of statistical inference developed during the twentieth century. Section 5.1 introduces how to measure uncertainty in probabilistic terms and looks at the basic ideas of statistical inference. In particular, it introduces the most used parametric probability model, the Gaussian distribution, in an operational way. Section 5.2 moves on to non-parametric and semiparametric modelling of the data, and shows how these approaches can be used to perform descriptive data mining on the observations. In particular, it introduces a probabilistic approach to cluster analysis, based on mixture models, as well as the basic ideas behind kernel density estimation.

Section 5.3 considers the normal linear model, the main tool for modelling the relationship between one or more response variables and one or more explanatory variables, to construct a decision rule that enables us to predict the values of the response variables, given the values of the explanatory variables. Section 5.4 introduces a more general class of parametric models, based on the exponential family of distributions; we derive a more general class of linear models that admits as special cases the linear model and the logistic regression model. Another important class of generalised linear models are the log-linear models; they are the most important data mining tool for descriptively analysing the interrelationships between variables. As log-linear models hold only for categorical variables (quantitative discrete and qualitative), Section 5.5 introduces graphical models that can achieve the same goal in a rather general fashion. Graphical models permit an extremely flexible and modular analysis of all the numerous interdependences present in a database. In particular, directed graphical models, known as expert systems or Bayesian networks, define sophisticated predictive models.

5.1   Uncertainty measures and inference

So far we have not assumed any probabilistic hypothesis on the considered statistical variables. However, the considered observations are generally only a subset

Applied Data Mining.   Paolo Giudici
© 2003 John Wiley & Sons, Ltd   ISBNs: 0-470-84679-8 (Paper); 0-470-84678-X (Cloth)

from a target population of interest, a sample. Furthermore, the very large size of the data often forces the analyst to consider only a sample of the available data matrix, either for computational reasons (storage and/or processing memory) or for interpretational reasons. Sampling theory gives a statistical explanation of how to sample from a population in order to extract the desired information efficiently; there is not space to cover it here but Barnett (1975) is a good reference. We shall assume that a sample has been drawn in a random way and is ready for analysis. When dealing with a sample, rather than with the whole population, it is necessary to introduce a probabilistic model that could adequately describe the sampling variability. More generally, a probabilistic model is a useful tool that is often used to model the informational uncertainty that affects most of our everyday decisions.

The introduction of a probabilistic model will lead us to take the estimated statistical summaries and attach measures of variability that describe the degree of uncertainty in the estimate due to sample variability. This will eventually lead us to substitute parametric point estimates with so-called interval estimates; we replace a number with an interval of real numbers that contains the parameter of interest in most cases. We can improve the diagnostic ability of a model by using statistical hypothesis testing; for example, we can introduce a critical threshold above which we retain a certain regression plane as a valid description of the relationship between the variables or we treat a certain clustering of the data as a valid partitioning of the observations. For descriptions of the various probabilistic models, see Mood, Graybill and Boes (1991) or Bickel and Doksum (1977).

5.1.1   Probability

An event is any proposition that can be either true or false and is formally a subset of the space Ω, which is called the space of all elementary events. Elementary events are events that cannot be further decomposed, and cover all possible occurrences. Let a be a class of subsets of Ω, called the event space. A probability function P is a function defined on a that satisfies the following axioms:

- $P(A) \geq 0, \forall A \in a$
- $P(\Omega) = 1$
- If $A_1, A_2, \ldots$ is a sequence of events of a that is pairwise mutually exclusive (i.e. $A_i \cap A_j = \emptyset$ for $i \neq j, i, j = 1, 2, \ldots,$) and if $A_1 \cup A_2 \cup \ldots = \bigcup_{i=1}^{\infty} A_i \in a$, then $P(\bigcup_{i=1}^{\infty} A_i) = \sum_{i=1}^{\infty} P(A_i)$.

A probability function will also be known as a probability measure or simply as probability. The three axioms can be interpreted in the following way. The first axiom says the probability is a non-negative function. The second axiom says the probability of the event Ω is 1; Ω is an event that will always be true as it coincides with all possible occurrences. Since any event is a subset of Ω, it follows that the probability of any event is a real number in [0,1]. The third axiom says the probability of occurrence of any one of a collection of events (possibly infinite, and mutually exclusive) is the sum of the probabilities of occurrence of each of them. This is the formal, axiomatic definition of probability due to Kolmogorov (1933). There are several interpretations of this probability. These interpretations will help us from an operational viewpoint when we come to construct a probability measure. In the classical interpretation, if an experiment gives rise to a finite number n of possible results, then $P(A) = n_A/n$, where n_A indicates the number of results in A (favourable results). In the more general frequentist interpretation, the probability of an event coincides with the relative frequency of the same event in a large (possibly infinite) sequence of repeated trials under the same experimental conditions. The frequentist interpretation allows us to take most of the concepts developed for frequencies (such as those in Chapter 3) and extend them to the realm of probabilities. In the even more general (although somewhat controversial) subjective interpretation, the probability is a degree of belief that an individual attaches to the occurrence of a certain event. This degree of belief is totally subjective but not arbitrary, since probabilities must obey coherency rules, that corresponds to the above axioms and all the rules derivable from those axioms. The advantage of the subjective approach is that it is always applicable, especially when an event cannot be repeated (a typical situation for observational data and data mining, and unlike experimental data).

We can use the three axioms to deduce the basic rules of probability. Here are the complement rule and the union rule:

- *Complement rule*: if A is any event in a, and $\overline{A}$ is its complement (negation), then $P(\overline{A}) = 1 - P(A)$.
- *Union rule*: For any pair of events A, $B \in a$, $P(A \cup B) = P(A) + P(B) - P(A \cap B)$, where the union event $A \cup B$ is true when either A or B is true; the intersection event $A \cap B$ is true when both A and B are true.

Probability has so far been defined in the absence of information. Similar to the concept of relative frequency, we can define the probability of an event A occurring, conditional on the information that the event B is true. Let A and B be two events in a. The conditional probability of the event A, given that B is true, is

$$P(A|B) = \frac{P(A \cap B)}{P(B)} \text{ with } P(B) > 0.$$

The previous definition extends to any conditioning sets of events. Conditional probabilities allows us to introduce further important rules:

- *Intersection rule*: Let A and B be two events in a. Then $P(A \cap B) = P(A|B)P(B) = P(B|A)P(A)$.

- *Independence of events*: If A is independent of B, the following relations hold:

$$P(A \cap B) = P(A)P(B)$$

$$P(A|B) = P(A)$$

$$P(B|A) = P(B)$$

In other words, if two events are independent, knowing that one of them occurs does not alter the probability that the other one occurs.

- *Total probability rule*: Consider n events $H_i, i = 1, \ldots, n$, pairwise mutually exclusive and exhaustive of Ω (equivalently, they form a partition of Ω), with $P(H_i) > 0$. Then the probability of an event B in a is given by

$$P(B) = \sum_{i=1}^{n} P(B|H_i)P(H_i)$$

- *Bayes' rule*: Consider n events $H_i, i = 1, \ldots, n$, pairwise mutually exclusive and exhaustive of Ω (equivalently, they form a partition of Ω), with $P(H_i) > 0$. Then the probability of an event B in a such that $P(B) > 0$ is given by

$$P(H_i|B) = \frac{P(B|H_i)P(H_i)}{\sum_j P(B|H_j)P(H_j)}$$

The total probability rule plays a very important role in the combination of different probability statements; we will see an important application in Section 5.7. Bayes' theorem is a very important rule, also known as the 'inversion rule' as it calculates the conditional probability of an event by using the reversed conditional probabilities. Note also that the denominator of Bayes' rule is the result of the total probability rule; it acts as a normalising constant of the probabilities in the numerator. This theorem lies at the heart of the inferential methodology known as Bayesian statistics.

5.1.2 Statistical models

Suppose that, for the problem at hand, we have defined all the possible elementary events Ω, as well as the event space a. Suppose also that, on the basis of one of the operational notions of probability, we have constructed a probability measure P. The triplet (Ω, a, P) defines a probability space; it is the basic for defining a random variable, hence for building a statistical model.

Given a probability space (Ω, a, P), a random variable is any function $X(\omega)$, $\omega \in \Omega$, with values on the real line. The cumulative distribution of a random variable X, denoted by F, is a function defined on the real line, with values on [0,1], that satisfies $F(x) = P(X \leq x)$ for any real number x. The cumulative distribution function, often called the distribution function, characterises the probability distribution for X. It is the main tool for defining a statistical model of the uncertainty in a variable X.

We now examine two important special cases of random variables and look at their distribution functions. A random variable is discrete if it can take only a finite, or countable, set of values. In this case

$$F(x) = \sum_{X \leq x} p(x) \text{ with } p(x) = P(X = x)$$

Therefore in this case $p(x)$, called the discrete probability function, also characterises the distribution. Both quantitative discrete variables and qualitative variables can be modelled using a discrete random variable, provided that numerical codes are assigned to qualitative variables. They are collectively known as categorical random variables.

A random variable is said to be continuous if there exist a function f, called the density function, such that the distribution function can be obtained from it:

$$F(x) = \int_{-\infty}^{x} f(u) \, du \text{ for any real number } x$$

Furthermore, the density function has these two properties:

$$f(x) \geq 0, \forall x$$

$$\int_{-\infty}^{\infty} f(x) \, dx = 1$$

In view of its definition, the density function characterises a statistical model for continuous random variables.

By replacing relative frequencies with probabilities, we can treat random variables like the statistical variables in Chapter 3. For instance, the discrete probability function can be taken as the limiting relative frequency of a discrete random variable. On the other hand, the density function corresponds to the height of the histogram of a continuous variable. Consequently, the concepts in Chapter 3 – mean, variance, correlation, association, etc. – carry over to random variables. For instance, the mean of a random variable, usually called the expected value, is defined by

$$\mu = \sum x_i p_i \text{ if } X \text{ is categorical}$$

$$\mu = \int x f(x) \, dx \text{ if } X \text{ is continuous}$$

The concept of a random variable can be extended to cover random vectors or other random elements, thereby defining a more complex statistical model. From here on, we use notation for random variables, but without loss of generality.

In general, a statistical model of uncertainty can be defined by the pair $(X, F(x))$, where X is a random variable, and $F(x)$ is the cumulative distribution attached to it. It is often convenient to specify F directly, choosing it from a catalogue of models available in the statistical literature, models which have been constructed specifically for certain problems. These models can be divided into three main classes: parametric models, for which the cumulative distribution is completely specified by a finite set of parameters, denoted by θ; non-parametric models, which, require the whole specification of F; and semiparametric models, where the specification of F is eased by having some parameters but these parameters do not fully specify the model.

We now examine the most used parametric model, the Gaussian distribution; Section 5.2 looks at non-parametric and semiparametric models. Let Z be a continuous variable with real values. Z is distributed according to a standardised Gaussian (or normal) distribution if the density function is

$$f(z) = \frac{1}{\sqrt{2\pi}} e^{-\frac{z^2}{2}}$$

This is a bell-shaped distribution (Section 3.1), with most of the probability around its centre, which coincides with the mean, the mode and the median of the distribution (equal to zero for the standardised Gaussian distribution). Since the distribution is symmetric, the probability of having a value greater than a certain positive quantity is equal to the probability of having a value lower than the negative of the same quantity, i.e. $P(Z > 2) = P(Z < -2)$. Having defined the Gaussian as our reference model, we can use it to calculate some probabilities of interest; these probabilities are areas under the density function. We cannot calculate them in closed form, so we must use numerical approximation. In the past this involved statistical tables but now it can be done with all the main data analysis packages. Here is a financial example.

Consider the valuation of the return of a certain financial activity. Suppose, as is often done in practice, that the future distribution of this return, Z, expressed in euros, follows the standardised Gaussian distribution. What is the probability of observing a return greater than 1 euro? To solve this problem it is sufficient to calculate the probability $P(Z > 1)$. The solution is not expressible in closed form, but using statistical software we find that the probability is equal to about 0.159. Now suppose that a financial institution has to allocate an amount of capital to be protected against the risk of facing a loss on a certain portfolio. This problem is a simplified version of a problem that daily faces credit operators – calculating value at risk (VaR). VaR is a statistical index that measures the maximum loss to which a portfolio is exposed in a holding period Δt and with a fixed level α of desired risk. Let Z be the change in value of the portfolio during the considered period, expressed in standardised terms. The VaR of the portfolio is then the loss (corresponding to a negative return), implicitly defined by

$$P(Z \le -\text{VaR}) = 1 - \alpha$$

suppose the desired level of risk is 5%. This corresponds to fixing the right-hand side at 0.95; the value of the area under the standardised density curve to the right of the value VaR (i.e. to the left of the value $-$VaR) is then equal to 0.05. Therefore the VaR is given by the point on the x-axis of the graph that corresponds to this area. The equation has no closed-form solution. But statistical software easily computes that VaR $= 1.64$. Figure 5.1 illustrates the calculation. The histogram shows the observed returns and the continuous line is the standard Gaussian distribution, used to calculate the VaR. In quantitative risk management this approach is known as the analytic approach or the delta normal approach, in contrast to simulation-based methods.

So far we have considered the standardised Gaussian distribution, with mean 0, and variance 1. It is possible to obtain a family of Gaussian distributions that differ only in their values for mean and variance. In other words, the Gaussian distribution is a parametric statistical model, parameterised by two parameters. Formally, if Z is a standard Gaussian random variable and $X = \sigma Z + \mu$ then X is distributed according to a Gaussian distribution with mean μ and variance σ^2. The family of Gaussian distributions is closed with respect to linear transformations; that is, any linear transformation of a Gaussian variable is also Gaussian. As a result, the Gaussian distribution is well suited to situations in which we hypothesize linear relationships among variables.

Our definition of the Gaussian distribution can be extended to the multivariate case. The resulting distribution is the main statistical model for the inferential analysis of continuous random vectors. For simplicity, here is the bivariate case. A bidimensional random vector (X_1, X_2) is distributed as a bivariate Gaussian distribution if there exist six real constants:

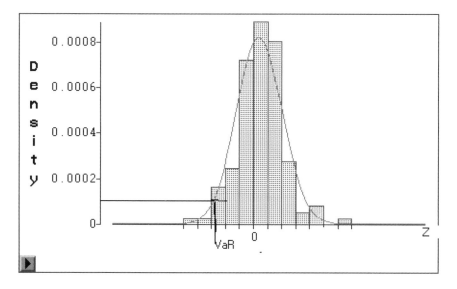

Figure 5.1 Calculation of VaR.

$$a_{ij}, 1 \le i, j \le 2$$

$$\mu_i, i = 1, 2$$

and two independent standardised Gaussian random variables, Z_1 and Z_2, such that

$$X_1 = \mu_1 + a_{11}Z_1 + a_{12}Z_2$$

$$X_2 = \mu_2 + a_{21}Z_1 + a_{22}Z_2$$

In matrix terms, the previous equation can be stated as $X = \mu + AZ$, which easily extends to the multivariate case. In general, a multivariate Gaussian distribution is completely specified by two parameters, the mean vector μ and the variance–covariance matrix $\Sigma = AA'$.

Using the Gaussian distribution, we can derive three distributions, of special importance for inferential analysis: the chi-squared distribution, the Student's t distribution and the F distribution.

The chi-squared distribution is obtained from a standardised Gaussian distribution. If Z is a standardised Gaussian distribution, the random variable defined by Z^2 is said to follow a chi-squared distribution with 1 degree of freedom; it is indicated by the symbol $\chi^2(1)$. More generally, a parametric family of chi-squared distributions, indexed by one parameter, is obtained from the fact that the sum of n independent chi-squared distributions is a chi-squared distribution with n degrees of freedom: $\chi^2(n)$. The chi-squared distribution has positive density only for positive real values. Probabilities from it have to be calculated numerically, as for the Gaussian distribution. Finally, the chi-squared value has an expected value equal to n and a variance equal to $2n$.

The Student's t distribution is characterised by a density symmetric around zero, like the Gaussian distribution but more peaked (i.e. with a higher kurtosis). It is described by one parameter, the degrees of freedom, n. As n increases, the Student's t distribution approaches the Gaussian distribution. Formally, let Z be a standard Gaussian (normal) distribution, in symbols $Z \sim N(0,1)$, and let U be a chi-squared distribution $T = \dfrac{Z}{\sqrt{U/n}} \sim t(n)$ with n degrees of freedom, $U \sim \chi_n^2$. If Z and U are independent, then,

$$T = \frac{Z}{\sqrt{U/n}} \sim t(n)$$

that is, T is a Student's t distribution with n degrees of freedom. It can be shown that the Student's t distribution has an expected value of 0 and a variance given by

$$\text{VaT}(T) = n/(n-2) \text{ for } n > 2$$

Finally, the F distribution is also asymmetric and defined only for positive values, like the chi-squared distribution. It is obtained as the ratio between two independent chi-squared distributions, U and V, with degrees of freedom m and n, respectively:

$$F = \frac{U/m}{V/n}$$

The F distribution is therefore described by two parameters, m and n; it has an expected value equal to $n/(n-2)$ and a variance that is a function of both m and n. An F distribution with $m = 1$ is equal to the square of a Student's t with n degrees of freedom.

5.1.3 Statistical inference

Statistical inference is mainly concerned with the induction of general statements on a population of interest, on the basis of the observed sample. First we need to derive the expression of the distribution function for a sample of observations from a statistical model. A sample of n observations on a random variable X is a sequence of random variables $X_1, X_2, \ldots, X_n$ that are distributed identically as X. In most cases it is convenient to assume that the sample is a simple random sample, with the observations drawn with replacement from the population modelled by X. Then it follows that the random variables $X_1, X_2, \ldots, X_n$ are independent and therefore they constitute a sequence of independent and identically distributed (i.i.d.) random variables. Let X indicate the random vector formed by such a sequence of random variables, $X = (X_1, X_2, \ldots, X_n)$, and let $X = (x_1, x_2, \ldots, x_n)$ indicate the sample value actually observed. It can be shown that, if the observations are i.i.d., the cumulative distribution of X simplifies to

$$F(x) = \prod_{i=1}^{n} F(x_i)$$

with $F(x_i)$ the cumulative distribution of X, evaluated for each of the sample values $(x_1, x_2, \ldots, x_n)$. If $x = (x_1, x_2, \ldots, x_n)$ are the observed sample values, this expression gives a probability, according to the assumed statistical model, of observing sample values less than or equal to the observed values. Furthermore, when X is a continuous random variable

$$f(x) = \prod_{i=1}^{n} f(x_i)$$

where f is the density function of X. And when X is a discrete random variable

$$p(x) = \prod_{i=1}^{n} p(x_i)$$

where p is the discrete probability function of X. If $x = (x_1, x_2, \ldots, x_n)$ are the observed sample values, this expression gives the probability, according to the assumed statistical model, of observing sample values exactly equal to the observed values. In other words, it measures how good is the assumed model for the given data. A high value of $p(x)$, possibly close to one, implies that the data is well described by the statistical model; a low value of $p(x)$ implies the data is poorly described. Similar conclusions can be drawn for $f(x)$ in the continuous case. The difference is that the sample density $f(x)$ is not constrained to be in [0,1], unlike the sample probability $p(x)$. Nevertheless, higher values of $f(x)$ also indicate that the data is well described by the model, and low values indicate the data is poorly described.

In both cases we can say that $p(x)$ or $f(x)$ express the *likelihood* of the model, for the given data.

These are fundamentals ideas when considering inference. A statistical model is a rather general model, in the sense that once a model is assumed to hold, it remains to specify precisely the distribution function or, if the model is parametric, the unknown parameters. In general, there remain unknown quantities to be specified. This can seldom be done theoretically, without reference to the observed data. As the observed data is typically observed on a sample, the main purpose of statistical inference is to 'extend' the validity of the calculations obtained on the sample to the whole population. In this respect, when statistical summaries are calculated on a sample rather than a whole population, it is more correct to use the term 'estimated' rather than 'calculated', to reflect the fact that the obtained values depend on the chosen sample and may therefore be different if a different sample is considered. The summary functions that produce the estimates, when applied to the data, are called statistics. The simplest examples of statistics are the sample mean and the sample variance; other examples are the statistical indexes in Chapter 3, when calculated on a sample.

The methodologies of statistical inference can be divided into estimation methods and hypothesis testing procedures. Estimation methods derive statistics, called estimators, of the unknown model quantities that, when applied to the sample data, can produce reliable estimates of them. Estimation methods can be divided into point estimate methods, where the quantity is estimated with a precise value, and confidence interval methods, where the quantity is estimated to have a high frequency of lying within a region, usually an interval of the real line. To provide a confidence interval, estimators are usually supplemented by measures of their sampling variability. Hypothesis testing procedures look at the use of the statistics to take decisions and actions. More precisely, the chosen statistics are used to accept or reject a hypothesis about the unknown quantities by constructing useful rejection regions that impose thresholds on the values of the statistics.

I briefly present the most important inferential methods. For simplicity, I refer to a parametric model. Starting with estimation methods, consider some desirable properties for an estimator. An estimator T is said to be unbiased, for a parameter θ, if $E(T) = \theta$. The difference $E(T) - \theta$ is called the bias of the estimator and is null if the estimator is unbiased. For example, the sample mean

$$\overline{X} = \frac{1}{n} \sum_{i=1}^{n} X_i$$

is always an unbiased estimator of the unknown population mean μ, as it can be shown that $E(\overline{X}) = \mu$. On the other hand, the sample variance

$$S^2 = \frac{1}{n} \sum_{i=1}^{n} (X_i - \overline{X})^2$$

is a biased estimator of the sample variance σ^2, as $E(S^2) = \dfrac{n^{-1}(n-1)\sigma^2}{n}$. Its bias is therefore

$$\text{bias}(S^2) = -\frac{1}{n}\sigma^2$$

This explains why an often used estimator of the population variance is the unbiased sample variance:

$$S^2 = \frac{1}{n-1} \sum_{i=1}^{n} (X_i - \overline{X})^2$$

A related concept is the efficiency of an estimator, which is a relative concept. Among a class of estimators, the most efficient estimator is usually the one with the lowest mean squared error (MSE), which is defined on the basis of the Euclidean distance by

$$\text{MSE}(T) = E[(T - \theta)^2]$$

It can be shown that

$$\text{MSE}(T) = [\text{bias}(T)]^2 + \text{Var}(T)$$

MSE is composed of two components: the bias and the variance. As we shall see in Chapter 6, there is usually a trade-off between these quantities: if one increases, the other decreases. The sample mean can be shown to be the most efficient estimator of the population mean. For large samples, this can be easily seen applying the definition.

Finally, an estimator is said to be consistent (in quadratic mean) if, for $n \to \infty$, $\lim(\text{MSE}(T)) = 0$. This implies, for $n \to \infty$, $P(\lim |T - \theta|) = 1$; that is, for a large sample, the probability that the estimator lies in an arbitrarily small neighbourhood of θ approximates to 1. Notice that the sample mean and the sample variances we have introduced are consistent.

In practice the two most important estimation methods are the maximum likelihood method and the Bayesian method.

Maximum likelihood methods

Maximum likelihood methods start by considering the likelihood of a model which, in the parametric case, is the joint density of X, expressed as a function of the unknown parameters θ:

$$p(x;\theta) = \prod_{i=1}^{n} p(x_i;\theta)$$

where θ are the unknown parameters and X is assumed to be discrete.

The same expression holds for the continuous case but with p replaced by f. In the rest of the text we will therefore use the discrete notation, without loss of generality.

If a parametric model is chosen, the model is assumed to have a precise form, and the only unknown quantities left are the parameters. Therefore the likelihood is in fact a function of the parameters θ. To stress this fact, the previous expression can also be denoted by $L(\theta;x)$. Maximum likelihood methods suggest that, as estimators of the unknown parameter θ, we take the statistics that maximise $L(\theta;x)$ with respect to θ. The heuristic motivation for maximum likelihood is that it selects the parameter value that makes the observed data most likely under the assumed statistical model. The statistics generated using maximum likelihood are known as maximum likelihood estimators (MLEs) and they have many desirable properties. In particular, they can be used to derive confidence intervals. The typical procedure is to assume that a large sample is available (this is often the case in data mining), then the maximum likelihood estimator is approximately distributed as a normal distribution. The estimator can thus be used in a simple way to derive an asymptotic (valid for large samples) confidence interval. Here is an example. Let T be a maximum likelihood estimator and let var(T) be its asymptotic variance. Then a $100(1 - \alpha)\%$ confidence interval is given by

$$\left(T - z_{(1-\alpha/2)}\sqrt{\mathrm{VaR}(T)}, T + z_{(1-\alpha/2)}\sqrt{\mathrm{VaR}(T)}\right)$$

where $z_{(1-\alpha/2)}$ is the $100(1 - \alpha/2)$ percentile of the standardised normal distribution, such that the probability of obtaining a value less than $z_{(1-\alpha/2)}$ is equal to $(1 - \alpha/2)$. The quantity $(1 - \alpha)$ is also known as the confidence level of the interval, as it gives the confidence that the procedure is correct: in $100(1 - \alpha)\%$ of the cases the unknown quantity will fall within the chosen interval. It has to be specified before to the analysis. For the normal distribution, the estimator of μ is the sample mean, $\overline{X} = n^{-1}\sum X_i$. So a confidence interval for the mean, assuming we known the variance σ^2, is given by

$$\left(\overline{X} - z_{(1-\alpha/2)}\sqrt{\mathrm{Var}(\overline{X})}, \overline{X} + z_{(1-\alpha/2)}\sqrt{\mathrm{Var}(\overline{X})}\right) \quad \text{where} \quad \mathrm{Var}(\overline{X}) = \frac{\sigma^2}{n}$$

When the distribution is normal from the start, as in this case, the expression for the confidence interval holds for any sample size. A common procedure in confidence intervals is to assume a confidence level of 95%; in a normal distribution this leads to $z_{(1-\alpha/2)} = 1.96$.

Bayesian methods

Bayesian methods use Bayes' rule, which expresses a powerful framework for combining sample information with (prior) expert opinion to produce an updated (posterior) expert opinion. In Bayesian analysis, a parameter is treated as a random variable whose uncertainty is modelled by a probability distribution. This distribution is the expert's prior distribution $p(\theta)$, stated in the absence of the sampled data. The likelihood is the distribution of the sample, conditional on the values of the random variable $\theta : p(x|\theta)$. Bayes' rule provides an algorithm to update the expert's opinion in light of the data, producing the so-called posterior distribution $p(\theta|x)$:

$$p(\theta|x) = c^{-1} p(x|\theta) p(\theta)$$

with $c = p(x)$, a constant that does not depend on the unknown parameter θ. The posterior distribution represents the main Bayesian inferential tool. Once it is obtained, it is easy to obtain any inference of interest. For instance, to obtain a point estimate, we can take a summary of the posterior distribution, such as the mean or the mode. Similarly, confidence intervals can be easily derived by taking any two values of θ such the probability of θ belonging to the interval described by those two values corresponds to the given confidence level. As θ is a random variable, it is now correct to interpret the confidence level as a probabilistic statement: $(1 - \alpha)$ is the coverage probability of the interval, namely, the probability that θ assumes values in the interval. The Bayesian approach is thus a coherent and flexible procedure. On the other hand, it has the disadvantage of requiring a more computationally intensive approach, as well as more careful statistical thinking, especially in providing an appropriate prior distribution.

For the normal distribution example, assuming as a prior distribution for θ a constant distribution (expressing a vague state of prior knowledge), the posterior mode is equal to the maximum likelihood estimator. Therefore, maximum likelihood estimates can be seen as a special case of Bayesian estimates. More generally, it can be shown that, when a large sample is considered, the Bayesian posterior distribution approaches an asymptotic normal distribution, with the maximum likelihood estimate as expected value. This reinforces the previous conclusion.

An important application of Bayes' rule arises in predictive classification problems. As explained in Section 4.4, the discriminant rule establishes that an observation x is allocated to the class with the highest probability of occurrence, on the basis of the observed data. This can be stated more precisely by appealing to Bayes' rule. Let C_i, for $i = 1, \ldots, k$, indicate a partition of mutually exclusive and exhaustive classes. Bayes' discriminant rule allocates each observation x to the class C_i that maximises the posterior probability:

$$p(C_i|x) = c^{-1} p(x|C_i) p(C_i) \text{ where } c = p(x) = \sum_{i=1}^{k} p(C_i) p(x|C_i)$$

and x is the observed sample. Since the denominator does not depend on C_i, it is sufficient to maximise the numerator. If the prior class probabilities are all equal to k^{-1}, maximisation of the posterior probability is equivalent to maximisation of the likelihood $p(x|C_i)$. This is the approach often followed in practice. Another common approach is to estimate the prior class probabilities with the observed relative frequencies in a training sample. In any case, it can be shown that the Bayes discriminant rule is optimal, in the sense that it leads to the least possible misclassification error rate. This error rate is measured as the expected error probability when each observation is classified according to Bayes' rule:

$$p_B = \int (1 - \max_i p(C_i|x)) p(x) \, dx$$

also known as the Bayes error rate. No other discriminant rule can do better than a Bayes classifier; that is, the Bayes error rate is a lower bound on the misclassification rates. Only rules that derive from Bayes' rule are optimal. For instance, the logistic discriminant rule and the linear discriminant rule (Section 4.4) are optimal, whereas the discriminant rules obtained from tree models, multilayer perceptrons and nearest-neighbour models are optimal for a large sample size.

Hypothesis testing

We now briefly consider procedures for hypothesis testing. A statistical hypothesis is an assertion about an unknown population quantity. Hypothesis testing is generally performed in a pairwise way: a null hypothesis H_0 specifies the hypothesis to be verified, and an alternative hypothesis H_1 specifies the hypothesis with which to compare it. A hypothesis testing procedure is usually built by finding a rejection (critical) rule such that H_0 is rejected, when an observed sample statistic satisfies that rule, and vice versa. The simplest way to build a rejection rule is by using confidence intervals. Let the acceptance region of a test be defined as the logical complement of the rejection region. An acceptance region for a (two-sided) hypothesis can be obtained from the two inequalities describing a confidence interval, swapping the parameter with the statistic and setting the parameter value equal to the null hypothesis. The rejection region is finally obtained by inverting the signs of the inequalities. For instance, in our normal distribution example, the hypothesis H_0: $\mu = 0$ will be rejected against the alternative hypotheses H_1: $\mu \neq 0$ when the observed value of $\overline{X}$ is outside the interval $(0 - z_{(1-\alpha/2)}\sqrt{\text{Var}(\overline{X})}, 0 + z_{(1-\alpha/2)}\sqrt{\text{Var}(\overline{X})})$.

The probability α has to be specified a priori and is called the significance level of the procedure. It corresponds to the probability of a type I error, namely, the probability of rejecting the null hypothesis when it is actually true. A common assumption is to take $\alpha = 0.05$, which corresponds to a confidence level of 0.95. The probability is obtained, in this case, by summing two probabilities relative to the random variable $\overline{X}$: the probability that $\overline{X} < 0 - z_{(1-\alpha/2)}\sqrt{\text{Var}(\overline{X})}$ and the probability that $\overline{X} > 0 + z_{(1-\alpha/2)}\sqrt{\text{Var}(\overline{X})}$. Notice that the rejection region is derived by setting $\mu = 0$. The significance level is calculated using the same assumption. These are general facts: statistical tests are usually derived under the assumption that the null hypothesis is true. For short, it is said that the test holds 'under the null hypothesis'. The limits of the interval are known as critical values. If the alternative hypothesis were one-sided, the rejection region would correspond to only one inequality. For example, if H_1: $\mu > 0$, the rejection region would be defined by the inequality

$$\overline{X} > 0 + z_{(1-\alpha)}\sqrt{\text{Var}(\overline{X})}$$

The critical value is different because the significance level is now obtained by considering only one probability.

There are other methods for deriving rejection rules; we will consider them in Section 5.4. An alternative approach to testing the validity of a certain null hypothesis is by calculating the p-value of the test. The p-value can be described as the probability, calculated under the null hypothesis, of observing a test statistic more extreme than actually observed, assuming the null hypothesis is true, where 'more extreme' means in the direction of the alternative hypothesis. For a two-sided hypothesis, the p-value is usually taken to be twice the one-sided p-value. Note that the p-value is calculated using the null hypothesis. In our normal distribution example, the test statistics is $\overline{X}$. Let $\overline{x}$ be the observed sample value of $\overline{X}$. The p-value would then be equal to twice the probability that $\overline{X}$ is greater than $\overline{x}$: p-value $= 2P(\overline{X} > \overline{x})$. A small p-value will indicate that $\overline{x}$ is far from the null hypothesis, which is thus rejected; a large p-value will mean that the null hypothesis cannot be rejected. The threshold value is usually the significance level of the test, which is chosen in advance. For instance, if the chosen significance level of the test is $\alpha = 0.05$, a p-value of 0.03 indicates that the null hypothesis can be rejected whereas a p-value of 0.18 indicates that the null hypothesis cannot be rejected.

5.2   Non-parametric modelling

A parametric model is usually specified by making a hypothesis about the distribution and by assuming this hypothesis is true. But this can often be difficult or uncertain. One possible way to overcome this is to use non-parametric procedures, which eliminate the need to specify the form of the distribution in advance. A non-parametric model only assumes that the observations come from a certain distribution function F, not specified by any parameters. But compared with parametric models, non-parametric models are more difficult to interpret and estimate. Semiparametric models are a compromise between parametric models and non-parametric models.

A non-parametric model can be characterised by the distribution function or by the density function (used for short to indicate the continuous and categorical cases), which need to be fully specified.

First consider the estimate of the distribution function. A valid estimator is the empirical distribution function, usually denoted by $S(x)$. Intuitively it is an analogous estimate of the distribution function $F(x)$ of the random variable X. Formally, the empirical distribution function is calculated, at any point x, by taking the proportion of sample observations less than or equal to it:

$$S(x) = \frac{1}{n} n\{x_i \leq x\}$$

It can be shown that the expected value of $S(x)$ is $F(x)$ and that

$$\text{Var}(S(x)) = \frac{1}{n} F(x)(1 - F(x))$$

Therefore the empirical distribution function is an unbiased estimator of $F(x)$ and it is consistent as, for $n \to \infty$, $\text{Var}(S(x)) \to 0$, so that $\text{MSE}(S(x)) \to 0$.

The sample distribution function can be used to assess a parametric model's goodness of fit in an exploratory way. To evaluate the goodness of fit of a distribution function, we usually use the Kolmogorov–Smirnov distance that leads to the well-known statistical test of the same name. In this test, the null hypothesis refers to a particular distribution that we shall call $F^*(x)$ (this distribution could be a normal distribution, for example). Therefore we have

$$H_0 : F(x) = F^*(x)$$

$$H_1 : F(x) \neq F^*(x)$$

To test H_0 against H_1, we consider the available random sample $X_1, \ldots, X_n$. The idea is to compare the observed distribution function, $S(x)$, with the theoretical distribution function F^* calculated using the observed values. The idea of Kolmogorov and Smirnov is simple and clever. Since $S(x)$ estimates $F(x)$ it is logical to hypothesis a 'distance' between $S(x)$ and $F(x)$. If $S(x)$ and $F(x)$ are close enough (i.e. they are similar enough), the null hypothesis can be accepted, otherwise it is rejected. But what kind of test statistics can we use to measure the discrepancy between $S(x)$ and $F(x)$? One of the easiest measurements is the supremum of the vertical distance between the two functions. This is the statistic suggested by Kolmogorov:

$$T_1 = \sup_{-\infty < x < +\infty} |S(x) - F^*(x)|$$

It relies on using the uniform distance, explained in Chapter 6. For 'high' T_1 values, the null hypothesis is rejected; for low T, values, the null hypothesis is accepted. The logic of the T_1 statistic is obvious but the calculation of the probability distribution is more complicated. Nevertheless, we can demonstrate that, under the null hypothesis, the probability distribution of the statistical test based on T_1 does not depend on the functional form of $F^*(x)$. This distribution is tabulated and included in the main statistical packages. It is therefore possible to determine critical values for T_1 and obtain a rejection region of the null hypotheses. Alternatively, it is possible to obtain p-values for the test. The

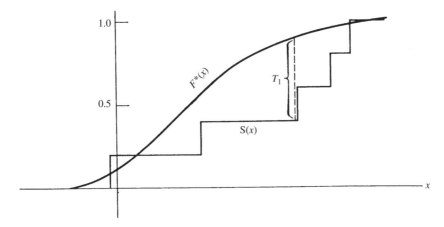

Figure 5.2   The Kolmogorov–Smirnov statistic.

Kolmogorov–Smirnov test is important in exploratory analysis. For example, when the qq-plot (Section 3.1) does not give any obvious indications that a certain empirical distribution is normal or not, we can check whether the distance of the normal distribution function from the empirical distribution function is large enough to be rejected. Figure 5.2 illustrates how the Kolmogorov–Smirnov statistic works.

The simplest type of density estimator is the histogram. A histogram assigns a constant density to each interval class. This density is easily calculated by taking the relative frequency of observations in the class and dividing it by the class width. For continuous densities the histogram can be interpolated by joining all midpoints of the top segment of each bar. However, histograms can depend heavily on the choice of the classes as well as on the sample, especially when considering a small sample. Kernel estimators represent a more refined class of density estimators. They represent a descriptive model that works locally, strongly analogous to nearest-neighbour models (Section 4.7). Consider a continuous random variable X, with observed values $x_1, \ldots, x_n$, and a kernel density function K with a bandwidth h. The estimated density function at any point x is

$$\hat{f}(x) = \frac{1}{n} \sum_{i=1}^{n} K\left(\frac{x - x_i}{h}\right)$$

In practice the kernel function is usually chosen as a unimodal function, with a mode at zero. A common choice is to take a normal distribution for the random variable $x - x_i$ with zero mean and variance corresponding to h^2, the square of the bandwidth of the distribution. The quality of a kernel estimate then depends on a good choice of the variance parameter h. The choice of h reflects the trade-off between parsimony and goodness of fit that we have already encountered: a low value of h means the estimated density values are fitted very locally, possibly on the basis of a single data point; a high value leads to a global estimate, smoothing the data too much. It is quite difficult to establish what a good value of h should be. One possibility is to use computationally intensive methods, such as cross-validation techniques. The training sample is used to fit the density and the validation sample is used to calculate the likelihood of the estimated density. A value of h can then be chosen that leads to a high likelihood.

Estimating high-dimensional density functions is more difficult but kernel methods can still be applied. Replacing the univariate normal kernel with a multivariate normal kernel yields a viable multivariate density estimator. Another approach is to assume that the joint density is the product of univariate kernels. However, the problem is that, as the number of variables increases, observations tend to be farther away and there is little data for the bandwidths. This parallels what happens with nearest-neighbour models. Indeed both are memory-based and the main difference is in their goals; kernel models are descriptive and nearest-neighbour models are predictive.

Kernel methods can be seen as a useful model for summarising a low-dimensional data set in a non-parametric way. This can be a helpful step towards the construction of a parametric model, for instance.

The most important semiparametric models are mixture models. These models are suited to situations where the data set can be clustered into groups of observations, each with a different parametric form. The model is semiparametric because the number of groups, hence the number of distributions to consider, is unknown. The general form of a finite mixture distribution for a random variable X is

$$f(x) = \sum_{i=1}^{g} w_i f_i(x; \theta_i)$$

where w_i is the probability that an observation is distributed as the ith population, with density f_i and parameter vector θ_i. Usually the density functions are all the same (often normal) and this simplifies the analysis. We can apply a similar techniques to a random vector X. The model can be used for (model-based) probabilistic cluster analysis. Its advantage is conducting cluster analysis in a coherent probabilistic framework, allowing us to draw conclusions based on inferential results rather than on heuristics. Its disadvantage is that the procedure is structurally complex and possibly time-consuming. The model can choose the number of components (clusters) and estimate the parameters of each population as well as the weight probabilities, all at the same time. The most challenging aspect is usually to estimate the number of components, as mixture models are non-nested so a log-likelihood test cannot be applied. Other methods are used, such as AIC, BIC, cross-validation and Bayesian methods (Chapter 6). Once the number of components is found, the unknown parameters are estimated by maximum likelihood or Bayesian methods.

5.3   The normal linear model

The most widely applied statistical model is the normal linear model. A linear model is defined essentially by two main hypotheses. Given the explanatory variables $X_1, \ldots, X_p$ and the response variable Y, with $x_{1i}, \ldots, x_{pi}$ the observed values of the explanatory variables $X_1, \ldots, X_p$ corresponding to the ith observation, the first hypothesis supposes that the corresponding observations $Y_1, \ldots, Y_n$ of the response variable Y are independent random variables, each normally distributed with different expected values $\mu_1, \ldots, \mu_n$ and equal variance σ^2:

$$E(Y_i|X_{1i} = x_{1i}, \ldots, X_{pi} = x_{pi}) = \mu_i$$

$$\text{Var}(Y_i|X_{1i} = x_{1i}, \ldots, X_{pi} = x_{pi}) = \sigma^2 \qquad (i = 1, \ldots, n)$$

Dropping the conditioning terms in the expressions for the means and the variances, we can write

$$E(Y_i) = \mu_i \qquad \text{Var}(Y_i) = \sigma^2 \qquad (i = 1, \ldots, n)$$

For each $i = 1, \ldots, n$, let

$$x_{i\bullet} = \begin{bmatrix} x_{0i} \\ x_{1i} \\ \vdots \\ x_{pi} \end{bmatrix} = \begin{bmatrix} 1 \\ x_{1i} \\ \vdots \\ x_{pi} \end{bmatrix} \qquad \beta = \begin{bmatrix} \beta_0 \\ \beta_1 \\ \vdots \\ \beta_p \end{bmatrix}$$

The second hypothesis states that the mean value of the response variable is a linear combination of the explanatory variables:

$$\mu_i = x'_{i\bullet}\beta = \beta_0 + \beta_1 x_{1i} + \cdots + \beta_p x_{pi} \qquad (i = 1, \ldots, n)$$

In matrix terms, setting

$$Y = \begin{bmatrix} Y_1 \\ Y_2 \\ \vdots \\ Y_n \end{bmatrix} \quad X = \begin{bmatrix} x'_{1\bullet} \\ x'_{2\bullet} \\ \vdots \\ x'_{n\bullet} \end{bmatrix} = \begin{bmatrix} x_{01} & x_{11} & \cdots & x_{p1} \\ x_{02} & x_{12} & \cdots & x_{p2} \\ \vdots & \vdots & \vdots & \vdots \\ x_{0n} & x_{1n} & \cdots & x_{pn} \end{bmatrix} \quad \beta = \begin{bmatrix} \beta_0 \\ \beta_1 \\ \vdots \\ \beta_p \end{bmatrix}$$

The two hypotheses can be summarised by saying that Y is a multivariate normal variable with mean vector $E(Y) = \mu = X\beta$ and variance–covariance matrix $\Sigma = E[(Y - \mu)(Y - \mu)'] = \sigma^2 I_n$, where I_n is an identity matrix of order n.

5.3.1 Main inferential results

Under the previous assumptions, we can derive some important inferential results that build on the theory in Section 4.3.

Result 1
For a point estimate, it can be demonstrated that the least squares fitted parameters in Section 4.3 coincide with the maximum likelihood estimators of β. We will use $\hat{\beta}$ to indicate either of the two estimators.

Result 2

A confidence interval for a slope coefficient of the regression plane is

$$\beta = \hat{\beta} \pm t_{n-p-1}(1 - \alpha/2)\mathrm{se}(\hat{\beta})$$

where $t_{n-p-1}(1 - \alpha/2)$ is the $100(1 - \alpha/2)$ percentile of a Student's t distribution with $n - p - 1$ degrees of freedom and se $(\hat{\beta})$ is an estimate of the standard error of $\hat{\beta}$.

Result 3

To test the hypothesis that a slope coefficient is 0, a rejection region is given by

$$R = \left\{ |T| \geq t_{n-p-1}(1 - \alpha/2) \right\} \text{ where } T = \frac{\hat{\beta}}{\mathrm{se}(\hat{\beta})}$$

If the observed absolute value of the statistic T is contained in the rejection region, the null hypothesis of the slope equal to 0 is rejected, and the slope coefficient is *statistically significant*. In other words, the considered explanatory variable significantly influences the response variable. Conversely, when the observed absolute value of the statistic T falls outside the rejection region, the explanatory variable is not significant. Alternatively, it is possible to calculate the p-value of the test, the probability of observing a value of T greater in absolute value than the observed value. If this p-value is small (e.g. lower than $\alpha = 0.05$), this means that the observed value is very distant from the null hypothesis, therefore the null hypothesis is rejected (i.e. the slope coefficient is significant).

Result 4

To test whether a certain regression plane, with p explanatory variables, constitutes a significant linear model, it can be compared with a trivial model, with only the intercept. The trivial model, set to be the null hypothesis H_0, is obtained by simultaneously setting all slope coefficients to 0. The regression plane will be significant when the null hypothesis is rejected. A rejection region is given by the following inequality:

$$F = \frac{R^2/p}{(1 - R^2)/(n - p - 1)} \geq F_{p,n-p-1}(1 - \alpha)$$

where R^2 is the coefficient of determination seen in Section 4.3 and $F_{p,n-p-1}(1 - \alpha)$ is the $100 (1 - \alpha)$ percentile of an F distribution, with p and $n - p - 1$ degrees of freedom. The degrees of freedom of the denominator represent the difference in dimension between the observation space (n) and the fitting plane ($p + 1$); those of the numerator represent the difference in dimension between the fitting plane ($p + 1$) and a fitting point (1) defined by the only intercept. A p-value for the test can be calculated, giving further support to the significance of the model.

Notice how we have introduced a precise threshold for evaluating whether a certain regression model is valid in making predictions, in comparison with the simple arithmetic mean. But this is a relative statement, which gives little indication of how well the linear model fits the data at hand. A statistic like this can be applied to cluster analysis, assuming that the available observations come from a normal distribution. Then the degrees of freedom are $c - 1$ and $n - c$. The statistic is called a pseudo-F statistic, because in the general case of a non-normal distribution for the observations, the statistic does not have an F distribution.

Result 5

To compare two nested regression planes that differ in a single explanatory variable, say the $(p + 1)$th, present in one model but not in the other, the simpler model can be set as the null hypothesis H_0, so the more complex model is chosen if the null hypothesis is rejected, and vice versa. A rejection region can be defined by the following inequality:

$$F = \frac{r^2_{Y,X_{p+1}|X_1,\ldots,X_p}/1}{(1 - r^2_{Y,X_{p+1}|X_1,\ldots,X_p})/(n - p - 2)} \geq F_{1,n-p-2}(1 - \alpha)$$

where $r^2_{Y,X_{p+1}|X_1,\ldots,X_p}$ is the partial correlation coefficient between X_{p+1} and the response variable Y, conditional on all present explanatory variables and $F_{1,n-p-2}(1 - \alpha)$ is the $100(1 - \alpha)$ percentile of an F distribution, with 1 and $n - p - 2$ degrees of freedom.

Notice that the degrees of freedom of the denominator represent the difference in dimension between the observation space (n) and the more complex fitting plane $(p + 2)$; the degrees of freedom of the numerator represent the difference in dimension between the more complex fitting plane $(p + 2)$ and the simpler one $(p + 1)$. Alternatively, we can do the comparison by calculating the p-value of the test. This can usually be derived from the output table that contains the decomposition of the variance, also called the analysis of variance (ANOVA) table. By substituting the definition of the partial correlation coefficient $r^2_{Y,X_{p+1}|X_1,\ldots,X_p}$, we can write the test statistic as

$$F = \frac{\mathrm{Var}(\hat{Y}_{p+1}) - \mathrm{Var}(\hat{Y}_p)}{(\mathrm{Var}(Y) - \mathrm{Var}(\hat{Y}_{p+1}))/(n - p - 2)}$$

therefore this F test statistic can be interpreted as the ratio between the additional variance explained by the $(p + 1)$th variable and the mean residual variance. In other words, it expresses the relative importance of the $(p + 1)$th variable. This test is the basis of a process which chooses the best model from a collection of possible linear models that differ in their explanatory variables. The final model is chosen through a series of hypothesis tests, each comparing two alternative models. The simpler of the two models is taken as the null hypothesis and the more complex model as the alternative hypothesis.

As the model space will typically contain many alternative models, we need to choose a search strategy that will lead to a specific series of pairwise comparisons. There are at least three alternative approaches. The forward selection procedure starts with the simplest model, without explanatory variables. It then complicates it by specifying in the alternative hypothesis H_1 a model with one explanatory variable. This variable is chosen to give the greatest increase in the explained variability of the response. The F test is used to verify whether or not the added variable leads to a significant improvement with respect to the model in H_0. In the negative case the procedure stops and the chosen model is the model in H_0 (i.e., the simplest model). In the affirmative case the model in H_0 is rejected and replaced with the model in H_1. An additional explanatory variable (chosen as before) is then inserted in a new model in H_1, and a new comparison is made. The procedure continues until the F test does not reject the model in H_0, which thus becomes the final model.

The backward elimination procedure starts with the most complex model, containing all the explanatory variables. It simplifies it by making the null hypotheses H_0 equal to the original model minus one explanatory variable. The eliminated variable is chosen to produce the smallest decrease in the explained variability of the response. The F test is used to verify whether or not the elimination of this variable leads to a significant improvement with respect to the model in H_1. In the negative case the chosen model is the model in H_1 (i.e. the most complex model) and the procedure stops. In the affirmative case the complex model in H_1 is rejected and replaced with the model in H_0. An additional variable is dropped (chosen as before) and the resulting model is set as H_0, then a new comparison is made. The procedure continues until the F test rejects the null hypothesis. Then the chosen model is the model in H_1.

The stepwise procedure is essentially a combination of the previous two. It begins with no variables; variables are then added one by one according to the forward procedure. At each step of the procedure, a backward elimination is carried out to verify whether any of the added variables should be removed. Whichever procedure is adopted, the final model should be the same. This is true most of the time but it cannot be guaranteed. The significance level used in the comparisons is an important parameter as the procedure is carried out automatically by the software and the software uses the same level for all comparisons. For example, the SAS procedure reg chooses a significance level of $\alpha = 0.15$ as a default. It is interesting to compare the model selection procedure of a linear model with the computational procedures in Chapter 4. The procedures in Chapter 4 usually require the introduction of heuristic criteria, whereas linear model selection can be fully automated but still remain within a formal procedure.

For large samples, stepwise procedures are often rather unstable in finding the best models. It is not a good idea to rely solely on stepwise procedures for selecting models.

5.3.2 Application

To illustrate the application of the normal linear model, we will again consider the data matrix with 262 rows and 6 columns containing observations on the behaviour of an investment fund return, and the five sector indexes that can be adopted as explanatory variables (Section 4.3). The objective is to determine the best linear model that describes the returns as a function of the sector indexes. We can do this by comparing different linear combinations of the predictors and choosing the best one. The exploratory procedures in Chapter 4 detected a strong correlation between the return and the predictors, encouraging us to apply a linear model. Before proceeding with model comparisons, it is useful to test whether the response variable satisfies the assumptions for the normal linear model, and whether it has an approximately normal distribution. If this is not the case, we will need to transform it to bring it closer to normality.

Table 5.1 shows the calculation of a few summary univariate indexes for the response variable. The values of the skewness and kurtosis do not depart much from those for the theoretical normal distribution (both equal to 0 in SAS). Figure 5.3 shows the qq-plot of the response variable, and confirms the validity of the normal approximation, apart from the possible presence of anomalous observations in the tail of the distribution. This means we can proceed with the

Table 5.1 Univariate statistics for the response variable.

▶|	Moments		
N	262.0000	Sum Wgts	262.0000
Mean	0.2537	Sum	66.4680
Std Dev	1.8799	Variance	3.5341
Skewness	-0.2595	Kurtosis	2.0901
USS	939.2511	CSS	922.3885
CV	741.0122	Std Mean	0.1161

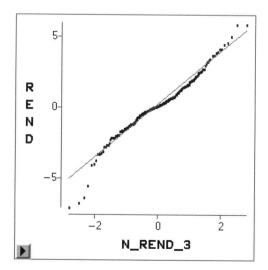

Figure 5.3 The qq-plot of the response variable.

Table 5.2   Estimates with the most complex linear model.

```
Backward Elimination Procedure for Dependent Variable REND
   Step 0      All Variables Entered      R-square = 0.81919887
   Source         DF       Sum of Squares    Mean Square      F      Prob>F
Regression          5       755.61964877    151.12392975   231.98   0.0001
   Error          256       166.76888880      0.65144097
   Total          261       922.38853757

                Parameter      Standard          Type II
Variable        Estimate        Error       Sum of Squares     F      Prob>F
INTERCEP       -0.00771196    0.05111640       0.01482805     0.02    0.8802
COMIT          -0.01453272    0.02254704       0.27063860     0.42    0.5198
JAPAN           0.07160597    0.02174317       7.06525395    10.85    0.0011
PACIFIC         0.08148180    0.02408673       7.45487776    11.44    0.0008
EURO            0.35309221    0.03924075      52.74444954    80.97    0.0001
NORDAM          0.35357909    0.02945975      93.84044089   144.05    0.0001
```

selection of the model. Although we are assuming a normal linear model, we could consider other linear models, such as constant variance and uncorrelated residuals. We will do this indirectly by examining the residuals of the final model. Econometrics textbooks give an introduction to more formal tests for choosing different kinds of linear model. Using the backward elimination procedure, we begin by fitting the most complex model, containing all the explanatory variables. Table 5.2 shows the typical output from applying the normal linear model. The first part of the table shows the results relative to the variance decomposition of the response variable; it is an ANOVA table. For each source of variability (regression, error, total) it shows the degrees of freedom (DF) and the sum of squares, which represents the explained variance. The mean square regression is the regression sum of squares divided by the regression DF. The mean square error is the error sum of squares divided by the error DF. The F statistic (from Result 4 on page 148) is the mean square regression divided by the mean square error. We can evaluate a p-value for F. The p-value is small (lower than 5%), so we reject the null hypothesis that the explanatory variables offer no predictive improvement over the mean alone. Therefore the model with five explanatory variables is significant. The multiple coefficient of determination R^2 is equal to 81.91%, a relatively large value that leads, through the application of the F test, to a significant model.

The second part of the table shows the maximum likelihood estimates of the six parameters of the regression plane (the intercept plus the five slope coefficients). These estimates match those obtained with the method of least squares (Table 4.5). But now the introduction of a statistical model allows us to attach measures of sampling variability (standard errors). Calculating the ratio between the value of the estimated parameters and their standard errors, we obtain the T statistic (from Result 3 on page 148). To test the hypothesis that the COMIT slope coefficient is 0, we obtain a T-value equal to -0.64, corresponding to a p-value of 0.54. This clearly indicates that the COMIT coefficient is not significantly different from 0 and therefore COMIT is not a significant predictor. The type II sum of squares is the additional contribution to the explained variability, with respect to a model that contains all other variables. Each type II sum of squares corresponds to the numerator of the F statistic (from Result 5 on page 149). The F statistic is the type II sum of squares divided by the mean square error in the first part of the table. The final column gives the corresponding p-values, which show that the response variable strongly depends on only four of the five explanatory variables.

Table 5.3 is a summary of the backward elimination procedure. We removed only the COMIT variable and then we stopped the procedure. The table shows the step of the procedure where the variable was removed, the number of variables remaining in the model (In = 4), the partial correlation coefficient (given all the others) of the excluded variable (0.0003), the coefficient of multiple determination of the model, for the remaining four variables (0.8189); it also gives the F statistic of Result 5 and its p-value, for inserting COMIT in a plane with all the other variables. The hypothesis is clearly rejected. Table 5.4 shows the final linear model, where all the remaining variables are significant.

Once a statistical model is chosen, it is useful to diagnose it, perhaps by analysing the residuals (Section 4.3). To facilitate comparisons, the residuals are often Studentised – they are divided by their estimated standard error. The name derives from the fact that we can take the resulting ratio and apply a Student's t test to see whether each residual significantly departs from the null value. If this

Table 5.3 Results of the backward selection procedure.

Summary of Backward Elimination Procedure for Dependent Variable REND

Step	Removed	In	Partial R**2	Model R**2	F	Prob>F
1	COMIT	4	0.0003	0.8189	0.4154	0.5198

Table 5.4 Estimates with the chosen final model.

Source	DF	Sum of Squares	Mean Square	F	Prob>F
Regression	4	755.34901017	188.83725254	290.54	0.0001
Error	257	167.03952741	0.64995925		
Total	261	922.38853757			

Variable	Parameter Estimate	Standard Error	Type II Sum of Squares	F	Prob>F
INTERCEP	-0.00794188	0.05105699	0.01572613	0.02	0.8765
JAPAN	0.07239498	0.02168398	7.24477432	11.15	0.0010
PACIFIC	0.08249154	0.02400838	7.67324503	11.81	0.0007
EURO	0.33825116	0.03173909	73.82028615	113.58	0.0001
NORDAM	0.35346510	0.02942570	93.78332454	144.29	0.0001

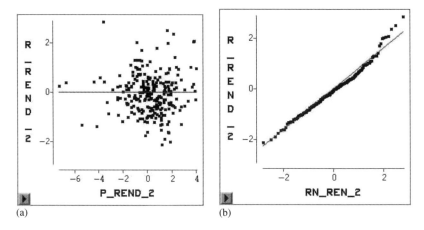

Figure 5.4 Diagnostics: (a) residuals against fitted values, (b) residuals qq-plot.

is so, it indicates a possible problem for the linear model. Using a significance level of 5%, the absolute value of the residuals should not exceed about 2, which approximates a 5% significance test. Figure 5.4 shows the analysis of the residuals for our chosen model. Figure 5.4(a) shows a plot of the observed residuals (y-axis) versus the fitted values (x-axis); Figure 5.4(b) is a qq-plot of the observed residuals (y-axis) against the theoretical normal ones (x-axis). Both plots show good behaviour of the model's diagnostics. In particular, all the residuals are included in the interval $(-2, +2)$ and there are no evident trends – no increasing or decreasing tendencies. The qq-plot confirms the hypothesis underlying the normal linear model. We can therefore conclude that we have chosen a valid model, on which it is reasonable to base predictions. The final model is described by the following regression plane:

$$REND = -0.0079 + 0.0724 \text{ JAPAN} + 0.0825 \text{ PACIFIC}$$
$$+ 0.3383 \text{ EURO} + 0.3535 \text{ NORDAM}$$

Comparing this model with the model in Table 4.5, there are slight differences in the estimated coefficients, due to the absence of the variable COMIT. The slight effect of COMIT on the response variable is absorbed by the other variables.

5.4 Generalised linear models

For several decades the linear model has been the main statistical model for data analysis. However, in many situations the hypothesis of linearity is not realistic. The second restrictive element of the normal linear model is the assumption of normality and constant variance of the response variable. In many applications the observations are not normally distributed nor do they have a constant variance, and this limits the usefulness of the normal linear model. Developments in statistical theory and computing power during the 1960s allowed researchers to take their techniques for linear models and develop them in other contexts. It turns out that many of the 'nice' proprieties of the normal distribution are shared by a wider class of statistical models known as the exponential family of distributions.

The numerical calculations for the parameter estimates have also benefited from refinements; as well as working on linear combinations $\mathbf{X}\boldsymbol{\beta}$, we can now work on functions of linear combinations such as $g(\mathbf{X}\boldsymbol{\beta})$. Improved computer hardware and software have helped with effective implementation, culminating in generalised linear models (Nelder and Wedderburn, 1972). In the normal linear model, the base distribution is the normal distribution; in generalised linear models it is one of the exponential family of distributions.

5.4.1 The exponential family

Consider a single random variable Y whose density function (or discrete probability function) depends on a single parameter θ (possibly vector-valued). The probability distribution of the variable is said to belong to the exponential family if the density can be written in the form

$$f(y;\theta) = s(y)t(\theta)e^{a(y)b(\theta)}$$

where a, b, s and t are known functions.

The symmetry existing between y and the parameter θ becomes more evident if the previous equation is rewritten in the form

$$f(y;\theta) = \exp[a(y)b(\theta) + c(\theta) + \mathrm{d}(y)]$$

where $s(y) = \exp[d(y)]$ and $t(\theta) = \exp[c(\theta)]$. If it holds that $a(y) = y$, the previous distribution is said to be in canonical form, and $b(\theta)$ is called the natural parameter of the distribution. If there are other parameters (let us say ϕ), besides the parameter of interest θ, they are considered as nuisance parameters that are usually dealt with as if they were known. Many familiar distributions belong to the exponential family; here are some of them.

Poisson distribution

The Poisson distribution is usually used to model the probability of observing integer numbers, corresponding to counts in a fixed period of time (e.g. the number of clients that enter a supermarket in an hour, or the number of phone calls received at a call centre in a day). The Poisson distribution is a discrete distribution that associates a non-zero probability to all the non-negative integers. It is parameterised by a parameter that represents the mean value of the counts. If a random variable Y has a Poisson distribution with mean λ, its discrete probability function is

$$f(y;\lambda) = \frac{\lambda^y e^{-\lambda}}{y!}$$

where y takes the values $0, 1, 2, \ldots$. Through simple algebra it is possible to rewrite the density as

$$f(y; \lambda) = \exp[y \log \lambda - \lambda - \log y!]$$

which shows that the Poisson distribution belongs to the exponential family, in canonical form, with natural parameter $b(\theta) = \log \lambda$.

Normal distribution
The normal distribution is a continuous distribution that associates a positive density to each real number. If Y is a normal random variable with mean μ and variance σ^2, its density function is

$$f(y; \mu) = \frac{1}{(2\pi\sigma^2)^{1/2}} \exp\left[-\frac{1}{2\sigma^2}(y - \mu)^2\right]$$

where μ is usually the parameter of interest and σ^2 is treated as a disturbance parameter. The density can be rewritten as

$$f(y; \mu) = \exp\left[y\frac{\mu}{\sigma^2} - \frac{\mu^2}{2\sigma^2} - \frac{1}{2}\log(2\pi\sigma^2) - \frac{y^2}{2\sigma^2}\right]$$

which shows that the normal distribution belongs to the exponential family, in canonical form, with natural parameter $b(\theta) = \mu/\sigma^2$.

Binomial distribution
The binomial distribution is used to model the probability of observing a number of successes (or events of interest) in a series of n independent binary trials, (e.g. how many among the n clients of a certain supermarket buy a certain product, or how many among n loans assigned to a certain credit institution have a good end). The binomial distribution is a discrete distribution that associates a non-zero probability to all the non-negative integers between 0 and n, representing the completed trials. It is parameterised by n and by the parameter π, which represents the probability of obtaining a success in each trial. Suppose that the random variable Y represents the number of successes in n binary independent experiments, in which the probability of success is always equal to π. In this case Y has a binomial distribution with discrete probability function

$$f(y; \pi) = \binom{n}{y} \pi^y (1 - \pi)^n - y$$

where Y takes the values $0,1,2, \ldots, n$. This function can be rewritten as

$$f(y; \pi) = \exp\left[y \log\left(\frac{\pi}{1 - \pi}\right) + n\log(1 - \pi) + \log\binom{n}{y}\right]$$

which shows that the binomial distribution belongs to the exponential family, in canonical form, with natural parameter $b(\theta) = \log[\pi/(1 - \pi)]$.

The exponential family
The exponential family of distributions is a very general class that contains these three important probabilistic models. The advantage of the general form is that it is possible to obtain inferential results common to all the distributions belonging to it. We will not dwell on these results; we will concentrate on some important consequences for data analysis. For more details see Agresti (1990) or Dobson (1990).

5.4.2 Definition of generalised linear models

A generalised linear model takes a function of the mean value of the response variable and relates it to the explanatory variables through an equation having linear form. It is specified by three components: a random component, which identifies the response variable Y and assumes a probability distribution for it; a systematic component, which specifies the explanatory variables used as predictors in the model; and a link function, which describes the functional relation between the systematic component and the mean value of the random component.

Random component
For a sample of size n, the random component of a generalised linear model is described by the sample random variables $Y_1, \ldots, Y_n$; these are independent, each has a distribution in exponential family form that depends on a single parameter θ_i, and each is described by the density function

$$f(y_i; \theta_i) = \exp[y_i b(\theta_i) + c(\theta_i) + d(y_i)]$$

All the distributions for the Y_i have to have the same form (e.g. all normal or all binomial) but their θ_i parameters do not have to be the same.

Systematic component
The systematic component specifies the explanatory variables and their roles in the model. It is specified by a linear combination:

$$\eta = \beta_1 x_1 + \cdots + \beta_p x_p = \sum_{j=1}^{p} \beta_j x_j$$

The linear combination η is called the linear predictor. The X_j represent the covariates, whose values are known (e.g. they can be derived from the data matrix). The β_j are the parameters that describe the effect of each explanatory variable on the response variable. The values of the parameters are generally unknown and have to be estimated from the data. The systematic part can be written in the following form:

$$\eta_i = \sum_{j=1}^{p} \beta_j x_{ij} \qquad (i = 1, \ldots, n)$$

where x_{ij} is the value of the jth explanatory variable for the ith observation. In matrix form it is

$$\eta = X\beta$$

where η is a vector of order $n \times 1$, X is a matrix of order $n \times p$, called the model matrix, and β is a vector of order $p \times 1$, called the parameter vector.

Link function
The third component of a generalised linear model specifies the link between the random component and the systematic component. Let the mean value of Y_i be denoted by

$$\mu_i = E(Y_i) \qquad (i = 1, \ldots, n.)$$

The link function specifies which function of μ_i linearly depends on the explanatory variables through the systematic component η_i. Let $g(\mu_i)$ be a function (monotone and differentiable) of μ_i. The link function is defined by

$$g(\mu_i) = \eta_i = \sum_{j=1}^{p} \beta_j x_{ij} \qquad (i = 1, \ldots, n)$$

In other words, the link function describes how the explanatory variables affect the mean value of the response variable, that is, through the function g. How do we choose g? In practice the more commonly used link functions are canonical and define the natural parameter of the particular distribution as a function of the mean response value. Table 5.5 shows the canonical link functions for the three important distributions in Section 5.4.1. The same table can be used to derive the most important examples of generalised linear models. The simplest link function is the normal one. It directly models the mean value through the link identity $\eta_i = \mu_i$, thereby specifying a linear relationship between the mean response value and the explanatory variables:

$$\mu_i = \beta_0 + \beta_1 x_{i1} + \cdots + \beta_p x_{ip}$$

The normal distribution and the identity link give rise to the normal linear model for continuous response variables (Section 5.3).

Table 5.5 Main canonical links.

Distribution	Canonical link
Normal	$g(\mu_i) = \mu_i$
Binomial	$g(\mu_i) = \log\left(\dfrac{\pi_i}{1 - \pi_i}\right)$
Poisson	$g(\mu_i) = \log \mu_i$

The binomial link function models the logarithm of the odds as a linear function of the explanatory variables:

$$\log\left(\frac{\mu_i}{1-\mu_i}\right) = \beta_0 + \beta_1 x_{i1} + \cdots + \beta_p x_{ip} \qquad (i = 1, \ldots, n)$$

This type of link is called a logit link and is appropriate for binary response variables, as in the binomial model. A generalised linear model that uses the binomial distribution and the logit link is a logistic regression model (Section 4.4). For a binary response variable, econometricians often use the probit link, which is not canonical. They assume that

$$\Phi^{-1}(\mu_i) = \beta_0 + \beta_1 x_{i1} + \cdots + \beta_p x_{ip} \qquad (i = 1, \ldots, n)$$

where Φ^{-1} is the inverse of the cumulative normal distribution function.

The Poisson canonical link function specifies a linear relationship between the logarithm of the mean response value and the explanatory variables:

$$\log(\mu_i) = \beta_0 + \beta_1 x_{i1} + \cdots + \beta_k x_{ik} \qquad (i = 1, \ldots, n)$$

A generalised linear model that uses the Poisson distribution and a logarithmic link is a log-linear model; it constitutes the main data mining tool for describing associations between the available variables. It will be examined in Section 5.5.

Inferential results

We now consider inferential results that hold for the whole class of generalised linear models; we will apply them to logistic regression and log-linear models. Parameter estimates are usually obtained using the method of maximum likelihood. The method computes the derivative of the log-likelihood with respect to each coefficient in the parameter vector $\boldsymbol{\beta}$ and sets it equal to zero, similar to the linear regression context in Section 4.3. But unlike what happens with the normal linear model, the resultant system of equations is non-linear in the parameters and does not generally have a closed-form solution. So to obtain maximum likelihood estimators of $\boldsymbol{\beta}$, we need to use iterative numerical methods, such as the Newton–Raphson method or Fisher's scoring method; for more details see Agresti (1990) or Hand, Mannila and Smyth (2001).

Once the parameter vector $\boldsymbol{\beta}$ is estimated, its significance is usually assessed by hypothesis testing. We will now see how to verify the significance of each parameter in the model. Later we will compute the overall significance of a model in the context of model comparison. Consider testing the null hypothesis $H_0 : \beta_i = 0$ against the alternative $H_1 : \beta_i \neq 0$. A rejection region for H_0 can be defined using the asymptotic procedure known as Wald's test. If the sample size is sufficiently large, the statistic

$$Z = \frac{\hat{\beta}_i}{\sigma(\hat{\beta}_i)}$$

is approximately distributed as a standardised normal; here $\sigma(\hat{\beta_i})$ indicates the standard error of the estimator in the numerator. Therefore, to decide whether to accept or reject the null hypothesis, we can build the rejection region

$$R = \{|Z| \geq z_{1-\alpha/2}\}$$

where $z_{1-\alpha/2}$ is the $100(1 - \alpha/2)$ percentile of a standard normal distribution. Or we can find the p-value and see whether it is less than a predefined significance level (e.g. $\alpha = 0.05$). If $p < \alpha$ then H_0 is rejected. The square of the Wald statistic Z has a chi-squared distribution with 1 degrees of freedom, for large samples (Section 5.1). That means it is legitimate for us to build a rejection region or to assess a p-value.

Rao's score statistic, often used as an alternative to the Wald statistic, computes the derivative of the observed log-likelihood function evaluated at the parameter values set by the null hypothesis, $\beta_i = 0$. Since the derivative is zero at the point of maximum likelihood, the absolute value of the score statistic tends to increase as the maximum likelihood estimate $\hat{\beta_i}$ gets more distant from zero. The score statistic is equal to the square of the ratio between the derivative and its standard error, and it is also asymptotically distributed as a chi-squared distribution with 1 degree of freedom. For more details on hypotheses testing using generalised linear models, see McCullagh and Nelder (1989), Dobson (1990) or Azzalini (1992).

Model comparison

Fitting a model to data can be interpreted as a way of replacing a set of observed data values with a set of estimated values obtained during the fitting process. The number of parameters in the model is generally much lower than the number of observations in the data. We can use these estimated values to predict future values of the response variable from future values of the explanatory variables. In general the fitted values, say $\hat{\mu_i}$, will not be exactly equal to the observed values, y_i. The problem is to establish the distance between the $\hat{\mu_i}$ and the y_i. In Chapter 6 we will start form this simple concept of distance between observed values and fitted values, then show how it is possible to build statistical measures to compare statistical models and, more generally, data mining methods. In this section we will consider the deviance and the Pearson statistic, two measures for comparing the goodness of fit of different generalised linear models.

The first step in evaluating a model's goodness of fit is to compare it with the models that produce the best fit and the worst fit. The best-fit model is called the saturated model; it has as many parameters as observations and therefore leads to a perfect fit. The worst-fit model is called the null model; it has only one intercept parameter and leaves all response variability unexplained. The saturated model attributes the whole response variability to the systematic component. In practice the null model is too simple and the saturated model is not informative because it does completely reproduces the observations. However, the saturated model is a useful comparison when measuring the goodness of fit of a model with p parameters. The resulting quantity is called the deviance, and it is defined as follows for a model M (with p parameters) in the class of generalised linear models:

$$G^2(M) = -2 \log \left\{ \frac{L(\hat{\beta}(M))}{L(\hat{\beta}(M^*))} \right\}$$

where the quantity in the numerator is the likelihood function, calculated using the maximum likelihood parameter estimates under model M, indicated by $\hat{\beta}(M)$; and the quantity in the denominator is the likelihood function of the observations, calculated using the maximum likelihood parameter estimates under the saturated model M^*. The expression in curly brackets is called the likelihood ratio, and it seems an intuitive way to compare two models in terms of the likelihood they receive from the observed data. Multiplying the natural logarithm of the likelihood ratio by -2, we obtain the maximum likelihood ratio test statistic.

The asymptotic distribution of the G^2 statistic (under H_0) is known: for a large sample size, $G^2(M)$ is approximately distributed as a chi-squared distribution with $n - k$ degrees of freedom, where n is the number of observations and k is the number of estimated parameters under model M, corresponding to the number of explanatory variables plus one (the intercept). The logic behind the use of G^2 is as follows. If the model M that is being considered is good, then the value of its maximised likelihood will be closer to that of the maximised likelihood under the saturated model M^*. Therefore 'small' values of G^2 indicate a good fit.

The asymptotic distribution of G^2 can provide a threshold beneath which to declare the simplified model M as a valid model. Alternatively, the significance can be evaluated through the p-value associated with G^2. In practice the p-value represents the area to the right of the observed value for G^2 in the χ^2_{n-k} distribution. A model M is considered valid when the observed p-value is large (e.g. greater than 5%). The value of G^2 alone is not sufficient to judge a model, because G^2 increases as more parameters are introduced, similar to what happens with R^2 in the regression model. However, since the threshold value generally decreases with the number of parameters, by comparing G^2 and the threshold we can reach a compromise between goodness of fit and model parsimony.

The overall significance of a model can also be evaluated by comparing it against the null model. This can be done by taking the difference in deviance between the considered model and the null model to obtain

$$D = -2 \log \left\{ \frac{L(\hat{\beta}(M_0))}{L(\hat{\beta}(M))} \right\}$$

Under H_0 'the null model is true', D is asymptotically distributed as a χ^2_p distribution, where p is the number of explanatory variables in model M. This can be obtained by noting that $D = G^2(M_0) - G^2(M)$ and recalling that the two deviances are independent and asymptotically distributed as chi-squared random variables. From the additive property of the chi-squared distribution, the degrees of freedom of D are $(n - 1) - (n - p - 1) = p$. The considered model is accepted (i.e. the null model in H_0 is rejected) if the p-value is small. This is equivalent to the difference D between the log-likelihoods being large. Rejection of the null hypothesis implies that at least one parameter in the systematic component is significantly different from zero. Statistical software often gives the log-likelihood maximised for each model of analysis, corresponding to $-2 \log(L(\hat{\beta}(M)))$, which can be seen as a score of the model under consideration. To obtain the deviance, this should be normalised by subtracting $-2 \log(L(\hat{\beta}(M^*)))$. On the other hand, D is often given with the corresponding p-values; This is analogous to the statistic in Result 4 on page 148. SAS calls it chi-square for covariate.

More generally, following the same logic used in the derivation of D, any two models can be compared in terms of their deviances. If the two models are nested (i.e. the systematic component of one of them is obtained by eliminating some terms from the other one), the difference of the deviances is asymptotically distributed as chi-squared with $p - q$ degrees of freedom, that is the number of variables excluded in the simpler model (which has q parameters) but not in the other one (which has p parameters). If the difference between the two is large (with respect to the critical value), the simpler model will be rejected in favour of the more complex model, and similarly when the p-value is small.

For the whole class of generalised linear models, it is possible to employ a formal procedure in searching for the best model. As with linear models, this procedure is usually forward, backward or stepwise elimination.

When the analysed data is categorical, or discretised to be such, an alternative to G^2 is Pearson's X^2:

$$X^2 = \sum_i \frac{(o_i - e_i)^2}{e_i}$$

where, for each category i, 'o_i' represents the observed frequencies and 'e_i' represents the frequencies expected according to the model under examination. As with the deviance G^2, we are comparing the fitted model (which corresponds to the e_i) and the saturated model (which corresponds to the o_i). However, the distance function is not based on the likelihood, but on direct comparison between observed and fitted values for each category. Notice that this statistic generalises the Pearson X^2 distance measure in Section 3.4. There the fitted model particularised to the model under which the two categorical variables were independent.

The Pearson statistic is asymptotically equivalent to G^2, therefore under H_0, $X^2 \approx \chi^2_{n-k}$. The choice between G^2 and X^2 depends on the goodness of the chi-squared approximation. In general, it can be said that X^2 is less affected by small frequencies, particularly when they occur in large data sets – data sets having many variables. The advantage of G^2 lies in its additivity, so it easily generalises to any pairwise model comparisons, allowing us to adopt a model selection strategy.

The statistics G^2 and X^2 indicate a model's overall goodness of fit; we need to do further diagnostic analysis to look for local lack of fit. Before fitting a model, it may be extremely useful to try some graphical representations. For example, we could plot the observed frequencies of the various categories, or functions of them, against the explanatory variables. It is possible to draw dispersion diagrams and fit straight lines for the response variable transformation described by the canonical link (e.g. the logit function for logistic regression). This can be useful to verify whether the hypotheses behind the generalised linear model are satisfied. If not, the graph itself may suggest further transformations of the response variable or the explanatory variables. Once a model is chosen as the best and fitted to the data, our main diagnostic tool is to analyse the residuals. Unlike what happens in the normal linear model, for generalised linear models there are different definitions of the residuals. Here we consider the deviance residuals that are often used in applications. For each observation, the residual from the deviance is defined by the quantity

$$_D r_i = (y_i - \hat{\mu}_i)\sqrt{d_i}$$

This quantity increases (or decreases) according to the difference between the observed and fitted values of the response variable $(y_i - \hat{\mu}_i)$ and is such that $\sum_D r_i^2 = G^2$. In a good model, the deviance residuals should be randomly distributed around zero, so plot the deviance residuals against the fitted values. For a good model, the points in the plane should show no evident trend.

5.4.3 The logistic regression model

The logistic regression model is an important model. We can use our general results to derive inferential results for the logistic regression model. The deviance of a model M assumes the following form:

$$G^2(M) = 2 \sum_{i=1}^{n} \left[y_i \log \left(\frac{y_i}{n_i \hat{\pi}_i} \right) + (n_i - y_i) \log \left(\frac{n_i - y_i}{n_i - n_i \hat{\pi}_i} \right) \right]$$

where the $\hat{\pi}_i$ are the fitted probabilities of success, calculated on the basis of the estimated β parameters for model M. The deviance G^2 assumes the form

$$G^2 = 2 \sum_i o_i \log \frac{o_i}{e_i}$$

where o_i indicates the observed frequencies y_i and $n_i - y_i$, and e_i indicates the corresponding fitted frequencies $n_i \hat{\pi}_i$ and $n_i - n_i \hat{\pi}_i$. Note that G^2 can be interpreted as a distance function, expressed in terms of entropy differences between the fitted model and the saturated model.

The Pearson statistic for the logistic regression model, based on the X^2 distance, takes the form

$$X^2 = \sum_{i=1}^{n} \frac{(y_i - n_i \hat{\pi}_i)^2}{n_i \hat{\pi}_i (1 - \hat{\pi}_i)}$$

Both G^2 and X^2 can be used to compare models in terms of distances between observed and fitted values. The advantage of G^2 lies in its modularity. For instance, in the case of two nested logistic regression models M_A, with q parameters, and M_B, with p parameters $(q < p)$, the difference between the deviances is given by

$$D = G^2(M_A) - G^2(M_B) = 2 \sum_{i=1}^{n} y_i \log \left(\frac{n_i \hat{\pi}_i^B}{n_i \hat{\pi}_i^A} \right) + (n_i - y_i) \log \left(\frac{n_i \hat{\pi}_i^B}{n_i \hat{\pi}_i^A} \right)$$

$$= 2 \sum_{i=1}^{n} o_i \log \left(\frac{e_i^B}{e_i^A} \right) \approx \chi_{p-q}^2$$

where $\hat{\pi}_i^A$ and $\hat{\pi}_i^B$ indicate the success probability fitted on the basis of models M_A and M_B, respectively. Note that the expression for the deviance boils down to an entropy measure between probability models, exactly as before. This is a general fact. The deviance residuals are defined by

$$_D r_i = \pm (y_i - \hat{\pi}_i) 2^{1/2} \left[y_i \log \left(\frac{y_i}{n_i \hat{\pi}_i} \right) + (n_i - y_i) \log \left(\frac{n_i - y_i}{n_i - n_i \hat{\pi}_i} \right) \right]^{1/2}$$

5.4.4 Application

We now consider a case study on correspondence sales for an editorial company. It is described at length in Chapter 10. The observations are the customers of the company. The response variable to be predicted distinguishes the clients into two categories: those that buy only one product and those that buy more, following the first purchase. All the explanatory variables are binary. The response variable is called Nacquist; it indicates whether or not the number of purchases is greater than one. The explanatory variables are Vdpflrat, islands, south, centre, north, age15_35, age36_50, age51_89, dim_g, dim_m, dim_p, sex.

The interpretation of the variables and the explanatory analysis are given in Chapter 10. Here we construct the logistic regression model, initially fitting a model with all the variables. The value of G^2 for this model is 3011.658. Table 5.6 gives the deviance and the maximum likelihood estimates for this model. It begins with information relative to the chosen model. The third row shows the log-likelihood score for the considered model and for the null model with only the intercept. The difference between the two deviances, D, is equal to 307.094. Using a chi-squared test with 9 degrees of freedom $(9 = 10 - 1)$, we obtain a significant difference, so we accept the considered model (the p-value is 0.00001). Even though there are 12 explanatory variables, the presence of the intercept means we have to eliminate three of them that we cannot estimate. For example, since there are three age classes, the three columns that indicate the presence or absence of each of them sum to a vector of ones, identical to the intercept vector. Therefore, in this model we eliminate the variable age15_35.

Table 5.6 Results of fitting the full logistic regression model.

```
        Model Fitting Information and Testing Global Null Hypothesis BETA=0
                                Intercept
                   Intercept      and
Criterion           Only       Covariates          Chi-Square for Covariates

AIC               3320.732     3031.658       .
SC                3326.556     3089.700       .
-2 LOG L          3318.752     3011.658       307.094 with g DF  (p=0.0001)
Score                 .            .          300.114 with g DF  (p=0.0001)

NOTE: The following parameters have been set to 0, since the variables are
   a linear combination of other variables as shown.
AGE15_35 = 1 * INTERCEPT - 1 * AGE51_89 - 1 * AGE36_50
NORTH = 1 * INTERCEPT - 1 * ISLANDS - 1 * SOUTH - 1 * CENTRE
DIM_P = 1 * INTERCEPT - 1 * DIM_G - 1 * DIM_M
```

Analysis of Maximum Likelihood Estimates

Variable	DF	Parameter Estimates	Standard Error	Wald Chi-Square	Pr > Chi-Square	Standardised Estimate	Odds Ratio
INTERCEPT	1	-1.2163	0.1510	64.9210	0.0001	.	.
VDPFLRAT	1	1.5038	0.0999	226.6170	0.0001	0.365878	4.498
ISLANDS	1	-0.2474	0.1311	3.5639	0.0590	-0.050827	0.781
SOUTH	1	-0.4347	0.1222	12.6525	0.0004	-0.098742	0.647
CENTRE	1	-0.1371	0.1128	1.4777	0.2241	-0.033399	0.872
AGE1_89	1	0.4272	0.1312	10.6086	0.0011	0.095633	1.533
AGE36_50	1	0.7457	0.1070	48.5289	0.0001	0.205547	2.108
DIM_G	1	-0.0689	0.1335	0.2667	0.6055	-0.016728	0.933
DIM_M	1	0.1294	0.1172	1.2192	0.2695	0.035521	1.138
AGE15_35	0	0	.	.	.	.	.
SEX	1	0.1180	0.0936	1.5878	0.2076	0.030974	1.125
NORTH	0	0	.	.	.	.	.
DIM_P	0	0	.	.	.	.	.

AIC and SC in the first two rows of the table are model choice criteria related to the numerator of the deviance. Chapter 6 covers them in more detail. The second part of the table shows, for each of the parameters, the estimates obtained plus the relative standard errors, as well as the Wald statistic for hypothesis testing on each coefficient. Using the p-value corresponding to each statistic, we can deduce that at least four variables are not significant (with a significance level of 0.05, five variables are not significant, as they have a greater p-value). Finally, the table shows the estimated odds ratios of the response variable with each explanatory variable. These estimates are derived using the estimated parameters, so they may differ from the odds ratios calculated during the exploratory phase (Section 4.4), which are based on a saturated model. The exploratory indexes are usually calculated marginally, whereas the present indexes take account of interactions among all variables.

We now look at a model selection procedure to see whether the model can be further simplified. We can choose forward, backward or stepwise selection.

In the normal linear model, these procedures are based on recursive application of the F test, but now they are based on the deviance differences. If the p-value for this difference is 'large', the simpler model will be chosen; if it is small, the more complex model will be chosen. The procedure stops when no further change will produce a significant change in the deviance. Table 5.7 shows the results obtained with a forward procedure (generically known as 'stepwise' by the software). It highlights for every variable the values of Rao's score statistic, in order to show the incremental importance of each inserted variable. The procedure stops after the insertion of five variables. Here they are in order of insertion: Vdpflrat, age15_35, north, age51_89, south. No other variable is retained at a significance level of $\alpha = 0.15$, the software default. Table 5.7 also reports the parameter estimates for the five variables selected in the final model, with the corresponding Wald statistics. Now, no variable appears to be not significant, using a significance level of 0.05. The variable Vdpflart indicates whether or not the price of the first purchase is paid in instalments; it is decisively estimated to be the variable most associated with the response variable.

For large samples, stepwise selection procedures, like the one we have just applied, might lead to high instability of the results. The forward and backward approaches may even lead to different final models. Therefore it is a good idea to consider other model selection procedures too; this is discussed in Chapter 6. Figure 5.5 presents a final diagnostic of the model, through analysis of the deviance residuals. It turns out that the standardised residuals behave quite well, lying in the interval $[-2,+2]$. But notice a slight decreasing tendency of the residuals (as opposed to being distributed around a constant line). This indicates a possible underestimation of observations with high success probability. For more details on residual analysis see Weisberg (1985).

Table 5.7   Results of forward procedure.

		Summary of Stepwise Procedure				
	Variable		Number	Score	Wald	Pr >
Step	Entered	Removed	In	Chi-Square	Chi-Square	Chi-Square
1	VDPFLRAT		1	234.7	.	0.0001
2	AGE15_35		2	45.0708	.	0.0001
3	NORTH		3	9.4252	. .	0.0021
4	AGE51_89		4	7.4656	.	0.0063
5	SOUTH		5	4.4325	.	0.0353

		Analysis of Maximum Likelihood Estimates					
Variable	DF	Parameter Estimate	Standard Error	Wald Chi-Square	Pr > Chi-Square	Standardized Estimate	Odds Ratio
INTERCEPT	1	-0.5281	0.0811	42.3568	0.0001	.	.
VDPFLRAT	1	1.5022	0.0997	226.9094	0.0001	0.365499	4.492
SOUTH	1	-0.2464	0.1172	4.4246	0.0354	-0.055982	0.782
AGE51_89	1	-0.3132	0.1130	7.6883	0.0056	-0.070108	0.731
AGE15_35	1	-0.7551	0.1063	50.5103	0.0001	-0.186949	0.470
NORTH	1	0.2044	0.0989	4.2728	0.0387	0.053802	1.227

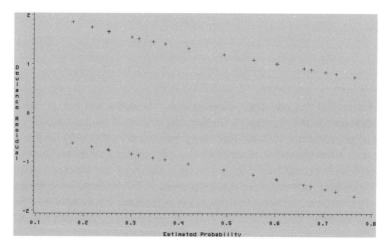

Figure 5.5 Residual analysis for the fitted logistic model.

5.5 Log-linear models

We can distinguish between symmetric and asymmetric generalised linear models. If the objective of the analysis is descriptive – to describe the associative structure among the variables – the model is called symmetric. If the variables are divided in two groups, response and explanatory – to predict the responses on the basis of the explanatory variables – the model is asymmetric. Asymmetric models we have seen are the normal linear model and the logistic regression model. We will now consider the most well-known symmetric model, the log-linear model. The log-linear model is typically used for analysing categorical data, organised in contingency tables. It represents an alternative way to express a joint probability distribution for the cells of a contingency table. Instead of listing all the cell probabilities, this distribution can be described using a more parsimonious expression given by the systematic component.

5.5.1 Construction of a log-linear model

We now show how a log-linear model can be built, starting from three different distributional assumptions about the absolute frequencies of a contingency table, corresponding to different sampling schemes for the data in the table. For simplicity but without loss of generality, we consider a two-way contingency table of dimensions $I \times J$ (I rows and J columns).

Scheme 1

The cell counts are independent random variables that are distributed according to a Poisson distribution. All the marginal counts, including the total number of observations n, are also random and distributed according to a Poisson distribution. As the natural parameter of a Poisson distribution with parameter m_{ij} is

$\log(m_{ij})$, the relationship that links the expected value of each cell frequency m_{ij} to the systematic component is

$$\log(m_{ij}) = \eta_{ij} \text{ for } i = 1, \ldots, I \text{ and } j = 1, \ldots, J$$

In the linear and logistic regression models, the total amount of information (which determines the degrees of freedom) is described by the number of observations of the response variable (indicated by n), but in the log-linear model this corresponds to the number of cells of the contingency table. In the estimation procedure, the expected frequencies will be replaced by the observed frequencies, and this will lead us to estimate the parameters of the systematic component. For an $I \times J$ table there are two variables in the systematic component. Let the levels of the two variables be indicated by x_i and x_j, for $i = 1, \ldots, I$ and $j = 1, \ldots, J$. The systematic component can therefore be written as

$$\eta_i = u + \sum_i u_i x_i + \sum_j u_j x_j \sum_{ij} u_{ij} x_i x_j$$

This expression is called the log-linear expansion of the expected frequencies. The terms u_i and u_j describe the single effects of each variable, corresponding to the mean expected frequencies for each of their levels. The term u_{ij} describes the joint effect of the two variables on the expected frequencies. The term u is a constant that corresponds to the mean expected frequency over all table cells.

Scheme 2
The total number of observations n is not random, but a fixed constant. This implies that the relative frequencies follow a multinomial distribution. Such a distribution generalises the binomial to the case where there are more than two alternative events for the considered variable. The expected values of the absolute frequencies for each cell are given by $m_{ij} = n\pi_{ij}$. With n fixed, specifying a statistical model for the probabilities π_{ij} is equivalent to modelling the expected frequencies m_{ij}, as in Scheme 1.

Scheme 3
The marginal row (or column) frequencies are known. In this case it can be shown that the cell counts are distributed as a product of multinomial distributions. It is also possible to show that we can define a log-linear model in the same way as before.

Properties of the log-linear model
Besides being parsimonious, the log-linear model allows us easily to incorporate in the probability distribution constraints that specify independence relationships between variables. For example, using results introduced in Section 3.4, when two categorical variables are independent, the joint probability of each cell probability

factorises as $\pi_{ij} = \pi_{i+}\pi_{+j}$, for $i = 1, \ldots, I$ and $j = 1, \ldots, J$. And the additive property of logarithms implies that

$$\log m_{ij} = \log n + \log \pi_{i+} + \log \pi_{+j}$$

This describes a log-linear model of independence that is more parsimonious than the previous one, called the saturated model as it contains as many parameters as there are table cells. In general, to achieve a unique estimate on the basis of the observations, the number of terms in the log-linear expansion cannot be greater than the number of cells in the contingency table. This implies some constraints on the parameters of a log-linear model. Known as identifiability constraints, they can be defined in different ways, but we will use a system of constraints that equates to zero all the u-terms that contain at least one index equal to the first level of a variable. This implies that, for a 2×2 table, relative to the binary variables A and B, with levels 0 and 1, the most complex possible log-linear model (saturated) is defined by

$$\log(m_{ij}) = u + u_i^A + u_i^B + u_{ij}^{AB}$$

with constraints such that: $u_i^A \neq 0$ for $i = 1$ (i.e. if $A = 1$); $u_i^B \neq 0$ for $j = 1$ (i.e. if $B = 1$); $u_{ij}^{AB} \neq 0$ for $i = 1$ and $j = 1$ (i.e. if $A = 1$ and $B = 1$). The notation reveals that, in order to model the four cell frequencies in the table, there is a constant term, u; two main effects terms that exclusively depend on a variable, u_i^A and u_i^B; and an interaction term that describes the association between the two variables, u_{ij}^{AB}. Therefore, following the stated constraints, the model establishes that the logarithms of the four expected cell frequencies are equal to the following expressions:

$$\log(m_{00}) = u$$
$$\log(m_{10}) = u + u_i^A$$
$$\log(m_{01}) = u + u_i^B$$
$$\log(m_{11}) = u + u_i^A + u_i^B + u_{ij}^{AB}$$

5.5.2 Interpretation of a log-linear model

Logistic regression models with categorical explanatory variables (also called logit models) can be considered as a particular case of log-linear models. To clarify this point, consider a contingency table with three dimensions for variables A, B, C, and numbers of levels $I, J, 2$ respectively. Assume that C is the response variable of the logit model. A logit model is expressed by

$$\log \left(\frac{m_{ij1}}{m_{ij0}} \right) = \alpha + \beta_i^A + \beta_j^B + \beta_{ij}^{AB}$$

All the explanatory variables of a logit model are categorical, so the effect of each variable (e.g. variable A) is indicated only by the coefficient (e.g. β_i^A) rather than by the product (e.g. βA). Besides that, the logit model has been expressed in terms of the expected frequencies, rather than probabilities, as in the last section. This is only a notational change, obtained through multiplying the numerator and the denominator by n. This expression is useful to show that the logit model which has C as response variable is obtained as the difference between the log-linear expansions of $\log(m_{ij1})$ and $\log(m_{ij0})$. Indeed the log-linear expansion for a contingency table with three dimensions $I \times J \times 2$ has the more general form

$$\log(m_{ijk}) = u + u_i^A + u_j^B + u_k^C + u_{ij}^{AB} + u_{ik}^{AC} + u_{jk}^{BC} + u_{ijk}^{ABC}$$

Substituting and taking the difference between the logarithms of the expected frequencies for $C = 1$ and $C = 0$:

$$\log(m_{ij1}) - \log(m_{ij0}) = u_1^C + u_{i1}^{AC} + u_{j1}^{BC} + u_{ij1}^{ABC}$$

In other words, the u-terms that do not depend on the variable C cancel out. All the remaining terms depend on C. By eliminating the symbol C from the superscript, the value 1 from the subscript and relabelling the u-terms using α and β, we arrive at the desired expression for the logit model. Therefore a logit model can be obtained from a log-linear model. The difference is that a log-linear model contains not only the terms that describe the association between the explanatory variables and the response – here the pairs AC, BC – but also the terms that describe the association between the explanatory variables – here the pair AB. Logit models do not model the association between the explanatory variables.

We now consider the relationship between log-linear models and odds ratios. The logarithm of the odds ratio between two variables is equal to the sum of the interaction u-terms that contain both variables. It follows that if in the considered log-linear expansion there are no u-terms containing both the variables A and B, say, then we obtain $\theta_{AB} = 1$; that is, the two variables are independent.

To illustrate this concept, consider a 2×2 table and the odds ratio between the binary variables A and B:

$$\theta = \frac{\theta_1}{\theta_2} = \frac{\pi_{1|1}/\pi_{0|1}}{\pi_{1|0}/\pi_{0|0}} = \frac{\pi_{11}/\pi_{01}}{\pi_{10}/\pi_{00}} = \frac{\pi_{11}\pi_{00}}{\pi_{01}\pi_{10}}$$

Multiplying numerator and denominator by n^2 and taking logarithms:

$$\log(\theta) = \log(m_{11}) + \log(m_{00}) - \log(m_{10}) - \log(m_{01})$$

Substituting for each probability the corresponding log-linear expansion, we obtain $\log(\theta) = u_{11}^{AB}$. Therefore the odds ratio between the variables A and B is $\theta = \exp(u_{11}^{AB})$. These relations, which are very useful for data interpretation, depend on the identifiability constraints we have adopted. For example, if we had used the default constraints of the SAS software, we would have obtained the relationship $\theta = \exp(1/4u_{11}^{AB})$.

We have shown the relationship between the odds ratio and the parameters of a log-linear model for a 2×2 contingency table. This result is valid for contingency tables of higher dimension, providing the variables are binary and, as usually happens in a descriptive context, the log-linear expansion does not contain interaction terms between more than two variables.

5.5.3 Graphical log-linear models

A key instrument in understanding log-linear models, and graphical models in general, is the concept of conditional independence for a set of random variables; this extends the notion of statistical independence between two variables, seen in Section 3.4. Consider three random variables X, Y, and Z. X and Y are conditionally independent given Z if the joint probability distribution of X and Y, conditional on Z, can be decomposed into the product of two factors: the conditional density of X given Z and the conditional density of Y given Z. In formal terms, X and Y are conditionally independent on Z if $f(x, y|Z = z) = f(x|Z = z)f(y|Z = z)$ and we write $X \perp Y|Z$. An alternative way of expressing this concept is that the conditional distribution of Y on both X and Z does not depend on X. So, for example, if X is a binary variable and Z is a discrete variable, then for every z and y we have

$$f(y|X = 1, Z = z) = f(y|X = 0, Z = z) = f(y|Z = z)$$

The notion of (marginal) independence between two random variables (Section 3.4) can be obtained as a special case of conditional independence. As seen for marginal independence, conditional independence can simplify the expression and interpretation of log-linear models. In particular, it can be extremely useful in visualising the associative structure among all variables at hand, using the so-called independence graphs. Indeed a subset of log-linear models, called graphical log-linear models, can be completely characterised in terms of conditional independence relationships and therefore graphs. For these models, each graph corresponds to a set of conditional independence constraints and each of these constraints can correspond to a particular log-linear expansion.

The study of the relationship between conditional independence statements, represented in graphs, and log-linear models has its origins in the work of Darroch, Lauritzen and Speed (1980). We explain this relationship through an example. For a systematic treatment see Whittaker (1990), Edwards (1995), or Lauritzen (1996). I believe that the introduction of graphical log-linear models helps to explain the problem of model choice for log-linear models. Consider a contingency table of three dimensions, each one corresponding to a binary variable, so the total number of cells in the contingency table is $2^3 = 8$. The simplest log-linear graphical model for a three-way contingency table assumes that the logarithm of the expected frequency of every cell is

$$\log(m_{jkl}) = u + u_j^A + u_k^B + u_l^C$$

This model does not contain interaction terms between variables, therefore the three variables are mutually independent. In fact, the model can be expressed in terms of cell probabilities as $p_{jkl} = p_{j++}p_{+k+}p_{++l}$, where the symbol $+$ indicates that the joint probabilities have been summed with respect to all the values of the relative index. Note that, for this model, the three odds ratios between the variables – (A, B), (A, C), (B, C) – are all equal to 1. To identify the model in a unique way it is possible to use a list of the terms, called generators, that correspond to the maximal terms of interaction in the model. These terms are called maximals in the sense that their presence implies the presence of interaction terms between subsets of their variables. At the same time, their existence in the model is not implied by any other term. For the previous model of mutual independence, the generators are (A, B, C); they are the main effect terms as there are no other terms in the model. To graphically represent conditional independence statements, we can use conditional independence graphs. These are built by associating a node to each variable and by placing a link (technically, an edge) to connect a pair of variables whenever the corresponding random variables are dependent. For the cases of mutual independence we have described, there are no edges and therefore we obtain the representation in Figure 5.6.

Consider now a more complex log-linear model among the three variables, described by the following log-linear expansion:

$$\log(m_{jkl}) = u + u_j^A + u_k^B + u_l^C + u_{jk}^{AB} + u_{jl}^{AC}$$

In this case, since the maximal terms of interaction are u_{jk}^{AB} and u_{jl}^{AC}, the generators of the model will be (AB, AC). Notice that the model can be reformulated in terms of cell probabilities as

$$\pi_{jkl} = \frac{\pi_{jk+}\pi_{j+l}}{\pi_{j++}}$$

or equivalently as

$$\frac{\pi_{jkl}}{\pi_{j++}} = \left(\frac{\pi_{jk+}}{\pi_{j++}}\right)\left(\frac{\pi_{j+l}}{\pi_{j++}}\right)$$

A

B  C

Figure 5.6 Conditional independence graph for mutual independence.

which, in terms of conditional independence, states that

$$P(B = k, C = l | A = j) = P(B = k | A = j) P(C = l | A = j)$$

This indicates that, in the conditional distribution (on A), B and C are independent. In other words, $B \perp C | A$. Therefore the conditional independence graph of the model is as shown in Figure 5.7. It can been demonstrated that, in this case, the odds ratio between all variable pairs are different from 1, whereas the two odds ratios for the two-way table between B and C, conditional on A, are both equal to 1.

We finally consider the most complex (saturated) log-linear model for the three variables:

$$\log(m_{jkl}) = u + u_j^A + u_k^B + u_l^C + u_{jk}^{AB} + u_{jl}^{AC} + u_{kl}^{BC} + u_{jkl}^{ABC}$$

which has (ABC) as generator. This model does not establish any conditional independence constraints on cell probabilities. Correspondingly, all odds ratios, marginal and conditional, will be different from 1. The corresponding conditional independence graph will be completely connected. The previous model (AB, AC) can be considered as a particular case of the saturated model, obtained by setting $u_{kl}^{BC} = 0$ for all k and l and $u_{jkl}^{ABC} = 0$ for all j, k, l. Equivalently, it is obtained by removing the edge between B and C in the completely connected graph, which corresponds to imposing the constraint, that B and C are conditionally independent on A. Notice that the mutual independence model is a particular case of the saturated model obtained by setting $u_{kl}^{BC} = u_{jl}^{AC} = u_{jk}^{AB} = u_{jkl}^{ABC} = 0$ for all j, k, l, or by removing all three edges in the complete graph. Consequently, the differences between log-linear models can be expressed in terms of differences between the parameters or as differences between graphical structures. I think it is easier to interpret differences between graphical structures.

All the models in this example are graphical log-linear models. In general, graphical log-linear models are definable as log-linear models that have as generators the cliques of the conditional independence graph. A clique is a subset of completely connected and maximal nodes in a graph. For example, in Figure 5.7 the subsets AB and AC are cliques, and they are the generators of the model. On the other hand, the subsets formed by the isolated nodes A, B and C are not cliques. To better understand the concept of a graphical log-linear model,

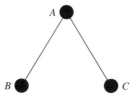

Figure 5.7   Conditional independence graph for $B \perp C | A$.

consider a non-graphical model for the trivariate case. Take the model described by the generator (AB, AC, BC):

$$\log(m_{jkl}) = u + u_j^A + u_k^B + u_l^C + u_{jk}^{AB} + u_{jl}^{AC} + u_{kl}^{BC}$$

Although this model differs from the saturated model by the absence of the three-way interaction term u_{jkl}^{ABC}, its conditional independence graph is the same, with one single clique ABC. Therefore, since the model generator is different from the set of cliques, the model is not graphical. To conclude, in this section we have obtained a remarkable equivalence relation between conditional independence statements, graphical representations and probabilistic models, with the probabilistic models represented in terms of cell probabilities, log-linear models or sets of odds ratios.

5.5.4 Log-linear model comparison

For log-linear models, including graphical log-linear models, we can apply the inferential theory derived for generalised linear models. We now insist on model comparison. This is because the use of conditional independence graphs permits us to interpret model comparison and choice between log-linear models in terms of comparisons between sets of conditional independence constraints. In data mining problems the number of log-linear models to compare increases rapidly with the number of considered variables. Therefore a valid approach may be to restrict the class of models. In particular, a parsimonious and efficient way to analyse large contingency tables is to consider interaction terms in the log-linear expansion that involve at most two variables. The log-linear models in the resulting class are all graphical. Therefore we obtain an equivalence relationship between the absence of an edge between two nodes, say i and j, conditional independence between the corresponding variables, X_i and X_j (given the remaining ones), and nullity of the interaction parameter indexed by both of them.

As we saw with generalised linear models, the most important tool for comparing models is the deviance. All three sampling schemes for log-linear models lead to an equivalent expression for the deviance. Consider, for simplicity, a log-linear model to analyse three categorical variables. The deviance of a model M is

$$G^2(M) = 2 \sum_{jkl} n_{jkl} \log\left(\frac{n_{jkl}}{\hat{m}_{jkl}}\right) = 2 \sum o_i \log \frac{o_i}{e_i}$$

where $\hat{m}_{jkl} = np_{jkl}$, the p_{jkl} are the maximum likelihood estimates of the cell probabilities, the o_i are the observed cell frequencies and the e_i indicate the cell frequencies estimated according to the model M. Notice the similarity with the deviance expression for the logistic regression model. What changes is essentially the way in which the cell probabilities are estimated. In the general case of a p-dimensional table, the definition is the same but the index set changes:

$$G^2(M_0) = 2 \sum_{i \in I} n_i \log \left(\frac{n_i}{\hat{m}_i^0} \right)$$

where, for a cell i belonging to the index set I, n_i is the frequency of observations in the ith cell and $\hat{m}_i^0$ are the expected frequencies for the considered model M_0. For model comparison, two nested models M_0 and M_1 can be compared using the difference between their deviances:

$$D = G_0^2 - G_1^2 = 2 \sum_{i \in I} n_i \log \left(\frac{n_i}{\hat{m}_i^0} \right) - 2 \sum_{i \in I} n_i \log \left(\frac{n_i}{\hat{m}_i^1} \right) = 2 \sum_{i \in I} n_i \log \left(\frac{\hat{m}_i^1}{\hat{m}_i^0} \right)$$

As in the general case, under H_0, D has an asymptotic chi-squared distribution whose degrees of freedom are obtained by taking the difference in the number of parameters for models M_0 and M_1.

The search for the best log-linear model can be carried out using a forward, backward or stepwise procedure. For graphical log-linear models we can also try adding or removing edges between variables rather than adding or removing interaction parameters. In the backward procedure we compare the deviance between models that differ by the presence of an edge and at each step we eliminate the less significant edge; the procedure stops when no arc removals produce a p-value greater than the chosen significance level (e.g. 0.05). In the forward procedure we add the most significance edges one at time until no arc additions produce a p-value lower than the chosen significance level.

5.5.5 Application

We can use a log-linear model to determine the associative structure among variables in a credit risk evaluation problem. The considered sample is made up of 8263 small and medium-sized Italian enterprises. The considered variables are A, a binary qualitative variable indicating whether the considered enterprise is deemed reliable (Good) or not (Bad); B, a qualitative variable with 4 levels that describes the age of the enterprise, measured from the year of its constitution; C, a qualitative variable with 3 levels that describes the legal status of the enterprise; D, a qualitative variable with 7 levels that describes the macroeconomic sector of activity of the enterprise; and E, a qualitative variable with 5 levels that describes the geographic area of residence of the enterprise.

Therefore the data is classified in a contingency table of five dimensions and the total number of cells is $2 \times 4 \times 3 \times 7 \times 5 = 840$. The objective of the analysis is to determine the associative structure present among the five variables. In the absence of a clear preliminary hypothesis on the associative structure, we will use a backward procedure for model comparison. Given the small number of variables to be determined, we can consider all log-linear models, including non-graphical models.

The first model to be fitted is the saturated model, which contains 840 parameters, equal to the number of cells. Here is the corresponding log-linear expansion embodying the identifiability constraints described earlier:

$$\log \mu_{ijklm}^{ABCDE} = u$$

$$+ u_i^A + u_j^B + u_k^C + u_l^D + u_m^E$$

$$+ u_{ij}^{AB} + u_{ik}^{AC} + + u_{il}^{AD} + u_{im}^{AE} + u_{jk}^{BC} + u_{jl}^{BD} + u_{jm}^{BE} + u_{kl}^{CD} + u_{km}^{CE} + u_{lm}^{DE}$$

$$+ u_{ijk}^{ABC} + u_{ijl}^{ABD} + u_{ijm}^{ABE} + u_{jkl}^{BCD} + u_{jkm}^{BCE} + u_{klm}^{CDE} + u_{ikl}^{ACD} + u_{ikm}^{ACE} + u_{ilm}^{ADE} + u_{jlm}^{BDE}$$

$$+ u_{ijkl}^{ABCD} + u_{ijkm}^{ABCE} + u_{jklm}^{BCDE} + u_{iklm}^{ACDE} + u_{ijlm}^{ABDE}$$

$$+ u_{ijklm}^{ABCDE}$$

Notice that the saturated model contains interaction terms of different order, for example, the constant (first row), terms of order 2 (third row) and one term of order 5 (fifth row).

The backward strategy starts by comparing the saturated model with a simpler model that omits the interaction term of order 5. At a significance level of 5% as the *p*-value for the deviance difference is 0.9946. We then look at interaction terms of order 4, removing them one at a time to find the simpler model in each comparison. We continue through the terms and down the orders until we can achieve no more simplification at our chosen significance level of 5%. The final model contains the constant term; the main effects and the interactions $AB, AC, BC, AD, AE, BE, ABC$ that is, 6 interactions of order 2 and one interaction of order 3. These interaction terms can be described by the generators (AD, AE, BE, ABC). Figure 5.8 shows the conditional independence graph for the final model.

Notice that Figure 5.8 contains three cliques: ABC, and ABE and AD. Since the cliques of the graph do not coincide with the generators of the log-linear model, the final model is not graphical. The log-linear model without the order 3 interaction term ABC would have the generators (AB, AC, BC, AD, AE, BE) and would be graphical. But on the basis of deviance difference, we need to

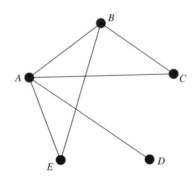

Figure 5.8 Conditional independence graph for the final selected model.

include the order 3 interaction. The model could be converted into a logistic regression model for variable *A* with respect to all the others. Then the logistic regression model would also have to contain the explanatory variable *B* * *C*, a multiplicative term that describes the joint effect of *B* and *C* on *A*.

5.6 Graphical models

Graphical models are models that can be specified directly through conditional independence relationships among the variables, represented in a graph. Although the use of graphics with statistical models is not a new idea, the work of Darroch, Lauritzen and Speed (1980) has combined the two concepts in a new and illuminating way. They showed that a subset of the log-linear models, the log-linear graphical models, can be easily interpreted in terms of conditional independence relationships. This finding has led to the development of a wide class of statistical models, known as graphical models, which give us considerable flexibility in specifying models to analyse databases of whatever dimension, containing both qualitative and quantitative variables, and admitting both symmetric and asymmetric relationships. Graphical models contain, as special cases, important classes of generalised linear models, such as the three seen in this book. For a detailed treatment see Whittaker (1990), Edwards (1995) or Lauritzen (1996).

Here are some definitions we will need. A graph $G = (V, E)$ is a structure consisting of a finite number V of vertices (nodes) that correspond to the variables present in the model, and a finite number of edges between them. In general, the causal influence of a variable on another is indicated by a directed edge (shown using an arrow) while an undirected edge (shown using a line) represents a symmetric association. Figure 5.8 is an example of an undirected graph, containing only undirected edges. Figure 5.9 is a directed graph for the same type of application, where we have introduced a new variable, X, which corresponds to the return on investments of the enterprises. We have made a distinction between vertices that represent categorical variables (empty circles) and vertices that represent continuous variables (filled circles).

Two vertices X and Y belonging to V are adjacent, written $X \sim Y$, if they are connected by an undirected arc; that is, if both the pairs (X, Y) and (Y, X) belong

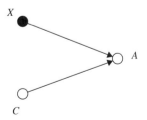

Figure 5.9 Example of a directed graph.

to E. A node X is a parent of node Y, written $X \rightarrow Y$, if they are connected by a directed edge from X to Y; that is, if $(X, Y) \in E$ and $(Y, X) \notin E$.

A complete graph is a graph in which all pairs of vertices are connected by an edge. A sequence of vertices $X_0, \ldots, X_n$ such that $X_{i-1} \sim X_i$ for $i = 1, \ldots, n$ is called a path of length n. A graph is connected when there exists at least one path between each pairs of vertices.

These are only some of the properties we can define for graphical models, but they are sufficient to understand the probabilistic assumptions implied by a conditional independence graph.

In general, a graphical model is a family of probability distributions that incorporates the rules of conditional independence described by a graph. The key to interpreting a graphical model is the relationship between the graph and the probability distribution of the variables. It is possible to distinguish three types of graph, related to the three main classes of graphical models:

- *undirected graphs* are used to model symmetric relations among the variables. (Figure 5.8); they give rise to the symmetric graphical models.
- *directed graphs* are used to model asymmetric relations among the variables. (Figure 5.9); they give rise to recursive graphical models, also known as probabilistic expert systems.
- *chain graphs* contain both undirected and directed edges, therefore they can model both symmetric and asymmetric relationships; they give rise to graphical chain models (Cox and Wermuth, 1996).

5.6.1 Symmetric graphical models

In symmetric graphical models, the probability distribution is Markovian with respect to the specified undirected graph. This is equivalent to imposing on the distribution a number of probabilistic constraints known as Markov properties. The constraints can be expressed in terms of conditional independence relationships. Here are two Markov properties and how to interpret them:

- *For the pairwise Markov property*, if two nodes are not adjacent in the fixed graph, the two corresponding random variables will be conditionally independent, given the others. On the other, hand, if the specified probability distribution is such that $X \perp Y|$ others, the edge between the nodes corresponding to X and Y has to be omitted from the graph.
- *For the global Markov property*, if two sets of variables, U and V, are graphically separated by a third set of variables, W, then it holds that $U \perp V|W$. For example, consider four discrete random variables, W, X, Y, and Z, whose conditional independence relations are described by the graph in Figure 5.10, from which we have that W and Z are separated from X and Y, and Y and Z are separated from X. A Markovian distribution with respect to the graph in Figure 5.10 has to satisfy the global Markov property and therefore it holds that $W \perp Z|(X, Y)$ and $Y \perp Z|(W, X)$.

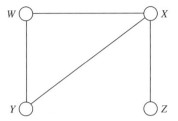

Figure 5.10   Illustration of the global Markov property.

It is useful to distinguish three types of symmetric graphical models:

- Discrete graphical models coincide with log-linear graphical models and are used when all the available variables are categorical.
- Graphical Gaussian models are used when the joint distribution of all variables is multivariate Gaussian.
- Mixed graphical models are used for a mixture of categorical variables and multivariate Gaussian variables.

We have seen discrete graphical models in the Section 5.5.3. A similar type of symmetric model, useful for descriptive data mining, can be introduced for continuous variables. An exhaustive description of these models can be found in Whittaker (1990), who has called them Gaussian graphical models even though they were previously known in the statistical literature as covariance selection models (Dempster, 1972). For these models, it is assumed that $Y = (Y_1, \ldots, Y_q)$ is a vector of continuous variables with a normal multivariate distribution. Markovian properties allow us to show that two variables are conditionally independent on all the others, if and only if the element corresponding to the two variables in the inverse of the variance–covariance matrix is null. This is equivalent to saying that the partial correlation coefficient between the two variables, given the others, is null. In terms of conditional independence graphs, given four variables X, Y, W, Z, if the elements of the inverse of the variance–covariance matrix $k_{x,z}$ and $k_{y,w}$ were null, the edges between the nodes X and Z and the nodes Y and W would have to be absent. From a statistical viewpoint, a graphical Gaussian model and, equivalently, a graphical representation are selected by successively testing hypotheses of edge removal or addition. This is equivalent to testing whether the corresponding partial correlation coefficients are zero.

Notice how the treatment of the continuous case is similar to the discrete case. This has allowed us to introduce a very general class of mixed symmetric graphical models. We now introduce them in a rather general way, including continuous and discrete graphical models as special cases. Let $V = \Gamma \cup \Delta$ be the vertex set of a graph, partitioned in a set of $|\Gamma|$ continuous variables, and a set of $|\Delta|$ discrete variables. If to each vertex v is associated a random variable X_v, the whole graph is associated with a random vector $X_V = (X_v, v \in V)$. A mixed graphical model is defined by a conditional Gaussian distribution for the vector X_V. Partition X_V into a vector X_Δ containing the categorical variables, and a vector X_Γ containing the continuous variables. Then X_V follows a conditional Gaussian distribution if it satisfies these two conditions:

- $p(i) = P(X_\Delta = i) > 0$
- $p(X_\Gamma | X_\Delta = i) = N_{|\Gamma|} \left(\xi(i), \sum(i) \right)$

where the symbol N indicates a Gaussian distribution of dimension $|\Gamma|$ with mean vector $\xi(i) = K(i)^{-1} h(i)$ and variance–covariance matrix $\sum(i) = K(i)^{-1}$, positive definite. In words, a random vector is distributed as a conditional Gaussian if the distribution of the categorical variables is described by a set of positive cell probabilities (this could happen through the specification of a log-linear model) and the continuous variables are distributed, conditional on each joint level of the categorical variables, as a Gaussian distribution with a null mean vector and a variance–covariance matrix that can, in general, depend on the levels of the categorical variables.

From a probabilistic viewpoint, a symmetric graphical model is specified by a graph and a family of probability distributions, which has Markov properties with respect to it. However, to use graphical models in real applications, it is necessary to completely specify the probability distribution, usually by estimating the unknown parameters on the basis of the data. This inferential task, usually accomplished by maximum likelihood estimation, is called quantitative learning. Furthermore, in data mining problems it is difficult to avoid uncertainty when specifying a graphical structure, so alternative graphical representations have to be compared and selected, again on the basis of the available data; this constitutes the so-called structural learning task, usually tackled by deviance-based statistical tests.

To demonstrate this approach, we can return to the European software industry application in Section 4.6 and try to describe the associative structure among all seven considered random variables. The graph in Figure 5.11 is based on hypotheses formulated through subject matter research by industrial economics experts; it shows conditional independence relationships between the available variables. One objective of the analysis is to verify whether the graph in Figure 5.11 can be simplified, maintaining a good fit to the data (structural learning). Another objective is to verify some research hypothesis on the sign of the association between some variables (quantitative learning).

We begin by assuming a probability distribution of conditional Gaussian type and given the reduced sample size (51 observations), a homogeneous model (Lauritzen, 1996). A homogeneous model means we assume the variance of the continuous variable does not depend on the level of the qualitative variables. So we can measure explicitly the effect of the continuous variable Y on the qualitative variables, we have decided to maintain, in all considered models, a link between Y and the qualitative variables, even when it is not significant on the basis of the data. The symmetric model for the complete graph will therefore

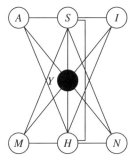

Figure 5.11   Initial conditional independence graph.

contain a total of 129 parameters. It is opportune to start the selection from the initial research graph (Figure 5.11). Since the conditional Gaussian distribution has to be Markovian with respect to this graph, all the parameters containing the pairs $\{M, A\}$, $\{N, I\}$, $\{M, N\}$, $\{M, I\}$, $\{A, N\}$, $\{A, I\}$ have to be 0, hence the total number of parameters in the model corresponding to Figure 5.11 is 29. Considering the low number of available observations, this model is clearly overparameterised.

A very important characteristic of graphical models is to permit local calculations on each clique of the graph (Frydenberg and Lauritzen, 1989). For instance, as the above model can be decomposed into 4 cliques, it is possible to estimate the parameters separately, on each clique, using the 51 available observations to estimate the 17 parameters of each marginal model. In fact, on the basis of a backward selection procedure using a significance level of 5%, Giudici and Carota (1992) obtained the final structural model shown in Figure 5.12. From the figure we deduce that the only direct significant associations between qualitative variables are between the pairs $\{H, I\}$, $\{N, S\}$ and $\{N, H\}$. These associations depend on the revenue Y but not on the remaining residual variables. Concerning quantitative learning, the same authors have used their final model to calculate the

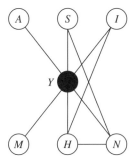

Figure 5.12   Final conditional independence graph.

odds ratios between the qualitative variables, conditional on the level of Y. They obtained the estimated conditional odds, relative to the pairs HI, NS, and NH:

$$\hat{\Theta}_{IH|R} = \exp(0.278 + 0.139R) \text{ therefore } \hat{\Theta}_{IH|R} > 1 \text{ for } R$$

$$> 0.135 \text{ (all enterprises)}$$

$$\hat{\Theta}_{NH|R} = \exp(-2.829 + 0.356R) \text{ therefore } \hat{\Theta}_{NH|R} > 1 \text{ for } R$$

$$> 2856 \text{ (one enterprise)}$$

$$\hat{\Theta}_{NS|R} = \exp(-0.827 - 0.263R) \text{ therefore } \hat{\Theta}_{NS|R} > 1 \text{ for } R$$

$$< 23.21 \text{ (23 enterprises)}$$

The signs of the association can be summarised as follows: the association between I and H is positive; the association between N and H is substantially negative; the association between N and S is positive only for enterprises having revenues less than the median.

From an economic viewpoint, these associations have a simple interpretation. The relationship between I and H confirms that enterprises which adopt a strategy of incremental innovations tend to increase their contacts with enterprises in the hardware sector. The strategy of creating radically new products is based on an opposite view. Looking at contacts exclusively within the software sector, small enterprises (having revenues less than the median) tend to fear their innovations could be stolen or imitated and they tend to not make contacts with other small companies. Large companies (having revenues greater than the median) do not fear initiations and tend to increase their contacts with other companies.

5.6.2   Recursive graphical models

Recursive graphical models, also known as probabilistic expert systems, can be considered as an important and sophisticated tool for predictive data mining. Their fundamental assumption is that the variables can be partially ordered so that every variable is logically preceded by a set of others. This precedence can be interpreted as a probabilistic dependency and, more strongly, as a causal dependency. Both interpretations exist in the field of probabilistic expert systems and this is reflected in the terminology: casual network if there is a causal interpretation, belief network if there is no causal interpretation.

To specify any recursive model, we need to specify a directed graph that establishes the (causal) relationships among the variables. Once this graph is specified, a recursive model is obtained by using a probability distribution that is Markov with respect to the graph (e.g. Lauritzen, 1996). The Markov properties include the following factorisation property of the probability distribution:

$$f(x_1, \ldots x_p) = \prod_{i=1}^{p} f(x_i | \text{pa}(x_i))$$

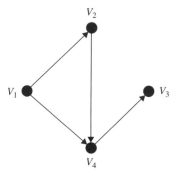

Figure 5.13   Example of a directed acyclic graph.

where pa(x_i) indicates the parent nodes of each of the p considered nodes. This specifies that the probability distribution of the p variables is factorised in a series of local terms, each of which describes the dependency of each of the considered variables, x_i, from the set of relevant explanatory variables, pa(x_i). It is a constructive way to specify a directed graphical model using a (recursive) sequence of asymmetric models, each of which describes the predictor set of each variable.

The conditional independence graphs are therefore directed, because the edges represent ordered pairs of vertices. They are also constrained to be acyclic–no sequence of connected vertices has to form a loop. Figure 5.13 is an example of an acyclic directed conditional in dependence graph. It states, for instance, that $V_3 \perp V_2|V_4$, and it corresponds to a recursive model that can be specified, for instance, by the following factorisation:

$$p(V_1, V_2, V_3, V_4) = p(V_1)p(V_2|V_1)p(V_4|V_1, V_2)p(V_3|V_4)$$

When it comes to specifying the local probability distributions (e.g. the distributions of V_1, V_2, V_3, and V_4), we could specify a recursive model as a recursion of generalised linear models. For example, Figure 5.13 corresponds to a model defined by a linear regression of V_3 on the explanatory variable V_4, of V_4 on the explanatory variables V_1 and V_2, and of V_2 on the explanatory variable V_1.

From a predictive data mining perspective, the advantage of recursive models is that they are simple to specify, interpret and summarise, thanks to the factorisation of the model into many local models of reduced dimensions. On the other hand, they do involve more sophisticated statistical thinking, especially in the context of structural learning. However, few mainstream statistical packages implement these types of model. Chapter 8 considers an application of directed graphical models using a recursive logistic model. Directed graphical models are typically used in artificial intelligence applications, where they are known as probabilistic expert systems or Bayesian networks (e.g. Heckerman, 1997).

Another important special case of directed graphical models are Markov chain models, which are particularly useful for modelling time series data. In particular, first-order Markov models are characterised by a short memory, and assume that $X_{i+1} \perp X_{j<i} | \{X_i\}$, where X_{i+1} is a random variable that describes the value of a certain quantity at time $i + 1$, i is the previous time point and $j < i$ indicates time points further back in time. In other words, the future occurrence of a random variable X_{i+1} does not depend on the past values $X_{j<i}$, if the present value X_i is known. If the data can be modelled by a Markov chain model, the joint probability distribution will factorise as

$$f(x_1, \ldots, x_p) = \prod_{i=1}^{p} f(x_i | x_{i-1})$$

Recursive graphical models can also be used to classify observations, when they are more commonly known as Bayesian networks. One of the simplest and most useful Bayesian networks is the naive Bayes model. It arises when there is one qualitative response variable that can assume M values, corresponding to M classes. The goal is to classify each observation in one of the three classes, and p explanatory variables can be used, described by a random vector X. As we have seen in Section 5.1, the Bayes classifier allocates each observation to the class C_i that maximises the posterior probability

$$p(C_i | X = x) = p(X = x | C_i) p(C_i) / p(X = x).$$

The naive Bayes model corresponds to a special case of this rule, obtained when the explanatory variables that appear in the vector X are assumed to be conditionally independent given the class label. A Bayesian network can be seen as a more sophisticated and more realistic version of a Bayes classifier, which establishes that among the explanatory variables there are relationships of conditional dependence specified by a directed graph.

5.6.3 Graphical models versus neural networks

We have seen that the construction of a statistical model is a long and conceptually complex process and it requires the formulation of a series of formal hypotheses. On the other hand, a statistical model allows us to make predictions and simulate scenarios on the basis of explicit rules that are easily scalable – rules that can be generalised to different data. In Chapter 4 we saw how computationally intensive techniques require a lighter analytical structure, allowing us to find precious information rapidly from large volumes of data. Their disadvantages are low transparency and low scalability. Here is a brief comparison to help underline the different concepts. We shall compare neural networks and graphical models; they can be seen as rather general examples of computational methods and statistical methods, respectively.

The nodes of a graphical model represent random variables, whereas in neural networks they are computational units, not necessarily random. In a graphical model an edge represents a probabilistic conditional dependency between the corresponding pair of random variables, whereas in a neural network an edge describes a functional relation between the corresponding nodes. Graphical models are usually constructed in three phases: (a) the qualitative phase establishes the conditional independence relationships among the random variables; (b) the probabilistic phase associates the graph with a vector of random variables having a Markovian distribution with respect to the graph; (c) the quantitative phase assigns the parameters (if known) that characterise the distribution in (b). Neural networks are constructed in three similar phases: (a) the qualitative phase establishes the organisation of the layers and the relationships among them; (b) the functional phase specifies the functional relationships between the layers; (c) the quantitative phase fixes the weights (if known) associated with the connections among the different nodes.

I believe that these two methodologies can be used in a complementary way. Taking a graphical model and introducing latent variables – variables that are not observed – confers two extra advantages. First, it allows us to represent a multilayer perceptron as a graphical model, so we can take formal statistical methods valid for graphical models and use them on neural networks (e.g. confidence intervals, rejection regions, deviance comparisons). Second the use of a neural network in a preliminary phase could help to reduce the structural complexity of graphical models, reducing the number of variables and edges present, and doing it in a more computationally efficient way. Adding latent variables to graphical models, corresponding to purely computational units, allows us to enrich the model with non-linear components, as occurs with neural networks. For more on the role of latent variables in graphical models, see Cox and Wermuth (1996).

5.7   Further reading

In this chapter we have reviewed the main statistical models for data mining applications. Their common feature is the presence of probabilistic modelling. This makes the results much easier to interpret but it may slow down the implementation and elaboration phases. I have tried to give an overview of the relevant literature.

We began with methods for modelling uncertainty and inference; there are many textbooks on this. One to consult is Mood, Graybill and Boes (1991); another is Azzalini (1992), which takes more of a modelling viewpoint. Non-parametric models are distribution-free, as they do not require heavy preliminary assumptions. They may be very useful, especially in an exploratory context. For a review of non-parametric methods see Gibbons and Chakraborti (1992). Semi-parametric models, based on mixture models, can provide a powerful probabilistic approach to cluster analysis. For an introductory treatment from a data mining viewpoint, see Hastie, Tibshirani and Friedman (2001).

Introduction of the Gaussian distribution allows us to bring regression methods into the field of normal linear models, and therefore to correlate the least squares method with measures of sample variability, as well as to provide thresholds for evaluating goodness of fit. For an introduction to the normal linear model, consult Mood, Graybill and Boes (1991) or a classic econometrics text such as Greene (1999). It is possible to develop the normal linear model into generalised linear models. For an introduction consult the original article of Nelder and Wedderburn (1972) and the books of Dobson (1990), McCullagh and Nelder (1989) and Agresti (1990).

Log-linear models are an important class generalised linear models. They are symmetric models and are mainly used to obtain the associative structure among categorical variables, whose observations are classified in multiple contingency tables. Graphical log-linear models are particularly useful for data interpretation. For an introduction to log-linear models, look at the earlier texts or at Christensen (1997). For graphical log-linear models it is better to consult texts on graphical models, for example Whittaker (1990).

We introduced the concept of conditional independence (and dependence); graphical representation of conditional independence relationships allowed us to take what we saw for graphical log-linear models and generalise it to a wider class of statistical models, known as graphical models. Graphical models are very general statistical models for data mining. In particular, they can adapt to different analytical objectives, from predicting multivariate response variables (recursive models) to finding associative structure (symmetric models), in the presence of both qualitative and quantitative variables. For an introduction to graphical models, consult Edwards (1995), Whittaker (1990) or Lauritzen (1996). For directed graphical models, also known as probabilistic expert systems, see Cowell *et al.* (1999) or Jensen (1996).

CHAPTER 6

Evaluation of data mining methods

In the previous two chapters we considered several classes of computational and statistical methods for data mining. For example, we looked at linear models, which differ in the number of explanatory variables; graphical models, which differ in the number of conditional dependences (edges in the graph); tree models, which differ in the number of leaves; and multilayer perceptrons, which differ in the numbers of hidden layers and nodes. Once a class of models has been established, the problem is to choose the 'best' model from it. In Chapter 5 we looked at the problem of comparing the various statistical models within the theory of statistical hypothesis testing. With this in mind we looked at the sequential procedures (forward, backward and stepwise) that allow a model to be chosen through a sequence of pairwise comparisons. These criteria are generally not applicable to computational data mining models, which do not necessarily have an underlying probabilistic model and therefore do not allow us to apply the statistical theory of hypothesis testing.

A particular data problem can often be tackled using several classes of models. For instance, in a problem in predictive classification it is possible to use logistic regression and tree models as well as neural networks.

Furthermore, model specification, hence model choice, is determined by the type of the variables. After exploratory analysis the data may be transformed or some observations may be eliminated; this will also affect the variables. So we need to compare models based on different sets of variables present at the start. For example, how do we take a linear model having the original explanatory variables and compare it with a model having principal components as explanatory variables?

All this suggests the need for a systematic study of how to compare and evaluate statistical models for data mining. In this chapter we will review the most important methods. As these criteria will be frequently used and compared in the second part of the text, this chapter will just offer a brief systematic summary without giving examples. Section 6.1 introduces the concept of discrepancy for a statistical model; it will make us look further at comparison criteria based on statistical tests. Although this leads to a very rigorous methodology, it allows only a partial ordering of the models. Scoring functions are a less structured approach developed in the field of information theory. Section 6.2 explains how they give

Applied Data Mining. Paolo Giudici
© 2003 John Wiley & Sons, Ltd ISBNs: 0-470-84679-8 (Paper); 0-470-84678-X (Cloth)

each model a score that puts the models into some kind of complete order. The Bayesian approach, covered in Section 6.3, possesses the structural advantages of discrepancy with the ordering advantages of scoring.

Section 6.4 looks at criteria for computational models, where it is difficult to develop formal statistic tests. One of the main computational criteria is cross-validation, which is based on calculating the predictive error in a validation data set. Computational criteria have the advantage of being generally applicable but the disadvantages of taking a long time to calculate and of being sensitive to the characteristics of the data. Section 6.4 concludes by looking at how to combine data mining models through model averaging, bagging and boosting; this is a very important concept. Section 6.5 explains how to compare model performance in terms of relative losses connected to the approximation errors when fitting data mining models. Loss functions are easy to understand but they still need formal improvements and mathematical refinements.

6.1   Criteria based on statistical tests

The choice of the statistical model used to describe a database is one of the main aspects of statistical analysis. A model is either a simplification or an approximation of the reality and therefore it does not entirely reflect reality. As we have seen in Section 5.1, a statistical model can be specified by a discrete probability function or by a probability density function $f(x)$ (for brevity we will refer to only one of them, but without loss of generality); this is what is considered to be 'underlying the data' or, in other words, it is the generating mechanism of the data. A statistical model is usually left unspecified, up to unknown quantities that have to be estimated from the data at hand. The observed sample is not sufficient to reconstruct each detail of $f(x)$, but it can be used to approximate $f(x)$ with a certain accuracy.

Often a density function is parametric or, rather, it is defined by a vector of parameters $\Theta = (\theta_1, \ldots, \theta_I)$ such that each value θ of Θ corresponds to a particular density function, $p_\theta(x)$. A model that has been correctly parameterised for a given unknown density function $f(x)$ is a model which gives $f(x)$ for particular values of the parameters. We can select the best model in a non-parametric context by choosing the distribution function that best approximates the unknown distribution function. But first of all we consider the notion of a distance between model f, which underlies the data, and model g, which is an approximating model.

6.1.1   Distance between statistical models

We can use a distance function to compare two models, say g and f. As explained in Section 4.1, there are different types of distance function; here are the most important ones.

In the categorical case, a distance is usually defined by comparing the estimated discrete probability distributions, denoted by f and g. In the continuous case, we often refer to two variables, X_f and X_g, representing fitted observation values obtained with the two models.

Entropic distance

The entropic distance is used for categorical variables and is related to the concept of heterogeneity reduction (Section 3.4). It describes the proportional reduction of the heterogeneity between categorical variables, as measured by an appropriate index. Because of its additive properties, the entropy is the most used hetero-geneity measure for this purpose. The entropic distance of a distribution g from a target distribution f is

$$_E d = \sum_i f_i \log \frac{f_i}{g_i}$$

which has the form of the uncertainty coefficient (Section 3.4) and also the form taken by the G^2 statistic. The G^2 statistic can be employed for most proba-bilistic data mining models. It can therefore be applied to predictive problems, such as logistic regression and directed graphical models, but also to descriptive problems, such as log-linear models and probabilistic cluster analysis. It also finds application with non-probabilistic models, such as classification trees. The Gini index can also be used as a measure of heterogeneity, giving rise to the concentration coefficient, with similar applications in classification trees.

Chi-squared distance

The Chi-squared distance between a distribution g and a target f is

$$_{\chi^2} d = \sum_i \frac{(f_i - g_i)^2}{g_i}$$

which corresponds to a generalisation of the Pearson statistic seen in Section 3.4. This distance is used for descriptive and predictive problems in the presence of categorical data, as an alternative to the entropic distance. It does not necessarily require an underlying probabilistic model; we have seen its application within the CHAID decision trees algorithm.

0–1 distance

The 0–1 distance applies to categorical variables, typically in the presence of a supervised classification problem. It is defined as

$$_{0-1} d = \sum_{r=1}^{n} 1(X_{fr} - X_{gr})$$

where $1(w, z) = 1$ if $w = z$ and 0 otherwise. It measures the distance in terms of a 0–1 function that counts the number of correct matches between the classifica-tions carried out using the two models. Dividing by the number of observations gives the misclassification rate, probably the most important evaluation tool in predictive classification models, such as logistic regression, categorical response multilayer perceptrons, classification trees and nearest-neighbour models.

Euclidean distance
Applied to quantitative variables, the Euclidean distance between a distribution g and a target f is

$$_2\,d(X_f, X_g) = \sqrt{\sum_{r=1}^{n} (X_{fr} - X_{gr})^2}$$

It represents the distance between two vectors in the Cartesian plane. The Euclidean distance leads to the R^2 index and to the F test statistics. Furthermore, by squaring it and dividing by the number of observations, we obtain the mean square error. The Euclidean distance is often used, especially for continuous predictive models such as linear models, regression trees, multilayer perceptrons and continuous probabilistic expert systems. But it is also used in descriptive models for the observations, such as cluster analysis and Kohonen maps. Notice that it does not necessarily require an underlying probability model. When there is an underlying model, it is usually the Gaussian distribution; consequently the Euclidean distance is often called the Gaussian distance.

Uniform distance
The uniform distance applies to comparisons between distribution functions. For two distribution functions F, G with values in [0, 1], the uniform distance is

$$\sup_{0 \le t \le 1} |F(t) - G(t)|$$

It is usually used in non-parametric statistics and leads to the Kolmogorov–Smirnov statistics in Section 5.2, typically employed to verify whether a non-parametric estimator is valid. It can also be used to verify whether a specific parametric method, for example the Gaussian model, is a good simplification with respect to a less restrictive non-parametric model.

6.1.2 Discrepancy of a statistical model

The distances in Section 6.1.1 can be used to define the notion of discrepancy for a model. Assume that f represents the unknown density of the population, and let $g = p_\theta$ be a family of density functions (indexed by a vector of I parameters, θ) that approximates it. The discrepancy of a statistical model g, with respect to a target model f, can be defined using the Euclidean distance as

$$\Delta(f, p_\vartheta) = \sum_{i=1}^{n} (f(x_i) - p_\vartheta(x_i))^2$$

For each observation, $i = 1, \ldots, n$, this discrepancy (which is a function of the parameters θ) considers the error made by replacing model f with the approximation obtained from model g, then it sums the squares of these errors. The discrepancy could have been calculated using another distance function, but to keep things simple we will concentrate on the Euclidean distance.

If we knew f, the real model, we would be able to determine which of the approximating statistical models, different choices for g, will minimise the discrepancy. Therefore the discrepancy of g (due to the parametric approximation) can be obtained as the discrepancy between the unknown probabilistic model and the best parametric statistical model, $p_{\theta_0}^{(I)}$:

$$\Delta\left(f, p_{\theta_0}^{(I)}\right) = \sum_{i=1}^{n} \left(f(x_i) - p_{\theta_0}^{(I)}(x_i)\right)^2$$

However, since f is unknown we cannot identify the best parametric statistical model. Therefore we will substitute f with a sample estimate, be denoted by $p_{\hat{\theta}}^{(I)}(x)$, for which the I parameters are estimated on the basis of the data. The discrepancy between this sample estimate of $f(x)$ and the best statistical model is called the discrepancy of g (due to the estimation process):

$$\Delta\left(p_{\hat{\theta}}^{(I)}, p_{\theta_0}^{(I)}\right) = \sum_{i=1}^{n} \left(p_{\hat{\theta}}^{(I)}(x_i) - p_{\theta_0}^{(I)}(x_i)\right)^2$$

Now we have a discrepancy that is a function of the observed sample. Bear in mind the complexity of the considered family of parametric models g. To get closer to the unknown model, it is better to choose a family where the models have a large number of parameters. In other words, the discrepancy due to parametric approximation is smaller for models having a large number of parameters – more complex models. But, the sample estimates obtained with a more complex model tend to overfit the data, producing a greater discrepancy due to estimation. The goal is to achieve a compromise between discrepancy due to parametric approximation and discrepancy due to estimation. The total discrepancy, known as the discrepancy between function f and the sample estimate $p_{\hat{\theta}}^{(I)}$, takes both these factors into account. It is given by the equation

$$\Delta\left(f, p_{\hat{\theta}}^{(I)}\right) = \sum_{i=1}^{n} \left(f(x_i) - p_{\hat{\theta}}^{(I)}(x_i)\right)^2$$

which represents the algebraic sum of two discrepancies, one from the parametric approximation and one from the estimation process. Generally, minimisation of the first discrepancy favours complex models, which are more adaptable to the data, whereas minimisation of the second discrepancy favours simple models, which are more stable when faced with variations in the observed sample.

The best statistical model to approximate f will be the model $p_{\hat{\theta}}^{(I)}$ that minimises the total discrepancy. The total discrepancy can rarely be calculated in practice as the density function $f(x)$ is unknown, so we resort to the notion of the total expected discrepancy, $E\Delta(f, p_{\hat{\theta}}^{(I)})$, where the expectation is taken with respect to the sample probability distribution. The problem becomes that of finding an appropriate estimator of the total expected discrepancy. Such an estimator defines an evaluation criterion for a model with I parameters. Model choice will then be based on comparing the corresponding estimators, known as minimum discrepancy estimators.

6.1.3 The Kullback–Leibler discrepancy

We now consider how to derive a model evaluation criterion. To define a general estimator, we need the Kullback–Leibler discrepancy; this is more general than the Euclidean discrepancy but the considerations in Section 6.1.2 still apply. The Kullback–Leibler (KL) discrepancy (or divergence) can be applied to any type of observations; it derives from the entropic distance and is defined as follows:

$$\Delta_{KL}\left(f, p_{\hat{\theta}}^{(I)}\right) = \sum_i f(x_i) \log\left(\frac{f(x_i)}{p_{\hat{\theta}}^{(I)}(x_i)}\right)$$

This can be easily mapped to the expression for the G^2 deviance; then the target density function corresponds to the saturated model. Kullback and Leibler proposed their measure in terms of information theory (Burnham and Anderson, 1998). The best model can be interpreted as the one with a minimal loss of information from the true unknown distribution. Like the entropic distance, the Kullback–Leibler discrepancy is not symmetric.

We can now show that the statistical tests used for model comparison are based on estimators of the total Kullback–Leibler discrepancy. Let p_θ indicate a probability density function parameterised by the vector $\Theta = \theta_1, \ldots, \theta_I$. The sample values $x_1, \ldots, x_n$ are a series of independent observations that are identically distributed, therefore the sample density function is expressed by the equation

$$L(\vartheta; x_1, \ldots, x_n) = \prod_{i=1}^{n} p_\vartheta(x_i)$$

Let $\hat{\vartheta}_n$ indicate the maximum likelihood estimator of the parameters, and let the likelihood function L be calculated at this point. Taking the logarithm of the resulting expression and multiplying by $-1/n$, we get

$$\Delta_{KL}\left(f, p_{\hat{\theta}}^{(I)}\right) = -\left(\frac{1}{n}\right) \sum_{i=1}^{n} \log\left[p_{\hat{\theta}}^{(I)}(x_i)\right]$$

known as the sample Kullback–Leibler discrepancy function. This expression can be shown to be the maximum likelihood estimator of the total expected

Kullback–Leibler discrepancy of a model p_θ. Notice that the Kullback–Leibler discrepancy gives a score to each model, corresponding to the mean (negative) log-likelihood of the observations. Practical applications often consider the log-likelihood score, which is equal to

$$2n \Delta_{KL}\left(f, p_{\hat{\theta}}^{(I)}\right) = -2 \sum_{i=1}^{n} \log\left[p_{\hat{\theta}}^{(I)}(x_i)\right]$$

The Kullback–Leibler discrepancy is fundamental to selection criteria developed in the field of statistical hypothesis testing. These criteria are based on successive comparisons between pairs of models. The idea is to compare the sample Kullback–Leibler discrepancy of two alternative models. Let us suppose that the expected discrepancy for two statistical models with respect to the same observed data is calculated as above, where the model p_θ is substituted by one of the two models considered. Let $\Delta_Z(f, z_{\hat{\vartheta}})$ be the sample discrepancy function estimated for the model with density z_θ and let $\Delta_G(f, g_{\hat{\vartheta}})$ be the sample discrepancy estimated for the model with density g_θ. Let us suppose that model g has a lower discrepancy, namely that $\Delta_Z(f, z_{\hat{\vartheta}}) = \Delta_G(f, g_{\hat{\vartheta}}) + \varepsilon$, where ε is a small positive number. Therefore, based on comparison of the discrepancy functions, we will choose the model with the density function g_θ.

This result may depend on the specific sample used to estimate the discrepancy function. We therefore need to carry out a statistical test to verify whether a discrepancy difference is significant; that is, whether the results obtained from a sample can be extended to all possible samples. Suppose we find that the difference ε is not significant, then the two models would be considered equal and it would be natural to choose the simplest model. The deviance difference criterion defined by G^2 (Section 5.4) is equal to twice the difference between sample Kullback–Leibler discrepancies. For nested models, the G^2 difference is asymptotically equivalent to the chi-squared comparison (and test), so this is also seen to derive from the Kullback–Leibler discrepancy. When a Gaussian distribution is assumed, the Kullback–Leibler discrepancy coincides with the Gaussian discrepancy, therefore we are justified in using F statistics.

To conclude, using a statistical test, it is possible to use the estimated discrepancy to make an accurate choice among the models, based on the observed data. The defect of this procedure is that it requires comparisons between model pairs, so when we have a large number of alternative models, we need to make heuristic choices regarding the comparison strategy (such as choosing among the forward, backward and stepwise criteria, whose results may diverge). Furthermore, we must assume a specific probabilistic model and this may not always be a reasonable assumption.

6.2 Criteria based on scoring functions

Often we will not be able to derive a formal test. Examples include choosing models for data analysis with missing values or for mixed graphical models. Furthermore, it may be important to have a complete ordering of models, rather than a partial one, based on pairwise comparisons. For this reason, it is important to develop scoring functions that attach a score to each model. The Kullback–Leibler discrepancy estimator is a scoring function that can often be approximated asymptotically for complex models.

A problem with the Kullback–Leibler score is that it depends on the complexity of a model, perhaps described by the number of parameters, hence its use may lead to us choosing complex models, similar to what happens with the R^2 index. Section 6.1 explained how a model selection strategy should reach a trade-off between model fit and model parsimony. We now look at this issue from a different perspective, based on a trade-off between bias and variance. In Section 5.1 we defined the mean square error of an estimator. Let us apply the same mean square principle to measure the Euclidean distance of the chosen model, $p_{\hat{\theta}}$, as the best approximator of the underlying model f:

$$\mathrm{MSE}(p_{\hat{\theta}}) = E[(p_{\hat{\theta}} - f)^2]$$

Note that $p_{\hat{\theta}}$ is estimated on the basis of the data and is therefore subject to sampling variability. In particular, for $p_{\hat{\theta}}$ we can define an expected value $E(p_{\hat{\theta}})$, roughly corresponding to the arithmetic mean over a large number of repeated samples, and a variance $\mathrm{Var}(p_{\hat{\theta}})$, measuring its variability with respect to this expectation. From the properties of the mean square error it then follows that

$$\mathrm{MSE}(p_{\hat{\theta}}) = [\mathrm{bias}(p_{\hat{\theta}})]^2 + \mathrm{Var}(p_{\hat{\theta}}) = [E(p_{\hat{\theta}}) - f]^2 + E[(p_{\hat{\theta}} - E(p_{\hat{\theta}}))^2]$$

This indicates that the error connected to a model $p_{\hat{\theta}}$ can be decomposed into two parts: a systematic error (bias), which does not depend on the observed data and reflects the error due to the parametric approximation; and a sampling error (variance), which reflects the error due to the estimation process. A model should therefore be selected to balance the two parts. A very simple model will have a small variance but a rather large bias (e.g. a constant model); a very complex model will have a small bias but a large variance. This is known as the bias–variance trade-off and emphasises the need to balance goodness of fit with model parsimony. This concept is central to data mining and can be shown in other ways. For instance, Vapnik (1995, 1998) has introduced the principle of structural risk minimisation for supervised learning problems, an idea that leads to similar conclusions.

We now define score functions that, related to the Kullback–Leibler principle, penalise for model complexity. The most important of these functions is the Akaike information criterion (AIC). To find AIC, in 1974 Akaike formulated the idea that (i) the parametric model is estimated using the method of maximum likelihood and (ii) the parametric family specified contains the unknown distribution $f(x)$ as a particular case. He therefore defined a function that assigns a score to each model by taking a function of the Kullback–Leibler sample discrepancy. In formal terms, AIC is defined by the following equation:

$$\mathrm{AIC} = -2\log L(\hat{\vartheta}; x_1, \ldots, x_n) + 2q$$

where $\log L(\hat{\vartheta}; x_1, \ldots, x_n)$ is the logarithm of the likelihood function calculated in the maximum likelihood parameter estimate and q is the number of parameters in the model. Notice that the AIC score essentially penalises the log-likelihood score using a term that increases linearly with model complexity.

AIC is based on the implicit assumption that q remains constant when the size of the sample increases. But this assumption is not always valid, so AIC does not lead to a consistent estimate for the dimension of the unknown model. An alternative and consistent scoring function is the Bayesian information criterion (BIC), also called SC. It was formulated by Schwarz (1978) and is defined by the following expression:

$$\text{BIC} = -2 \log L(\hat{\vartheta}; x_1, \ldots, x_n) + q \log n$$

BIC differs from AIC only in the second part, which now also depends on the sample size n. When n increases, BIC favours simpler models than AIC. As n gets large, the first term (linear in n) will dominate the second term (logarithmic in n). This corresponds to the fact that, for large n, the variance term in the MSE expression tends to be negligible. Despite the superficial similarity between AIC and BIC, AIC is usually justified by resorting to classical asymptotic arguments, whereas BIC is usually justified by appealing to the Bayesian framework.

To conclude, the scoring function criteria we have examined are easy to calculate and lead to a total ordering of the models. From most statistical packages we can get the AIC and BIC scores for all the models considered. A further advantage of these criteria is that they can be used to compare non-nested models and, more generally, models that do not belong to the same class (e.g. a probabilistic neural network and a linear regression model). The disadvantage of these criteria is the lack of a threshold, as well as the difficulty of interpreting their measurement scale. In other words, it is not easy to determine whether or not the difference between two models is significant, and how it compares with another difference.

6.3 Bayesian criteria

From an operational perspective, the Bayesian criteria are an interesting compromise between the statistical criteria based on the deviance differences and the criteria based on scoring functions. They are based on coherent statistical modelling and therefore their results can be easily interpreted. They provide a complete ordering of the models and can be used to compare non-nested models as well as models belonging to different classes. In the Bayesian derivation each model is given a score that corresponds to the posterior probability of the model itself. A model becomes a discrete random variable that takes values on the space of all candidate models. This probability can be calculated from Bayes' rule:

$$P(M|x_1, \ldots, x_n) = P(x_1, \ldots, x_n|M)P(M)/P(x_1, \ldots, x_n)$$

The model which maximises this posterior probability will be chosen. Unlike the information criteria, the Bayesian criteria use probability and therefore define a distance that can be easily interpreted to compare models.

For further information about Bayesian theory and selection criteria for Bayesian models, see Bernardo and Smith (1994) and Cifarelli and Muliere (1989). There are also difficulties with the Bayesian scoring methods. These are related to the practical application of Bayes' rule. The first problem is to calculate the likelihood of a model, $P(x_1, \ldots, x_n|M)$. To calculate this, the parameters of the model must be integrated out, and integration may be a rather difficult task. For a model M indexed by a vector ϑ of parameters, we have to calculate

$$P(x_1, \ldots, x_n|M) = \int P(x_1, \ldots, x_n|\vartheta, M) P(\vartheta|M) \, d\vartheta$$

where $P(\vartheta|M)$ is the prior distribution of the parameters, given that model M is under consideration. Although calculations like these long prevented the widespread use of Bayesian methods, Markov chain Monte Carlo (MCMC) techniques emerged during the 1990s, providing a successful, albeit computationally intensive, way to approximate such integration problems, even in highly complex settings. For a review of MCMC methods, see Gilks, Richardson and Spiegelhalter (1996). The most common software for implementing MCMC is BUGS, which can be found at www.mrc-bsu.cam.ac.uk/bugs.

A further advantage of Bayesian methods is that the model scores are probabilities, so they can also be used to draw model-averaged inferences from the various competing models, rather than making inferences conditional on a single model being chosen. This takes model uncertainty into account. Consider the problem of predicting the value of a certain variable Y. In the presence of uncertainty over which model to choose, among the K available models, the Bayesian prediction will be

$$E(Y|x_1, \ldots, x_n) = \sum_{j=1}^{K} E(Y|M, x_1, \ldots, x_n) P(M|x_1, \ldots, x_n)$$

Notice how the prediction correctly reflects the uncertainty on the statistical model. Rather than choosing a single model, and drawing all inferences based on it, we consider a plurality of models, averaging the inferences obtained from each model, using posterior probabilities as weights. Application of Bayesian model averaging to complex models usually requires careful design of MCMC approximations. This issue is considered in detail in Brooks, Giudici and Roberts (2003) and for graphical models in Giudici and Green (1999). Green, Hjort and Richardson (2003) is an important reference on Bayesian inference and computational approximations for highly structured stochastic systems.

6.4   Computational criteria

The widespread use of computational methods has led to the development of computationally intensive model selection criteria. These criteria are usually based on using data sets that are different from the one being analysed (external validation) and are applicable to all the models considered, even when they belong to different classes (e.g. in comparing logistic regression, decision trees and neural networks, even when the latter two are non-probabilistic). A possible problem with these criteria is that they take a long time to design and implement, although general-purpose packages such as SAS Enterprise Miner have made this task easier. We now consider the main computational criteria.

The cross-validation criterion
The idea of cross-validation is to divide the sample into two subsamples: a training sample having $n - m$ observations and a validation sample having m observations. The first sample is used to fit a model and the second is used to estimate the expected discrepancy or to assess a distance. We have already seen how to apply this criterion to neural networks and decision trees. Using this criterion the choice between two or more models is made by evaluating an appropriate discrepancy function on the validation sample.

We can see that the logic of this criterion is different. The other criteria are all based on a function of internal discrepancy on a single data set, playing the roles of the training data set and the validation data set. With these criteria we directly compare predicted and observed values on an external validation sample. Notice that the cross-validation idea can be applied to the calculation of any distance function. For example, in the case of neural networks with quantitative output, we usually employ a Gaussian discrepancy

$$\frac{1}{m} \sum_i \sum_j (t_{ij} - o_{ij})^2$$

where t_{ij} is the fitted output and o_{ij} the observed output, for each observation i in the validation set and for each output neuron j.

One problem with the cross-validation criterion is in deciding how to select m, the number of observations in the validation data set. For example, if we select $m = n/2$ then only $n/2$ observations are available to fit a model. We could reduce m but this would mean having few observations for the validation data set and therefore reducing the accuracy with which the choice between models is made. In practice proportions of 75% and 25% are usually used for the training and validation data sets, respectively.

The cross-validation criterion can be perfected in different ways. One limitation is that if the validation data set is used to choose a model, the results obtained are not real measurements of the model's performance that can be compared with the measurements obtained from other models. The reason for this is that the validation data set is in fact also used to construct the model. Therefore the idea is to generalise what we have seen by dividing the sample into more than two data sets.

The most frequently used method, especially in the field of neural networks, is to divide the data set into three blocks: training, validation and testing. The test data will not be used in the modelling phase. Model fit will be carried out on the training data, using the validation data to choose a model. Finally, the model chosen and estimated on the first two data sets will be adapted to the test data and the error found will provide a correct estimate of the prediction error. The disadvantage is that it reduces the amount of data available for training and validation.

A further improvement could be to use all the data for the training. The data is divided into k subsets of equal size; the model is fitted k times, leaving out one of the subsets each time, which could be used to calculate a prediction error rate. The final error is the arithmetic average of the errors obtained. This method is known as k-fold cross-validation. Another common alternative is the leaving-one-out method, in which one observation only is left out in each of the k samples, and this observation is used to calibrate the predictions. The disadvantage of these methods is the need to retrain the model several times, which makes the elaboration process very computationally intensive.

The bootstrap criterion

The bootstrap method was introduced by Efron (1979) and is based on the idea of reproducing the 'real' distribution of the population with a resampling of the observed sample. Application of the method is based on the assumption that the observed sample is in fact a population, a population for which we can calculate the underlying model $f(x)$ – it is the sample density. To compare alternative models, a sample can be drawn (or resampled) from the fictitious population (the available sample) and then we can use out earlier results on model comparison. For instance, we can calculate the Kullback–Leibler discrepancy directly, without resorting to estimators. The problem is that the results depend on resampling variability. To get around this, we resample many times, and we assess the discrepancy by taking the mean of the obtained results. It can be shown that the expected discrepancy calculated in this way is a consistent estimator of the expected discrepancy of the real population. We will therefore choose the statistical model which minimises it. Application of the bootstrap method requires us to assume a probabilistic model, either parametric or non-parametric, and it can also be rather computationally intensive.

Bagging and boosting

Bootstrap methods can be used not only to assess a model's discrepancy and therefore its accuracy, but also to improve the accuracy. Bagging and boosting methods are recent developments that can be used for combining the results of more than one data mining analysis. In this respect they are similar to Bayesian model-averaging methods, as they also lead to model-averaged estimators, which often improve on estimators derived using a single model.

Bagging (bootstrap aggregation) methods can be described as follows. For each loop of the procedure, we draw a sample with replacement from the available training data set. Typically, the sample size corresponds to the size of the training data itself. This does not mean that the drawn sample will be the same as the training sample, because observations are drawn with replacement. Consider B loops of the procedure; the value of B depends on the computational resources available and time. A data mining method can be applied to each bootstrapped sample, leading to a set of estimates for each model; these can then be combined to obtain a bagged estimate. For instance, the optimal classification tree can be searched for one sample, and each observation allocated to the class with the highest probability. The procedure is repeated, for each sample $i = 1, \ldots, B$, leading to B classifications. The bagged classification for an observation corresponds to the majority vote, namely, to the class in which it is most classified by the B fitted trees. Similarly, a regression tree can be fitted for each of the B samples, producing a fitted value $\hat{y}_i$, in each of them, for each observation. The bagged estimate is the mean of these fitted values:

$$\frac{1}{B} \sum_{i=1}^{B} \hat{y}_i$$

With reference to the bias–variance trade-off, as a bagged estimate is a sample mean, it will not alter the bias of a model but it may reduce the variance. This occurs especially for highly unstable models, such as decision trees, complex neural networks and nearest-neighbour models. On the other hand, if the applied model is simple, the variance may not decrease, because variability is added by bootstrapping.

So far we have assumed that the same model is applied to the bootstrap samples; this does not need to be the case. Different models can be combined, provided the estimates are compatible and expressed on the same scale. Bagging is related to the use of bootstrap samples, but this is not strictly the case for boosting. Although there are now many variants, the early versions of boosting fitted models on several weighted versions of the data set, where the observations with the poorest fit receive the greatest weight. For instance, in a classification problem, the well-classified observations will get lower weights as the iteration proceeds, allowing the model to concentrate on estimating the most difficult cases. The case studies explain how to apply these methods, and more details can be found in Han and Kamber (2001) and Hastie, Tibshirani and Friedman (2001).

Genetic algorithms
Genetic algorithms are not strictly for data mining. They are a class of optimisation methods that can be used within any data mining model; this makes them similar to any other optimisation method, such as maximum likelihood or least squares. Here is a brief description. Like neural networks, genetic algorithms are based on analogies with biological mechanisms. Evolutionary theory

links a species' survival chances to how well it can adapt to the surrounding environment. These adaptations optimise the efficiency of the following generations, propagating the best genetic traits from one generation to the next. Genetic algorithms apply the same idea; they simulate these evolutionary mechanisms to create an adaptive method for solving optimisation problems. To solve a problem, they work on a population of individuals, each representing a possible solution; at the end of the process, they indicate the best solution. More concretely, individuals can represent parameters or models, therefore the algorithm furnishes the best estimate or the best model.

Genetic algorithms can be very important for model evaluation. They allow us to manage the process of model choice in a very flexible way, because they do not have an underlying modelling hypothesis. They can be used as part of Bayesian model averaging, bagging and boosting; they can be used alongside them or instead of them. One of the advantages of genetic algorithms is the ability to work, in a general way, with all types of data. Two disadvantages are the long coding times of the algorithms and the need for large computational resource to run them.

6.5   Criteria based on loss functions

One aspect of data mining is the need to communicate the final results in a way that suits the aims of the analysis. With business data we need to evaluate the models not only by comparing them among themselves but also by comparing the advantages to be had by using one model rather than another. In other words, we need to compare the results obtained from the models, not just the models themselves. Since the main problem dealt with by data analysis is to reduce uncertainties in the risk factors or loss factors, we often talk about developing criteria to minimise the loss connected with a problem. In other words, the best model is the one that leads to the lowest loss. The best way to introduce these rather specific criteria is to give some practical examples. As these criteria are mostly used in predictive classification problems, that is where we will concentrate. The confusion matrix is used as an indication of the properties of a classification (discriminant) rule. It contains the number of elements that have been correctly or incorrectly classified for each class. The main diagonal shows the number of observations that have been correctly classified for each class; the off-diagonal elements indicate the number of observations that have been incorrectly classified. If it is assumed, explicitly or implicitly, that each incorrect classification has the same cost, the proportion of incorrect classifications over the total number of classifications is called the misclassification error, or misclassification rate; this is the quantity we must minimise. The assumption of equal costs can be replaced by weighting errors with their relative costs.

Table 6.1 shows a confusion matrix for a classification problem. The diagonal shows the correct predictions. We can see that the model classifies 38 out of 46 observations correctly as belonging to class B (2 + 38 + 6). Of the 8 observations that have been incorrectly classified, 2 belong to class A and 6 belong to class C.

Table 6.1 Example of a confusion matrix.

Observed / Predicted	Class A	Class B	Class C
Class A	45	2	3
Class B	10	38	2
Class C	4	6	40

This is much more informative than saying the accuracy of the model is 82% (123 correct classifications out of 150). If there are different costs for different errors, a model with a lower general level of accuracy is preferable to one that has greater accuracy but also much higher costs. For example, if we suppose that in Table 6.1 each correct answer has a value of €1000 and that each error for class A costs €500s, each error for class B costs €1000 and each error for class C costs €2000, the cost associated with the matrix will be $(123 \times 1000) - (5 \times 500) - (12 \times 1000) - (10 \times 2000) = €88\,500$.

We now consider the lift chart and the ROC curve, two graphs that can be used to assess model costs. Both are presented with reference to a binary response variable, the area where evaluation methods have developed most quickly. For a comprehensive review see Hand (1997).

Lift chart

The lift chart puts the observations in the validation data set into increasing or decreasing order on the basis of their score, which is the probability of the response event (success), as estimated on the basis of the training data set. It subdivides these scores into deciles then calculates and graphs the observed probability of success for each of the decile classes in the validation data set. A model is valid if the observed success probabilities follow the same order (increasing or decreasing) as the estimated probabilities. To improve interpretation, a model's lift chart is usually compared with a baseline curve, for which the probability estimates are drawn in the absence of a model, that is, by taking the mean of the observed success probabilities.

Figure 6.1 compares the lift charts of three logistic regression models. The scores are ordered in a decreasing way, so the more the curve is decreasing, the better the corresponding model. The performances of the three models are quite close, but model C seems to be better than the others, especially because in the first deciles it captures the successes better. Dividing the values of each curve by the baseline, we obtain a relative index of performance called the lift. The lift measures a model's worth. For model C, in the first decile (containing 164 observations) the lift is 4.46 (i.e. 22.7%/5.1%); this means that using model C we are 4.5 times more likely to get a success than if we chose randomly, without a model.

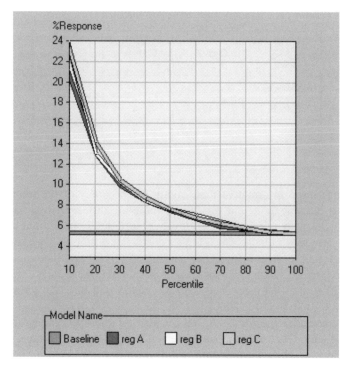

Figure 6.1   Example of a lift chart.

ROC curve

The receiver operating characteristic (ROC) curve is a graph that measures the predictive accuracy of a model. It is based on the confusion matrix in Table 6.2. The term 'event' stands for the value $Y = 1$ (success) of the binary response. Table 6.2 classifies the observations of a validation data set into four possible categories:

- Observations predicted as events and effectively such (with absolute frequency equal to a)

Table 6.2   Theoretical confusion matrix.

Observed \ Predicted	Event (1)	Non-event (0)	Total
Event (1)	a	b	$a + b$
Non-event (0)	c	d	$c + d$
Total	$a + c$	$b + d$	$a + b + c + d$

- Observations predicted as events and effectively non-events (with frequency equal to c)
- Observations predicted as non-events and effectively events (with frequency equal to b)
- Observations predicted as non-events and effectively such (with frequency equal to d)

Given an observed table, and a cut-off point, the ROC curve is calculated on the basis of the resulting joint frequencies of predicted and observed events (successes) and non-events (failures). More precisely, it is based on the following conditional probabilities:

- *Sensitivity* $\dfrac{a}{a+b}$ is the proportion of events predicted as such.
- *Specificity* $\dfrac{d}{c+d}$ is the proportion of non events predicted as such.
- *False positives* $\dfrac{c}{c+d} = 1 -$ specificity is the proportion of non-events predicted as events (type II error).
- *False negatives* $\dfrac{b}{a+b} = 1 -$ sensitivity is the proportions of events predicted as non-events (type I error).

The ROC curve is obtained by graphing, for any fixed cut-off value, the false positives (1 − specificity) on the horizontal axis and the sensitivity on the vertical axis. Each point on the curve corresponds to a particular cut-off. The ROC curve can also be used to select a cut-off point, trading off sensitivity and specificity. In terms of model comparison, the ideal curve coincides with the vertical axis, so the best curve is the leftmost curve. Figure 6.2 shows ROC curves for the same problem considered in Figure 6.1. It turns out that the best model is C. However, the three models are substantially similar.

The ROC curve is the basis of an important summary statistic called the Gini index of performance. Recall the concentration curve in Figure 3.2. For any given value of F_i, the cumulative frequency, there corresponds a value of Q_i, the cumulative intensity. F_i and Q_i take values in [0,1] and $Q_i \leq F_i$ Therefore the concentration curve joins a number of points in the Cartesian plane determined by taking $x_i = F_i$ and $y_i = Q_i$, for $i = 1, \ldots, n$. The area between the curve and the 45° line gives a summary measure for the degree of concentration. The ROC curve can be treated in a similar way. In place of F_i and Q_i we need to consider two cumulative distributions constructed as follows.

First, the data contains both events ($Y_i = 1$) and non-events ($Y_i = 0$). It can therefore be divided into two samples, one containing all events (labelled E) and one containing all non-events (labelled N). As explained in Chapter 4, any statistical model for predictive classification takes each observation and attaches to it a score that is the fitted probability of success π_i. In each of the two samples, E and N, the observations can be ordered (in increasing order) according to

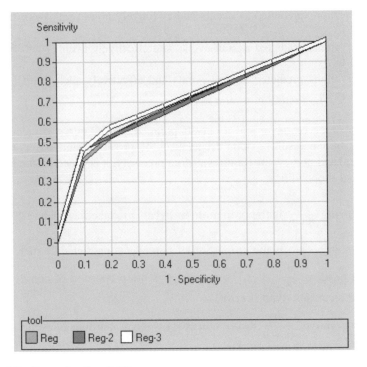

Figure 6.2 Example of an ROC curve.

this score. Now, for any fixed value of i (a percentile corresponding to the cut-off threshold), a classification model would consider all observations below it as non-events and all observations above it as events.

Correspondingly, the predicted proportion of events can be estimated for populations E and N. For a reasonable model, in population E this proportion has to be higher than in population N. Let F_i^E and F_i^N be these proportions corresponding to the cut-off i, and calculate coordinate pairs (F_i^N, F_i^E) as i varies. The coordinates will be different for each model. We have that, for $i = 1, \ldots, n$, both F_i^E and F_i^N take values in [0,1]; indeed they both represent cumulative frequencies. Furthermore, $F_i^N \leq F_i^E$. The ROC curve is obtained by joining points with coordinates $y_i = F_i^E$ and $x_i = F_i^N$. This is because F_i^E equals the sensitivity and F_i^N equals 1 − specificity.

Notice that the curve will always lie above the 45° line. However, the area between the curve and the line can also be calculated, and gives the Gini index of performance. The higher the area, the better the model.

6.6 Further reading

In this chapter we have systematically compared the main criteria for evaluating the statistical methods used in data mining. These methods can be classified into criteria based on statistical tests, criteria based on scoring functions, Bayesian criteria, computational criteria, and criteria based on loss functions. Criteria based on statistical tests start from the theory of statistical hypothesis testing, so there is a lot of detailed literature; see for example Mood, Graybill and Boes (1991). The main limitation of these methods is that the choice is made by pairwise comparisons, which introduces an element of discretion, further reinforced by the choice of significance levels.

Criteria based on scoring functions offer a high generality of application, complete ordering and simple calculation. Their main disadvantage is that they do not define threshold levels which allow us to choose one model rather than another. Therefore they are especially useful in an exploratory phase. Zucchini (2000) and Hand, Mannila and Smyth (2001) examine these criteria and compare them with criteria based on statistical tests. Bayesian criteria are a possible compromise between the previous two. They can be developed in an interesting way, but their limited application is probably due to the absence of general software. For data mining using Bayesian criteria see Giudici (2001a) and Giudici and Castelo (2001).

Computational criteria have an important advantage in being applicable to statistical methods that are not necessarily model based, such as those in Chapter 4. They are the main methods of universal comparison among the different types of model. Since most of them are non-probabilistic, they may be too dependent on the observed *sample*. One way to overcome this problem is to consider model combination methods, such as bagging and boosting. For a thorough description of these recent methodologies, see Hastie, Tibshirani and Friedman (2001).

Criteria based on loss functions have recently appeared, although related ideas have long been known in Bayesian decision theory (Bernardo and Smith, 1994). They are very interesting and have considerable potential, but at present they are mainly concerned with solving classification problems. For a more detailed treatment see Hand (1997), Hand, Mannila and Smyth (2001), or the reference manuals that accompany data mining software, such as Enterprise Miner (SAS Institute, 2001).

I think the topics in this chapter are of great interest for developing statistical methods in data mining. The second part of the book shows how to apply them in different contexts.

PART II

Business cases

CHAPTER 7

Market basket analysis

7.1 Objectives of the analysis

This case study looks at market consumer behaviour using the marketing methodology known as market basket analysis. Market basket analysis has the objective of individuating products, or groups of products, that tend to occur together (are associated) in buying transactions (baskets). The knowledge obtained from a market basket analysis can be very valuable; for instance, it can be employed by a supermarket to reorganise its layout, taking products frequently sold together and locating them in close proximity. But it can also be used to improve the efficiency of a promotional campaign: products that are associated should not be put on promotion for the same periods. By promoting just one of the associated products, it should be possible to increase the sales of that product and get accompanying sales increases for the associated products.

The databases usually considered in a market basket analysis consist of all the transactions made in a certain sale period (e.g. one year) and in certain sale locations (e.g. a chain of supermarkets). Consumers can appear more than once in the database. In fact, consumers will appear in the database whenever they carry out a transaction at a sales location. The objective of the analysis is to individuate the most frequent combinations of products bought by the customers. The association rules in Section 4.8 represent the most natural methodology here; indeed they were actually developed for this purpose. Analysing the combinations of products bought by the customers, and the number of times these combinations are repeated, leads to a rule of the type 'if condition, then result' with a corresponding interestingness measurement. Each rule of this type describes a particular local pattern. The set of association rules can be easily interpreted and communicated. Possible disadvantages are locality and lack of probabilistic modelling.

This case study takes a real market basket analysis and compares association rules with log-linear models (Section 5.5), which represent a powerful method of descriptive data mining. It also shows how an exploratory analysis, based on examining the pairwise odds ratios, can help in building a comprehensive log-linear model. Odds ratios can be directly compared with association rules. Similar analyses can be found in Giudici and Passerone (2002) and Castelo and Giudici (2003); Castelo and Giudici take a Bayesian viewpoint.

Applied Data Mining. Paolo Giudici
© 2003 John Wiley & Sons, Ltd ISBNs: 0-470-84679-8 (Paper); 0-470-84678-X (Cloth)

7.2 Description of the data

The statistical analysis in this chapter was carried out on a data set kindly provided by AC Nielsen, concerning transactions at a large supermarket in southern Italy. The data set is part of a larger database for 37 shop locations of a chain of supermarkets in Italy. In each shop the recorded transactions are all the transactions made by someone holding one of the chain's loyalty cards. Each card carries a code that identifies features about the owner, including important personal characteristics such as sex, birthdate, partner's birthdate, number of children, profession and education. The card allows the analyst to follow the buying behaviour of its owner: how many times they go to the supermarket in a given period, what they buy, whether they follow the promotions, etc. Our aim here is to consider only transaction data on products, in order to investigate the associations between these products. Therefore we shall not consider the influence of demographic variables or the effect of promotions.

The available data set is organised in a collection of 37 transactional databases, one for each shop location. For each shop, a statistical unit (a row in the database) corresponds to one loyalty card code and one product bought. For each card code there may be more than one product and, in the file, the same card code may appear more than once, each time corresponding to one visit to a particular shop.

Table 7.1 The considered product categories and corresponding frequency counts.

	Count	Item
1	4541	pasta
2	4428	milk
3	3452	water
4	3371	biscuits
5	2703	coffee
6	2680	brioches
7	2493	yoghurt
8	2484	frozen vegetables
9	2464	tunny
10	1970	beer
11	1958	tomato souce
12	1883	coke
13	1822	rice
14	1681	juices
15	957	crackers
16	775	oil
17	759	frozen fish
18	445	ice cream
19	432	mozzarella
20	177	tinned meat

The considered period consists of 75 days between 2 January and 21 April 2001. To suit the aims of the analysis and the complexity of the overall data set, we will choose one representative shop, in southern Italy, with an area of about $12\,000\,m^2$. This shop has a mean number of visits in the considered period of 7.85, which is roughly equivalent to the overall mean for the 37 shops. But the total number of loyalty cards issued for the shop is 7301, the largest out of all the shops; this is one of the main reasons for choosing it. Finally, the average expenditure per transaction is about € 28.27, slightly lower than the overall mean.

The total number of products available in the shop is about 5000 ignoring the brand, format and specific type (e.g. weight, colour, size). Products are usually grouped into categories. The total number of available categories in the considered supermarket is about 493. For clarity we will limit our analysis to 20 categories (items), which correspond to those most sold. They are listed in Table 7.1, along with their frequency of occurrence, namely, the number of transactions that contain the item at least once. Notice that all considered product categories – shortened to products from now on–concern food products. These categories are used to produce a transaction database and Table 7.2 presents an extract. This extract will be called the transactions data set.

From Table 7.2 notice that the transaction database presents, for each card and each purchase date (i.e. for each transaction), a list of the products that have been

Table 7.2 The transactions data set.

	COD_CARD	DATE			PRODUCT
1	0460202004099	01	02	2001	tinned meat
2	0460202004099	01	02	2001	tunny
3	0460202004099	01	02	2001	mozzarella
4	0460202007021	01	02	2001	milk
5	0460202033648	01	02	2001	milk
6	0460202033648	01	02	2001	coke
7	0460202033648	01	02	2001	pasta
8	0460202033648	01	02	2001	crackers
9	0460202033648	01	02	2001	milk
10	0460202035871	01	02	2001	water
11	0460202035871	01	02	2001	water
12	0460202039190	01	02	2001	tunny
13	0460501000020	01	02	2001	crackers
14	0460501000020	01	02	2001	milk
15	0460501000020	01	02	2001	pasta
16	0460501000020	01	02	2001	biscuits
17	0460501000020	01	02	2001	pasta
18	0460501000020	01	02	2001	biscuits
19	0460501000204	01	02	2001	juices
20	0460501000204	01	02	2001	milk
21	0460501000204	01	02	2001	biscuits
22	0460501000303	01	02	2001	pasta
23	0460501000723	01	02	2001	oil
24	0460501000853	01	02	2001	biscuits
25	0460501000853	01	02	2001	biscuits
26	0460501001744	01	02	2001	tinned meat
27	0460501001966	01	02	2001	milk
28	0460501001966	01	02	2001	coffee
29	0460501001966	01	02	2001	pasta

Table 7.3   The card owners database.

	COD_CART	TIN_MEAT	MOZZAR	TUNNY	MILK	COKE	CRACKERS	PASTA	WATER	BISCUITS	JUICES	OIL	COFFEE
1	0460202004099	1	1	1	0	0	0	0	0	0	0	0	0
2	0460202007021	0	0	0	1	0	0	0	0	0	0	0	0
3	0460202033648	0	0	0	1	1	1	1	0	0	0	0	0
4	0460202035871	0	0	0	0	0	0	0	1	0	0	0	0
5	0460202039190	0	0	1	0	0	0	0	0	0	0	0	0
6	0460501000020	0	0	0	1	0	1	1	0	1	0	0	0
7	0460501000204	0	0	0	1	0	0	0	0	1	1	0	0
8	0460501000303	0	0	0	0	0	0	1	0	0	0	0	0
9	0460501000723	0	0	0	0	0	0	0	0	0	0	1	0
10	0460501000853	0	0	0	0	0	0	0	0	1	0	0	0
11	0460501001744	1	0	0	0	0	0	0	0	0	0	0	0
12	0460501001966	0	0	1	0	0	0	1	0	0	0	0	1
13	0460501001980	0	0	1	1	0	0	1	0	0	1	0	0
14	0460501002017	0	0	0	1	0	0	0	0	0	0	0	0
15	0460501002024	0	0	0	0	0	0	1	0	0	0	0	0
16	0460501002291	0	0	0	0	0	0	0	0	0	0	0	0
17	0460501002994	0	0	0	1	0	1	0	0	1	0	0	0
18	0460501003038	0	0	0	0	0	0	1	0	0	0	0	0
19	0460501003052	0	0	0	1	0	0	1	0	0	0	0	0
20	0460501003403	0	0	0	0	0	0	1	0	0	1	0	1
21	0460501004578	0	0	0	0	0	0	0	0	0	1	0	0
22	0460501004875	0	0	0	0	0	0	0	0	1	0	0	0
23	0460501005131	0	0	0	0	0	0	1	0	0	0	0	0
24	0460501005476	0	0	0	1	0	0	0	0	0	0	0	0
25	0460501005780	0	0	0	1	0	0	0	1	0	0	0	1
26	0460501006008	0	0	0	0	0	0	1	0	0	0	0	0
27	0460501006077	0	0	0	0	1	0	0	0	0	0	0	0
28	0460501006572	0	0	0	1	0	0	1	0	0	0	0	0
29	0460501006718	0	1	0	0	0	0	0	0	1	0	0	0

put in the basket. For example, on 2 January 2002, card owner 0460202004099 bought tinned meat, tunny and mozzarella. The transaction database may conveniently be expressed as a data matrix, with each row representing one transaction of one owner of a card code; the columns are binary variables that represent whether or not each specific product has been bought (at least once) in that transaction. We will call this the card owners database; an extract is shown in Table 7.3. The total number of transactions is 46 727, which corresponds to the number of rows in the card owners database.

7.3   Exploratory data analysis

To understand the associations between the 20 products considered, we have considered 190 two-way contingency tables, one for each pair of products. Table 7.4 shows one of these tables. It can be used to study the association between the products ice cream and Coke. In each cell of the contingency table we have the absolute frequency, the relative frequency (as a percentage), and the conditional frequency by row and by column. Below the table we report the association measure, the odds ratio between the two variables, along with the corresponding confidence interval. According to Section 3.4, an association is deemed significant if the value 1 is external to the confidence interval. Here we can say there is a strong positive association between the two products. Recall that the total sample size is quite large (46 727 transactions), therefore even a small odds ratio can

Table 7.4 Example of a two-way contingency table and calculation of the odds ratios.

ICE CREAM Frequency Percent Row Pct Col Pct	COKE 0	 1	 Total
0	41 179 88.13 89.60 98.57	4779 10.23 10.40 96.56	45 958 98.35
1	599 1.28 77.89 1.43	170 0.36 22.11 3.44	769 1.65
Total	41 778 89.41	4949 10.59	46 727 100.00

	Value	95% Confidence Limits	
Odds Ratio	2.4455	2.0571	2.9071

be significant. We have calculated all 190 possible odds ratios between products; the largest values are shown in Table 7.5. Notice that the largest associations are detected between tinned meat and tunny, tinned meat and mozzarella, and frozen fish and frozen vegetables. In all these cases the two paired products are fast food products. Next comes an association between two drinks: Coke and beer. In general, all the associations in Table 7.5 appear fairly reasonable from a subject-matter viewpoint. In calculating the odds ratios, each pair of variables is considered independently from the remaining 18. It is possible to relate them to each other by drawing a graph whose nodes are the binary product variables. An edge is drawn between a pair of nodes if the corresponding odds ratio is significantly different from 1; in other words, if the confidence interval for the odds ratio does not contain the value 1. The resulting graph is not a conditional independence graph, like those in Section 5.6, but a marginal independence graph. Nevertheless, it may be useful in an exploratory stage.

It is difficult to visualise a graph with perhaps as many as 190 links. Therefore we will represent only positive associations with an odds ratio greater than 2 (i.e. those in Table 7.5). This reduces the number of links in the graph and Figure 7.1 shows what it looks like. Using Figure 7.1 we can group together products that are linked. Notice that five products appear isolated from the others, not (strongly) positively associated with anything: milk, biscuits, water, coffee and yoghurt. All other products are related, either directly or indirectly. It is possible to individuate at least three groups, by connecting links but also by

Table 7.5 The largest odds ratios between pairs of products and the corresponding confidence interval.

Product 1	Product 2	ODDS RATIO	Confidence	Interval
tin. meat	tunny	5.0681	3.9101	6.5689
tin. meat	mozzar	4.8847	2.9682	8.0386
froz. veg	froz. fish	3.3610	2.9521	3.8265
coke	beer	2.8121	2.6109	3.0289
brioches	juices	2.8094	2.6094	3.0248
juices	ice cream	2.5333	2.1018	3.0534
coke	ice cream	2.4455	2.0571	2.9071
tomato j.	pasta	2.3773	2.2446	2.5179
crackers	ice cream	2.2839	1.7061	3.0574
brioches	crackers	2.2833	2.0276	2.5713
tin. meat	rice	2.1433	1.4762	3.1120
rice	pasta	2.1129	1.9618	2.2756
brioches	ice cream	2.0211	1.7178	2.3781
crackers	juices	2.0486	1.7633	2.3800
froz. fish	mozzar	2.0785	1.4721	2.9347
oil	tomato j.	2.0713	1.8318	2.3420

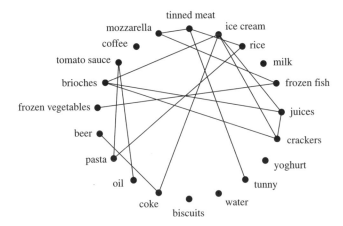

Figure 7.1 Graph showing the strong positive associations between the products.

logical relationships between products. These groups are very interesting because they identify fairly typical buying behaviours. There is one group with five nodes: tunny, tinned meat, mozzarella, frozen fish and frozen vegetables. These nodes, highly related with each other, correspond to fast food products, quick and easy to prepare. A second group contains four nodes: rice, pasta, tomato sauce and oil. This group can be identified with food bought for ordinary meals (ordinary by Mediterranean standards). A third group contains six other products: beer, Coke, juice, ice cream, brioches, crackers. All relate to break items, food and drink typically consumed outside of regular meals. This group seems less logically homogeneous than the other two. We shall return to this in the next section. We have not detected any significant negative association in the data at hand. This has important implications; for instance, a promotion on pasta will presumably increase the sales of this product but is very unlikely to decrease the sales of other products, such as rice and water. Negative associations are rarely considered in market basket analysis.

7.4   Model building

7.4.1   Log-linear models

Log-linear models are very useful for descriptive data mining; they investigate the associations between the considered variables. Fitting a log-linear model to all our 20 binary variables may require too many parameters to be estimated. Furthermore, the conditional independence graph may be difficult to interpret. Therefore, to be parsimonious and to satisfy computational restrictions, we will analyse the results in Figure 7.1 using an exploratory approach.

Figure 7.1 suggests the existence of five isolated nodes that can be deemed independent from the others: milk, biscuits, water, coffee and yoghurt. We will therefore try to fit a graphical log-linear model to the remaining 15 variables, in order to see whether the results from the exploratory analysis can be confirmed. Table 7.6 presents the maximum likelihood estimates of the parameters of the log-linear model with interactions up to order 2, fitted on the 15-way contingency table corresponding to the 15 considered variables.

Table 7.6 Maximum likelihood estimates of the log-linear parameters.

Parameter	Estimate	Standard Error	Chi-Square	Pr > ChiSq
TIN_MEAT	−1.6186	0.2206	53.85	<.0001
MOZZAR	−0.0100	0.1320	0.01	0.9396
TIN_MEAT*MOZZAR	0.6607	0.0660	100.31	<.0001
TUNNY	−0.3920	0.0635	38.07	<.0001
TIN_MEAT*TUNNY	0.3994	0.0344	134.72	<.0001
MOZZAR*TUNNY	0.1483	0.0290	26.17	<.0001
COKE	−0.1740	0.0750	5.38	0.0203
TIN_MEAT*COKE	0.2215	0.0501	19.58	<.0001
MOZZAR*COKE	0.0769	0.0326	5.58	0.0182
TUNNY*COKE	0.0592	0.0117	25.63	<.0001
CRACKERS	−0.2079	0.1228	2.87	0.0904
TIN_MEAT*CRACKERS	0.4715	0.0768	37.71	<.0001
MOZZAR*CRACKERS	0.1389	0.0616	5.08	0.0242
TUNNY*CRACKERS	0.1504	0.0188	63.80	<.0001

(continued overleaf)

Table 7.6   (*continued*)

Parameter	Estimate	Standard Error	Chi-Square	Pr > ChiSq
COKE*CRACKERS	0.1068	0.0199	28.68	<.0001
PASTA	−0.2935	0.0516	32.35	<.0001
TIN_MEAT*PASTA	0.0294	0.0346	0.72	0.3957
MOZZAR*PASTA	0.00751	0.0206	0.13	0.7156
TUNNY*PASTA	0.0872	0.00796	120.20	<.0001
COKE*PASTA	0.0267	0.00805	11.01	0.0009
CRACKERS*PASTA	0.0219	0.0144	2.30	0.1291
JUICES	−0.3191	0.0807	15.62	<.0001
TIN_MEAT*JUICES	0.2942	0.0543	29.32	<.0001
MOZZAR*JUICES	0.1089	0.0347	9.84	0.0017
TUNNY*JUICES	0.0879	0.0126	48.95	<.0001
COKE*JUICES	0.1238	0.0119	107.57	<.0001
CRACKERS*JUICES	0.1683	0.0200	70.84	<.0001
PASTA*JUICES	0.0304	0.00901	11.41	0.0007
OIL	0.0318	0.1195	0.07	0.7902
TIN_MEAT*OIL	0.4508	0.0770	34.28	<.0001
MOZZAR*OIL	0.1343	0.0569	5.57	0.0183
TUNNY*OIL	0.1219	0.0180	45.90	<.0001
COKE*OIL	0.0466	0.0204	5.20	0.0226
CRACKERS*OIL	0.1644	0.0361	20.76	<.0001
PASTA*OIL	0.0792	0.0131	36.54	<.0001
JUICES*OIL	0.0630	0.0230	7.52	0.0061
TOMATO_J	−0.1715	0.0712	5.80	0.0160
TIN_MEAT*TOMATO_J	0.2314	0.0469	24.34	<.0001
MOZZAR*TOMATO_J	0.1121	0.0284	15.62	<.0001
TUNNY*TOMATO_J	0.0605	0.0112	29.23	<.0001
COKE*TOMATO_J	0.0958	0.0108	78.92	<.0001
CRACKERS*TOMATO_J	0.0589	0.0211	7.77	0.0053
PASTA*TOMATO_J	0.1887	0.00747	637.43	<.0001
JUICES*TOMATO_J	0.0831	0.0122	46.54	<.0001
OIL*TOMATO_J	0.1780	0.0163	119.22	<.0001
BRIOCHES	−0.2412	0.0620	15.14	0.0001
TIN_MEAT*BRIOCHES	0.1530	0.0414	13.64	0.0002
MOZZAR*BRIOCHES	0.0955	0.0254	14.17	0.0002
TUNNY*BRIOCHES	0.0774	0.00995	60.57	<.0001
COKE*BRIOCHES	0.0965	0.00966	99.71	<.0001
CRACKERS*BRIOCHES	0.1860	0.0156	141.60	<.0001
PASTA*BRIOCHES	0.0343	0.00689	24.81	<.0001
JUICES*BRIOCHES	0.2342	0.00962	592.76	<.0001
OIL*BRIOCHES	0.0251	0.0176	2.02	0.1552
TOMATO_J*BRIOCHES	0.0608	0.00967	39.54	<.0001
BEER	−0.0287	0.0742	0.15	0.6987
TIN_MEAT*BEER	0.2098	0.0462	20.62	<.0001
MOZZAR*BEER	0.0700	0.0333	4.42	0.0356

Table 7.6 (*continued*)

Parameter	Estimate	Standard Error	Chi-Square	Pr > ChiSq
TUNNY*BEER	0.0864	0.0113	58.89	<.0001
COKE*BEER	0.2415	0.00965	626.64	<.0001
CRACKERS*BEER	0.0721	0.0210	11.76	0.0006
PASTA*BEER	0.00755	0.00802	0.89	0.3464
JUICES*BEER	0.1201	0.0119	102.14	<.0001
OIL*BEER	0.0805	0.0192	17.61	<.0001
TOMATO_J*BEER	0.0602	0.0111	29.56	<.0001
BRIOCHES*BEER	0.0621	0.00985	39.83	<.0001
FROZ_VEG	−0.2247	0.0704	10.18	0.0014
TIN_MEAT*FROZ_VEG	0.1938	0.0490	15.64	<.0001
MOZZAR*FROZ_VEG	0.1211	0.0276	19.25	<.0001
TUNNY*FROZ_VEG	0.0634	0.0114	31.14	<.0001
COKE*FROZ_VEG	0.0398	0.0116	11.75	0.0006
CRACKERS*FROZ_VEG	0.0630	0.0214	8.70	0.0032
PASTA*FROZ_VEG	0.0381	0.00773	24.30	<.0001
JUICES*FROZ_VEG	0.0496	0.0129	14.76	0.0001
OIL*FROZ_VEG	0.0720	0.0188	14.59	0.0001
TOMATO_J*FROZ_VEG	0.0847	0.0106	63.29	<.0001
BRIOCHES*FROZ_VEG	0.0406	0.00993	16.75	<.0001
BEER*FROZ_VEG	0.0224	0.0118	3.61	0.0575
RICE	−0.2743	0.0840	10.67	0.0011
TIN_MEAT*RICE	0.2987	0.0514	33.83	<.0001
MOZZAR*RICE	0.1887	0.0355	28.34	<.0001
TUNNY*RICE	0.1460	0.0131	124.67	<.0001
COKE*RICE	0.0626	0.0149	17.65	<.0001
CRACKERS*RICE	0.1909	0.0235	65.96	<.0001
PASTA*RICE	0.1481	0.00975	231.01	<.0001
JUICES*RICE	0.1024	0.0155	43.40	<.0001
OIL*RICE	0.1225	0.0237	26.75	<.0001
TOMATO_J*RICE	0.1090	0.0129	70.90	<.0001
BRIOCHES*RICE	0.0228	0.0128	3.15	0.0759
BEER*RICE	0.0362	0.0151	5.74	0.0166
FROZ_VEG*RICE	0.0949	0.0136	49.02	<.0001
F_FISH	−0.0494	0.1337	0.14	0.7119
TIN_MEAT*F_FISH	0.4792	0.0894	28.74	<.0001
MOZZAR*F_FISH	0.2417	0.0527	21.04	<.0001
TUNNY*F_FISH	0.1034	0.0224	21.40	<.0001
COKE*F_FISH	0.0504	0.0258	3.82	0.0507
CRACKERS*F_FISH	0.1047	0.0494	4.48	0.0342
PASTA*F_FISH	0.0536	0.0156	11.78	0.0006
JUICES*F_FISH	0.1032	0.0274	14.22	0.0002
OIL*F_FISH	0.1232	0.0419	8.66	0.0033
TOMATO_J*F_FISH	0.0750	0.0221	11.49	0.0007
BRIOCHES*F_FISH	0.0545	0.0207	6.92	0.0085

(*continued overleaf*)

Table 7.6   (*continued*)

Parameter	Estimate	Standard Error	Chi-Square	Pr > ChiSq
BEER*F_FISH	0.0735	0.0243	9.16	0.0025
FROZ_VEG*F_FISH	0.2954	0.0169	305.75	<.0001
RICE*F_FISH	0.1711	0.0262	42.64	<.0001
ICECREAM	−0.4074	0.1882	4.68	0.0304
TIN_MEAT*ICECREAM	0.6214	0.1579	15.49	<.0001
MOZZAR*ICECREAM	0.1597	0.0828	3.73	0.0536
TUNNY*ICECREAM	0.1106	0.0293	14.28	0.0002
COKE*ICECREAM	0.2095	0.0235	79.35	<.0001
CRACKERS*ICECREAM	0.2912	0.0417	48.72	<.0001
PASTA*ICECREAM	−0.00983	0.0200	0.24	0.6233
JUICES*ICECREAM	0.2335	0.0255	83.69	<.0001
OIL*ICECREAM	0.1632	0.0534	9.33	0.0023
TOMATO_J*ICECREAM	0.0961	0.0286	11.31	0.0008
BRIOCHES*ICECREAM	0.1393	0.0220	40.05	<.0001
BEER*ICECREAM	0.1133	0.0278	16.57	<.0001
FROZ_VEG*ICECREAM	0.2202	0.0240	84.07	<.0001
RICE*ICECREAM	0.1967	0.0347	32.13	<.0001
F_FISH*ICECREAM	0.1872	0.0560	11.18	0.0008

The results to Table 7.6 are obtained using the SAS procedure CATMOD. To compare Table 7.6 with Table 7.5, recall that the odds ratio between each pair of parameters can be obtained by exponentiating a value which is about four times the estimated interaction parameter. Therefore the threshold odds ratio of 2, adopted in Table 7.5 corresponds to a threshold value of the interaction parameter equal to about 0.1732. We can thus select the interactions that pass this threshold and consider the corresponding pair as being (strongly) positively associated.

From Table 7.6 it turns out that all interactions found in Table 7.5 remain strongly significant, except for (rice, pasta), (brioches, ice cream) and (crackers, juices), which have an estimated odds ratio slightly lower than 2. Furthermore, there are 14 more (strongly) positive associations: 9 of them concern tinned meat associated with Coke, crackers, juices, oil, tomato, beer, frozen vegetables, frozen fish and ice cream; 3 of them concern ice cream associated with frozen vegetables, rice, and frozen fish; the final 2 are (mozzarella, rice) and (crackers, rice). The difference with Table 7.5 is that we have now taken into account conditional dependences between the variables, and as all variables are positively associated, more interactions have been found significant. Table 7.6 reveals, that no significant negative interactions are found.

7.4.2   Association rules

The most common way to analyse of market basket data is to use association rules, a local data mining method explained in Section 4.8. We begin with a simple setting. Consider the products ice cream and Coke. As order is not relevant, to study the association between the two products, the data set can be collapsed to the two-way contingency table in Table 7.4. This shows that the support for the rule 'if ice cream, then Coke' is

$$\text{support (ice cream} \longrightarrow \text{Coke)} = \frac{170}{46\,727} = 0.0036$$

indicating low support for the rule. This means these two products are bought together only occasionally. The support corresponds to only one of the four joint frequencies in Table 7.4, corresponding to the occurrence of both buying events. A support of 0.0036 means that only 0.36% of the transactions considered will have both ice cream and Coke in the basket. The support of an association rule is symmetric; the support of the rule 'if Coke, then ice cream' would be the same.

The confidence of a rule, even when calculated for an association, where order does not matter, depends on the body and head of the rule:

$$\text{confidence (ice cream} \longrightarrow \text{Coke)} = \frac{170}{769} = 0.22$$

which corresponds to the second row conditional frequency of Coke $= 1$, and

$$\text{confidence (Coke} \longrightarrow \text{ice cream)} = \frac{170}{4949} = 0.034$$

which corresponds to the second column conditional frequency of ice cream $= 1$. The confidence is really a particular conditional frequency. In the first case it indicates the proportion, among those that buy ice cream, of those that also buy Coke. In the second case it indicates the proportion, among those that buy Coke, of those that also buy ice cream. The lift is a normalised measure of interestingness; it is also symmetric:

$$\text{lift (ice cream} \longrightarrow \text{Coke)} = \frac{0.22}{0.11} = 2$$

$$\text{lift (Coke} \longrightarrow \text{ice cream)} = \frac{0.034}{0.017} = 2$$

This is always the case, as can be seen from the formula in Section 4.8. Section 4.8 goes on to derive an asymptotic confidence interval for the lift. Here the asymptotic confidence interval goes from 1.17 to 3.40, so the association can be considered significant.

Notice that the odds ratio between the two products was calculated as 2.44, a rather similar value (and also with a significant confidence interval). The main difference is that the odds ratio depends explicitly on all four cell frequencies of a contingency table, whereas the lift is the ratio between the frequency of the levels $(A = 1, B = 1)$ and the product of the two marginal frequencies, $(A = 1)$ and

($B = 1$), so it depends only implicitly on the frequencies of the complementary events ($A = 0$, $B = 0$).

In any case the support of the considered rule is rather limited – ice cream and Coke are present in only 0.36% of all transactions – therefore conclusions based on it may not be of much practical value, even when supported by a high confidence and/or a high lift value. But this conclusion is relative; it depends on the support of other rules. To discover this and obtain a more comprehensive picture of the interesting association rules, we now move to a full application of association rule modelling. The Apriori algorithm and a threshold support rule of 0.05*support(mode), where mode is the rule with maximum support among all rules of a fixed order, leads to the selection of several relevant rules.

Table 7.7 presents the order 2 association rules with the highest support out of the 190 possible rules. For each rule it shows the lift, the support and the confidence as well as the transaction count, which is the absolute frequency of the rule. It turns out that the (ice cream, Coke) rule does not appear among the most frequent. Other rules have a higher support, and the rule with the highest support is milk $\rightarrow$ pasta, which appears in almost 50% of the transactions. This is followed by biscuits $\rightarrow$ pasta, milk $\rightarrow$ biscuits, water $\rightarrow$ pasta and milk $\rightarrow$ water, all occurring in about 39% of the transactions.

Table 7.7 Association rules with highest support.

	Relations	Lift	Support(%)	Confidence(%)	Transaction Count	Rule
1	2	1.13	49.84	75.86	3359.0	milk ==> pasta
2	2	1.13	49.84	73.97	3359.0	pasta ==> milk
3	2	1.18	39.90	79.77	2689.0	biscuits ==> pasta
4	2	1.18	39.90	59.22	2689.0	pasta ==> biscuits
5	2	1.21	39.86	60.66	2686.0	milk ==> biscuits
6	2	1.21	39.86	79.68	2686.0	biscuits ==> milk
7	2	1.15	39.72	77.55	2677.0	water ==> pasta
8	2	1.15	39.72	58.95	2677.0	pasta ==> water
9	2	1.18	39.69	60.41	2675.0	milk ==> water
10	2	1.18	39.69	77.49	2675.0	water ==> milk
11	2	1.23	33.21	82.80	2238.0	coffee ==> pasta
12	2	1.23	33.21	49.28	2238.0	pasta ==> coffee
13	2	1.24	32.71	81.54	2204.0	coffee ==> milk
14	2	1.24	32.71	49.77	2204.0	milk ==> coffee
15	2	1.19	31.96	47.43	2154.0	pasta ==> brioches
16	2	1.19	31.96	80.37	2154.0	brioches ==> pasta
17	2	1.24	31.84	63.66	2146.0	biscuits ==> water
18	2	1.24	31.84	62.17	2146.0	water ==> biscuits
19	2	1.19	31.09	78.17	2095.0	brioches ==> milk
20	2	1.19	31.09	47.31	2095.0	milk ==> brioches
21	2	1.25	30.92	83.90	2084.0	frozen vegetables ==> pasta
22	2	1.25	30.92	45.89	2084.0	pasta ==> frozen vegetables
23	2	1.26	30.92	45.89	2084.0	pasta ==> tunny
24	2	1.26	30.92	84.58	2084.0	tunny ==> pasta
25	2	1.22	29.72	45.23	2003.0	milk ==> yoghurt
26	2	1.22	29.72	80.34	2003.0	yoghurt ==> milk
27	2	1.22	29.57	80.23	1993.0	frozen vegetables ==> milk
28	2	1.22	29.57	45.01	1993.0	milk ==> frozen vegetables

Table 7.8 Association rules with highest confidence.

	Relations	Lift	Support(%)	Confidence(%)	Transaction Count	Rule
1	2	1.34	24.38	90.18	1643.0	rice ==> pasta
2	2	1.32	2.34	89.27	158.00	tinned meat ==> pasta
3	2	1.32	25.86	89.02	1743.0	tomato souce ==> pasta
4	2	1.30	9.88	87.75	666.00	frozen fish ==> pasta
5	2	1.27	9.85	85.68	664.00	oil ==> pasta
6	2	1.26	5.46	85.19	368.00	mozzarella ==> pasta
7	2	1.29	5.61	84.94	378.00	ice cream ==> milk
8	2	1.29	9.56	84.85	644.00	frozen fish ==> milk
9	2	1.26	30.92	84.58	2084.0	tunny ==> pasta
10	2	1.25	11.95	84.12	805.00	crackers ==> pasta
11	2	1.28	11.92	83.91	803.00	crackers ==> milk
12	2	1.25	30.92	83.90	2084.0	frozen vegetables ==> pasta
13	2	1.27	5.36	83.56	361.00	mozzarella ==> milk
14	2	1.23	20.74	83.16	1398.0	juices ==> pasta
15	2	1.23	33.21	82.80	2238.0	coffee ==> pasta
16	2	1.23	5.46	82.70	368.00	ice cream ==> pasta
17	2	1.23	23.10	82.69	1557.0	coke ==> pasta
18	2	1.26	20.58	82.51	1387.0	juices ==> milk
19	2	1.26	22.30	82.49	1503.0	rice ==> milk
20	2	1.25	23.80	81.92	1604.0	tomato souce ==> milk
21	2	1.24	32.71	81.54	2204.0	coffee ==> milk
22	2	1.20	23.67	80.96	1595.0	beer ==> pasta
23	2	1.19	31.96	80.37	2154.0	brioches ==> pasta
24	2	1.22	29.72	80.34	2003.0	yoghurt ==> milk
25	2	1.22	22.44	80.30	1512.0	coke ==> milk
26	2	1.22	29.57	80.23	1993.0	frozen vegetables ==> milk
27	2	1.18	39.90	79.77	2689.0	biscuits ==> pasta
28	2	1.21	39.86	79.68	2686.0	biscuits ==> milk

As Table 7.7 contains the rules with the highest support and as support is symmetric, it is obvious that reciprocal rules are always adjacent to each other. Table 7.8 presents the order 2 association rules with the highest confidence out of the 190 possible rules. From Table 7.8 we can see, for example, that rice → pasta has a confidence equal to 90.18. This means that if a transaction contains rice, it will also contain pasta about 90% of the time. On the other hand, pasta → rice is not among the rules in Table 7.8; it has a confidence of 36.18. This can be interpreted as saying that if a transaction contains pasta, it will also contain rice only 36.18% of the time. Notice that the confidence of pasta → rice can be obtained by multiplying the confidence of rice → pasta by a factor of 0.401, which corresponds to the ratio between the number of transactions containing rice (1822) and the number of transactions containing pasta (4541), as obtained from Table 7.1. More generally, notice that in Table 7.8 the head of the rule is always either pasta or milk, as these are the most supported products.

Finally, to obtain a relative measure of a rule's interestingness, we can also consider the lift. Table 7.9 reports the rules with the highest lift out of the 190 possible rules. Notice that frozen fish → mozzarella and ice cream → crackers come first, both with a lift of about 2.36. And notice that Coke → ice cream is well ranked. Table 7.9 can be usefully compared with the odds ratios in Table 7.5,

Table 7.9 Association rules with highest lift.

	Relations	Lift	Support(%)	Confidence(%)	Transaction Count	Rule
1	2	2.36	1.71	15.15	115.00	frozen fish ==> mozzarella
2	2	2.36	1.71	26.62	115.00	mozzarella ==> frozen fish
3	2	2.36	2.21	33.48	149.00	ice cream ==> crackers
4	2	2.36	2.21	15.57	149.00	crackers ==> ice cream
5	2	2.17	1.62	14.36	109.00	frozen fish ==> ice cream
6	2	2.17	1.62	24.49	109.00	ice cream ==> frozen fish
7	2	1.98	3.65	55.28	246.00	ice cream ==> coke
8	2	1.98	3.65	13.06	246.00	coke ==> ice cream
9	2	1.98	1.90	72.32	128.00	tinned meat ==> tunny
10	2	1.96	1.39	53.11	94.00	tinned meat ==> rice
11	2	1.91	7.91	70.22	533.00	frozen fish ==> frozen vegetables
12	2	1.91	7.91	21.46	533.00	frozen vegetables ==> frozen fish
13	2	1.86	3.07	12.31	207.00	juices ==> ice cream
14	2	1.86	3.07	46.52	207.00	ice cream ==> juices
15	2	1.86	2.40	21.34	162.00	frozen fish ==> oil
16	2	1.86	2.40	20.90	162.00	oil ==> frozen fish
17	2	1.84	2.94	20.69	198.00	crackers ==> frozen fish
18	2	1.84	2.94	26.09	198.00	frozen fish ==> crackers
19	2	1.83	1.35	11.74	91.00	oil ==> mozzarella
20	2	1.83	1.35	21.06	91.00	mozzarella ==> oil
21	2	1.82	6.08	20.94	410.00	tomato souce ==> oil
22	2	1.82	6.08	52.90	410.00	oil ==> tomato souce
23	2	1.82	6.44	25.82	434.00	juices ==> crackers
24	2	1.82	6.44	45.35	434.00	crackers ==> juices
25	2	1.82	1.38	12.00	93.00	oil ==> ice cream
26	2	1.82	1.38	20.90	93.00	ice cream ==> oil
27	2	1.80	7.12	25.49	480.00	coke ==> crackers
28	2	1.80	7.12	50.16	480.00	crackers ==> coke

which were used to build the exploratory graph in Figure 7.1. It turns out that similar products appear in both tables, except for pasta, which appears only in the odds ratios table. However, the pairs are sometimes different. Isolated products in Figure 7.1 – milk, biscuits, water, coffee and yoghurt – have a high support but a low lift, therefore they do not appear in Table 7.9. The rules we obtain depend on the measure of interestingness that we choose. It is interesting to consider the rules jointly in terms of support, confidence and lift.

Figure 7.2 is a graphical representation of the rules with the highest support (i.e. the 28 rules in Table 7.7). Support decreases with distance up the vertical axis; confidence decreases with distance along the horizontal axis. The larger the volume of the geometric figure, the greater the lift. Figure 7.2 is a valuable joint visualisation of the rules that need to be selected. For instance, we can see that pasta → milk has the highest confidence of all the rules that have pasta in their body, but it has a low value of lift.

Now consider associations between more than two products. Table 7.10 shows the associations with the highest support, for associations up to order 4.

Notice that some order 2 associations in Table 7.7 are also present in Table 7.10. There are also some order 3 associations, typically for break items and for combinations of isolated products such as pasta, milk and biscuits. Table 7.11 shows similar results, this time ordered by confidence.

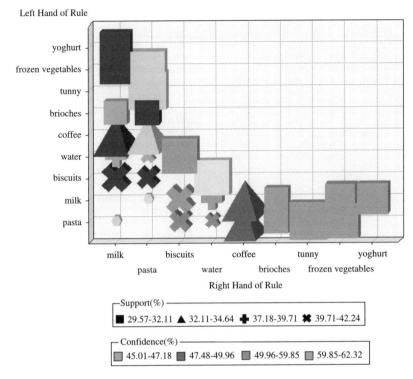

Figure 7.2 Graphical representation of association rules, based on support, confidence and lift.

Notice that the confidences values are now rather high. For instance, if a transaction contains tomato sauce, oil and crackers, it will certainly contain pasta as well, as the confidence is equal to 100%. However, the support of this rule is only 1.41%. As in table 7.8, milk and pasta are the only heads selected. Unlike Table 7.10, there are no order 2 associations.

Next we try a methodology based on tree models (Section 4.8). We have chosen pasta, the most frequent product and the most frequent head of the rule in the associations. We have built a tree model having pasta as target variable and all the other products as predictors. Among the different paths leading to the terminal nodes, we consider those paths where all variables in the path have the value 1. These paths corresponds to rules with high confidence. Using a CHAID tree (CART gives similar results), we obtain the following rules:

tunny & tomato sauce → pasta
tomato sauce & rice → pasta
rice & biscuits → pasta

Table 7.10 Higher-order association rules ordered in terms of support.

	Relations	Lift	Support(%)	Confidence(%)	Transaction Count	Rule
1	2	1.13	49.84	73.97	3359.0	pasta ==> milk
2	2	1.13	49.84	75.86	3359.0	milk ==> pasta
3	2	1.18	39.90	59.22	2689.0	pasta ==> biscuits
4	2	1.18	39.90	79.77	2689.0	biscuits ==> pasta
5	2	1.21	39.86	79.68	2686.0	biscuits ==> milk
6	2	1.21	39.86	60.66	2686.0	milk ==> biscuits
7	2	1.15	39.72	77.55	2677.0	water ==> pasta
8	2	1.15	39.72	58.95	2677.0	pasta ==> water
9	2	1.18	39.69	60.41	2675.0	milk ==> water
10	2	1.18	39.69	77.49	2675.0	water ==> milk
11	3	1.36	33.94	68.09	2287.0	pasta & milk ==> biscuits
12	3	1.26	33.94	50.36	2287.0	pasta ==> milk & biscuits
13	3	1.29	33.94	51.65	2287.0	milk ==> pasta & biscuits
14	3	1.26	33.94	85.15	2287.0	milk & biscuits ==> pasta
15	3	1.36	33.94	67.84	2287.0	biscuits ==> pasta & milk
16	3	1.29	33.94	85.05	2287.0	pasta & biscuits ==> milk
17	3	1.25	33.51	84.41	2258.0	water & milk ==> pasta
18	3	1.31	33.51	65.41	2258.0	water ==> pasta & milk
19	3	1.28	33.51	50.99	2258.0	milk ==> water & pasta
20	3	1.31	33.51	67.22	2258.0	pasta & milk ==> water
21	3	1.25	33.51	49.72	2258.0	pasta ==> water & milk
22	3	1.28	33.51	84.35	2258.0	water & pasta ==> milk
23	2	1.23	33.21	82.80	2238.0	coffee ==> pasta
24	2	1.23	33.21	49.28	2238.0	pasta ==> coffee
25	2	1.24	32.71	81.54	2204.0	coffee ==> milk
26	2	1.24	32.71	49.77	2204.0	milk ==> coffee
27	2	1.19	31.96	47.43	2154.0	pasta ==> brioches
28	2	1.19	31.96	80.37	2154.0	brioches ==> pasta

and their respective measures of interestingness:

lift 1.41, confidence 95.24%, support 14.84%
lift 1.44, confidence 96.80%, support 12.14%
lift 1.40, confidence 94.23%, support 18.43%

Notice that all three rules, have a high confidence. This is to be expected, as a tree model tries to develop the best predictive rules for the target variable.

7.5 Model comparison

It is quite difficult to assess local models such as association rules, simply because a global measure of evaluation conflicts with the local nature of the model. Furthermore, as the idea of searching for local patterns and rules is very recent, there is little consensus in the data mining literature on how to measure their performance (Hand, Mannila and Smyth, 2001). A natural idea is to measure the utility of patterns in terms of how interesting or unexpected they are to the analyst. As it is quite difficult to model an analyst's opinion, we usually assume a situation of completely uninformed opinion. The measures of interestingness for

Table 7.11 Higher-order association rules ordered in terms of confidence.

	Relations	Lift	Support(%)	Confidence(%)	Transaction Count	Rule
1	4	1.48	2.66	100.00	179.00	oil & juices & frozen vegetables ==> pasta
2	4	1.48	1.41	100.00	95.00	tomato souce & oil & crackers ==> pasta
3	4	1.48	3.29	99.55	222.00	tomato souce & rice & oil ==> pasta
4	4	1.48	3.22	99.54	217.00	rice & crackers & beer ==> pasta
5	4	1.48	3.10	99.52	209.00	rice & oil & brioches ==> pasta
6	4	1.48	3.03	99.51	204.00	yoghurt & rice & oil ==> pasta
7	4	1.48	2.79	99.47	188.00	rice & oil & beer ==> pasta
8	4	1.47	2.15	99.32	145.00	frozen fish & crackers & brioches ==> pasta
9	4	1.47	2.08	99.29	140.00	yoghurt & tomato souce & mozzarella ==> pasta
10	4	1.51	1.87	99.21	126.00	yoghurt & mozzarella & juices ==> milk
11	4	1.47	1.72	99.15	116.00	rice & frozen fish & crackers ==> pasta
12	4	1.47	1.66	99.12	112.00	tomato souce & frozen fish & crackers ==> pasta
13	4	1.47	1.65	99.11	111.00	juices & frozen fish & crackers ==> pasta
14	4	1.47	1.63	99.10	110.00	frozen fish & crackers & coke ==> pasta
15	4	1.47	1.51	99.03	102.00	oil & frozen fish & brioches ==> pasta
16	4	1.47	1.42	98.97	96.00	rice & oil & crackers ==> pasta
17	4	1.47	1.41	98.96	95.00	rice & oil & frozen fish ==> pasta
18	4	1.47	4.21	98.95	284.00	tunny & tomato souce & crackers ==> pasta
19	4	1.47	2.58	98.86	174.00	rice & oil & coke ==> pasta
20	4	1.47	3.68	98.80	248.00	tomato souce & crackers & coke ==> pasta
21	4	1.47	2.34	98.75	158.00	frozen fish & crackers & biscuits ==> pasta
22	4	1.47	2.31	98.73	156.00	rice & oil & juices ==> pasta
23	4	1.46	2.21	98.68	149.00	tomato souce & mozzarella & frozen vegetables ==> pasta
24	4	1.46	6.62	98.67	446.00	yoghurt & rice & juices ==> pasta
25	4	1.46	3.22	98.64	217.00	oil & frozen vegetables & coke ==> pasta
26	4	1.46	2.11	98.61	142.00	tomato souce & mozzarella & coffee ==> pasta
27	4	1.50	2.11	98.61	142.00	mozzarella & juices & biscuits ==> milk
28	4	1.46	2.09	98.60	141.00	tunny & frozen fish & crackers ==> pasta

a rule (Section 4.8), can then be used to assess performance. In this case study we have considered support, confidence and lift as the main measures for validating a set of association rules. But the needs of the user will govern which of these three is the best one for selecting a set of rules. The support can be used to assess the importance of a rule in terms of its frequency in the database; the confidence can be used to investigate possible dependences between variables; and the lift can be used to measure the distance from the situation of independence.

Ultimately, a set of rules has to be assessed on its ability to meet the analysis objectives. Here the objectives are primarily to reorganise the layout of a sales outlet and to plan promotions so as to increase revenues. Once the associations have been identified, it is possible to organise promotions within the outlet so the products that are put on offer at the same time are products which are not associated. Correspondingly, by putting one product on promotion, we also increase the sales of the associated products.

At the beginning of the chapter we saw that odds ratios and log-linear models can also be employed to determine a global association structure between the buying variables; in this case traditional statistical measures, such as G^2, or AIC and BIC, can be employed to assess the overall quality of a model. Although they have a different purpose, classification trees can also be seen as a global model capable of producing an association structure. Although association rules are much easier to detect and interpret, I believe that good global modelling, as expressed by log-linear and tree models, allows more stable and coherent conclusions. With enough time and sufficient knowledge to implement a global model, I think this approach should be preferred.

7.6 Summary report

- *Context*: this case study concerns the understanding of associations between buying behaviours. A similar kind of analysis can be applied to problems in which the main objective is cross-selling to increase the number of products that are bought in a given commercial unit (a supermarket, a bank, a travel agency, or more generally, a company offering more than one product or services). A related class of problems arise in promotional campaigns: it is desirable to put on promotion the fewest possible number of products but to derive any benefits on the largest possible number of products. This is achieved by an efficient layout of the products, putting together those that are most associated with each other.
- *Objectives*: the aim of the analysis is to track the most important buying patterns, where a pattern means a group of products bought together. The chosen measure of importance determines the results of the analysis. The most common measures refer to the occurrence probability of a certain sequence (support) or to the conditional probability of buying a certain product, having bought others (confidence). There are strong analogies with the class of problems that can be analysed using the methods in Chapter 8. The crucial difference is that here we are not interested in the order in which the products are bought.
- *Organisation of the data*: data is extracted from a large database containing all commercial transactions in a supermarket in a given amount of time. The transactions are made by someone holding one of the chain's loyalty cards. Although data is structured in a transactional database, it can be simplified into a data matrix format, with rows identifying clients and columns associated with binary variables describing whether or not each product has been bought. After some simplification the data matrix contains 46 727 rows and 20 columns
- *Exploratory data analysis*: exploratory data analysis was performed by looking at all pairwise odds ratios between the 20 products, for a total of 190 association measures. The results can be visualised graphically and already give important suggestions for the analysis objectives.
- *Model specification*: we compared association rules, originally devised for market basket analysis problems, with more structured log-linear models, the most important symmetric statistical models for analysing contingency table data.
- *Model comparison*: it is rather difficult to compare association rules, which are local, with log-linear models, which are global. The most effective measure of comparison has to be the practical utility of a rule; this can be measured in terms of cross-selling or by using the efficacy of a promotional campaign.

- *Model interpretation*: association rules seem to be easier to understand than the results from log-linear models, but it depends on how the results are presented. Results from a log-linear model can be expressed graphically, using dependences and odds ratios, and these measures can be understood. The advantage of log-linear models is that they are based on inferential statements and, can therefore provide confidence intervals for an association statement or a threshold able to 'filter' out relevant rules from the many possible rules and in a coherent way.

CHAPTER 8

Web clickstream analysis

8.1 Objectives of the analysis

This case study considers how visitor behaviour on a website can be predicted by analysing existing data on the order in which the site's webpages are visited. Whenever a user links to a website, the server keeps track of all their actions in a log file. What is captured is the click flow, or clickstream, of the mouse and the keys the user employs to navigate the website. Usually every click of the mouse corresponds to the viewing of a webpage, therefore we can define the clickstream as the sequence of webpages requested. A user session describes the succession of webpages seen by one user during one period logged on to the web. This may contain pages from more than one site. A server session, or session, is the set of pages for one particular site during the user session. Collectively these pages are often known as a visit.

The objective of the analysis is to show how web clickstream data can be used to understand the most likely navigation paths in a website, with the aim of predicting, possibly online, which pages a visitor will view, given the path they have taken so far. This can be very useful in finding the probability that a visitor will view a certain page, perhaps a buying page in an e-commerce site. It can also find the probability of entering (or exiting) the website from any particular page. Note that since most pages are now dynamically generated, the idea of viewing a particular page may need to be replaced with the idea of viewing a particular class of page, or type of page; a class could be defined by meta information in the header.

8.2 Description of the data

The data set comes from the log file for an e-commerce site. The source of the data cannot be specified, but it is the website of a company that sells hardware and software products; it will be known as a webshop. The accesses to the website were registered in a log file for a period of about two years, 30 September 1997 to 30 June 1999. The log file was then processed to produce a data set called sequences. This data set contains the userid (c_value), a variable with the date and the instant the visitor has linked to a specific page (c_time) and the

Applied Data Mining. Paolo Giudici
© 2003 John Wiley & Sons, Ltd   ISBNs: 0-470-84679-8 (Paper); 0-470-84678-X (Cloth)

Table 8.1 The considered data set.

c_value	c_time	c_caller
70ee683a6df...	14OCT97:11:09:01	home
70ee683a6df...	14OCT97:11:09:08	catalog
70ee683a6df...	14OCT97:11:09:14	program
70ee683a6df...	14OCT97:11:09:23	product
70ee683a6df...	14OCT97:11:09:24	program

webpage seen (c_caller). Table 8.1 reports a small extract of the available data set, corresponding to one visit. Table 8.1 shows that the visitor corresponding to the identifier (cookie) 70ee683a6df... entered the site on 14 October 1997 at 11:09:01 and visited, in sequence, the pages home, catalog, program, product, program, leaving the website at 11:09:24.

The whole data set contains 250 711 observations, each corresponding to a click, that describe the navigation paths of 22 527 visitors among the 36 pages which compose the site of the webshop. The visitors are taken as unique; that is, no visitors appears with more than one session. But a page can occur more than once in the same session. This data set is an example of a transaction dataset. However, unlike the market basket data in Chapter 7, the order in which the pages are seen is important, and it may be the very objective of the analysis to understand the patterns that produce it. The data set can be used directly in a form like Table 8.1, with as many rows as the number of total clicks, to determine association and sequence rules. Alternatively, we can use a derived data set called visitors. It is organised by sessions and contains variables that can characterise each of these sessions. The variables include important quantitative variables, such as the total duration of the server session (length), the total number of clicks made in a session (clicks), and the time at which the session starts (start, setting 0 as midnight of the preceding day). More importantly for our analysis, this data set contains binary variables that describe whether each page is visited at least once (level 1) or not (level 0). Table 8.2 shows an extract from visitors that corresponds to the session in Table 8.1.

The rows in Table 8.1 correspond to clicks, but the rows in Table 8.2 correspond to sessions (or, equivalently, visitors, as they are unique). There are as many rows as the total number of visits to the website. In particular, looking at the last five columns, we obtain a binary data matrix that expresses which pages, among the 36 considered, have been visited at least once in each session. Other binary variables, derived from the original 36, can be inserted in visitors; for instance, it is of interest for e-commerce to insert a variable Purchase

Table 8.2 The derived data set.

c_value	c_time	length	clicks	time	home	catalog	addcart	program	product
70ee683a6df...	14OCT97:11:09:01	24	5	11:09:01	1	1	0	1	1

that indicates whether the session has led to at least one commercial transaction. However, in this case study we will be mainly concerned with understanding the navigation patterns, so we will mainly consider the 36 binary variables describing the available webpages. To give an idea of the types of page, here are some of the most common ones:

- Home: the homepage of the website.
- Login: where a user has to enter their name and other personal information, during the first registration, to access certain services and products reserved for customers.
- Logpost: prompts a message that informs whether the login has been successful or whether it has failed.
- Logout: where the user can leave the personal characterisation given in the login page.
- Register: to be recognised later on, the visitor has to obtain a userid and password.
- Regpost: shows the partial results of the registration, asking for missing information.
- Results: once the registration is accomplished, this page summarises the information given.
- Regform1: here the visitor has to insert data that enables them to buy a product; the data could be a personal identification number.
- Regform2: here the visitor has to subscribe to a contract in which they accept the conditions for online commerce.
- Help: it answers questions that may arise during navigation through the website.
- Fdback: a page that allows the user to go back to the previous page they have visited.
- Fdpost: a page that allows the user to go back to a previously viewed page in determined areas of the site.
- News: presents the most up-to-date products.
- Shelf: contains a list of the programs that can be downloaded from the website.
- Program: gives detailed information about the software programs that can be bought.
- Promo: demonstrates the features of a program.
- Download: allows the user to download software programs of interest.
- Catalog: contains a complete list of products on sale in the website.
- Product: shows detailed information on each product that can be purchased.
- P_info: sets out the payment terms for purchasing products on the website.
- Addcart: where the virtual basket can be filled with items to be purchased.
- Cart: shows the current status of the basket, i.e. the items it contains.
- Mdfycart: allows the user to modify the current content of the basket, perhaps by removing an item.
- Charge: indicates the required payment to buy the items contained in the basket.

- Pay_req: displays the amount final amount to pay for the products in the basket.
- Pay_res: here the visitor agrees to pay, and payment data is inserted (e.g. credit card number).
- Freeze: where the requested payment can be suspended, perhaps to add new products to the basket.

The data set in this chapter has also been analysed by Blanc and Giudici (2002) and Di Scala and La Rocca (2002).

8.3   Exploratory data analysis

Our main aim is to discover the most frequent sequence rules among the 36 binary variables describing whether any single page has been visited. To obtain valid conclusions, the considered data has to be homogeneous. To assess whether visitors (and, correspondingly, sequence) is homogeneous, we decide to do an exploratory analysis on it. The available quantitative variables, which are ancillary to the analysis, can be used in the exploratory phase. We now examine the univariate distributions of clicks, length and start.

Table 8.3 shows summary measures for clicks. It turns out that the mean number of clicks is 11. However, the mean is affected by the presence of extreme observations to the right of the distribution, as the mode and the median consist, respectively, of 5 and 8 clicks. In most of the cases more than 5 clicks (1% quantile) and less than 47 clicks (99% quantile) are seen. The maximum number of clicks is 192; this appears as an anomalous observation. To investigate this further, we consider the boxplot in Figure 8.1. The distribution is heavily skewed to the right, and the skewness coefficient in Table 8.3 is 4.7.

Table 8.4 shows summary statistics for length. Notice that this distribution behaves like the previous one – the mean is considerably higher than the mode

Table 8.3 Summary measures for click.

Mean	11,13	clicks
Mode	5	clicks
Minimum	1	click
Quantile 1%	5	clicks
First quartile	6	clicks
Median	8	clicks
Third quartile	13	clicks
Quantile 99%	47	clicks
Maximum	192	clicks
Skewness	4.7	
Kurtosis	40.8	

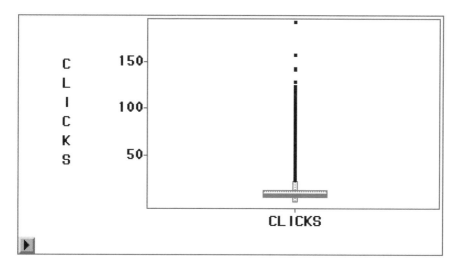

Figure 8.1 Boxplot of the variable `clicks`.

Table 8.4 Summary measures for `length`.

Mean	12.33	minutes
Mode	2.08	minutes
Minimum	0	seconds
Quantile 1%	45	seconds
First quartile	2.65	minutes
Median	5.12	minutes
Third quartile	11.4	minutes
Quantile 99%	108	minutes
Maximum	65.5	hours
Asymmetry	58.6	
Kurtosis	5666	

and the median. This reflects the fact that there may be anomalous observations (sessions). Indeed, as the 95% quantile is equal to 47.6 minutes, we have that 95% of the sessions terminate after 47.6 minutes and 99% after 1 hour and 48 minutes. Notice that the minimum time is 0 seconds; this must be an error in the log file or in the transcription of the data from the log file, so this observation can be safely eliminated as an outlier.

Table 8.5 shows summary statistics for `start`, which indicates the time when the website is first entered. The distribution appears skewed to the left. The mean and median starting time of connection are around 14:30, the beginning of the afternoon. Figure 8.2 shows the boxplot of the distribution, measuring time in

Table 8.5 Summary measures
for start.

Mean	14:30
Mode	9:49
Minimum	2:30
First quartile	11:11
Median	14:43
Third quartile	18:17
Quantile 99%	23:40
Maximum	23:59
Asymmetry	−0.49
Kurtosis	0.19

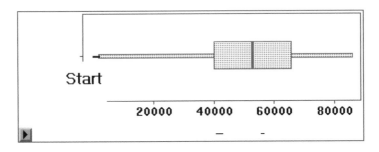

Figure 8.2 Boxplot of the variable start.

seconds. It shows a distribution that is indeed skewed to the left, but the skewness is reflected in a large bunch of observations in the left tail (night visitors) not in an asymmetric aspect of the central box (containing 75% of the observations).

On the basis of the previous results we decide to remove the outliers. From now on, for clarity, we will express start in hours and length in minutes. We eliminate all observations above the 99th percentile of the distributions for clicks and length, which behave in a similar way. But we do not remove the possible outliers for start. This is because of the nature of start and the appearance of the observed distribution. Furthermore, these extreme users may well be the most valuable customers. After removing the outliers, visitors contains 22 152 observations, instead of the initial 22 527.

We now consider a descriptive analysis of the 36 binary variables at hand, on the cleaned data set. The fourth column of Table 8.6 contains the relative frequency of visit (support) for each of the 28 most frequent pages. Furthermore, for e-commerce purposes, we have indicated the frequency distribution of the same variables, conditional on the values of purchase. The overall proportion of purchasers is 7.21%, therefore the third column can be obtained as a weighted average of the other two, with weights equal to 7.21% and 92.79%.

Table 8.6 Frequency distribution of the visits, and of the purchase.

	Frequency of visit		
	Purchase = 0	Purchase = 1	Frequency of visit
ADDCART	26.33%	99.56%	31.61%
AGB	5.12%	8.33%	5.35%
CART	15.67%	55.73%	18.56%
CATALOG	42.68%	68.13%	44.52%
CHARGE	0.06%	1.63%	0.17%
DOWNLOAD	3.96%	65.44%	8.40%
FDBACK	2.47%	1.88%	2.42%
FDPOST	0.78%	0.81%	0.79%
FREEZE	19.00%	99.94%	24.84%
HELP	8.49%	8.58%	8.50%
HOME	49.32%	40.89%	48.71%
LOGIN	40.18%	65.87%	42.03%
LOGOUT	1.90%	4.01%	2.05%
LOGPOST	30.42%	73.64%	33.53%
MDFYCART	3.46%	10.33%	3.96%
NEWS	9.60%	4.76%	9.25%
P_INFO	49.52%	32.50%	48.29%
PAY_REQ	10.45%	97.43%	16.73%
PAY_RES	5.05%	90.61%	11.22%
PRODUCT	83.69%	96.49%	84.62%
PROGRAM	76.81%	75.89%	76.74%
PROMO	0.27%	0.88%	0.32%
REGFORM1	1.24%	2.07%	1.30%
REGFORM2	1.28%	1.31%	1.29%
REGISTER	26.17%	35.94%	26.88%
REGPOST	16.79%	32.25%	17.91%
RESULT	4.15%	4.45%	4.18%
SHELF	15.90%	74.64%	20.13%

Table 8.7 Conditional means of the quantitative variables with respect to purchase.

Purchase	N. Obs.	Variable	Mean
0	20555	clicks	10
		length	9
		start	14
1	1597	clicks	17
		length	21
		start	14

The most visited pages are, in decreasing order, product (84.62%), program (76.74%), home (48.71%), p_info (48.29%) and catalog (48.71%). Although we are not interested here in studying the dependence of purchase on the other variables, we can draw interesting preliminary conclusions from Table 8.6. For instance, notice that, even if the 31.61% of visitors add at least one product to the virtual basket (addcart =1), the application of Bayes' rule (Section 5.1) shows that the percentage of them who actually purchases something is only equal to (99.56% × 7.21%)/31.61% = 22.61%. Further conclusions about purchase can be drawn by considering the mean values of the quantitative variables, conditional on the values of purchase. They are described in Table 8.7.

From Table 8.7 notice that the time of entering the website (start) is about the same, but the purchasers make, on average, more clicks (17 against 10) and stay longer in the site (21 minutes against 9 minutes) This could occur because purchasing might take a long time and require many clicks to confirm the order. Given the heterogeneous nature of the navigators, we decide to perform a cluster analysis, in order to find homogeneous clusters of behaviours. Our primary goal is not cluster analysis per se, so cluster analysis can be seen as preliminary to the local models we are seeking.

The clustering variables we consider are the three quantitative variables start, length and clicks, plus the binary variable purchase, all of them instrumental to our objective of understanding navigation patterns. We begin with a hierarchical method to find the number of groups and then try a non-hierarchical method to allocate observations into the determined number of groups. We use the Euclidean distance as our distance function and Ward's method (Section 4.2) as our hierarchical method, after some comparative experiments. To allocate observations we choose the K-means non-hierarchical method. From the hierarchical method, we obtain the number of clusters as 4. In fact, a further reduction in the number of clusters leads to a noticeable decrease in R^2 and an increase in SPRSQ. This can be seen in Figure 8.3, which plots R^2 and SPRSQ versus the number of groups in the hierarchical agglomerative algorithm.

We then apply the K-means algorithm to the data, with the number of clusters set to 4. Table 8.8 summarises the results; it shows the size of each cluster and the mean values of the four variables used in the classification. For purchase

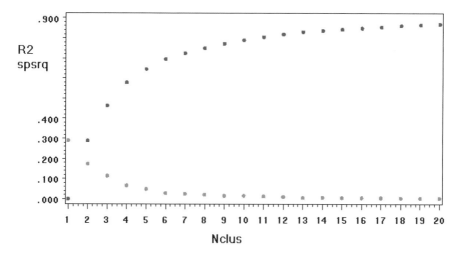

Figure 8.3 Behaviour of R^2 (increasing) and SPRSQ (decreasing).

Table 8.8 Results of the cluster analysis.

Cluster	N. obs.	Variables	Cluster mean	Overall mean
1	8802	clicks length start purchase	8 6 min 18 h 0.034	10 10 min 14 h 0.072
2	2859	clicks length start purchase	22 17 min 15 h 0.241	
3	1240	clicks length start purchase	18 59 min 13 h 0.194	
4	9251	clicks length start purchase	8 6 min 10 h 0.039	

the mean represents the proportion of actual purchases. Notice that there are two bigger groups, 1 and 4. From this final cluster allocation we have $R^2 = 59\%$, which indicates a good performance given the complexity of the data. To better understand the cluster configurations, the percentages of visits to the 36 webpages can be calculated separately for each cluster. There is not enough space to publish all the results, so here is a summary description of the mean profile of each cluster, obtained by interpreting the percentages and the conditional means in Table 8.8:

- *Cluster 1*: they connect in the late afternoon, at about 18; they visit about 2 pages (2 less than the overall mean); the length of the visit is about 6 minutes (4 less than the overall mean), and they purchase less than the mean (about 3.4% against 7.21%). They are particularly interested in the pages product (82% viewed) and program (75.74% viewed); the other pages are viewed in a proportion well below the overall mean.
- *Cluster 2*: they link up at about 15; they visit many pages (22, 12 more than the overall mean); they stay connected for a long time (17 minutes) and purchase much more than the others (24% against the overall 7.22%). Consequently, they are very interested in all pages related to purchase: product (95% viewed), addcart (63% viewed) and freeze (55% viewed). They are also frequent visitors, as the register page is visited less than the average (47%).
- *Cluster 3*: they link up at about 13; they visit many pages (18); they stay connected for a very long time (1 hour) and purchase more than the others (19% against the overall 7.22%). They seem to be very similar to the visitors in cluster 2 with respect to the visited pages, but they seem to be less frequent visitors and they stay connected for longer.
- *Cluster 4*: they link up at about 10, four hours before than the mean; they visit fewer pages (8); they stay connected as the overall population (10 minutes) and purchase little (only 3.9%) They are similar to the visitors in cluster 1, as they often visit product (83%) and program (75%). The difference between the two clusters seems to be in the starting time.

The results obtained from cluster analysis confirm heterogeneity of behaviours. To find navigation patterns, we decide to concentrate on only one cluster and we choose cluster 3. This choice is obviously subjective but it has two important features. First, the visitors in this cluster stay connected for a long time and visit many pages. This will help us explore the navigation sequences between the webpages. Second, this cluster has a high probability of purchase; it seems important to consider the typical navigation pattern for a group of high purchasers. We shall therefore consider a reduced data set, corresponding to cluster 3, with 1240 sessions and 21 889 clicks.

8.4   Model building

8.4.1   Sequence rules

To meet the objectives in Section 8.1 and for the type of data available, we begin by applying the associative local models in Section 4.8. Since the transactions considered here are visit sessions, the order in which pages are visited is important, so we shall consider the application of sequence rules, which are associative rules ordered by a variable. In our case such variable is start. Sequence rules are to be calculated on the sequence data set corresponding to cluster 3, which looks like the data in Table 8.1. Furthermore, to obtain useful results, we have appended two extra pages: at the beginning of each session there is a start_session page and at the end of each session there is an end_session page. The total number of pages is therefore 38. To choose a sequence model, we have applied the Apriori algorithm implemented in SAS Enterprise Miner, setting a support threshold equal to $0.05 \times$ support (mode), where support(mode) indicates the support of the most seen page among the 38 considered.

As a result of the algorithm, we can obtain the sequence rules with the highest interestingness, as measured by the support and confidence. Consider a sequence $A \rightarrow B$. Suppose for simplicity that it is an indirect sequence of order 2 and indicate with $N_{A \rightarrow B}$ the number of visits which appear in the sequence at least once. Let N be the total number of server sessions. Based on Section 4.8, the

Table 8.9 The most frequent indirect sequences of order 2.

	Support(%)	Confidence(%)	Transaction Count	Rule
1	100.00	100.00	1240	start_session ==> end_session
2	88.79	88.79	1101	start_session ==> product
3	88.79	100.00	1101	product ==> end_session
4	77.66	77.66	963	start_session ==> program
5	77.66	100.00	963	program ==> end_session
6	73.39	94.50	910	program ==> product
7	64.68	72.84	802	product ==> product
8	62.10	62.10	770	start_session ==> home
9	62.10	100.00	770	home ==> end_session
10	56.13	56.13	696	start_session ==> catalog
11	56.13	100.00	696	catalog ==> end_session
12	53.23	53.23	660	start_session ==> login
13	53.23	100.00	660	login ==> end_session
14	52.26	93.10	648	catalog ==> program
15	51.37	91.52	637	catalog ==> product
16	50.32	81.04	624	home ==> product
17	49.92	56.22	619	product ==> program
18	49.76	100.00	617	addcart ==> end_session
19	49.76	49.76	617	start_session ==> addcart
20	48.71	54.86	604	product ==> addcart
21	48.39	48.39	600	start_session ==> logpost
22	48.39	100.00	600	logpost ==> end_session
23	48.15	61.99	597	program ==> program
24	45.89	73.90	569	home ==> program
25	44.76	44.76	555	start_session ==> p_info
26	44.76	100.00	555	p_info ==> end_session

support for $A \rightarrow B$ is obtained by dividing the number of server sessions which satisfy the rule by the total number of server sessions. Therefore the support is a relative frequency that indicates the percentage of users for which the two pages have been visited in succession. The confidence of $A \rightarrow B$ is obtained by taking the number of server sessions which satisfy the rule and dividing it by the number of sessions containing page A. Therefore the confidence expresses the probability that during a server session where page A has been viewed then page B has subsequently been viewed.

Table 8.9 reports the most likely sequences of order 2, for the sequence data set of cluster 3. In other words, we search a pattern of sequences characterised by maximum support among all sequences of order 2. Notice that most of the sequences involve start_session and/or end_session; this is obvious as each session will contain both of them and we are considering indirect rules. Among the other sequences, program $\rightarrow$ product is the sequence with the highest frequency, followed by product $\rightarrow$ product; product $\rightarrow$ product will not be detected by an association rule that is not sequential. Table 8.9 establishes that the estimated probability is 64.68% that the product page is seen at least twice in a session.

We now search the most supported indirect sequences among those of any order. Table 8.10 reports the results from the Apriori algorithm.

Table 8.10 The most frequent indirect sequences of any order.

	Chain Length	Support(%)	Confidence(%)	Transaction Count	Rule
1	2	100.00	100.00	1240	start_session ==> end_session
2	2	88.79	88.79	1101	start_session ==> product
3	2	88.79	100.00	1101	product ==> end_session
4	3	88.79	100.00	1101	start_session ==> product ==> end_session
5	3	77.66	100.00	963	start_session ==> program ==> end_session
6	2	77.66	100.00	963	program ==> end_session
7	2	77.66	77.66	963	start_session ==> program
8	2	73.39	94.50	910	program ==> product
9	3	73.39	94.50	910	start_session ==> program ==> product
10	3	73.39	100.00	910	program ==> product ==> end_session
11	4	73.39	100.00	910	start_session ==> program ==> product ==> end_session
12	4	64.68	100.00	802	start_session ==> product ==> product ==> end_session
13	3	64.68	72.84	802	start_session ==> product ==> product
14	3	64.68	100.00	802	product ==> product ==> end_session
15	2	64.68	72.84	802	product ==> product
16	2	62.10	100.00	770	home ==> end_session
17	2	62.10	62.10	770	start_session ==> home
18	3	62.10	100.00	770	start_session ==> home ==> end_session
19	3	56.13	100.00	696	start_session ==> catalog ==> end_session
20	2	56.13	56.13	696	start_session ==> catalog
21	2	56.13	100.00	696	catalog ==> end_session
22	2	53.23	100.00	660	login ==> end_session
23	2	53.23	53.23	660	start_session ==> login
24	3	53.23	100.00	660	start_session ==> login ==> end_session
25	3	52.26	93.10	648	start_session ==> catalog ==> program
26	3	52.26	100.00	648	catalog ==> program ==> end_session
27	2	52.26	93.10	648	catalog ==> program
28	4	52.26	100.00	648	start_session ==> catalog ==> program ==> end_session
29	4	51.45	100.00	638	program ==> product ==> product ==> end_session

Table 8.11 The most frequent direct sequences of order 2.

	Support(%)	Confidence(%)	Transaction Count	Rule
1	60.65	78.09	752	program ==> product
2	46.21	82.33	573	catalog ==> program
3	45.81	45.81	568	start_session ==> home
4	35.73	67.12	443	login ==> logpost
5	31.77	63.86	394	addcart ==> freeze
6	25.56	28.79	317	product ==> addcart
7	25.24	28.43	313	product ==> p_info
8	24.68	67.85	306	pay_req ==> pay_res
9	24.19	54.55	300	freeze ==> pay_req
10	19.68	43.96	244	p_info ==> product
11	19.52	61.58	242	register ==> regpost
12	17.02	17.02	211	start_session ==> program
13	15.48	17.44	192	product ==> product
14	14.52	14.52	180	start_session ==> product
15	14.35	45.41	178	shelf ==> download
16	12.66	20.39	157	home ==> program
17	12.18	42.66	151	pay_res ==> shelf
18	11.77	24.33	146	logpost ==> catalog
19	11.69	26.13	145	p_info ==> p_info
20	11.53	38.03	143	cart ==> freeze
21	10.97	17.66	136	home ==> login
22	10.97	17.66	136	home ==> catalog
23	9.84	20.33	122	logpost ==> cart
24	9.76	15.71	121	home ==> product
25	9.68	18.18	120	login ==> register
26	9.19	9.19	114	start_session ==> logpost
27	9.03	47.66	112	download ==> download

Besides those already examined, notice that the most frequent sequences are sequences to do with visiting the most seen pages in the cluster, namely start_session → product → end_session and start_session → program → end_session. We now search the most likely direct sequences. Although direct sequences of order 2 can be easily obtained from the software, this is not the case for higher-order sequences. Table 8.11 reports the most likely direct sequences of order 2. Notice that program → product is the most likely direct sequence, but its support is now about 0.60, against 0.73 for indirect sequences (Table 8.10). This means that other pages are viewed between program and product on 13% of occasions. Table 8.11 also allows us to make sensible conclusions about which pages are the entrance pages: home, program, product, logpost. These are listed among those having the highest support of occurring with start_session. But there are no sequences containing end_session as head of a rule; this means that the site is typically entered from a few pages (the four that are listed) but it is exited from a wide variety of pages. Sequence rules can also be deduced by using a classification tree that has as its target variable one of the considered pages, which acts as a supervisor.

8.4.2   Link analysis

We now consider how we can take the results from the sequence rules and use link analysis to build up a global model. In the Enterprise Miner implementation, link analysis takes as its input those sequences having a prespecified support. For comparison we will consider all indirect sequences of any order up to a maximum of 10. As in Section 8.4.1, we will use the default threshold of support(mode), which is 0.05. Link analysis considers each of the obtained sequences as a row observation in a data set called link. It then counts how many of the observations include a certain sequence. This is called the count of a sequence and is the fundamental measure for link analysis.

The main output of a link analysis is a graph of nodes and links. Figure 8.4 shows the graph for our webshop data.

In the graph each page is represented by a node, and links are drawn between the nodes. A link is drawn between two nodes if the count of the corresponding sequence of order 2 is non-null (i.e. the sequence is contained at least once in the link data set). The graph therefore tells us which nodes are connected and which are not. Usually the thickness of a link is directly related to the size of the count. For instance, the link between home and program is quite

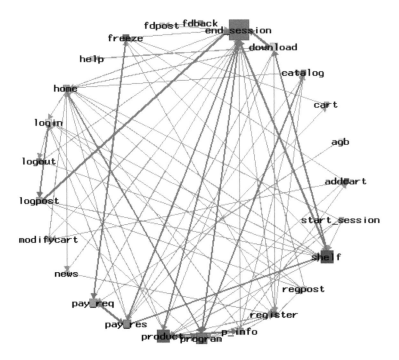

Figure 8.4   Link analysis graph.

thick, as the corresponding sequence appears often in the link data set. Links are directed; for instance, to orientate an edge between two nodes A, B the two counts of $A \rightarrow B$ and $B \rightarrow A$ in the link data set are compared and the higher count determines the orientation. Both orientations will be present when there is substantial parity. For instance, shelf precedes download in the graph, as the count of shelf $\rightarrow$ download is higher than that of download $\rightarrow$ shelf.

The size of the nodes typically depends on a so-called centrality measure. This concepts comes from ideas in social networks. A first-order centrality measure (C1) basically means that the importance of a node depends on the number of connections it has. On the other hand, a second-order centrality measure (C2) means that the importance of a node depends on the number of connections that the nodes connected to it have. In both cases each connection and link can be weighted according to its count in the link data set. We will describe the size of a node using an unweighted first-order centrality measure. Therefore in Figure 8.4 the pages end_session, product, program and shelf turn out to be the largest nodes, as they are connected to many others. Table 8.12 gives the values of the variables used to plot Figure 8.4.

The position of a node may also depend on the counts. The counts between each pair of pages are put in a proximity matrix. Multidimensional scaling is then used to reproduce these proximities with a bidimensional Euclidean distance, and correspondingly to derive two (X, Y) points. The higher the count, the closer the points on a Cartesian graph. For instance, product and program have a large count and their points are close together.

Table 8.12 Coordinates from the link analysis.

	C1	C2	VALUE	COUNT	ID	X	Y
A1	0.0172735761	0.2782446312	addcart	24	A1	456	240
A2	0.0009337068	0.0620915033	agb	2	A2	449.59097564	189.26730496
A3	0.010270775	0.1209150327	cart	15	A3	430.76660446	141.72232638
A4	0.0214752568	0.5084033613	catalog	32	A4	400.70968893	100.3524851
A5	0.0536881419	0.9253034547	download	99	A5	361.30881244	67.757196017
A6	0.2450980392	0.9150326797	end_session	525	A6	315.03967279	45.984537588
A7	0.0009337068	0.0018674136	fdback	2	A7	264.80952531	36.402563716
A8	0.0018674136	0.246031746	fdpost	2	A8	213.7745096	39.613344048
A9	0.0476190476	0.578898226	freeze	65	A9	165.141338	55.415133785
A10	0.0046685341	0.1073762838	help	5	A10	121.96580641	82.815050032
A11	0.0485527544	1.3636788049	home	86	A11	86.960787698	120.09145817
A12	0.048085901	0.5336134454	login	60	A12	62.325772244	164.90214833
A13	0.0046685341	0.4463118581	logout	5	A13	49.608666066	214.43150477
A14	0.0452847806	0.6087768441	logpost	50	A14	49.608530372	265.5674211
A15	0.0037348273	0.3109243697	modifycart	4	A15	62.325373689	315.09684503
A16	0.0028011204	0.3225957049	news	4	A16	86.960151324	359.90766593
A18	0.0620915033	0.4878618114	pay_req	101	A18	121.9649722	397.18425985
A19	0.0732959851	0.7044817927	pay_res	99	A19	165.14035838	424.58440524
A20	0.1652661064	1.0322128852	product	276	A20	213.77344611	440.38645308
A21	0.1479925303	0.8986928105	program	228	A21	264.80844478	443.59750426
A17	0.0616246499	0.839869281	p_info	93	A17	315.03864311	434.01579697
A22	0.0289449113	0.9561157796	register	35	A22	361.30789831	412.2433841
A23	0.0144724556	0.4159663866	regpost	31	A23	400.70894779	379.64830413
A24	0.1531279178	0.8520074697	shelf	260	A24	430.76608288	338.27862236
A25	0.0182072829	0.5149393091	start_session	39	A25	449.59070639	290.73374369

8.4.3 Probabilistic expert systems

Probabilistic expert systems build up global statistical models by means of subsequent local factorisations. Although there are strong similarities with sequence rules, the difference is substantial. In the application considered here, sequence rules state that the visit to page B depends on the visit to page A, and establishes that this is true if the support (and possibly the confidence) of the rule $A \rightarrow B$ is higher than a prefixed threshold. In a probabilistic expert system the binary random variable B depends on the occurrences of the binary random variable A if P($B|A$, others) $\neq P(B|$others), where others are the other variables considered. Therefore probabilistic expert systems are global models for the dependence between variables, whereas association rules are local models for the dependence between the occurrence of events. In our present context the pages start_session and end_session are not random variables, hence they will not appear in the model, which will contain at most 36 variables. A further difference is that discrete probabilistic expert systems are actually calculated using contingency tables in a similar way to odds ratios (Chapter 7), therefore they cannot easily take account of temporal order.

To compare probabilistic expert systems and association rules, we will fit a probabilistic expert system to the available data set, with 1240 sessions. This methodology is not yet fully implemented in SAS, so we have to build it using a sequence of logistic regressions. The problem with this approach is that no a priori ordering of the variables is given, so each attempted logistic regression has been based on all the chosen variables, except the one adopted as response. Alternatively, we could have used a software package that supports probabilistic expert systems, such as Hugin (www.hugin.com).

The graphical model in Figure 8.5 is has been obtained on the basis of 17 logistic regression models, one for each of the 17 pages with highest support. The relevant page is taken as the target variable and the other 16 binary variables are used as explanatory variables. The model is built from the logistic regression results by supposing that if a significantly positive odds ratio occurs, this corresponds to the existence of a link from the relevant explanatory variable to the target variable. The link is represented on the graph by an arrow from the explanatory variable to the target variable. Because we have no a priori logical ordering of the variables, we have not obtained a single model, but a graph that can be compatible with different orderings.

Figure 8.5 can be compared with the results obtained from the indirect and direct sequence rules. In general, sequences can contain start_session and end_session, but the expert systems cannot contain them as they are not random variables. Consequently, most of the selected sequences are not in the graph. Another main difference is that the expert systems cannot contain rules of the type $A \rightarrow A$, they are based on an unordered data set (visitors); this is especially noticeable with indirect rules. Here most of the direct rules chosen correspond to a link in the expert systems. Indeed probabilistic expert systems can be deemed closer to direct rules. The model in Figure 8.5 determines the pages variable that most influences webpage selection; since this model does not

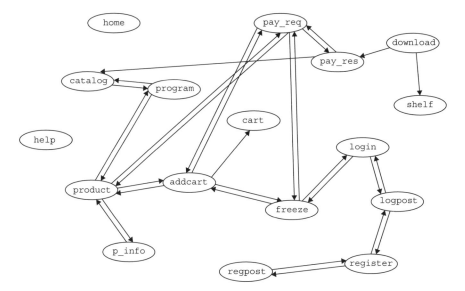

Figure 8.5 Directed graph built by recursive logistic regression.

consider the order of the visits, these pages can precede or follow the visit to the target page. In the graph there are double arrows, so the model is not a true probabilistic expert system; that would require us to specify the order of the variables. For instance, we could use the order specified by the selected indirect or direct rules.

Even though this is a global model, it can still give precise local statements. For instance, the odds ratios for the variable `product` with all other 16 variables can be estimated from the local logistic regression of `product` on all others. These odds ratios are reported in Table 8.13. It turns out that `product` is significantly positively associated with `p_info`, `pay_req`, `addcart` and `program`, and these are precisely the nodes to which it is linked in Figure 8.5. Blanc and Tarantola (2002) give a different analysis of this data set, comparing probabilistic expert systems and dependency networks, a class of more elaborate recursive graphical models (Heckerman *et al.*, 2000).

8.4.4   Markov chains

Probabilistic expert systems are global models for analysing the dependence between variables; they are different from sequence rules, which model dependence between events. Markov chain models, (Section 5.7), can be used as global models for sequences of events. Here we consider discrete Markov chains. The idea is to introduce dependence between time-specific variables. In each session, to each time point i, corresponding to the ith click, there corresponds a discrete random variable with as many levels as the number of pages; these are called

Table 8.13 Estimated odds ratios of the page product.

| | Odds Ratio Estimates | | |
Effect	Point Estimate	95% Wald Confidence Limits	
PROGRAM	9.461	5.105	17.534
HOME	0.593	0.321	1.096
CATALOG	1.358	0.724	2.547
LOGIN	2.066	0.790	5.403
ADDCART	17.889	5.305	60.323
LOGPOST	0.494	0.190	1.284
P_INFO	36.115	10.821	120.535
FREEZE	2.136	0.357	12.769
PAY_REQ	21.256	0.489	924.314
REGISTER	0.315	0.140	0.708
SHELF	0.384	0.161	0.916
CART	0.375	0.168	0.836
PAY_RES	0.202	0.007	5.906
REGPOST	1.663	0.645	4.288
DOWNLOAD	0.353	0.125	0.997
HELP	1.613	0.543	4.794

states of the chain. The observed ith page in the session is the observed realisation of the Markov chain, at time i, for that session. Time can go from $i = 1$ to $i = T$, and T can be any finite number. A session can stop well before T; in this case the last page viewed is an absorbing state (end_session for our data).

A Markov chain model establishes a probabilistic dependence between what is seen before time i and what will be seen at time i. In particular, a first-order Markov chain, which is the model we consider here, establishes that what is seen at time i depends only on what is seen at time $i - 1$. This short-memory dependence can be assessed by a transition matrix that establishes the probability of going from any one page to any other page in a single step. For 36 pages there are 36×36 probabilities of this kind. The conditional probabilities in the transition matrix can be estimated from the available conditional frequencies. By making the assumption that the transition matrix is constant in time (homogeneity of the Markov chain), we can use the frequencies of any two adjacent pairs of time-ordered clicks to estimate the conditional probabilities. Note the analogy of Markov chains with direct sequences. Conditional probabilities in a first-order Markov model correspond to the confidence of order 2 direct sequence rules, therefore a first-order Markov chain is a model for direct sequences of order 2. Furthermore, it can be shown that a second-order Markov model is a model for direct sequences of order 3, and so on. The difference is that the Markov chain model is global not local. This is mainly reflected in the fact that Markov chains consider all pages, not just those with a high support. The Markov model is a probabilistic model, hence it allows inferential results to be obtained.

Table 8.14 The data set page for the Markov chain model.

	page_now	page_tomorrow
1	start_session	home
2	home	program
3	program	product
4	product	home
5	home	program
6	program	product
7	product	home
8	home	end_session
9	start_session	program
10	program	catalog
11	catalog	program
12	program	product
13	product	program
14	program	program
15	program	end_session
16	start_session	program

To build a Markov chain model (first-order and homogeneous), we have reorganised the data in a new data set called page, in which there are two variables: page_now and page_tomorrow. page_now indicates what is viewed by the visitor at a certain click and page_tomorrow indicates what is viewed immediately afterwards. Table 8.14 is an extract from this data set. Each row in Table 8.14 corresponds to a pair of pages that are seen one after the other. For a given visitor, the second term in a row becomes the first term in the next row. For a new visitor, we start with a new pair of pages and apply the same rule. The transition matrix can be calculated from this data set. It is a table with 37 rows (the 36 pages and start_session) and 37 columns (the 36 pages and end_session). The rows represent page_now (they thus exclude end_session, which cannot appear first) and the columns represent page_tomorrow (they exclude start_session, which cannot appear second). Therefore a transition matrix contains a total of $37 \times 37 = 1369$ estimated probabilities. There is not enough space to publish the whole transition matrix.

First of all, we can evaluate where a visitor is most likely to enter the site. To obtain this we have to consider the transition probabilities of the row start_session. Figure 8.6 is a graph of the probabilities, excluding those estimated to have a null probability. The most frequent entrance page is home (48.81%), followed by program (17.02%), product (14.52%), logpost (9.19%) and catalog (6.77%). This is consistent with the nature of the visitors belonging to this cluster. Unlike what happens with association rules, the transition probabilities sum to 1 by row and column. We can then consider the

most likely exit pages. To obtain this we have to consider the transition probabilities of the column end_session. Figure 8.7 is a graph of the probabilities,
excluding those estimated to have a null probability. The most likely exit page
is product (20.81%), followed by logpost (12.10%), download (10.56%),
home (9.19%) and p_info (6.94%).

From the transition matrix we can establish a path that connects nodes
through the most likely transitions. One possibility is to proceed forward from
start_session. From start_session we can connect to the page with
which start_session has the highest probability of transition; this is home.
Next follows program, then product and then p_info. From p_info the

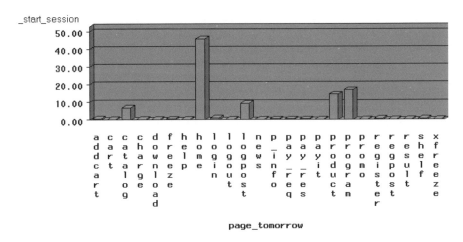

Figure 8.6 Representation of the transition probabilities from the page
start_session.

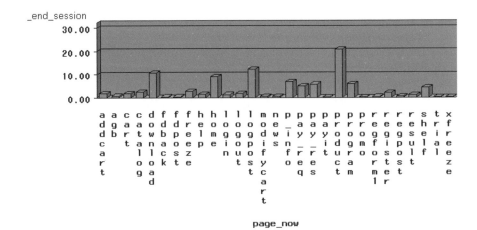

Figure 8.7 Representation of the transition probabilities from the page end_session.

most likely transition is back to product, so the path ends. This information can be represented graphically as in Figure 8.8, which includes estimates for the conditional probabilities of transition. We can compare what the previous path would be, using the confidence index in the sequence rule algorithm. Initially, from start_session the highest confidence is reached for home (45.81%, as obtained by Markov chains), followed by program (20.39%, more than with Markov chains), product (78.09% as against 70.18%). The next most probable link is now with addcart (28.79%) rather than p_info. The differences with Markov chains are due to the fact that the direct sequences consider only pages which pass a certain support.

Following similar logic, we can also construct a backward path as in Figure 8.9, which is built starting from end_session. The page with the highest transition probability to end_session is product (20.81%). Then the highest transition to product is program (42.41%), and so on. Here the path is complete, as is it reaches start_session. The paths in Figure 8.8 and 8.9 are not the most likely ones; these could be calculated by comparing all Markov chains of all orders, a formidable computational task. Alternatively, sequence rules can be used (Section 8.4.1); they are local, easy to calculate and easy to implement, even for large data sets. But because they are local, they are not normalised, therefore they do not sum to 1. We conclude this Markov chain analysis by describing the estimated transitions for some typical pages:

- addcart: the highest transition is to freeze (57.01%), followed by modifycart (8.24%), addcart (7.49%), login (7.38%). On the other hand, addcart is mostly reached by product (78.82%).

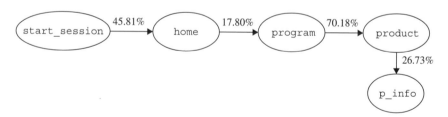

Figure 8.8 The forward path of the most likely transitions.

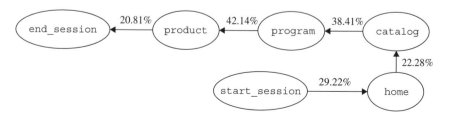

Figure 8.9 The backward path of the most likely transitions.

- shelf: once the programs in shelf are seen, most visits go to download (39.35%), back to shelf (16.06%) or to cart (8.09%).

- download: once a program is downloaded, visitors return to the same page (46.88%), or leave the site (end_session is 20.47%) and on 13.44% of occasions they go to shelf.

- catalog: after catalog, the most seen page is program (78.73%), while all others are visited on less than 5% of occasions. On the other hand, catalog is reached from home (22.28%), logpost (13.60%) and product (10.87%)

- pay_res: having consented to pay, a visitor goes to shelf with a probability of 33.77%, to cart (14.83%) or to end_session (11.70%). On the other hand, pay_res reached from pay_req on 81.55% of occasions.

8.5 Model comparison

As discussed in Chapter 6, it is quite difficult to evaluate local models. Here the situation is complicated by the fact that in Section 8.4 we compared local models with global models. For global models, such as probabilistic expert systems and Markov chains, statistical evaluation can proceed as in Sections 6.2, 6.4 and 6.5, or in terms of computationally intensive methods. But the real problem is how to compare them with sequence rules. In the absence of other considerations, a simple and natural scoring function for a sequence rule is its support, which gives the proportion of the population to which the rule applies. Alternatively, if the objective is to predict visiting behaviour, in terms of conditional probabilities of moving from one page to another, the confidence or the lift may be used.

Among the considered models, direct sequences and Markov chains are comparable with each other and can be more easily interpreted, as they lead to statements having a unique meaning (these are direct sequence rules to which a conditional probability is attached). Indirect sequences can be seen as more exploratory; they lead to the link analysis representation, which is a very helpful global picture of the relationships between pages. On the other hand, probabilistic expert systems do model problems of a different nature, in which the modelled dependency is between random variables rather than event occurrences.

We now compare briefly the results obtained with direct sequence rules and Markov chain models.

The set of rules selected in Table 8.11 can be scored in terms of support, as we have already done. To measure how usefully the body of a rule predicts the head of the rule, we can calculate its lift. We do this by taking each confidence in the table and dividing it by the support of the corresponding head (which consists of a single page); these supports are given in Table 8.15.

Dividing the confidences in Table 8.11 by the corresponding supports in Table 8.15, we find that 24 of them have a lift greater than one; some have a high lift value and are therefore very informative. This is the case for the sequences program → product (lift = 4.35) and catalog → program (lift = 7.64). The lift of 7.64 is saying that the probability of visiting program is about 7.64 times greater when catalog is seen beforehand than what it would be by chance. On the other hand, the rules product → product, start_session → product and home → product are not informative, as their lift values are close to 1 (indeed slightly lower).

Similar conclusions can be drawn from the Markov chain model; the lift of each transition can be calculated from dividing the transition probabilities by the initial state probabilities, corresponding to the probabilities which are (partly) reproduced in Table 8.15. It can thus be deduced, for example, that the lift of program → product is 0.7018/0.1793 = 3.91, and the lift of catalog → program is 0.7873/0.1077 = 7.31. Notice that both lifts are slightly lower than for sequence rules; this is because sequence rules only consider as transition candidates those pages whose joint support is higher than a certain threshold, whereas Markov chains consider them all.

Table 8.15 Support of the most frequent pages in cluster 3.

C_CALLER		
C_caller	Frequency	Percent
product	4366	17.93%
program	2622	10.77%
home	1944	7.99%
p_info	1715	7.04%
catalog	1279	5.25%
End_session	1240	5.09%
start_session	1240	5.09%
login	1135	4.66%
freeze	1120	4.60%
addcart	935	3.84%
pay_req	879	3.61%
logpost	857	3.52%
shelf	803	3.30%
cart	644	2.65%
download	640	2.63%
Register	631	2.59%
pay_res	607	2.49%
Regpost	504	2.07%

Ultimately, though, a set of rules has to be assessed on its ability to meet the analysis objectives. In this case study the informative value of start_session → end_session is null, but in Table 8.10 it has the largest support and confidence (100%). On the other hand, the informative value of the rules that go from start_session to other pages, and from other pages to end_session can be extremely important when designing the website.

8.6 Summary report

- *Context*: this case study concerns the identification of navigation patterns in a website. A similar kind of analysis can be applied to problems in which there is discrete time-ordered data identifying behavioural patterns; for instance, in consecutive commercial transactions (online or otherwise), or in studying people's careers. The peculiarity of web behaviour is that the average number of transactions per individual, in a given period, is higher than in other contexts.
- *Objectives*: the aim of the analysis is to track the most important patterns of visits, where a pattern means a time-ordered sequence of pages, possibly repeated. The chosen measure of importance determined the results of the analysis. The most common measures refer to the occurrence probability of a certain viewing sequence (support) or to the conditional probability of viewing a certain page, having viewed others in the past (confidence).
- *Organisation of the data*: data is extracted from the log file that registers the access to a website. It is structured in a transaction database. It may be further simplified into a data matrix format, but then the temporal order will be lost.
- *Exploratory data analysis*: this phase of the analysis is necessary to draw valid conclusions. On the basis of three continuous variables related to visitor characteristics – the number of clicks in the session, the time of the connection and the length of the connection – we removed outlying observations, which are bound to arise in this context. Furthermore, a preliminary cluster analysis identified four distinct behaviours. This allows us to identify patterns for homogeneous groups of visitors. We concentrated on one cluster.
- *Model specification*: the data mining analysis needed here is an example of a local model or pattern. We therefore compared sequence rules, based on the Apriori algorithm, with link analysis. Furthermore, we considered more traditional statistical techniques, based on the whole data set but using local computations – probabilistic expert systems and Markov chain models.
- *Model comparison*: it is rather difficult to assess local models; consequently, it is also hard to compare them with global based statistical models. Another difficulty when comparing local models with global models is that they are based on different assumptions. Sequence rules can be compared directly with Markov chains. It turns out that the most probable patterns identified by the two procedures are rather similar. The choice between the two methods therefore depends on the scope of the rules themselves.

- *Model interpretation*: the rules can be easily interpreted, but there may be a problem if the analysis produces a very large number. Statistical models, such as Markov chains, make it considerably easier to select the most relevant rules, as they can be evaluated in a more coherent way.

CHAPTER 9

Profiling website visitors

9.1 Objectives of the analysis

The aim of this case study is to analyse web access data to classify the visitors into homogeneous groups on the basis of their behaviour. This will lead us to identify typical visiting profiles. In other words, we are trying to match each visitor to a specific cluster, depending on their surfing habits on that particular site. This will give us a behavioural segmentation of the users that we can use in future marketing decisions. We can also monitor the evolution of the kind of 'customer' who comes to the site by looking at how the distribution of users in the different behavioural segments evolves over time. Then we can see how our business decisions affect the different segments, whether they increase visits by a particular segment or whether they decrease them. Examples of business decisions are changes to the webpages and the use of publicity. The data set in this chapter has also been analysed by Cadez *et al.* (2000) and Giudici and Castelo (2001); Giudici and Castelo take a Bayesian viewpoint.

9.2 Description of the data

The data set contains data about the pages visited of the website www.microsoft.com by 32 711 anonymous visitors. For each visitor we have indicated the pages of the site that have been visited in the first week of February 1998. Visitors are identified with an identification number (from 10 001 to 42 711) and no personal information is given. The total number of visited pages is 296. The pages are identified by a number that corresponds to a title and a corresponding address. For example, number 1057 refers to the page 'MS PowerPoint News' of the PowerPoint group of pages. The numeric codes associated with the pages are integers that go from 1000 up to 1295. To give a better idea of the data set, here are its first few lines:

```
C, ``10908'', 10908
V, 1108
V, 1017
C, ``10909'', 10909
V, 1113
```

Applied Data Mining.   Paolo Giudici
© 2003 John Wiley & Sons, Ltd   ISBNs: 0-470-84679-8 (Paper); 0-470-84678-X (Cloth)

```
V,  1009
V,1034
C,  ''10910'',  10910
V,  1026
V,  1017
```

Each visitor is indicated by a line (beginning with the letter C) that identifies them using with a numerical code. The code is converted into a number. The visitor's line is then followed by one or more lines that show which pages are visited. The pages that are not visited do not appear. Unlike in Chapter 8, this time it is convenient to work with a derived data matrix, organised by visitors. This matrix will describe, for each visitor, how many times each page has been viewed. We will therefore have one categorical variable for each page. And also unlike Chapter 8, we count how many times a page is viewed, not just whether the page has been viewed at least once. As a result, we now have a discrete quantitative random variable, not a binary variable.

There is a problem with setting up the data matrix. The number of variables in the data set corresponds to the number of webpages viewed, and at 296 it is too large. It will be likely that many combinations of these variables will never arise, or they will arise very rarely, so there will not be much statistical information. To perform a valid cluster analysis of visitors into groups, we need to clean and summarise the original file so we obtain a less complex data matrix. To do this, we group the webpages into 13 homogeneous categories, reflecting their logical meaning in the Microsoft website. The number of discrete variables is then reduced from 296 to 13. Each variable corresponds to one of the 13 groups:

- *Initial*: this includes all the general access pages and all the pages dedicated to research.
- *Support*: this includes all the pages related to the requests for help and support.
- *Entertainment*: this includes all the pages that refer to entertainment, games and cultural software.
- *Office*: this has all the pages which refer to the Office software.
- *Windows*: this groups together all the pages related to the Windows operating system.
- *Othersoft*: this refers to all the pages relating to software other than Office.
- *Download*: this includes all the pages regarding software downloading or updating.
- *Otherint*: this has all the pages dedicated to services through the internet for IT professionals; these pages are different from the download pages.
- *Development*: this has all the pages dedicated to professional developers (e.g. Java).
- *Hardware*: this includes the pages relating to Microsoft hardware.
- *Business*: this has pages dedicated to businesses.
- *Info*: this includes all the pages which give information about new products and services.
- *Area*: this has all the pages which refer to local access, depending on the specific language.

Table 9.1 Extract from the visitors data matrix.

	client_code	initial	help	entertainment	office	windows	othersf	download	otherint	development	hardware	business	information	area
1	10001	1	1	1	0	0	0	0	0	0	0	0	0	0
2	10002	1	1	0	0	0	0	0	0	0	0	0	0	0
3	10003	2	1	0	0	0	0	0	0	0	0	0	0	0
4	10004	0	0	0	0	0	0	0	0	0	0	0	0	1
5	10005	0	0	0	0	0	0	0	1	0	0	0	0	0
6	10006	2	0	0	0	0	0	0	0	0	0	0	0	0
7	10007	0	0	0	1	0	0	0	0	0	0	0	0	0
8	10008	1	0	0	0	0	0	0	0	0	0	0	0	0
9	10009	0	0	0	0	1	0	1	0	0	0	0	0	0
10	10010	1	1	0	1	0	1	0	0	2	0	0	0	0
11	10011	2	0	0	3	0	0	0	0	0	0	0	0	0
12	10012	0	0	0	0	0	1	0	0	1	0	0	0	0
13	10013	0	0	0	0	0	0	1	0	0	0	0	0	0
14	10014	0	0	0	0	0	0	0	0	0	0	0	0	1
15	10015	0	0	0	0	0	0	0	0	0	1	0	0	0
16	10016	0	0	0	0	0	0	0	1	1	0	0	0	0
17	10017	1	0	0	0	0	0	0	0	3	0	0	0	0
18	10018	1	0	0	0	0	0	0	0	0	0	0	0	0
19	10019	4	0	2	1	0	0	2	0	0	1	1	0	0
20	10020	0	1	1	1	0	0	1	0	0	0	0	0	0
21	10021	3	1	1	1	2	1	1	3	2	0	1	1	0
22	10022	2	0	0	0	0	0	1	0	0	0	0	0	0
23	10023	0	0	0	0	0	0	1	0	0	0	0	0	0
24	10024	0	0	0	0	0	0	0	0	1	0	0	0	0
25	10025	0	0	0	0	1	0	0	0	0	0	0	0	0
26	10026	0	0	0	1	0	0	0	0	0	0	0	0	0
27	10027	0	1	0	1	0	0	1	0	0	0	0	0	0
28	10028	0	0	0	0	0	0	0	0	0	0	1	0	0

Using this grouping, we can derive a visitor data matrix with 32 711 rows and 13 columns. Table 9.1 shows part of it. Corresponding to each page there is a discrete variable that shows the number of times each person has visited the specific group of pages. It does not include information on the order in which the pages are visited. We have already commented on this point in Chapter 8. To achieve our initial aims, we carry out the analysis in three stages: (1) an exploratory phase looks at preliminary considerations; (2) an analysis phase determines the behavioural classes of users by applying cluster analysis and Kohonen maps; (3) a comparison phase evaluates the performance of the two descriptive models in terms of grouping and predictive ability.

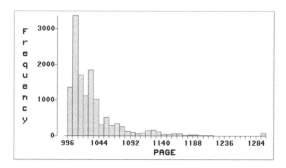

Figure 9.1 Frequency of visits to the webpages of the website being analysed.

9.3   Exploratory analysis

The exploratory analysis reveals a high level of dispersion with respect to the pages visited. Figure 9.1 shows the absolute frequency distribution of visits to each page. Notice that the pages coded with the lowest numbers (from 1000 onwards) have the highest frequencies, and there appears to be a decreasing pattern, as higher-numbered pages are being considered. From a preliminary examination of the data it turns out that the most frequently visited page is page number 1008, 'Free Downloads'. We have also discovered that each visitor looks, on average, at 4 pages, as this is the sample mean. However, the mode is only 2, reflecting a positively skewed distribution of the variable 'number of visited pages'. Given the size of the available data, the number of pages to be considered (296) is too large for a valid categorical data analysis. If all variables were considered, there would be too many parameters to be estimated, with a consequent loss in statistical efficiency of the procedure. It becomes necessary to have a preliminary transformation of the data and in particular to group the pages together, as we discussed in Section 9.2.

9.4   Model building

The first part of the analysis aims to identify the different behavioural segments within the sample of users. We use two different descriptive data mining techniques: cluster analysis and the unsupervised networks known as Kohonen maps. Both techniques allow us to partition the data to identify homogeneous groups or types possessing internal cohesion that differentiates them from the other groups. We use two techniques so we can compare their efficiency, but also to check that they produce consistent results. We will use the results of the cluster analysis to help us determine the optimal number of clusters for the Kohonen map implementation.

9.4.1   Cluster analysis

Chapter 4 explained the main techniques of hierarchical cluster analysis as well as the non-hierarchical K-means method. A variation of the K-means method is used in the SAS procedure `fastclus` that we will employ. The basic idea is to introduce seeds, or centroids, to which statistical units may be attracted, forming a cluster. It is important to specify the maximum number of clusters, say G, in advance. As discussed in Section 4.2, hierarchical and non-hierarchical methods of cluster analysis do have some disadvantages. Hierarchical cluster analysis does not need to know the number of clusters in advance but it may require too much computing power. For moderately large quantities of data, as in this case study, the calculations may take a long time. Non-hierarchical methods are fast, but they require us to choose the number of clusters in advance.

To avoid these disadvantages and to try to exploit the potential of both the methods, we can adopt two possible approaches. We can extract from the data a sample of limited size, then carry out a hierarchical cluster analysis to determine G, the optimal number of clusters. Once we have a value for G we take the G means of the clusters as our seeds; then we continue with a non-hierarchical analysis on the whole data set using a number of clusters equal to G and allocating each observation to one of them. Alternatively we can work on the whole data set, carrying out a non-hierarchical analysis with a large value of G. We then consider a new data set, made up from the G group means, each endowed with two measurements, one indicating the cluster size and one the dispersion within the cluster. A hierarchical analysis is then carried out on this data set to see whether any groups can be merged. It is essential to indicate the frequency and the dispersion of each cluster, otherwise the analysis will not take account of clusters having different numbers and variabilities.

The Clustering node of Enterprise Miner implements a mixture of both approaches in a three-stage procedure. Initially a non-hierarchical clustering procedure is run on the whole data, having chosen a large value of G. Seeds are initially set as the first G available observations. Then an iterative procedure is run; at each step of the procedure, temporary clusters are formed, allocating each observation to the cluster with the seed nearest to it. Each time an observation is allocated to a cluster, the seed is substituted with the mean of the cluster, called the centroid. The process is repeated until convergence is achieved, namely, until there are no substantial changes in the cluster seeds. At the end of the procedure, a total of G clusters are available, with corresponding cluster centroids. This is the input of the second stage.

In the second stage a hierarchical clustering method is run on a sample of the data to find the optimal number of clusters. As the number of clusters cannot be greater than G, the procedure is agglomerative, starting at G and working downwards. The previous cluster means are used as seeds, and a non-hierarchical procedure is run to allocate the observations to the clusters. A peculiar aspect of this stage is that the optimal number of clusters is chosen with respect to a test statistic, a function of the R^2 index known as the cubic clustering criterion (CCC).

As discussed in Section 4.2, it may be too restrictive to assume, a Gaussian distribution for the observations to be clustered. But in order to derive a statistical test, we need to make some kind of assumptions. Suppose that we want to verify the significance of a number of clusters equal to G. A rather general assumption is to assume that, under the null hypotheses H_0, the observations are distributed uniformly over a hypercube with dimension equal to the number of variables, each cube representing a cluster, adjacent to the others. Under the alternative hypothesis, clusters are distributed as a mixture of multivariate Gaussian distributions, centred at the mean of each cluster, and with equal variances. The cubic clustering criterion is a function of the ratio between the observed R^2 and the expected R^2 under the null hypothesis. From empirical Monte Carlo studies, it turns out that a value of CCC greater than 2 represents sufficient evidence against the null hypothesis and, therefore, for the validity of the chosen G clusters. Although it is approximate, the criterion tends to be conservative – it may have a bias towards a low number of clusters.

   Once the optimal number of clusters has been chosen, the algorithm proceeds with a non-hierarchical clustering to allocate the observations into the
G chosen groups, whose initial seeds are the centroids obtained in the previous step. In this way, we obtain a final configuration of the observations. The
procedure is similar to the first non-hierarchical stage, and can be summarised
as follows:

Repeat the following two steps until convergence: (1) scan the data and assign
   each observation to the nearest seed (nearest using the Euclidean distance);
   (2) replace each seed with the mean of the observations assigned to its cluster.

Here we choose $G = 40$ for the first non-hierarchical stage. The hierarchical
stage is then carried out on a sample of 2000 observations from the available
data, obtained by sampling randomly with replacement. The distance function is
the Euclidean distance, and Ward's method is used to recompute the distances
as the clusters are formed. To choose the number of clusters, we set the CCC
threshold at 3 (rather conservative) and the maximum number of clusters at 40.
To obtain valid cluster means for use as seeds in the third stage, we impose a
minimum of 100 observations in each cluster.

   Table 9.2 is the dendrogram for the agglomerative clustering procedure,
expressed in tabular form. Each of the 40 observations in fact corresponds to
a cluster, as formed in the previous non-hierarchical stage. It is quite difficult to
choose the optimal number of clusters on the basis of R^2 (RSQ) or the semipartial
R^2 (SPSRQ); a threshold criteria is definitely required. Figure 9.2 shows the
behaviour of CCC as the number of clusters increases from 2 to 40. Notice that
CCC reaches a threshold value of 3 when there are 10 groups. And in Table 9.2,
when moving from 9 groups to 10, there is a considerable increase in SPRSQ from
0.0163 to 0.0165 and a corresponding reduction in RSQ from 0.440 to 0.424. A
final non-hierarchical procedure was therefore run on the whole data set using
10 clusters.

   The results of the final procedure are shown in Table 9.3. For each of the
10 clusters, it gives the total number of observations in the cluster, (the frequency) and a measure of internal cohesion (the root mean square standard
deviation within the cluster). It also gives the maximum distance from the
cluster seed as a further measure of internal cohesion, and the distance from
the cluster seed to the nearest other cluster seed. We have $R^2 = 0.45$ for the
final configuration, which can be treated as a summary evaluation measure of
the model.

   To better interpret the cluster configurations, Table 9.4 gives the means of
each cluster. Notice that clusters 1 and 3 have similar centroids, expressed by a

Table 9.2 Dendrogram of the first-stage hierarchical cluster analysis.

NCL	-Clusters Joined -		FREQ	SPRSQ	RSQ
39	OB15	OB18	2	0.0012	.626
38	OB17	OB34	2	0.0013	.625
37	OB16	OB40	4	0.0016	.623
36	OB5	CL39	3	0.0017	.622
35	OB9	OB14	5	0.0019	.620
34	OB19	OB35	6	0.0020	.618
33	OB7	CL37	10	0.0020	.616
32	OB20	OB33	2	0.0021	.614
31	OB28	OB39	8	0.0025	.611
30	OB13	CL34	22	0.0029	.608
29	OB24	CL31	9	0.0031	.605
28	OB11	OB23	29	0.0033	.602
27	OB10	OB21	11	0.0033	.599
26	CL35	CL38	7	0.0034	.595
25	CL26	OB31	18	0.0040	.591
24	CL36	CL29	12	0.0041	.587
23	OB2	OB12	51	0.0046	.583
22	CL33	CL32	12	0.0064	.576
21	OB29	OB32	57	0.0068	.569
20	CL25	CL30	40	0.0069	.562
19	OB4	OB8	80	0.0081	.554
18	OB30	OB36	204	0.0082	.546
17	CL24	CL27	23	0.0084	.538
16	OB3	OB27	159	0.0091	.529
15	OB6	OB37	174	0.0130	.516
14	CL28	CL21	86	0.0130	.503
13	CL23	CL20	91	0.0146	.488
12	CL22	CL14	98	0.0154	.473
11	OB1	OB22	971	0.0158	.457
10	OB25	OB38	156	0.0163	.440
9	CL11	CL10	1127	0.0165	.424
8	CL19	CL17	103	0.0172	.407
7	CL9	OB26	1171	0.0239	.383
6	CL13	CL16	250	0.0263	.357
5	CL7	CL18	1375	0.0269	.330
4	CL6	CL15	424	0.0380	.292
3	CL8	CL12	201	0.0653	.226
2	CL4	CL3	625	0.0834	.143
1	CL5	CL2	2000	0.1429	.000

similar mean number of mean visits to each page. On the other hand, clusters 4 and 9 appear to have rather different behaviours, concentrated mainly on one page (respectively, `development` and `initial`). Before interpreting the final profiles in Table 9.4, we will have a look at Kohonen maps.

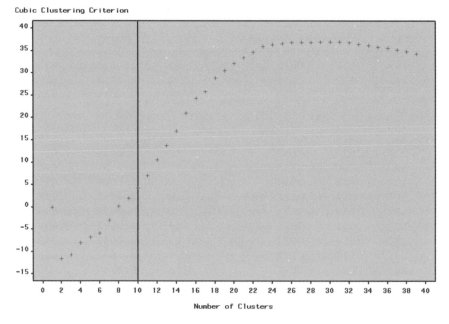

Figure 9.2   Choice of the optimum number of clusters according to CCC.

Table 9.3   Results from the final K-means cluster configuration.

CLUSTER	Frequency of Cluster	Root-Mean-Square Standard Deviation	Maximum Distance from Cluster Seed	Nearest Cluster	Distance to Nearest Cluster
1	1175	0.4077094652	4.6142280795	3	1.3276315967
2	1521	0.5393549212	6.9258181788	3	2.2614834767
3	18840	0.3233800952	4.05658574	8	1.2538340446
4	249	0.9791822971	8.1644334316	5	2.7987810396
5	966	0.5383445025	4.193097119	8	1.6299394922
6	342	0.5696658578	7.2180747852	8	2.3624871965
7	1633	0.4112438629	5.8786940253	10	2.0418866825
8	2972	0.322350282	3.3252215083	3	1.2538340446
9	1123	0.5986841515	8.8387678346	10	2.1423510802
10	3890	0.4412040095	4.4863266971	3	1.5129488616

9.4.2   Kohonen maps

Kohonen maps require us to specify the number of rows and the number of columns in the grid space characterising the map. Large maps are usually the best choice, as long as each cluster has a significant number of observations. The learning time increases significantly with the size of the map. The number of rows and the number of columns are usually established by conducting several trials until a satisfactory result is obtained. We will use the results of the cluster analysis to help us. It makes sense in terms of optimality but it will also be useful when we compare the two techniques later on. Having identified 10 as the optimal number of clusters, we will consider a 5×2 map. The Kohonen mapping algorithm in SAS Enterprise Miner essentially replaces the third step of the clustering algorithm with the following iterative procedure:

Table 9.4 The K-means cluster means.

CLUSTER	initial	help	entertainment	office	windows	othersft	download	otherint	development	hardware	business	information	area
1	0.6212765957	0.1336170213	0.0510638298	0.2178723404	0.1991489362	0.0510638298	0.2791489362	0.1182978723	0.090212766	1.2765957447	0.1421276596	0.0519148936	0.1038297872
2	1.0874424721	0.2024983563	0.0979618672	2.4944115713	0.2273042735	0.0696909928	0.6015779093	0.1847468771	0.2222222222	0.067061144	0.1137409599	0.3017751479	0.1078238001
3	0.3627388535	0.078343949	0.0904458599	0.4093418259	0.1083333333	0.0397027601	0.3339171975	0.0944798301	0.0023888535	0	0.0706944798	0.05	0.0989915074
4	2.140562249	0.7630522088	0.1726907631	1.59437751	0.8915662651	1.2409638554	0.7630522088	1.4297188755	3.8032128514	0.9799196787	0.3975903614	0.3333333333	0.1606425703
5	0.6966873706	0.1428571429	0.0755693582	0.6304347826	0.2122153209	0.2432712215	0.5020703934	0.900621118	2.4875776398	0.1252587992	0.1014492754	0.0703933747	0.115942029
6	0.716374269	0.134502924	0.0614035088	0.4152046784	0.1754385965	2.3771929825	0.4210526316	0.3598491228	0.9970760234	0.1783625731	0.1286549708	0.0964912281	0.1169590643
7	1.2400489896	2.2339252909	0.0789957134	0.2345376607	0.0404164115	0.0404164115	0.2241273729	0.1206366647	0.0838946724	0.0826699326	0.0679730557	0.0624617269	0.0508266993
8	0.1857335128	0.0309555855	0.0390309556	0.1864064603	0.0057370121	0.1271870794	0.1591520861	0.5437415882	1.1160834455	0.0144683715	0.0333109017	0.0312920592	0.0629205922
9	3.2306322351	1.7720391808	0.1727515583	0.5333926981	0.6892252894	0.0926090828	0.4603739982	0.2813891362	0.2235084595	0.3125556545	0.1576135352	0.1620658949	0.1219946572
10	1.7059125964	0.3192802057	0.1231362468	0.2917737789	0.7254498715	0.0588688946	0.416966581	0.1452442159	0.0915167095	0.1059125964	0.1102827763	0.0732647815	0.101285347

Table 9.5   Results from the final Kohonen map configuration.

SEGMNT	Frequency of Cluster	Root-Mean-Square Standard Deviation	Nearest Cluster	Distance to Nearest Cluster	Row	Column
1	2227	0.5585999839	7	2.1138923707	1	1
2	6458	0.3168822791	3	1.3688591161	1	2
3	5438	0.315939344	4	1.2231685601	1	3
4	4309	0.2372281956	8	1.0251448942	1	4
5	1699	0.6478801746	3	2.4774676782	1	5
6	803	0.6970150444	8	2.7724147776	2	1
7	2165	0.3370936593	2	1.6026234411	2	2
8	4628	0.2687942614	4	1.0251448942	2	3
9	3232	0.375643876	2	1.5607210793	2	4
10	1752	0.2918243329	3	1.2233723027	2	5

Repeat the following two steps until convergence: (1) scan the data and assign
each observation to the nearest seed (nearest using the Euclidean distance);
(2) replace each seed with a weighted mean of the cluster means for the clusters
that lie in the grid neighbourhood of the seed's cluster

The weights correspond to the frequencies of each cluster. In this way the cluster
configuration is such that any two clusters which are close to each other in the
map grid will have centroids close to each other. The initial choice of the seeds
can be made in different ways; we will choose them randomly. Alternatively, we
could have used the centroids obtained from the second stage of the K-means
clustering procedure.

Table 9.5 shows the summary statistics for the final 5×2 configuration. For
each of 10 map clusters, it gives the total number of observations in the cluster
(the frequency) and the root mean square standard deviation within the cluster,
as a measure of internal cohesion. It also gives the distance from the cluster
seed to the nearest cluster seed. Table 9.5 should be compared with Table 9.3,
which gives similar information for the K-means procedure. Notice that the
groups in Table 9.5 are more homogeneous in their numbers of observations.
In Table 9.3 there is one large cluster (cluster 3) but now most clusters have a
similar size. We also have $R^2 = 0.51$, which is 0.06 higher than we obtained
using the K-means procedure.

To better interpret the cluster configurations, Table 9.6 gives the centroids
of each cluster in the final Kohonen configuration; it confirms the findings in
Table 9.4. For instance, clusters 1 and 6 seem to describe visitors that visit the
initial pages a high number of times, whereas cluster 5 describes visitors that
often click on the development pages. These behaviours correspond, respectively to clusters 4, 9 and 4, 5 in Table 9.4. Notice there is a degree of overlapping:
two kinds of behaviour appear in the same cluster, number 4.

9.5   Model comparison

An important consideration concerns the economic value of the results. Broadly
speaking, a visitor profile is better if the cluster profiles are more distinct and
if their separation reflects a truly distinct behaviour rather than being due to
randomness. We have already commented that the Kohonen map seems to do

Table 9.6 The Kohonen map cluster means.

SEGMNT	initial	help	entertainment	office	windows	othersft	download	otherint	development	hardware	business	information	area
1	2.5972159856	1.7790749888	0.1418949259	0.3515940727	0.5514144589	0.0880107768	0.4342164347	0.2281095644	0.1733273462	0.2537045352	0.1230354737	0.1091154019	0.1028289178
2	1.3186745122	0.0481573242	0.0868669997	0.0884174667	0.0328275008	0.0850108393	0.1503561474	0.1060699907	0.0755651905	0.1062248374	0.1087023846	0.0520284918	0.0277175596
3	0.0049650607	0.0029422582	0.1588819419	0.0020228025	0.0108495771	0.1362633321	0.2532180949	0.3641044502	0.3001103347	0.0709819787	0.1166708716	0.0748436925	0.0007355645
4	0.3109770248	0.0239034579	0.0378278023	1.0872592249	0.0178695753	0.0245996751	0	0.0953817591	0.070782084	0.0239034579	0.0394523091	0.0765838942	0.0060338826
5	0.7086521483	0.1730429665	0.0741612713	0.5609181872	0.2536786345	0.4714537964	0.443790465	0.810476751	2.5026486168	0.2313125368	0.1147733961	0.0841671572	0.1024131842
6	2.0473225405	0.4508094645	0.1419676214	2.986301369	0.4408468244	0.1892901619	0.6226650062	0.3611457036	0.504358655	0.198007472	0.2117061021	0.4308841843	0.102117061
7	0.6198614319	1.4868360277	0.0605080831	0.1385681293	0.0521939954	0.0378752887	0.1270207852	0.1043879908	0.0512702079	0.0748267898	0.0605080831	0.048960739	0.0295612009
8	0.2642610199	0.0494814175	0.0611495246	1.1006914434	0.084701815	0.0417026793	1.0190146932	0.0888072602	0.0667675022	0.0324114088	0.0334917891	0.0417026793	0.0592048401
9	0.6017945545	0.2277227723	0.0943688119	0.1689356436	1.3530321782	0.0402227723	0.5142326733	0.0594059406	0.0609529703	0.0872524752	0.0609529703	0.0405321782	0.0529084158
10	0.276826484	0.0313926941	0.0599315068	0.1369863014	0.053652968	0.0559360731	0.0622146119	0.0930365297	0.0890410959	0.0473744292	0.0559360731	0.0416666667	1.1078767123

this better. It achieves it by exploiting the dependence between adjacent clusters. A second consideration is that the statistical evaluation of the results should be based mainly on R^2, or measures derived from it, because this is a descriptive analysis. We have already seen that the overall R^2 is larger with the Kohonen networks. It is interesting to examine for each variable (page) the ratio of the between sum of squares and the total sums of squares that lead to R^2. This can give a measure of the goodness of the cluster representation, specific for each variable. By examining all such R^2 we can get an overall picture of which aspects of the observations are more used in the clustering process.

Table 9.7 presents all variable-specific R^2 and the overall R^2 for the K-means procedure and the Kohonen procedure. For both procedures the group pages that have a high R^2 and are therefore most influential in determining the final results, are Initial, help, office and download. There are also pages that are influential only for the K-means procedure: othersoftware and hardware. And, there are pages that are influential only for the Kohonen procedure: windows, download, and area. The choice between the two procedures therefore depends on which pages to choose as discriminant for the behaviour. In the absence of other considerations, the choice should consider the procedure which leads to the highest overall R^2, here the Kohonen map.

Further considerations may arise when the results will be used to make predictions. For instance, suppose that once the grouping has been accomplished, we receive some new observations to be classified into clusters. One reasonable

Table 9.7 Comparison of the variable-specific R^2.

Page	R^2 for (K-means)	R^2 for Kohonen map
initial	0.60	0.65
support	0.68	0.66
entertainment	0.01	0.02
office	0.44	0.70
windows	0.18	0.56
othersoft	0.47	0.07
download	0.04	0.43
otherint	0.21	0.15
development	0.79	0.64
hardware	0.49	0.03
business	0.02	0.02
infor	0.05	0.05
area	0.01	0.56
Overall	0.45	0.51

way to proceed is to assign them to one of the clusters previously determined, according to a discriminant rule. Alternatively, the analysis could be redone on the old and new observations. The first choice is more valid from a decision-making viewpoint. In that case, clustering methods can be compared in terms of predictive performance, perhaps by using cross-validation techniques. We begin by creating two data sets. We take the original data set and append one column of values, corresponding to the categorical variable that assigns each observation to a cluster (namely, the allocation variable). The allocation variable obviously differs between the K-means analysis and the Kohonen analysis, hence we create two different data sets.

To compare the two clustering procedures, we then split the two data sets into a training sample with 75% of the observations and a validation sample with the remaining 25%. A classification tree procedure is then run on both training data sets, with the allocation variable as the target response variable. We will take entropy as the impurity measure. We can then compare the predictive performance of the tree model on the two data sets, in terms of misclassification errors. This is because we know, from the cluster analysis, the actual allocation of each observation in the validation sample. Note that the two data sets only differ for the target variable, and the tree model applied is the same. The difference in the misclassification rates will therefore measure the performance of the two clustering methods in terms of predictive ability. For each cluster and for both methods, Table 9.8 shows the proportion of observations classified correctly; we can obtain the misclassification rates by subtracting these values from 100%. Once again the Kohonen map performs better on this data set, as in 9 of the 10 cases it leads to a lower misclassification error.

Table 9.8 Comparison of the predictive performances between the K-means method and the Kohonen map network.

Actual cluster	Predicted cluster	Percentage correctly classified by K-means	Percentage correctly classified by Kohonen map
1	1	92	86
2	2	98	99
3	3	99	97
4	4	73	96
5	5	82	99
6	6	57	69
7	7	92	98
8	8	93	97
9	9	80	86
10	10	58	92

Therefore, on the basis of all viewpoints, Kohonen maps are to be preferred for this problem. We now proceed with a more detailed interpretation of its results. Table 9.6 characterises each cluster in terms of the most clicked pages. But this interpretation can be improved by producing a graphical representation of the same information. More precisely, for each cluster we compare graphically the overall mean of each page variable with that found in the different visitor segments. For our study we use the mean number of visits made to the 13 areas for each behavioural profile. By comparing the 13 mean values with the whole population (as if there were just one cluster), we can suggest an interpretation of the profile.

To make interpretation easier, we will make the comparison with respect to the normalised mean (the mean divided by the maximum value in the 13 group

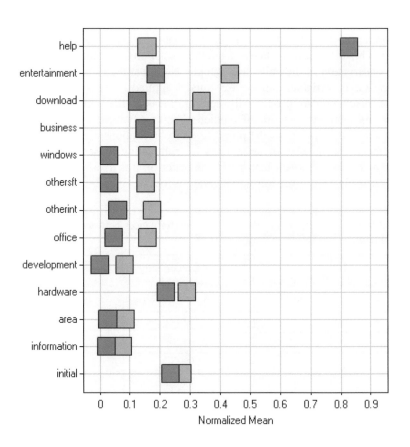

Figure 9.3 Interpretation of cluster 7.

pages), which varies between 0 and 1. For each behavioural segment, we shall use a graph that has the normalised mean on the horizontal axis and the 13 webpages on the vertical axis, plotted in decreasing order of their normalised mean. There is insufficient space to show all the clusters, but we do illustrate a few typical ones. First of all we have clusters that represent monothematic behaviours, people who visit mostly one specific area of the website. This behaviour occurs for the visitors in cluster 7, and Figure 9.3 shows that it describes visitors who mostly go to help. In other words, this group of users visits the site to ask for help about how to use the different products. The visitors in clusters 10, 9, 8 and 4 also exhibit monothematic behaviours; they correspond to visitors who go mainly to area, windows, download and office, respectively.

A second type of behaviour is polythematic behaviour, illustrated by cluster 6. Figure 9.4 shows that these visitors exploit all areas of the site. They are curious visitors who surf the pages reserved for hardware, the pages reserved

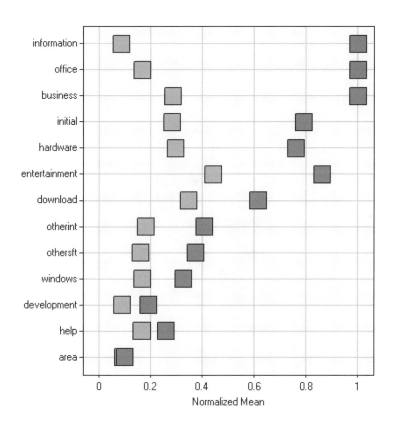

Figure 9.4   Interpretation of cluster 6.

for businesses and the pages which give information about new products and services. They are also interested in areas connected to technical help, entertainment, downloads and Office products. A similar behaviour is seen in cluster 1, which is perhaps less business-oriented than cluster 6.

A third type of behaviour is intermediate between the previous two, but it can also be interpreted as profiling specific categories of visitor. An example is cluster 5. Figure 9.5 shows that this cluster can represent software developers, namely IT professionals in the field of programming and the development of software solutions. They often visit pages on development, specialised software, hardware and downloads. And they are probably involved in the care and development of their company's computing power, hence the high number of visits to the business area.

Other intermediate behaviours are exhibited by clusters 2 and 3. Cluster 2 can represent workers who do their duty, people who use the site mostly for

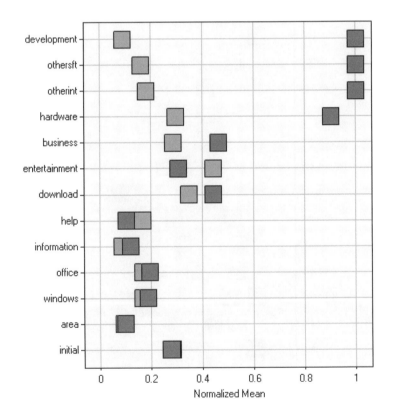

Figure 9.5 Interpretation of cluster 5.

business and initial. In other words, it is the profile of people who use the site for work reasons without being distracted by other things. Cluster 3 can represent workers in pause, people who mainly visit entertainment; they also go to pages reserved for businesses and other interests pages. In other words, it is the profile of people visiting the site for work reasons but who are also taking a break.

9.6 Summary report

- *Context*: this case study concerns customer profiling on the basis of web behaviour. The context is very broad, as the analysis refers to any type of problem involved with classifying people, companies or any other statistical units into homogeneous groups.
- *Objectives*: the aim of the analysis is to classify customers into an unknown number of homogeneous classes that will then be interpreted on the basis of their statistical characteristics, such as mean values of the variables employed. The classification is unsupervised: there is no target variable and all the available information should be used to form homogeneous groups, or clusters.
- *Organisation of the data*: in this case study the data was elaborated from the log file that registers access to a website. Consequently, there is a data matrix that records for each visitor the number of times they have viewed a collection of pages. For computational tractability, the pages were grouped into 13 web areas, homogeneous in terms of their content. Therefore the data matrix considered in the analysis contains 32 711 rows (visitors) and 13 columns (one counting variable for each area).
- *Exploratory data analysis*: this phase of the analysis revealed a high level of dispersion with respect to the pages visited. Each visitor looks, on average, at 4 pages, and this confirms the validity of grouping the 104 visited pages into 13 areas.
- *Model specification*: the analysis objectives suggested a descriptive model that would group observations into homogeneous classes. Given the size of the data set, we considered non-hierarchical cluster analysis models based on the K-means algorithm and Kohonen maps. To compare the two approaches fairly, we considered a 5×2 Kohonen map, which corresponds to the same number of clusters (10) obtained with the K-means algorithm.
- *Model comparison*: models were first compared by splitting the total variability into within-group variability and between-group variability, leading to the calculation of the overall R^2 and R^2 for specific area variables. The result of the comparison favours Kohonen maps, which also have the advantage that the groups obtained tend to be more distinct than the groups from K-means clustering. We then compared the models in terms of their predictive ability. We did this by using the clustering variable as a 'target' variable, fitting a classification tree and following a cross-validation approach. Yet again the results favour Kohonen maps.

- *Model interpretation*: the interpretation of the results should be based on the obtained cluster profiles. For the Kohonen map, which performed better, we interpreted each cluster profile by looking at the comparison between the overall mean and the cluster-specific mean of each of the 13 variables. This allowed us to identify each cluster profile. Expert knowledge is needed to elucidate the business meaning of each profile.

CHAPTER 10

Customer relationship management

10.1 Objectives of the analysis

This case study looks at statistical aspects of customer relationship management (CRM). In this context a company has as a primary objective to encourage customer loyalty, to obtain from them as much value as possible. The necessity of having loyal customers motivates companies to know them well. One way to do this is by using valid management and processing of the customer database. Data mining methods represent a valid approach to extracting precious information from such a database, and the information is then used to manage relations with existing and prospective clients. Companies increasingly personalise their services to suit each client. The data in this case study is from a company that foresaw the potential and has long been using statistically driven CRM to help manage its sales network. I cannot mention its name, but it sells mail-order merchandise in Italy.

The objective is to study the buying behaviour of the company's clients and, in particular, to understand from the outset which factors might create an, occasional buyer or a loyal shopper. This may indicate at an early stage which customers will be really profitable and where to concentrate any marketing efforts. In data mining terms, we are concerned with a problem of predictive classification. Another common data mining problem, churn analysis, can be seen as somewhat similar to loyalty analysis, as churners can be identified as disloyal clients. So this case study can also help with churn models.

10.2 Description of the data

Although schematic and concise, the analysis here is a complete representation of the data mining process, from the construction of the data matrix to the communication of the final results. It can therefore give an idea of what is involved in setting up the whole data mining process (Section 1.2). Information on the

Applied Data Mining. Paolo Giudici
© 2003 John Wiley & Sons, Ltd   ISBNs: 0-470-84679-8 (Paper); 0-470-84678-X (Cloth)

reference population, the company's current customers, is distributed across three distinct databases, containing the list of customers and their characteristics; the list of orders collected by the local agencies, later transmitted to the company; and the list of buying orders transmitted by the agencies to the company. All three databases contain variables on the customers, mainly socio-demographic and behavioural variables. These variables refer to the ways in which the first commercial contact has been established (e.g. the number of products bought and the method of payment).

To achieve the goals of the analysis, it is useful to analyse a homogeneous cohort of consumers, that is, to analyse the behaviour over time of people whose first contact with the company occurred at roughly the same time, the entry period. This eliminates possible bias effects due to structural changes in the economy, or in the structure of the company. We first consider all clients that have entered the customer database between 1992 and 1996; the total number is very large, equal to 210 085. It would be very expensive and time-consuming to analyse the whole data set, so we will take a stratified sample and analyse that. We will take the same number of clients from each time slot over the whole entry period; this sample contains a total of 2470 customers. Generally it is not necessary to sample the data; the main reason for doing it here is the low quality of the available data.

Finally, as data is spread across three databases, we need to construct a marketing database (datamart) that organises all the information we require; this is not a simple procedure. The input data sets contain data collected for operational purposes and the records differ in their type and structure. We need to obtain a coherent and informative data set by eliminating a great deal of information. The end result is a data matrix with one row for each customer and one column for each customer characteristic (statistical variable). After a long process of database management, we obtain the variables in Table 10.1.

Table 10.1   The available customer variables.

• Marketing status	• Dimension of the shop
• Whether the client is active	• Age
• Whether the client is in a debt position	• Area of residence
• Total number of orders	• Sex
• Date of first order	• Whether first payment is with instalments
• Date of last order	• First amount spent
• Total amount ordered	• Number of products at first order
• Total amount paid	
• Current balance	
• Whether payments have been delayed	
• Time lag between first and second order	
• Amount of current instalment	
• Residual number of instalments	

10.3   Exploratory data analysis

Before starting the actual data analysis, we need to identify a response variable; we need to define the explanatory variables and suggest possible transformations. The main objective is to classify the customers in two categories: those that place only one order, and those that make further orders. This binary variable, indicated by Y, can be deduced from the 'total number of orders' variable in Table 10.1. We shall set $Y = 0$ when the number of orders is equal to one and $Y = 1$ if the number of orders is greater than one. In the stated objectives, the two levels of the response variable correspond to consumers deemed disloyal ($Y = 0$) and loyal ($Y = 1$). Therefore a customer is deemed loyal if they place at least two orders with the company. Table 10.2 shows the distribution of this response variables for our sample. We could have chosen other variables to represent Y, such as the total expenditure and the number of items bought. Notice that the sample is well divided between the two categories. There are also more than 19 observations for which the value of the response variable is missing. We will ignore these observations.

Consider now the choice of explanatory variables. We want variables that will help us with predictive classification. Intuitively it seems important to consider variables that concern the first order, that describe how the first contact with the company is established, as well as the socio-demographic variables available on the customers 'age, sex, area of residence' and the dimension of the corresponding agency (see later). These are the variables on the right-hand side of Table 10.1. A few data items are missing for the explanatory variables, but as there are only a few, we can substitute a location measure for the distribution of the valid data, such as the mean (continuous variables) the median (ordinal variables) and the mode (nominal variables).

Table 10.3 shows the conditional distribution of the response variable on the socio-demographic variables. We can draw the following conclusions:

- *Sex*: at first sight, it does not seem very influential on the response variable, as there is no substantial difference in the distribution for males and females.
- *Area of residence*: see how the conditional probability of $Y = 1$ decreases when the area changes from North to Centre and from Centre to South (of Italy). This seems to be a predictive variable. South includes the Italian islands, and sometimes we will call it 'south and islands'.
- *Age*: the odds for $Y = 1$ are close to 1 for the oldest group, but noticeably lower than 1 for the other two classes, and especially for the youngest

Table 10.2   Distribution of the response variable.

Modality	Absolute frequency	Relative frequency (%)
$Y = 0$	1457	59.71
$Y = 1$	1013	40.29

Table 10.3 Conditional distribution of the response variable on the socio-demographic explanatory variables.

Sex	Y=0	Y=1
Female	61.04%	38.96%
Male	57.88%	42.12%

Area	Y=0	Y=1
North	55.40%	44.60%
Center	58,22%	41.78%
South	62.73%	37.27%

Age	Y=0	Y=1
15-35	68.80%	31.20%
36-50	53.44%	46.56%
51-89	60.42%	39.58%

Dimension	Y=0	Y=1
Small	60.39%	39,61%
Medium	56.95%	43.05%
Large	62.11%	37.89%

Table 10.4 Contingency table classifying the response variable and the instalment variable.

Y Frequency Percent Row Pct Col Pct	instalment		
	0	1	Total
0	1239 50.16 85.04 68.04	218 8.83 14.96 33.59	1457 58.99
1	582 23.56 57.45 31.96	431 17.45 42.55 66.41	1013 41.01
Total	1821 73.72	649 26.28	2470 100.00

group. This variable may be a relevant predictor, as the probability of $Y = 1$ increases noticeably with age.

- *Dimension of the agency*: this represents the only information we can use to reconstruct the location of the agency, an important variable that we do not have. Dimension of the agency subdivides the agencies into three classes on the basis of number of clients served: if the number is less than 15, the agency is considered small; if the number is between 15 and 30, it is considered medium; if it is greater than 30 (up to a maximum of 60), it is considered large. In Table 10.3 notice how the conditional probability of $Y = 1$ gets lower for large agencies. Unlike the previous variables, the effect on the response variable is not monotone with respect to the order of the explanatory variable, as medium agencies appear to show the highest conditional probability.

Besides socio-demographic variables, we also have behavioural variables that refer to the customer's first order:

- *Instalment*: a binary variable that indicates whether the first purchase is paid for in instalments (level 1) or not (level 0). It indicates the length of the relationship between the customer and the company. If a person pays in instalments, the contact with the company will tend to be longer. Table 10.4 shows the contingency table that cross-classifies the response variable with the modalities of instalment. Notice the positive association of this variable with Y, as the odds ratio is about 4.20.
- *First amount spent and number of products at first order (numb)*: these two quantitative variables seem particularly informative about the behaviour of

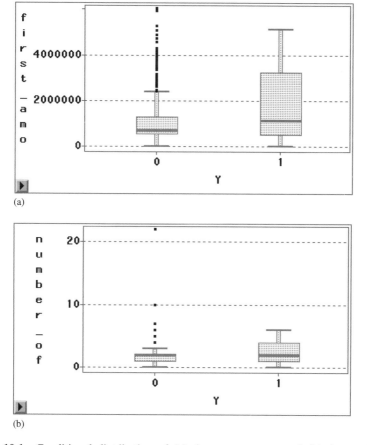

(a)

(b)

Figure 10.1 Conditional distribution of (a) the amount spent and (b) the number of products with respect to the levels of Y.

the client at the first commercial contact. The first amount spent is expressed in Italian lire (€1 = L1936.27). Figure 10.1 shows the boxplots for these two variables. If the two resulting boxplots differ markedly in position (e.g. in terms of the median), the corresponding variable can be deemed relevant. The amount spent seems to be relevant, but the number of products bought does not. And there appear to be outliers in the right tail of the distribution. We proceed by removing observations above the 99th percentile of the two variables.

We will not transform the two quantitative variables; we will leave them as they are. But to help with interpretation, we will binarise the qualitative variables age, area and dimension of the agency, all of which have three levels. This gives a total of nine binary variables. In fitting linear models, to avoid perfect collinearity, it is necessary to remove the intercept or to remove one binary variable for each of the three variables. We will leave the intercept. Table 10.5 shows an extract of the available data matrix, summarising the variables we will use in the analysis.

10.4 Model building

We will employ different types of model, and some of them we will not be able to compare using statistical techniques. In Section 10.5 we will therefore rely on cross-validation.

10.4.1 Logistic regression models

Having selected our explanatory variables, we need to find the ones that can effectively predict the response variable. The first model we consider is the logistic regression model. In order to choose a model, we follow a stepwise procedure, based in the G^2 deviance difference, with a level of significance equal to 0.05. Table 10.6 presents the results obtained from the stepwise procedure, namely the selected model along with the corresponding parameter estimates and estimated odds ratios. Only three of the available seven variables significantly affect Y: the binary instalment variable, with a strong positive association measured by an odds ratio of about 5; the age variable or, more precisely, the youngest class variable, with a negative effect determined by an odds ratio of about 0.580; and the numb variable, with a mild positive association expresses by an odds ratio of about 1.356. As numb is discrete, the effect should be interpreted by saying that a unitary increase in the number of products determines an increase in the odds of $Y = 1$ of about 1.356. For the age variable, there is no significant distinction between the adult class (36–50) and the mature class (51–89); what matters is whether or not the customer is young (15–35).

The model as a whole is significant, with a log-likelihood score equal to 254.928, leading to rejection of the null model; the degrees of freedom for this test is 3. In the next section we will assess the predictive ability of the logistic

Table 10.5 The considered data matrix.

	installment	first_amount_spen	numb	Y	center	age51_89	age36_50	dim_big	dim_medium	age15_35	sex	north	south_and_islands	dim_small
1	0	520000	0	0	0	0	0	0	1	1	1	0	1	0
2	1	1484000	2	0	0	0	1	0	0	0	0	0	1	1
3	0	2459000	1	0	0	1	0	1	1	0	1	0	1	0
4	0	3389000	0	0	1	0	1	1	0	0	1	0	0	0
5	1	3823000	2	0	0	0	0	0	0	1	0	0	1	1
6	1	1391000	2	0	0	0	0	0	1	0	1	0	1	1
7	0	2459000	1	0	0	1	0	0	0	1	1	1	0	0
8	1	1460000	1	0	0	0	1	0	1	0	0	0	1	1
9	0	1190000	0	0	1	0	0	0	1	0	0	0	0	1
10	1	3181000	2	0	0	0	1	0	0	1	1	0	1	1
11	1	2385000	1	0	0	0	0	0	0	0	1	0	1	1
12	1	1395000	1	0	0	0	0	0	0	1	1	0	1	1
13	1	1395000	1	0	0	0	1	0	0	0	0	0	1	1
14	0	2658000	3	0	0	0	0	0	0	1	1	0	1	1
15	1	2333000	3	0	0	0	1	0	0	0	0	0	1	1
16	1	3555000	1	0	0	0	0	0	0	1	1	0	1	1
17	1	1563000	1	0	0	0	1	0	0	0	0	0	1	1
18	0	1953000	3	0	0	0	0	0	1	0	1	0	1	0
19	0	738000	3	0	0	0	1	0	1	0	0	0	1	0
20	0	5106000	3	1	0	0	0	0	1	1	1	0	1	0
21	0	3808000	2	1	0	1	0	0	1	0	0	0	1	0
22	0	1953000	3	0	0	0	1	0	1	0	1	0	1	0
23	0	5259000	0	0	0	0	1	0	1	0	1	0	1	0
24	0	2480000	1	0	0	0	0	0	1	0	0	0	1	0
25	0	4041000	4	0	0	1	0	0	0	1	0	0	1	1
26	1	3645000	1	0	0	0	0	0	0	1	1	0	1	1
27	1	2940000	1	0	0	0	0	0	0	1	1	0	1	1
28	1	2940000	1	0	0	0	0	0	0	0	0	0	1	1
29	0	3645000	1	0	0	0	1	0	1	0	1	0	1	0

Table 10.6 The selected logistic regression model.

	Estimates	Stderr	Wald	Pr>Chi-square	Odds ratio
Intercept	0.3028	0.1248	108.93	<.0001	–
age15_35	-0.5440	0.1367	15.84	<.0001	0.580
installment	1.6107	0.1371	137.98	<.0001	5.006
number_of_products	0.3043	0.0465	42.78	<.0001	1.356

regression model, which has the advantage of producing transparent results interpretable in a linear form. The logistic discriminant rule in this case study allows us to distinguish a priori customers that are profitable ($Y = 1$) from those that are less profitable, therefore we can devise different ways of targeting customers. On the basis of the estimated model in Table 10.6, we can see how the discriminant rule works. For each new customer that has placed a first order, we need to know three things: whether they are young (variable A), whether they pay in instalments (B) and how many products they order (C). Let t_a, t_b, t_c be the estimated parameters of the three variables, whose values are given in Table 10.6, and let t be the estimated intercept. A customer will be profitable if the estimated probability of ordering more than once is greater than 0.5, and this corresponds to checking whether the inequality $t + t_a A + t_b B + t_c C > 0$ is true. For instance, if a customer is not young, pays in instalments and buys one product, they are profitable as $(-1.3028 \times 1) + (1.6107 \times 0) + (0.3043 \times 1) = 0.6122 > 0$. If a customer is not young, does not pay in instalments and buys one product, they are likely to be less profitable as $-1.3028 + 1.6107 + 0.3043 = -0.9985$. The estimated probability of reordering is about 0.648 in the first example and 0.269 in the second. The logistic regression model can therefore provide a simple scoring mechanism for each customer that can be used for decision making.

10.4.2 Radial basis function networks

For a neural network model, we will choose a radial basis function (RBF) with one hidden node. This is because there may be a neighbourhood structure in the input variable space and we might be able to explain it. We have considered 13 explanatory variables: all those present in Table 10.5 apart from the response variable Y. As a combination function for the input variables, we will take a Gaussian radial basis function with equal widths and equal heights. The activation function for the hidden node is the identity function and the activation function for the output node is the softmax function, so we obtain normalised output values corresponding to the estimated probabilities of $Y = 1$. The parameters of the network are learned by minimising the misclassification rate in the validation data set. Figure 10.2 shows how the misclassification rate evolves with successive iterations. The process can be stopped when the misclassification rate stabilises, and Figure 10.2 indicates that seven iterations are sufficient.

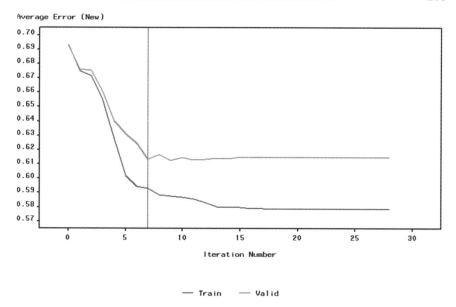

Figure 10.2   Evolution of the misclassification rate for the RBF network.

A neural network of this kind produces a list of fitted weights, with no assessment of their significance. We will not publish the list here; in any case, the largest weights correspond to the variables selected using the logistic regression model. It is not advisable to use the fitted weights of a neural network to build a discriminant rule, because the fitted weights are not corrected for sample variability, so they may depend heavily on the sample at hand. We will suspend comment on the RBF discriminant rule for the time being.

10.4.3   Classification tree models

We begin by comparing two CART tree models, based on the entropy and the Gini impurity. The better model is based on the Gini impurity. The results from the better tree are based on a pruning algorithm that leads to an optimal number of terminal nodes. It does this by minimising the misclassification rate. Figure 10.3 shows the behaviour of the classification accuracy (the complement of the misclassification rate) as the number of terminal nodes (leaves) increases. Notice that the optimal configuration of the decision tree is obtained when the number of leaves equals 11. The corresponding tree can be described in terms of 11 association rules, pointing towards the leaves, that take the 1465 customers in the training data set and split them into 11 target groups, each with a different estimated probability of ordering again ($Y = 1$). Table 10.7 gives the list of these rules.

In Table 10.7 each rule is stated according to the path that leads from the root node to the terminal node. But the list of conditions that express a rule is

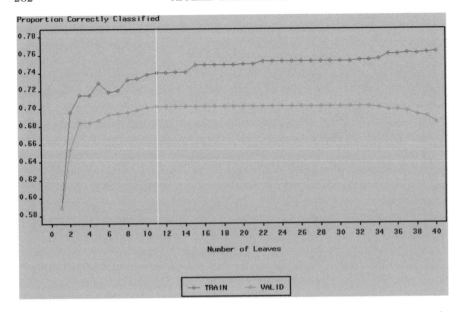

Proportion Correctly Classified

Figure 10.3 Evolution of the classification accuracy for the classification tree as the number of leaves increases.

written in reverse order, so that nodes farther from the leaf come closer to it in the rule. Here is the association rule with the highest support; about 48.3% of the customers follow this rule:

```
IF (375000 ≤ FIRST_AMOUNT_SPENT < 2659000) AND
   (INSTALMENT = 0),   THEN (Y =0)
```

This rule corresponds to a leaf obtained from splitting all observations by instalment, and then by the inequality $375000 \leq$ FIRST_AMOUNT_SPENT <2659000. Customers that obey the conditions of this rule are estimated to be not profitable, as the estimated probability of $Y = 1$ is only 18.6%. This explains why the head of the rule is $Y = 0$. In general, the head of the rule follows the classical discriminant rule: if the fitted probability is less than 50% then $Y = 0$; otherwise $Y = 1$.

Table 10.7 The rules for the classification tree.

```
IF     2659000 <=FIRST_AMOUNT_SPENT

AND INSTALMENT EQUALS 0
THEN
  N : 226
  1 : 56.2%
```

Table 10.7 (*continued*)

```
IF    2659000 <=FIRST_AMOUNT_SPENT
 0 : 43.8%

IF FIRST_AMOUNT_SPENT <    515000
AND INSTALMENT EQUALS 1
THEN
 N : 55
 1 : 89.1%
 0 : 10.9%

IF   375000 <=FIRST_AMOUNT_SPENT <    2659000
AND INSTALMENT EQUALS 0
THEN
 N : 709
 1 : 18.6%
 0 : 81.4%

IF NORTH EQUALS 0
AND NUMBER_OF_PRODUCTS < 2.5
AND    515000 <=FIRST_AMOUNT_SPENT
AND INSTALMENT EQUALS 1
THEN
 N : 99
 1 : 47.5%
 0 : 52.5%

IF NORTH EQUALS 1
AND NUMBER_OF_PRODUCTS < 2.5
AND    515000 <=FIRST_AMOUNT_SPENT
AND INSTALMENT EQUALS 1
THEN
 N : 42
 1 : 73.8%
 0 : 26.2%

IF    2.5 <=NUMBER_OF_PRODUCTS < 5.5
AND    515000 <=FIRST_AMOUNT_SPENT
AND INSTALMENT EQUALS 1
THEN
 N : 178
 1 : 78.7%
 0 : 21.3%

IF    5.5 <=NUMBER_OF_PRODUCTS
AND  515000 <=FIRST_AMOUNT_SPENT
AND INSTALMENT EQUALS 1
THEN
 N : 3
```

(*continued overleaf*)

Table 10.7 (*continued*)

```
IF    2659000 <=FIRST_AMOUNT_SPENT

 1 : 0.0%
 0 : 100.0%

IF FIRST_AMOUNT_SPENT < 105000
AND NORTH EQUALS 1
AND INSTALMENT EQUALS 0
THEN
 N : 7
 1 : 0.0%
 0 : 100.0%

IF    105000 <=FIRST_AMOUNT_SPENT < 375000
AND NORTH EQUALS 1
AND INSTALMENT EQUALS 0
THEN
 N : 59
 1 : 72.9%
 0 : 27.1%

IF AGE36_50 EQUALS 1
AND NORTH EQUALS 0
AND FIRST_AMOUNT_SPENT < 375000
AND INSTALMENT EQUALS 0
THEN
 N : 47
 1 : 25.5%
 0 : 74.5%

IF AGE36_50 EQUALS 0
AND NORTH EQUALS 0
AND FIRST_AMOUNT_SPENT < 375000
AND INSTALMENT EQUALS 0
THEN
 N : 40
 1 : 52.5%
 0 : 47.5%
```

The classification tree thus provides an immediate discriminant rule, based on partitions of the explanatory variables. To allocate a new customer, we begin at the root and take the path corresponding to the characteristics of the customer; then we see whether the terminal leaf gives a probability higher than 50% to $Y = 1$. The difference with the logistic regression model is that the discriminant rule is a hierarchical logical statement (based on partitions of the data) rather than an additive score (based on all the data). The variables that appear relevant for classification are instalment, number of products, and age, which correspond

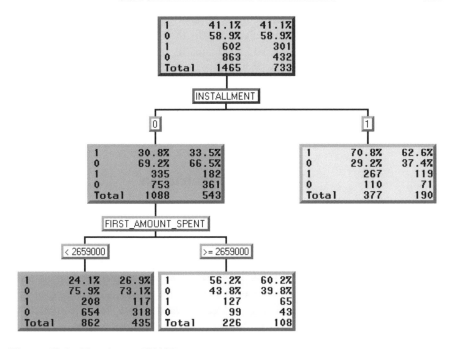

Figure 10.4 The chosen CHAID tree.

to the significant variables in the logistic regression model. The tree also ascribes relevance to the first amount spent and the geographic area.

For completeness, we also implement a CHAID tree model, with a significance level of 0.01, in order to obtain a more parsimonious classification tree. The resulting model has a higher misclassification rate than our Gini-based CART model, but it is parsimonious. Figure 10.4 shows the CHAID tree. The two discriminant variables are instalment and first amount spent. These two variables are also the ones first chosen in the CART tree of Table 10.7. The difference is that the CHAID tree does not go into as much depth. On the other hand, comparing the results with logistic regression, the instalment variable appears in both, but age and number of products are now replaced by first amount spent.

10.4.4   Nearest-neighbour models

In a nearest-neighbour model, the main parameter to choose is the width K; this establishes the size of the neighbourhood of the explanatory variables that will be used to predict Y. We begin with a very large value, $K = 732$, which corresponds to half the total number of observations in the training data set. Then we try a very low value, $K = 10$. It turns out that $K = 10$ is a better choice, in terms of misclassification rate: for $K = 732$ it is 0.41; for $K = 100$ it is 0.328; and for $K = 10$ it is 0.316. The misclassification rate increases for lower values of K. We will thus choose $K = 10$.

For nearest-neighbour models there is no analytic form to comment upon, as the method is memory-based, namely, it recalls the neighbouring data only when a prediction is in order. Section 10.5 evaluates its predictive performance.

A nearest-neighbour model works well when the observations are well separated in the space of the explanatory variables and when the corresponding groups are fairly pure. In an ideal situation, observations should be partitioned in non-overlapping regions, possibly of a small size, and each region should contain observations with a similar value of the response variable (here 0 or 1).

10.5   Model comparison

We first compare models in terms of the confusion matrices obtained on the validation data set. For all models, we have chosen a cut-off threshold of 50%, and the errors are derived on that basis. Table 10.8 shows the confusion matrix for the final logistic regression model. In this table and the following ones, frequencies are expressed as percentages. Table 10.8 shows that the model predicts as non-profitable ($Y = 0$ predicted) customers that in fact are profitable ($Y = 1$ observed) in 22.92% of the cases; this is the type I error. On the other hand, it predicts as profitable ($Y = 1$ predicted) those that are not ($Y = 0$ observed) in 10.91% of the cases; this is the type II error.

Whether the logistic regression model leads to a valid discriminant rule, depends on marketing evaluations on the relative costs of the two errors. Usually, if a customer is targeted to be profitable, a direct marketing campaign is dedicated to them by mail, telephone calls, etc. If a customer is not targeted to be profitable, they will not be part of the campaign. Therefore the cost of the type I error depends on the probability of losing customers that are not targeted, although they would be profitable; the cost of the type II error is the money allocated by the company to follow customers that are probably not worthy of attention. From Table 10.8 the logistic regression model leads to a higher type I error, and should be chosen if type II error is deemed more costly than type I error. Table 10.9 shows the confusion matrix for the chosen CART tree model. Notice that the total misclassification rate for the classification tree is slightly

Table 10.8   Confusion matrix for the logistic regression model.

		Predicted	
		0	1
Observed	0	48.02	10.91
	1	22.92	18.14

lower than for the logistic regression model, 29.74% against 33.83%. Furthermore, the probabilities of the two types of error are rather balanced. The tree model should therefore be chosen in the absence of information on the costs of the two errors, or when the costs are roughly equivalent.

Table 10.10 shows the confusion matrix for the RBF network. Notice that the total misclassification rate is about 32.47%, lower than for logistic regression but higher than for CART. The probabilities of the two errors are unbalanced, as with logistic regression. Overall we can draw the same conclusions as for logistic regression. However, the slight improvement does not justify the increased model complexity and difficulty of interpretation compared with logistic regression.

Table 10.11 shows the confusion matrix for the nearest-neighbour model. It turns out that the nearest-neighbour model has the same total misclassification rate as the tree model, 29.74%, and is therefore as good overall. But the probabilities for type I and type II errors are slightly more unbalanced, and the nearest-neighbour model has the lowest type I error probability among all the considered models. Therefore, if type I error costs are higher than type II error costs, a nearest-neighbour model should be chosen. If the relative error costs are not a consideration, both the CART tree and the nearest-neighbour model can be chosen, as they minimise the misclassification error rate over the validation set.

Table 10.9 Confusion matrix for the CART classification tree.

		Predicted	
		0	1
Observed	0	43.52	15.42
	1	14.32	26.74

Table 10.10 Confusion matrix for the RBF neural network.

		Predicted	
		0	1
Observed	0	47.34	11.60
	1	20.87	20.19

Table 10.11 Confusion matrix for
the nearest-neighbour model.

		Predicted	
		0	1
Observed	0	41.34	17.60
	1	12.14	28.92

So far we have drawn our conclusions using the validation data set. But since some data mining models are often built using results on the validation data set, it may be of interest to compare models on a third data set, named the test data set. To do this, the available data should be partitioned into three data sets instead of two: a training data set (60% of the data), a validation dataset (20% of the data) and a test data set (20% of the data). Then the predictive power of the models can be compared on the test data set, to obtain a more neutral evaluation. When there are only two data sets, not three, the second data set (for validation) is sometimes indirectly used to build a model (e.g. to prune a tree, to choose the number of hidden nodes in a neural network, or to choose the number of neighbours in a nearest-neighbour method); consequently, the outcome of the validation may be too optimistic. Splitting the data set into three implies a loss of information, as the test data set is never used, and the number of observations in the training data set is reduced. The extra sampling process introduces a new source of variability and it could increase the instability of the results.

We consider a threefold partitioning accomplished in a stratified way to maintain the proportion of $Y = 1$ and $Y = 0$ in each of the three data sets. We have placed 60% of the data in the training data set, 20% in the validation data set and 20% in the test data set. Table 10.12 shows the misclassification rates for the models on all three partitions training, validation and test. On the test set, the tree model has the lowest error, followed by the nearest-neighbour model, called MBR for memory-based reasoning, then the RBF network and finally the logistic regression model. The same ranking of the models is obtained on the training data set, but on the validation data set there is a tie between MBR and the tree model. The CHAID tree in Figure 10.4 leads to a misclassification error of 0.3237 on the test set, higher than the CART tree and MBR.

Table 10.12 Summary comparison of misclassification errors.

Tool	Misclassification Rate	Valid:Misclassification Rate	Test:Misclassification Rate
Tree	0.2593856655	0.2974079127	0.2909836066
MBR	0.2894197952	0.2974079127	0.3155737705
Regression	0.3071672355	0.3383356071	0.3770491803
Neural Network	0.3051194539	0.3246930423	0.3360655738

Now would be the time to approach marketing experts for a cost function using the costs of the type I and type II errors. But even without this information, we can still go a bit further in our model selection. Up to now we have used a cut-off threshold of 50%, but this need not be the only choice. In particular, the costs of the errors may lead us to change the cut-off. For instance, if type II error is deemed more costly, a higher cut-off can be chosen, so as to predict fewer events $Y = 1$ and decrease type II errors; but this will increase type I errors. Conversely, if type I error is deemed more costly, a lower cut-off can be chosen.

In the absence of cost considerations, the models should be compared using ROC curves. Figure 10.5 shows the ROC curves of the four models being compared. The vertical axis is the sensitivity, equal to $1 -$ the probability of type I error, and the horizontal axis plots $1 -$ specificity, equal to the probability of a type II error. Notice that the ROC curves for all four models are rather similar, apart from a gap in the central part of the curve, where the tree model and the nearest-neighbour model (called user) are better. This is the area where the

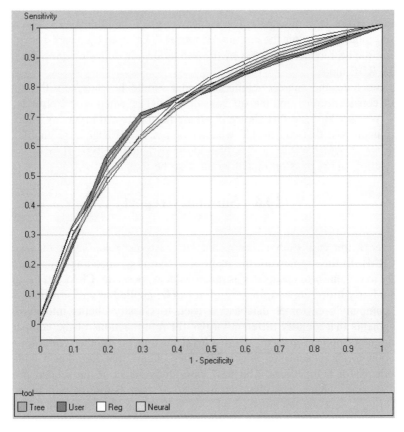

Figure 10.5 ROC curves for the considered models. The curve called user is the MBR model.

Table 10.13 Comparison of Gini indexes of performance.

	Logistic regression	RBF	Tree	Nearest neighbour
Gini index	0.4375	0.4230	0.4445	0.5673

50% cut-off error probabilities fall. Conversely, in the upper right part of the graph, the neural network model and the logistic regression model are better, as they lead to a higher sensitivity (lower type I error). All the curves are similar for high values of the cut-off, corresponding to low values of sensitivity and 1 − specificity.

To decide between the curves, we need more information about the costs. But without this information we can calculate a summary measure of performance for the models, which corresponds to the area between the ROC curve and the 45° line; it is called the Gini index of performance (Section 6.6). We calculate the Gini index for all four models on the test data set, and for nine equally spaced cut-off points (from 10% onwards). The values are given in Table 10.13. The higher the Gini index, the better the considered model. Therefore the nearest-neighbour model is the best model, followed by the tree model, the logistic regression model and the RBF model.

To conclude, the nearest-neighbour model should be chosen in the absence of cost considerations (and cut-off considerations) or when type I error is more costly. We should make this choice if we are not interested in having an explicit discriminant rule that can decide whether or not a customer is profitable. Otherwise we should consider a classification tree model. If type II error is more costly, a logistic regression model would also be fine.

10.6 Summary report

- *Context*: this case study concerns analytic customer relationship management (CRM). In this framework the main objective is to encourage customer loyalty to obtain from customers as much value as possible. CRM can be applied in a fairly broad context; in general, it can be applied to any situations where a company's customer database is used to classify clients into classes or segments that identify different targets for future actions of the company. A common application is to identify loyal customers; another common application is churn analysis, which identifies clients that abandon a company, perhaps for competitors. The next case study looks at the related problem of scoring, where each client is assigned a score before classification. The scoring aspect was not emphasised here, as the main interest was in classifying the customers.
- *Objectives*: the aim of the analysis is to classify customers into homogeneous classes that identify different target profiles. Customers are divided into more

valuable customers (more than one order in the considered period) and less valuable customers (only one order in the considered period).

- *Organisation of the data*: data is usually contained in a so-called customer table, or marketing database (data mart). We considered a common situation, especially for small and medium-sized companies, in which there is not a data warehouse and therefore a customer database has to be built up from operational databases. This process is rather difficult and typically eliminates much information due to inconsistencies or missing data. To consider a clean and statistically representative data mart (e.g. with regard to the entrance time in the database), we had to take a sample whose size appears very small when compared with the original customer database. This shows just how important it is to consider how the data will be analysed when building up a data warehouse or a system of operational databases. At the end of the process, besides the binary response variable indicating the value of a customer, we obtained seven explanatory variables, five discrete and two continuous.

- *Exploratory data analysis*: this was conducted by analysing the bivariate distributions involving the binary response variable and the seven candidate predictors taken one at a time.

- *Model specification*: the analysis objective suggested a predictive classification model that allocates customers to the classes more valuable and less valuable. We considered four types of model: logistic regression, classification trees, RBF networks and nearest-neighbour models.

- *Model comparison*: the models were compared using a computational cross-validation approach. We compared classification errors of the models on a validation data set and then on a more independent test dataset. We used the standard discriminant threshold rule of 50%. Then we compared ROC curves, which are drawn by varying the discriminant threshold. To give a summary performance measure, we calculated the Gini index for each ROC curve. The result is that, in the absence of considerations on error costs or when type I error is deemed more costly, the classification tree performs best with a 50% threshold and the nearest-neighbour model performs best with a varying threshold. If type II error is more costly, a logistic regression model would also be fine.

- *Model interpretation*: on the basis of model comparison, it seems that classification trees and nearest-neighbour models are the best tools for the considered predictive task. However, there is an interpretational difference that should be taken into account. Classification trees produce rules that are easily interpretable in logical terms but nearest-neighbour models do not deliver explicit rules. Nearest-neighbour models are non-parametric tools, hence they have the advantage of not requiring strong modelling assumptions but they are harder to interpret. The choice between the two tools depends on who will be using the results. If the results will go to trained statisticians or IT. experts, then it probably does not matter which model is chosen, but trees are probably better for business experts who would like a more user-friendly picture of what is going on.

CHAPTER 11

Credit scoring

11.1   Objectives of the analysis

This case study applies data mining methods to the problem of credit scoring for consumer credit. It looks at how to evaluate the credit reliability of individuals who ask for credit when buying goods or services. The various credit operators (e.g. banks, investment companies and credit card societies) receive thousands of applications every day, so they need a system to help them grant or refuse requests. Recent studies have proposed decision support systems, or scoring models. They are fast, objective and inexpensive, which makes them extremely efficient when compared with traditional scores based on experience. This is especially true for consumer credit, where the monetary value of each loan is quite small. We will take customer data from an important bank in southern Germany and use it to construct a scoring model for consumer credit.

Automatic systems are widely used for evaluating creditworthiness, especially by banks and investment companies. There are many reasons for this development, including the regulatory policy that was recently established by the Basel Committee of central banks (www.bis.org). These regulations include a detailed prescription of how credit risk should be calculated by financial institutions and they apply to different types of credit, including consumer credit and business credit. Consumer credit means lending to individuals and households for the acquisition of goods or services. The exercise of this activity is reserved by law to banks, specialised intermediary backers and, in some forms, to the sellers of goods or services.

The term 'credit scoring' describes the statistical methods used to classify possible creditors into two classes of risk: good and bad. Statistical models for credit scoring, often known as scorecard models, use explanatory variables obtained from information about the applicant to estimate the probability of a loan's non-repayment. A credit request is granted or refused by comparing the estimated probability with a suitable threshold chosen by the management. The statistical methods most often used to develop scorecards are neural networks, logistic regression and classification trees. The literature on credit scoring and credit scorecard models is quite vast; see for instance Hand and Henley (1996).

The data to construct a scorecard is generally obtained from a sample of applicants to whom credit has already been granted, and for whom it is known

Applied Data Mining.   Paolo Giudici
© 2003 John Wiley & Sons, Ltd   ISBNs: 0-470-84679-8 (Paper); 0-470-84678-X (Cloth)

whether or not the creditor was reliable. To calculate the score for a specific credit request, the customer's data is compared with the scorecard, in order to classify the new applicant into one of the observed behavioural patterns and determine a predictive score. Often a scorecard model is able to assign a score to every measurable characteristic of the applicant. These scores are then summed to produce an overall score.

11.2   Description of the data

The data set is 1000 observations on 1000 credit applicants to an important bank in southern Germany; see Fahrmeir and Hamerle (1994) for a more detailed description of the data. We consider 21 variables; one of them is the binary variable Y, credit reliability ($Y = 0$ for the reliables, $Y = 1$ for the non-reliables), which we treat as the response or target variable. The other 20 variables are treated as explanatory variables. They can be grouped in the following way. Table 11.1 shows the data matrix.

- *Socio-demographic variables*
  - sex and marital status
  - age
  - residence: number of years resident in the present home
- *Personal and financial variables*
  - account: whether owners of a bank account
  - bank book: whether owners of a bank book
  - previous rep: history of past repayments
  - debts: amount of previous debts
  - concurrent: whether other fundings have been required
  - employment: type of employment
  - working years: number of working years
  - foreign: whether foreign worker
  - family: number of people in charge of
- *Variables specific to the loan*
  - loan: amount of the loan
  - purpose: purpose of the loan

Table 11.1   The structure of the data matrix.

Applicant	Y	X1	X2	...	X3	...	...	...	...	...	X20
1	1	1	18	...	1049			...			1
⋮											
34	1	4	24	...	1376			...			1
⋮											
1000	0	1	30	...	6350			...			1

- deadline: deadline of the loan
- monthly interests
- others: whether other concurrent debtors are specified
- *Indicators of wealth*
  - house: whether owner of a house
  - effects: whether has other personal guarantees
  - telephone: whether a telephone is available

Only 3 of the 20 explanatory variables are continuous: deadline, loan and age. The other 17 are discrete but only 2 of these are binary: telephone and foreigner. The other 15 discrete variables have different numbers of levels; purpose has 11.

The data is stratified into 300 customers selected as non-reliable ($Y = 1$, loans not repaid) and 700 as reliable ($Y = 0$, loans repaid). Therefore the percentages of good and bad customers are already fixed. This kind of stratification affects the results obtained from the statistical models; they will not be the same as the results from a simple random sample. The data set has an inherent bias as it contains only those individuals actually given a loan. There are others that did not get a loan and we do not know whether or not they would have been at risk. Although these considerations do not alter the validity of the analysis, we should remember them when we come to interpretation.

Even though we will lose information, to simplify the analysis, we will modify the original data set to obtain exclusively binary variables. Binarisation allows us to investigate the odds ratio. For the quantitative variables we mainly calculate the median; we create two levels, one corresponding to values higher than the median, another to values lower than the median. For example, deadline had values in the interval of 0–72 months, but we have modified it as in Table 11.2 For all the other variables, we give the value 0 to the category that is less reliable, and the value 1 to the category that is more reliable. Take previous rep as an example. We give the value 1 to the category corresponding to impeccable previous repayments and the value 0 to the category corresponding to late previous repayments.

Some discrete variables have to be reclassified. For instance, account is subdivided into two new binary variables: good_account and bad_account. Table 11.3 shows the new and old classifications. The variable sex and marital status is divided into two distinct binary variables: sex and marital status. Table 11.4 summarises this representation.

Table 11.2 Classification of the deadline variable.

Previous classes	New classes	Interpretation
Deadline > 18 months	1	Long-term
Deadline < 18 months	0	Short-term

Table 11.3   Classification of the account variable.

New variables		Original variable	
bad_account	good_account	account	
1	0	2 negative balance	Bad
0	1	4 balance > DM 200	Good
0	0	3 balance in [0–200]	Neutral
0	0	1 no account	Neutral

Table 11.4   Classification of the sex and marital status variables.

New variables		Original Variable
sex	marital status	sex and marital status
0	0	1 man: bachelor, divorced or separated
1	0	2 woman: bachelor, divorced or separated
0	1	3 man: married or widow
1	1	4 woman: married or widow

11.3 Exploratory data analysis

We begin with a univariate analysis to investigate the intensity of the existing links between every explanatory variable and the response variable. This will indicate the efficiency of each explanatory variable in identifying the non-reliable clients $(Y = 1)$. The explanatory variables that are more associated with the response variable should be better able to determine client's reliability. Although it neglects interactions between the variables, univariate analysis often proves very useful. It is an important preliminary step in setting up a multivariate model.

To investigate the association between the response variable and each of the 22 explanatory variables, we construct the odds ratio. Here we put $Y = 1$ first and $Y = 0$ second to help with interpretation. The resulting odds ratio is the reciprocal of the one we would obtain using the conventional order (Section 3.4). Now the higher the odds ratio, the more negative the association of the explanatory variable with the response variable and the higher the positive association with credit reliability. In other words, the results indicate the efficiency of each individual variables as an indicator of creditworthiness.

Table 11.5 shows the odds ratios and the corresponding 95% confidence intervals; the last column shows the p-value of the chi-squared Pearson statistic. The 22 explanatory variables are tabulated in decreasing order of the odds ratio. The first eight variables in the table have a negative association with the response variable; in fact, the odds ratio shows a value higher than 1, and 1 does not fall in the confidence interval. The last five variables have a positive association with the response variable, since the odds ratio takes values in the interval [0,1], and

Table 11.5 Univariate odds ratios with the response variable.

Variable	Odds ratio	95% Confidence interval	Association	Chi-square p-value
good_account	5.459	(3.857; 7.725)	(−)	1.41E-24
previous rep	3.958	(2.529; 6.193)	(−)	1.21E-09
bank book	2.758	(1.957; 3.888)	(−)	3.05E-09
deadline	1.842	(1.402; 2.421)	(−)	1.22E-05
working years	1.781	(1.311; 2.421)	(−)	2.47E-04
purpose	1.679	(1.269; 2.220)	(−)	2.85E-04
age	1.676	(1.274; 2.206)	(−)	2.48E-04
marital status	1.532	(1.160; 2.022)	(−)	3.17E-03
monthly interests	1.342	(1.008; 1.787)	(−?)	0.045
loan	1.241	(0.946; 1.627)	NO	0.129
debts	1.233	(0.928; 1.639)	NO	0.153
telephone	1.177	(0.892; 1.554)	NO	0.261
residence	1.031	(0.785; 1.354)	NO	0.835
family	1.018	(0.700; 1.481)	NO	1.000
others	0.994	(0.624; 1.583)	NO	1.000
employment	0.904	(0.651; 1.257)	NO	0.563
sex	0.769	(0.584; 1.011)	NO	0.067
effects	0.642	(0.489; 0.842)	(+)	1.49E-03
bad_account	0.568	(0.423; 0.763)	(+)	1.88E-04
concurrent	0.550	(0.395; 0.765)	(+)	4.06E-04
house	0.531	(0.398; 0.710)	(+)	1.99E-05
foreign	0.273	(0.096; 0.778)	(+)	9.42E-03

1 does not fall in the confidence interval. The variable monthly interests exhibits a probable negative association since the odds ratio is greater than 1, but 1 is slightly out of the confidence interval. We will leave it in for now and use the multivariate analysis to make a firmer decision. The rest of the explanatory variables show no significant association with the response variable, since the confidence interval contains the value 1. These conclusions are all confirmed by the p-values of the chi-squared statistics in the last column of the table.

- For the first eight variables and the last five variables the p-value is less than 0.05; this means that the null hypothesis is rejected and the existence of an association is accepted:
- For monthly interests the p-value is slightly under 0.05; this means the association with the response variable is borderline significant.
- The remaining variables have a p-value greater than 0.05; this means the null hypothesis is accepted

Table 11.6 shows how we derive the odds ratios and allows us to draw the following conclusions:

Table 11.6 Interpretation of the odds ratios.

Variable	Odds for $X = 1$, θ_1	Odds for $X = 0$, θ_2	Odds ratio	Association
good_account	0.594	3.243	5.459	(−)
previous rep	0.291	1.152	3.958	(−)
bank book	0.078	2.143	2.758	(−)
deadline	0.730	1.344	1.842	(−)
working years	0.650	1.157	1.781	(−)
purpose	0.720	1.209	1.679	(−)
age	0.788	1.322	1.676	(−)
marital status	0.767	1.175	1.532	(−)
monthly interests	0.901	1.210	1.342	(−?)
loan	0.901	1.116	1.241	N0
debts	0.928	1.114	1.233	N0
telephone	0.937	1.104	1.177	N0
residence	0.983	1.041	1.031	N0
family	0.997	1.016	1.018	N0
others	1.000	0.996	0.994	N0
employment	1.081	0.978	0.904	N0
sex	1.115	0.857	0.769	N0
effects	1.253	0.804	0.642	(+)
bad_account	1.178	0.669	0.568	(+)
concurrent	1.129	0.620	0.550	(+)
house	1.217	0.646	0.531	(+)
foreign	3.541	0.966	0.273	(+)

- The applicants who possess a good current account (more than DM 200) with a creditor bank are more reliable. In fact, in going from customers who have a medium account or a negative balance (good_account = 0) to customers who have a good account (good_account = 1) the probability of repayment increases; it goes from an odds of 0.594 to an odds of 3.243. Therefore there exists a negative association between unreliability and the possession of a good current account; the exact measure of this association is given by the odds ratio. In the case of good_account, when the account balance is greater than DM 200 then the probability of repayment is about 5.46 times the probability of repayment for clients who have a medium account or a negative balance.
- German workers are more reliable than foreign workers. In going from clients who are German workers (foreign = 0) to clients who are foreign workers (foreign = 1) the odds of repayment is reduced from 3.541 to 0.966. This means that a positive association exists between being a foreign worker and being non-reliable. The exact measure of this association is expressed by the odds ratio, and the probability of repayment for foreign workers is 0.273 times that for German workers. In other words, the probability of repayment for

German workers is around 3.6 times (1/0.273) the probability of repayment for foreign workers.

- those who own effects (`effects` = 1) or who own a house (`house` = 1) are less reliable than those who do not own effects or who do not own a house. This could be because house owners have already taken out credit in the form of mortgage. Having to cope with a mortgage could make someone a non-reliable client.

11.4 Model building

Having performed a univariate exploratory analysis, we move on to a multivariate analysis, by specifying a statistical model. We are trying to combine all the signals from the different explanatory variables to obtain an overall signal that indicates the reliability of each applicant. In order to choose a model, we have to clarify the nature of the problem. It is clear that we have a predictive classification problem, as the response variable is binary and our aim is to predict whether a credit applicant will be reliable or non-reliable. We will concentrate on logistic regression, classification trees and multilayer perceptrons, the methods most often used for predictive classification in general and credit scoring in particular. We also consider an approach based on bagging, which combines the results from different models. Other methods can also be adopted, notably nearest-neighbour models and probabilistic expert systems, but we will not consider them here.

11.4.1 Logistic regression models

We choose a logistic regression model using a forward selection procedure with a significance level of 0.05. To check the model, we try a stepwise procedure and a backward procedure then verify that all three models are similar. Table 11.7 describes the forward selection procedure. The starting point is the

Table 11.7 Results of the forward selection procedure.

Step	Effect entered	Effect removed	df	Number in	Score chi-square	Wald chi-square	$P >$ chi-square
1	good_account	–	1	1	103.9648	–	<0.0001
2	previous rep	–	1	2	24.4942	–	<0.0001
3	bank book	–	1	3	17.3725	–	<0.0001
4	deadline	–	1	4	18.8629	–	<0.0001
5	house	–	1	5	8.3749	–	0.0038
6	age	–	1	6	7.0758	–	0.0078
7	purpose	–	1	7	8.4775	–	0.0036
8	foreign	–	1	8	7.9316	–	0.0049
9	monthly interests	–	1	9	6.9678	–	0.0083
10	marital status	–	1	10	5.7610	–	0.0164

simplest model, containing only the intercept. Then, at every step, we compare the deviances to decide whether or not to add an explanatory variable.

SAS Enterprise Miner uses the score chi-squared statistic in the forward procedure and the Wald chi-squared statistic in the backward procedure. According to Table 11.7, the final model is obtained in step 10; besides `intercept`, it includes the following explanatory variables:

```
X1 = deadline            X6 = age
X2 = previous rep        X7 = house
X3 = purpose             X8 = foreign
X4 = bank book           X9 = good_account
X5 = monthly interests   X10 = marital status
```

To check the overall quality of the final model, we calculate the likelihood ratio test G^2 for the final model (H_1) against the null model (H_0). It turns out that $G^2 = 219.89$ with 10 degrees of freedom. As the corresponding p-value of the test is lower than 0.0001, the null hypothesis is rejected, implying that at least one of the model's coefficients in Table 11.7 is significant. The model has an AIC score of 1023.828, and a BIC score of 1077.814. The total misclassification rate is 0.244. The misclassification rate of a model with all variables present (i.e. without any stepwise model selection) is 0.252, slightly higher than 0.244.

Table 11.8 shows the maximum likelihood estimates corresponding to the final model and the statistical significance of the parameters. For all the explanatory variables we obtain a p-value lower than 0.05, therefore the null hypothesis is always rejected. This means that all the 10 explanatory variables selected using the stepwise procedure are significantly associated with the response variable and are useful in explaining whether an applicant is reliable ($Y = 0$) or not ($Y = 1$).

Table 11.8 Maximum likelihood estimates of the parameters.

Parameter	df	Estimate	Standard error	Wald chi-square	$P >$ chi-square
intercept	1	0.5030	0.6479	0.6029	0.4375
deadline	1	−0.6027	0.1567	14.7914	0.0001
previous rep	1	−1.0479	0.2573	16.5875	<0.0001
purpose	1	−0.5598	0.1632	11.7703	0.0006
bank book	1	−0.7870	0.1937	16.5063	<0.0001
monthly interests	1	−0.4754	0.1660	8.2009	0.0042
age	1	−0.4203	0.1603	6.8701	0.0088
house	1	0.4934	0.1683	8.5914	0.0034
foreign	1	1.3932	0.5794	5.7825	0.0162
good_account	1	−1.4690	0.1863	62.1582	<0.0001
marital status	1	−0.3910	0.1633	5.7325	0.0167

Now that we have a model, we need to interpret it. A stepwise procedure may be unstable in the estimates, which are conditional on the selected model. A model-averaging approach, such as a full Bayesian approach, may solve this problem, but it will make the model more complicated (Giudici, 2001a). The obtained logistic regression model can be described by the following formula:

$$\log \frac{P(Y=1)}{P(Y=0)} = \beta_0 + \beta_1 X_1 + \beta_2 X_2 + \cdots + \beta_{10} X_{10}$$

in which the response variable is credit reliability ($Y = 0$ if yes, $Y = 1$ if no) and the explanatory variables are as described in Section 11.2. Table 11.9 shows the parameter estimates and the estimated odds ratios for each variable. We can interpret Table 11.9 using the model formula. This formula is constructed by setting $Y = 1$ when the debtor is non-reliable, so we can say that a parameter with a positive sign indicates that the corresponding variable reduces the debtor's reliability. Conversely, a parameter with a negative sign indicates that the corresponding variable increases the debtor's reliability.

The variable good_account has a parameter with a negative sign ($\hat{\beta} = -1.4690$); this means that clients who have a good current account, above DM 200, present a probability of repayment greater than clients who have a medium account or a negative balance. Analogous arguments are valid for deadline, previous rep, purpose, bank book, monthly interests, age and marital status. We can therefore list eight variables that reduce the risk of non-repayment, or increase the probability of repayment:

- A good current account
- Previous impeccable repayments
- The possession of a bank book
- A loan with a short-term deadline

Table 11.9 Interpretation of the estimated model.

Variables	$\hat{\beta}$	$e^{-\hat{\beta}}$
intercept	0.5030	0.605
deadline	−0.6027	1.827
previous rep	−1.0479	2.852
purpose	−0.5598	1.750
bank book	−0.7870	2.197
monthly interests	−0.4754	1.609
age	−0.4203	1.522
house	0.4934	0.611
foreign	1.3932	0.248
good-account	−1.4690	4.345
marital status	−0.3910	1.479

- A business purpose for the loan
- The presence of high rates of interest
- Not being single
- Age above 33 years

Foreign workers that ask for a loan (foreign = 1) are less reliable than German workers. This is indicated by the positive sign of the coefficient, $\hat{\beta} = 1.3932$. Consequently, there is a direct relationship between being a foreign worker and being a non-reliable applicant. As we saw during the exploratory phase, clients who own a house and perhaps have a mortgage (house = 1) are less reliable than clients who do not own their own house. This is indicated by the coefficient $\hat{\beta} = 0.4934$, which has a positive sign.

The odds ratio measures the strength of association between each explanatory variable and the response variable. Table 11.10 compares the estimated odds ratio with the values from the exploratory analysis. When a client possesses a good current account (good_account = 1) their probability of repayment is 4.345 times greater than for a client without an account. Analogous arguments are valid for previous rep, bank book, deadline, purpose, age, monthly interests and marital status. The variables house and foreign are positively associated with the response variable. The probability of repayment for foreign workers (foreign =1) is 0.248 times that for German workers. In other words, the probability of repayment for German workers is around 4 times the value for foreign workers. These multivariate odds ratios are more reliable than the univariate odd ratios. They give a better description of the interrelationships between the variables, as each individual association is

Table 11.10 Comparison between univariate and multivariate odds ratios.

Variable	Odds ratios	
	Multivariate	Univariate
deadline	1.827	1.842
previous rep	2.852	3.958
purpose	1.750	1.679
bank book	2.197	2.758
monthly interests	1.609	1.342
age	1.522	1.676
house	0.611	0.531
foreign	0.248	0.273
good_account	4.345	5.459
marital status	1.479	1.532

corrected by taking into account the indirect effects on the response variable that occur through the remaining explanatory variables.

11.4.2   Classification tree models

SAS Enterprise Miner allows us to fit three types of tree model. We begin with one based on the CHAID algorithm and the chi-squared impurity measure. To obtain a parsimonious tree, we use a significance level of 0.05 in the stopping rule. Figure 11.1 and Table 11.11 present the results from the CHAID classification tree analysis. Figure 11.1 is self-explanatory; the total number of terminal nodes is 6, each obtained through successive splits of the chosen binary variables. At each split, the only choice is to decide which variable to use for the split.

The total number of splitting variables in the final tree is 4: good_account, bank book, previous rep and deadline. These variables are the first four obtained by the forward selection procedure for logistic regression (Table 11.7). From the classification tree we can see good_account acts on its own, but the other variables interact with each other. This reveals a possible lack of fit when using a logistic regression model that considers only the separate effects of each explanatory variable and no interaction effects. Interactions can obviously

Table 11.11   Results for the CHAID classification tree.

Condition	Results
IF GOOD_ACCOUNT EQUALS 1	N : 394 1 : 11.7% 0 : 88.3%
IF BANK_BOOK EQUALS 0 AND PREVIOUS_REP EQUALS 0 AND GOOD_ACCOUNT EQUALS 0	N : 59 1 : 76.3% 0 : 23.7%
IF BANK_BOOK EQUALS 1 AND PREVIOUS_REP EQUALS 0 AND GOOD_ACCOUNT EQUALS 0	N : 14 1 : 28.6% 0 : 71.4%
IF DEADLINE EQUALS 1 AND PREVIOUS_REP EQUALS 1 AND GOOD_ACCOUNT EQUALS 0	N : 295 1 : 29.5% 0 : 70.5%
IF BANK_BOOK EQUALS 1 AND DEADLINE EQUALS 0 AND PREVIOUS_REP EQUALS 1 AND GOOD_ACCOUNT EQUALS 0	N : 52 1 : 28.8% 0 : 71.2%
IF BANK_BOOK EQUALS 0 AND DEADLINE EQUALS 0 AND PREVIOUS_REP EQUALS 1 AND GOOD_ACCOUNT EQUALS 0	N : 186 1 : 55.4% 0 : 44.6%

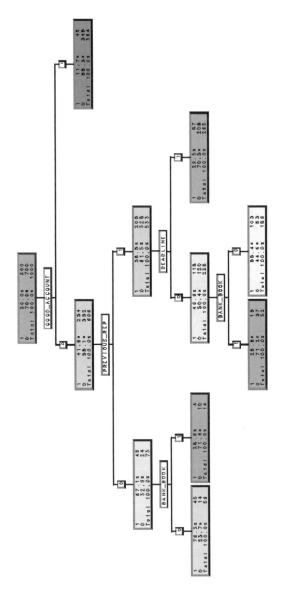

Figure 11.1 Results for the CHAID classification tree.

be introduced, but this considerably increases the calculations and makes the model harder to interpret.

Table 11.11 shows the chosen tree in the form of if-then rules, where the if condition corresponds to a tree path that leads to the then result of a terminal node, characterised by the indicated absolute frequencies (N), percentage of bad applicants (1) and percentage of good applicants (0). The six tree rules can be interpreted as association rules (Section 4.8), all having as their body either $Y = 0$, or $Y = 1$. To do this, we need to consider as primitive items not only the level 1 of each variable, but also the complements, for a total of 44 items. Then we obtain results like this:

- GOOD_ACCOUNT → NOT RELIABLE has a support of 39.4% and a confidence of 11.7%.
- BANK BOOK = 1 AND NO PREVIOUS REP AND NO GOOD ACCOUNT → NOT RELIABLE has a support of 1.4% (14/1000) and a confidence of 28.6%.

We can calculate the misclassification rate as an overall performance measure. In each leaf we classify all the observations according to the majority vote, that is, the class with the highest fitted probability of being present. This corresponds to a cut-off threshold of 0.5. The misclassification rate is 0.249, slightly higher than we obtained with the logistic regression model.

We now look at a tree model using the CART algorithm and the Gini impurity. For pruning, we calculate the misclassification rate on the whole data set using the penalty parameter $\alpha = 1$. This can be considered as the default choice, in the absence of other considerations. Table 11.12 shows the chosen tree in the form of if-then rules. A graphical representation can easily be constructed from Table 11.12. Compared with the CHAID tree, this one is rather complex and has 33 terminal nodes. The 33 paths in the model can be interpreted as association rules. The extra complexity has lowered the misclassification rate to 0.212, obtained on the training data set. But this improvement may not justify the increased complexity.

Almost all the explanatory variables are represented in the tree model, except for sex and marital status. This is a remarkable result. There is no difference in reliability by sex or by marital status. It is also interesting to note that all the paths are rather long, with lengths between 4 and 6. We could reduce the complexity of the model by increasing α, but we will leave it at $\alpha = 1$ so we can compare it with the CHAID tree.

Table 11.13 shows a CART model using the entropy impurity and keeping $\alpha = 1$. This model is also rather complex; it has 34 terminal nodes, one more than the Gini model. The results are also rather similar, but they are not exactly the same. The misclassification rate of the entropy model is 0.211 on the training data set, compared with 0.212 for the Gini model. In Section 4.5 we considered the same tree as in Table 11.13, but we stopped at 4 leaves. On the basis of misclassification rates it seems that the CART models are better than the CHAID model, and the entropy impurity is slightly better than the Gini impurity. But so far we have only compared goodness of fit, not predictive ability.

Table 11.12 Results for the CART classification tree with Gini impurity.

IF FAMILY EQUALS 0 AND BANK_BOOK EQUALS 1 AND PREVIOUS_REP EQUALS 0 AND GOOD_ACCOUNT EQUALS 0	N : 10 1 : 10.0% 0 : 90.0%
IF FAMILY EQUALS 1 AND BANK_BOOK EQUALS 1 AND PREVIOUS_REP EQUALS 0 AND GOOD_ACCOUNT EQUALS 0	N : 4 1 : 75.0% 0 : 25.0%
IF EFFECTS EQUALS 0 AND DEADLINE EQUALS 1 AND PREVIOUS_REP EQUALS 1 AND GOOD_ACCOUNT EQUALS 0	N : 194 1 : 24.7% 0 : 75.3%
IF FAMILY EQUALS 0 AND AGE EQUALS 1 AND CONCURRENT EQUALS 0 AND GOOD_ACCOUNT EQUALS 1	N : 144 1 : 2.8% 0 : 97.2%
IF DEBTS EQUALS 0 AND PURPOSE EQUALS 0 AND CONCURRENT EQUALS 1 AND GOOD_ACCOUNT EQUALS 1	N : 9 1 : 22.2% 0 : 77.8%
IF AGE EQUALS 0 AND PURPOSE EQUALS 1 AND CONCURRENT EQUALS 1 AND GOOD_ACCOUNT EQUALS 1	N : 19 1 : 0.0% 0 : 100.0%
IF AGE EQUALS 1 AND HOUSE EQUALS 0 AND BANK_BOOK EQUALS 0 AND PREVIOUS_REP EQUALS 0 AND GOOD_ACCOUNT EQUALS 0	N : 10 1 : 90.0% 0 : 10.0%
IF FOREIGN EQUALS 0 AND HOUSE EQUALS 1 AND BANK_BOOK EQUALS 0 AND PREVIOUS_REP EQUALS 0 AND GOOD_ACCOUNT EQUALS 0	N : 1 1 : 0.0% 0 : 100.0%
IF FOREIGN EQUALS 1 AND HOUSE EQUALS 1 AND BANK_BOOK EQUALS 0 AND PREVIOUS_REP EQUALS 0 AND GOOD_ACCOUNT EQUALS 0	N : 28 1 : 92.9% 0 : 7.1%
IF MONTHLY_INTERESTS EQUALS 0 AND BANK_BOOK EQUALS 0 AND DEADLINE EQUALS 0	N : 119 1 : 61.3% 0 : 38.7%

Table 11.12 (*continued*)

AND PREVIOUS_REP EQUALS 1 AND GOOD_ACCOUNT EQUALS 0	
IF DEBTS EQUALS 1 AND EFFECTS EQUALS 1 AND DEADLINE EQUALS 1 AND PREVIOUS_REP EQUALS 1 AND GOOD_ACCOUNT EQUALS 0	N : 30 1 : 26.7% 0 : 73.3%
IF OTHERS EQUALS 0 AND WORKING_YEARS EQUALS 0 AND AGE EQUALS 0 AND CONCURRENT EQUALS 0 AND GOOD_ACCOUNT EQUALS 1	N : 31 1 : 22.6% 0 : 77.4%
IF OTHERS EQUALS 1 AND WORKING_YEARS EQUALS 0 AND AGE EQUALS 0 AND CONCURRENT EQUALS 0 AND GOOD_ACCOUNT EQUALS 1	N : 2 1 : 100.0% 0 : 0.0%
IF EMPLOYMENT EQUALS 1 AND WORKING_YEARS EQUALS 1 AND AGE EQUALS 0 AND CONCURRENT EQUALS 0 AND GOOD_ACCOUNT EQUALS 1	N : 107 1 : 9.3% 0 : 90.7%
IF OTHERS EQUALS 0 AND FAMILY EQUALS 1 AND AGE EQUALS 1 AND CONCURRENT EQUALS 0 AND GOOD_ACCOUNT EQUALS 1	N : 34 1 : 5.9% 0 : 94.1%
IF OTHERS EQUALS 1 AND FAMILY EQUALS 1 AND AGE EQUALS 1 AND CONCURRENT EQUALS 0 AND GOOD_ACCOUNT EQUALS 1	N : 1 1 : 100.0% 0 : 0.0%
IF OTHERS EQUALS 1 AND DEBTS EQUALS 1 AND PURPOSE EQUALS 0 AND CONCURRENT EQUALS 1 AND GOOD_ACCOUNT EQUALS 1	N : 1 1 : 0.0% 0 : 100.0%
IF RESIDENCE EQUALS 0 AND AGE EQUALS 1 AND PURPOSE EQUALS 1 AND CONCURRENT EQUALS 1 AND GOOD_ACCOUNT EQUALS 1	N : 3 1 : 66.7% 0 : 33.3%

(*continued overleaf*)

Table 11.12   (*continued*)

IF RESIDENCE EQUALS 1 AND AGE EQUALS 1 AND PURPOSE EQUALS 1 AND CONCURRENT EQUALS 1 AND GOOD_ACCOUNT EQUALS 1	N : 16 1 : 12.5% 0 : 87.5%
IF LOAN EQUALS 0 AND AGE EQUALS 0 AND HOUSE EQUALS 0 AND BANK_BOOK EQUALS 0 AND PREVIOUS_REP EQUALS 0 AND GOOD_ACCOUNT EQUALS 0	N : 12 1 : 33.3% 0 : 66.7%
IF LOAN EQUALS 1 AND AGE EQUALS 0 AND HOUSE EQUALS 0 AND BANK_BOOK EQUALS 0 AND PREVIOUS_REP EQUALS 0 AND GOOD_ACCOUNT EQUALS 0	N : 8 1 : 75.0% 0 : 25.0%
IF TELEPHONE EQUALS 0 AND BAD_ACCOUNT EQUALS 0 AND BANK_BOOK EQUALS 1 AND DEADLINE EQUALS 0 AND PREVIOUS_REP EQUALS 1 AND GOOD_ACCOUNT EQUALS 0	N : 15 1 : 60.0% 0 : 40.0%
IF TELEPHONE EQUALS 1 AND BAD_ACCOUNT EQUALS 0 AND BANK_BOOK EQUALS 1 AND DEADLINE EQUALS 0 AND PREVIOUS_REP EQUALS 1 AND GOOD_ACCOUNT EQUALS 0	N : 10 1 : 20.0% 0 : 80.0%
IF OTHERS EQUALS 0 AND BAD_ACCOUNT EQUALS 1 AND BANK_BOOK EQUALS 1 AND DEADLINE EQUALS 0 AND PREVIOUS_REP EQUALS 1 AND GOOD_ACCOUNT EQUALS 0	N : 26 1 : 11.5% 0 : 88.5%
IF OTHERS EQUALS 1 AND BAD_ACCOUNT EQUALS 1 AND BANK_BOOK EQUALS 1 AND DEADLINE EQUALS 0 AND PREVIOUS_REP EQUALS 1 AND GOOD_ACCOUNT EQUALS 0	N : 1 1 : 100.0% 0 : 0.0%
IF LOAN EQUALS 0 AND MONTHLY_INTERESTS EQUALS 1 AND BANK_BOOK EQUALS 0	N : 61 1 : 41.0% 0 : 59.0%

Table 11.12 (*continued*)

AND DEADLINE EQUALS 0 AND PREVIOUS_REP EQUALS 1 AND GOOD_ACCOUNT EQUALS 0	
IF LOAN EQUALS 1 AND MONTHLY_INTERESTS EQUALS 1 AND BANK_BOOK EQUALS 0 AND DEADLINE EQUALS 0 AND PREVIOUS_REP EQUALS 1 AND GOOD_ACCOUNT EQUALS 0	N : 6 1 : 83.3% 0 : 16.7%
IF LOAN EQUALS 1 AND DEBTS EQUALS 0 AND EFFECTS EQUALS 1 AND DEADLINE EQUALS 1 AND PREVIOUS_REP EQUALS 1 AND GOOD_ACCOUNT EQUALS 0	N : 42 1 : 52.4% 0 : 47.6%
IF LOAN EQUALS 0 AND DEBTS EQUALS 0 AND EFFECTS EQUALS 1 AND DEADLINE EQUALS 1 AND PREVIOUS_REP EQUALS 1 AND GOOD_ACCOUNT EQUALS 0	N : 29 1 : 31.0% 0 : 69.0%
IF BANK_BOOK EQUALS 0 AND EMPLOYMENT EQUALS 0 AND WORKING_YEARS EQUALS 1 AND AGE EQUALS 0 AND CONCURRENT EQUALS 0 AND GOOD_ACCOUNT EQUALS 1	N : 11 1 : 18.2% 0 : 81.8%
IF BANK_BOOK EQUALS 1 AND EMPLOYMENT EQUALS 0 AND WORKING_YEARS EQUALS 1 AND AGE EQUALS 0 AND CONCURRENT EQUALS 0 AND GOOD_ACCOUNT EQUALS 1	N : 4 1 : 75.0% 0 : 25.0%
IF EMPLOYMENT EQUALS 1 AND OTHERS EQUALS 0 AND DEBTS EQUALS 1 AND PURPOSE EQUALS 0 AND CONCURRENT EQUALS 1 AND GOOD_ACCOUNT EQUALS 1	N : 11 1 : 81.8% 0 : 18.2%
IF EMPLOYMENT EQUALS 0 AND OTHERS EQUALS 0 AND DEBTS EQUALS 1 AND PURPOSE EQUALS 0 AND CONCURRENT EQUALS 1 AND GOOD_ACCOUNT EQUALS 1	N : 1 1 : 0.0% 0 : 100.0%

Table 11.13 Results for the CART classification tree with entropy impurity.

IF FAMILY EQUALS 0 AND BANK_BOOK EQUALS 1 AND PREVIOUS_REP EQUALS 0 AND GOOD_ACCOUNT EQUALS 0	N : 10 1 : 10.0% 0 : 90.0%
IF FAMILY EQUALS 1 AND BANK_BOOK EQUALS 1 AND PREVIOUS_REP EQUALS 0 AND GOOD_ACCOUNT EQUALS 0	N : 4 1 : 75.0% 0 : 25.0%
IF EFFECTS EQUALS 0 AND DEADLINE EQUALS 1 AND PREVIOUS_REP EQUALS 1 AND GOOD_ACCOUNT EQUALS 0	N : 194 1 : 24.7% 0 : 75.3%
IF FAMILY EQUALS 0 AND AGE EQUALS 1 AND CONCURRENT EQUALS 0 AND GOOD_ACCOUNT EQUALS 1	N : 144 1 : 2.8% 0 : 97.2%
IF DEBTS EQUALS 0 AND PURPOSE EQUALS 0 AND CONCURRENT EQUALS 1 AND GOOD_ACCOUNT EQUALS 1	N : 9 1 : 22.2% 0 : 77.8%
IF AGE EQUALS 0 AND PURPOSE EQUALS 1 AND CONCURRENT EQUALS 1 AND GOOD_ACCOUNT EQUALS 1	N : 19 1 : 0.0% 0 : 100.0%
IF AGE EQUALS 1 AND HOUSE EQUALS 0 AND BANK_BOOK EQUALS 0 AND PREVIOUS_REP EQUALS 0 AND GOOD_ACCOUNT EQUALS 0	N : 10 1 : 90.0% 0 : 10.0%
IF CONCURRENT EQUALS 0 AND HOUSE EQUALS 1 AND BANK_BOOK EQUALS 0 AND PREVIOUS_REP EQUALS 0 AND GOOD_ACCOUNT EQUALS 0	N : 18 1 : 100.0% 0 : 0.0%
IF LOAN EQUALS 1 AND BANK_BOOK EQUALS 0 AND DEADLINE EQUALS 0 AND PREVIOUS_REP EQUALS 1 AND GOOD_ACCOUNT EQUALS 0	N : 43 1 : 69.8% 0 : 30.2%
IF DEBTS EQUALS 1 AND EFFECTS EQUALS 1	N : 30 1 : 26.7%

Table 11.13   (*continued*)

AND DEADLINE EQUALS 1 AND PREVIOUS_REP EQUALS 1 AND GOOD_ACCOUNT EQUALS 0	0 : 73.3%
IF OTHERS EQUALS 0 AND WORKING_YEARS EQUALS 0 AND AGE EQUALS 0 AND CONCURRENT EQUALS 0 AND GOOD_ACCOUNT EQUALS 1	N : 31 1 : 22.6% 0 : 77.4%
IF OTHERS EQUALS 1 AND WORKING_YEARS EQUALS 0 AND AGE EQUALS 0 AND CONCURRENT EQUALS 0 AND GOOD_ACCOUNT EQUALS 1	N : 2 1 : 100.0% 0 : 0.0%
IF EMPLOYMENT EQUALS 1 AND WORKING_YEARS EQUALS 1 AND AGE EQUALS 0 AND CONCURRENT EQUALS 0 AND GOOD_ACCOUNT EQUALS 1	N : 107 1 : 9.3% 0 : 90.7%
IF OTHERS EQUALS 0 AND FAMILY EQUALS 1 AND AGE EQUALS 1 AND CONCURRENT EQUALS 0 AND GOOD_ACCOUNT EQUALS 1	N : 34 1 : 5.9% 0 : 94.1%
IF OTHERS EQUALS 1 AND FAMILY EQUALS 1 AND AGE EQUALS 1 AND CONCURRENT EQUALS 0 AND GOOD_ACCOUNT EQUALS 1	N : 1 1 : 100.0% 0 : 0.0%
IF RESIDENCE EQUALS 1 AND DEBTS EQUALS 1 AND PURPOSE EQUALS 0 AND CONCURRENT EQUALS 1 AND GOOD_ACCOUNT EQUALS 1	N : 3 1 : 100.0% 0 : 0.0%
IF RESIDENCE EQUALS 0 AND AGE EQUALS 1 AND PURPOSE EQUALS 1 AND CONCURRENT EQUALS 1 AND GOOD_ACCOUNT EQUALS 1	N : 3 1 : 66.7% 0 : 33.3%
IF RESIDENCE EQUALS 1 AND AGE EQUALS 1 AND PURPOSE EQUALS 1 AND CONCURRENT EQUALS 1 AND GOOD_ACCOUNT EQUALS 1	N : 16 1 : 12.5% 0 : 87.5%

(*continued overleaf*)

Table 11.13 (*continued*)

IF LOAN EQUALS 0 AND AGE EQUALS 0 AND HOUSE EQUALS 0 AND BANK_BOOK EQUALS 0 AND PREVIOUS_REP EQUALS 0 AND GOOD_ACCOUNT EQUALS 0	N : 12 1 : 33.3% 0 : 66.7%
IF LOAN EQUALS 1 AND AGE EQUALS 0 AND HOUSE EQUALS 0 AND BANK_BOOK EQUALS 0 AND PREVIOUS_REP EQUALS 0 AND GOOD_ACCOUNT EQUALS 0	N : 8 1 : 75.0% 0 : 25.0%
IF WORKING_YEARS EQUALS 0 AND CONCURRENT EQUALS 1 AND HOUSE EQUALS 1 AND BANK_BOOK EQUALS 0 AND PREVIOUS_REP EQUALS 0 AND GOOD_ACCOUNT EQUALS 0	N : 2 1 : 0.0% 0 : 100.0%
IF WORKING_YEARS EQUALS 1 AND CONCURRENT EQUALS 1 AND HOUSE EQUALS 1 AND BANK_BOOK EQUALS 0 AND PREVIOUS_REP EQUALS 0 AND GOOD_ACCOUNT EQUALS 0	N : 9 1 : 88.9% 0 : 11.1%
IF TELEPHONE EQUALS 0 AND BAD_ACCOUNT EQUALS 0 AND BANK_BOOK EQUALS 1 AND DEADLINE EQUALS 0 AND PREVIOUS_REP EQUALS 1 AND GOOD_ACCOUNT EQUALS 0	N : 15 1 : 60.0% 0 : 40.0%
IF TELEPHONE EQUALS 1 AND BAD_ACCOUNT EQUALS 0 AND BANK_BOOK EQUALS 1 AND DEADLINE EQUALS 0 AND PREVIOUS_REP EQUALS 1 AND GOOD_ACCOUNT EQUALS 0	N : 10 1 : 20.0% 0 : 80.0%
IF OTHERS EQUALS 0 AND BAD_ACCOUNT EQUALS 1 AND BANK_BOOK EQUALS 1 AND DEADLINE EQUALS 0 AND PREVIOUS_REP EQUALS 1 AND GOOD_ACCOUNT EQUALS 0	N : 26 1 : 11.5% 0 : 88.5%

Table 11.13 (*continued*)

IF OTHERS EQUALS 1 AND BAD_ACCOUNT EQUALS 1 AND BANK_BOOK EQUALS 1 AND DEADLINE EQUALS 0 AND PREVIOUS_REP EQUALS 1 AND GOOD_ACCOUNT EQUALS 0	N : 1 1 : 100.0% 0 : 0.0%
IF MONTHLY_INTERESTS EQUALS 0 AND LOAN EQUALS 0 AND BANK_BOOK EQUALS 0 AND DEADLINE EQUALS 0 AND PREVIOUS_REP EQUALS 1 AND GOOD_ACCOUNT EQUALS 0	N : 82 1 : 58.5% 0 : 41.5%
IF MONTHLY_INTERESTS EQUALS 1 AND LOAN EQUALS 0 AND BANK_BOOK EQUALS 0 AND DEADLINE EQUALS 0 AND PREVIOUS_REP EQUALS 1 AND GOOD_ACCOUNT EQUALS 0	N : 61 1 : 41.0% 0 : 59.0%
IF LOAN EQUALS 1 AND DEBTS EQUALS 0 AND EFFECTS EQUALS 1 AND DEADLINE EQUALS 1 AND PREVIOUS_REP EQUALS 1 AND GOOD_ACCOUNT EQUALS 0	N : 42 1 : 52.4% 0 : 47.6%
IF LOAN EQUALS 0 AND DEBTS EQUALS 0 AND EFFECTS EQUALS 1 AND DEADLINE EQUALS 1 AND PREVIOUS_REP EQUALS 1 AND GOOD_ACCOUNT EQUALS 0	N : 29 1 : 31.0% 0 : 69.0%
IF BANK_BOOK EQUALS 0 AND EMPLOYMENT EQUALS 0 AND WORKING_YEARS EQUALS 1 AND AGE EQUALS 0 AND CONCURRENT EQUALS 0 AND GOOD_ACCOUNT EQUALS 1	N : 11 1 : 18.2% 0 : 81.8%
IF BANK_BOOK EQUALS 1 AND EMPLOYMENT EQUALS 0 AND WORKING_YEARS EQUALS 1 AND AGE EQUALS 0 AND CONCURRENT EQUALS 0 AND GOOD_ACCOUNT EQUALS 1	N : 4 1 : 75.0% 0 : 25.0%

(*continued overleaf*)

Table 11.13 *(continued)*

IF BANK_BOOK EQUALS 0 AND RESIDENCE EQUALS 0 AND DEBTS EQUALS 1 AND PURPOSE EQUALS 0 AND CONCURRENT EQUALS 1 AND GOOD_ACCOUNT EQUALS 1	N : 8 1 : 75.0% 0 : 25.0%
IF BANK_BOOK EQUALS 1 AND RESIDENCE EQUALS 0 AND DEBTS EQUALS 1 AND PURPOSE EQUALS 0 AND CONCURRENT EQUALS 1 AND GOOD_ACCOUNT EQUALS 1	N : 2 1 : 0.0% 0 : 100.0%

11.4.3 Multilayer perceptron models

To specify a multilayer perceptron, we need to decide on its architecture. Given the nature of this problem, we choose a single layer of hidden nodes and we make both activation functions logistic, from the input to the hidden nodes and from the hidden nodes to the output. The output nodes are combined through a softmax function. According to the SAS Enterprise Miner implementation of the multilayer perceptron, we choose a back propagation estimation algorithm for the weights, with a momentum parameter of 0.1. The error function is binomial, as in Section 4.6.

To choose the optimal number of nodes in the hidden layer, we begin with a single node and proceed stepwise until the misclassification rate starts to decrease. With 3 nodes it is 0.182, with 4 it is 0.141 and with 5 its 0.148. This suggests a multilayer perceptron with 4 nodes. Therefore the architecture of our final network contains 22 input nodes, 4 hidden nodes and 1 output node. The corresponding number of weight parameters is 97.

Unlike logistic regression and tree models, neural networks are black boxes. There are no interesting structures to see, besides the fitted 0–1 values for each observation, obtained according to the 0.5 threshold rule, from which we derive the misclassification rate. Unlike tree models, the multilayer perceptron can be embedded in a parametric (binomial) framework. This allows us to obtain the model scores, which can then be compared with logistic regression scores. For our final neural network model, we have AIC = 1634.30 and BIC = 2110.35. Both are considerably higher than for the final logistic regression model, indicating a possible improvement.

11.5 Model comparison

To help us choose a final model, we extend our performance analysis to include criteria based on loss functions. For all our models we begin by splitting the available data into a training data set, containing 75% of the observations, and a validation data set, containing 25% of the observations. We do this in a stratified way to maintain the proportions 70% reliable and 30% non-reliable in the new data sets. After fitting each model on the training data set, we use it to classify the observations in the validation data set. This classification is reached by producing a score and then using a threshold cut-off to classify those above the threshold as $Y = 1$ and as those below the threshold as $Y = 0$. Finally, each model is evaluated by assessing the misclassification rate.

We begin with the logistic regression model and classification errors for a cut-off threshold of 50% (corresponding to the discriminant rule). According to this threshold, all the applicants whose estimated probability of non-reliability ($Y = 1$) is greater than 50% are predicted as non-reliable clients, otherwise they are classified as reliable clients. This model correctly predicts 90.29% of the reliable clients ($Y = 0$). The probability of committing a type II error is 9.71%. A type II error means taking a reliable client and predicting it as non-reliable. The model is less effective at predicting non-reliable clients; in fact, it predicts only 39.56% of them correctly. The probability of committing a type I error is 60.44%. A type I error means taking a non-reliable client and predicting it as reliable. It seems that the model has greater difficulty in predicting non-reliable clients than reliable ones.

This is quite common in credit-scoring problems. The main difficulty of score-card models is in predicting the bad risks. But we need models that can predict bad risk effectively, because type I errors are usually more costly than type II errors. The previous error rates are obtained for a 50% cut-off, but a lower cut-off might allow us to catch a greater number of bad repayers. A 30% cut-off reduces the type I error to 24.44%, but the type II error rises from 9.71% to 22.80%.

The cut-off threshold should be chosen to suit the costs of the type I and type II errors. If the costs are similar, at 50% cut-off will be fine; otherwise, a different threshold may be better. In credit-scoring problems, where type I error is usually more costly, a cut-off lower than 50% is probably advisable. How much below depends on the cost function. The ROC curve, which shows how the errors change when the threshold varies, can be used for this purpose. Before looking at the ROC curve, we compare the predictive misclassification rates, at 50% cut-off, for the logistic regression model, the classification tree and the neural network. It turns out that the tree model has the best performance, with a misclassification rate of 0.244, followed by the multilayer perceptron at 0.248 and the logistic regression model at 0.280. Concerning type I errors, the logistic regression model shows a 60.44% probability against 54.67% for the tree model and 64.79% for the neural network.

We now compare the three models in terms of their ROC curves and the Gini index of performance. The higher the point on the curve, the lower the cut-off threshold, before applicants are estimated to be non-reliable. Figure 11.2 shows the ROC curves for our three final models; all are calculated using the same random partitioning of the data. It shows the point for 50% cut-off using the decision tree, which is the best model when using 50% cut-off. The predictive behaviour of the three models is rather similar. The logistic regression

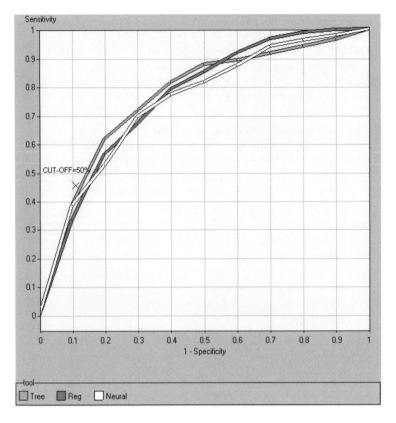

Figure 11.2   ROC curves for the final models.

model appears slightly inferior to the other two, but not as bad as it appeared on the misclassification rates alone. For a clearer comparison, we calculate the Gini index of performance; the classification tree has the highest value (0.6260), followed by the logistic regression model (0.5798) and then the neural network (0.5738).

Figure 11.3 is a lift chart. A lift chart gives, for each decile, the percentage of predicted events (here non-reliable applicant). If the model were perfect, this percentage would be 100% for the first three deciles (as this is the proportion of true events) and equal to zero for the other seven deciles. From Figure 11.3 it appears that the models are rather similar for the last seven deciles (with the neural network a bit worse, probably due to overfitting); and in the first three deciles, the most critical region for credit scoring, the tree outperforms the logistic regression model, and although they are very different in nature, the tree and the neural network have a similar performance.

To summarise, the tree seems to be the best-performing model, but the differences are rather slight.

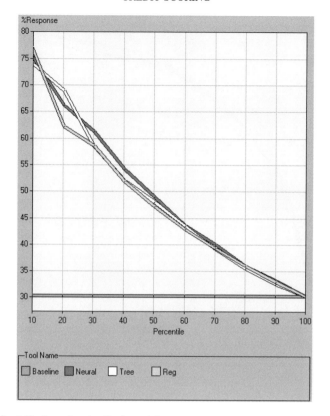

Figure 11.3 Lift chart for the final models.

We now consider whether a combined model leads to a better classification performance. Given the potential instability of the tree model, we try to improve it using the bagging algorithms in SAS Enterprise Miner. We take 10 random samples for both algorithms. Each sample is split randomly and in a stratified way into a training data set and a validation data set, and the observations in the validation data set are calculated according to the majority rule out of the 10 classification from the CART model using entropy impurity. As a result, we obtain a total misclassification rate of 0.224, with a type I error probability of about 48%. This shows a notable improvement over the single-tree model (which had a total misclassification rate of 0.244 and a type I error probability of about 54%).

Figure 11.4 shows the ROC curves plus the 50% cut-off point using the combined tree model. The combined model is rather similar to the single-tree model. Indeed the Gini index of performance for the combined tree model is 0.5724, slightly worse than for the single tree. Therefore, if the cut-off threshold is to be chosen, not fixed at 50%, then perhaps it would be better to keep a single tree. But if the cut-off is fixed at 50%, then the combined tree is the better performer.

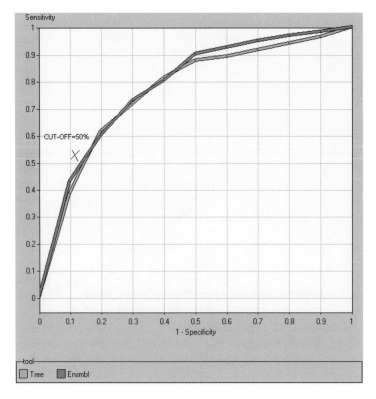

Figure 11.4   ROC curves for the bagged tree model and the single-tree model.

Table 11.14   Comparison of the bagged model with the three individual models.

Tool	Target	Target Event	Root ASE	Valid:Root ASE	Schwarz Bayesian Criterion	Misclassification Rate	Valid:Misclassification Rate
Ensemble	BAD	1	0.3956453665	0.4062584929		0.2213333333	0.248
Neural Network	BAD	1	0.4011945038	0.4131136493	2107.7858823	0.24	0.248
Tree	BAD	1	0.4001167793	0.4097238635		0.2226666667	0.244
Regression	BAD	1	0.4068947285	0.4177366486	825.63597147	0.2493333333	0.28

Now we use unweighted majority voting to combine the results from the regression model the tree model and the neural network. Table 11.14 shows the results. Although the combined model is the best one on the training data set, in terms of predictive classification it is outperformed by the tree model, which proves to be the best one. However, notice that the difference in performance is very small, no more than 0.04. The type I error probability of the combined model is 56%, worse than the single tree. Figure 11.5 shows the ROC curves for this comparison. Notice that the combined model does better than the tree for low cut-off values, but then the type I error is too high. The Gini index of performance for the combined model is 0.5699, lower than

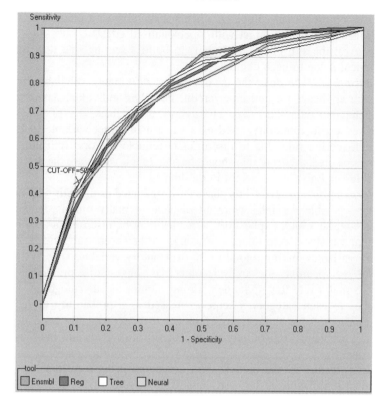

Figure 11.5 ROC curves for the bagged tree model and its component models.

before. Therefore the tree model, which does better at high cut-off values, is to be preferred.

To conclude, the best model for classifying the data set is the single-tree model, or if computational resources allow, the bagged tree model. However, all the final models have a rather similar performance, so it may make sense to choose the most transparent model, namely, logistic regression.

11.6 Summary report

- *Context*: this case study concerns credit scoring. It may also be applied to any situations where the objective is to score the past behaviour of an individual or company in order to plan a future action on the same individual or company in a CRM framework. The score can then be used to evaluate credit reliability, customer loyalty or customer churnability. Furthermore, it can be used to select clients in order to maximise the return on an investment (e.g. clients to receive a promotional campaign, clients to involve in a one-to-one banking relationship, clients to target with a personalised gift).

- *Objectives*: the aim of the analysis is to build a scoring rule that attaches a numerical value to each client.

- *Organisation of the data*: the data is all the information available in a bank on each applicant for consumer credit, including individual data and banking behaviour data. There are 21 categorical variables, one of which is the observed credit reliability, used as a supervisor target variable to build up a credit-scoring rule able to discriminate reliable debtors from non-reliable debtors. A credit-scoring rule should be able to tell which are the discriminant variables and give their weight in the final score.

- *Exploratory data analysis*: this phase was conducted using odds ratio analysis, as the available variables were all discrete (actually binarised). The odds ratios suggest which explanatory variables may be discriminant. Two of the original variables were rather confusing, so they were subdivided into new binary variables, giving a total of 22 explanatory variables.

- *Model specification*: the analysis objective suggested a predictive model, able to find a rule that splits debtors into homogeneous categories and then attaches to each category a score expressed as a probability of reliability. We considered the three types of model that are typically used in credit-scoring problems: logistic regression, classification trees and multilayer perceptrons.

- *Model comparison*: the models were compared using statistical or scoring-based criteria, such as G^2, AIC and BIC as well as the misclassification rate on the whole data set. There was not enough data to rely on cross-validation alone. The goodness-of-fit comparison showed that neural networks performed best, followed by logistic regression and classification trees. We then considered a cross-validation approach, and compared classification errors on a validation data set. To convert a score into a 0–1 estimate (good or bad debtors) we assumed a threshold of 50%. Then the tree model had the best performance, followed by the multilayer perceptron and then the logistic regression model. However, in terms of type I errors, which are usually more costly in these types of problem, logistic regression outperformed neural networks. To obtain a result independent of the chosen threshold, we compared the ROC curves and calculated the Gini index of performance. This time the classification tree came out best, confirmed by the lift chart. Given the rather limited amount of data and the potential instability of tree models, we tried to improve our model by bagging; the results for the bagged model were considerably better when a 50% threshold was chosen.

- *Model interpretation*:: on the basis of model comparison, it seems that classification trees, or their bagged version, do the best job for this problem. But logistic regression models are not so inferior on this considered data set, especially if type I errors are emphasised. The choice should also depend on how the results will be used. If decision makers look for hierarchical 'what if' rules, which classify clients into risk class profiles, then classification trees are very good. On the other hand, if they desire analytic rules, which attach an impact weight to each explanatory variable (measured by a regression coefficient or an odds ratio), then logistic regression is better.

CHAPTER 12

Forecasting television audience

12.1 Objectives of the analysis

This case study compares a number of statistical techniques for forecasting television audiences in the Italian market. Programme planners want a forecasting method that will help them devise schedules to maximise audiences. To do this, they need to know which programmes on a channel reach the maximum audience, for a given choice of the competing channels. There are essentially two strategies: counterplanning reacts to competitors' programmes with a programme that is very different, in order to capture the remaining public; and competitive programming reacts to competitors' programmes with programmes of the same type, hoping to attract a higher audience share based on the programme's quality. Television schedules are planned in advance. The data in this study consists of programme plans for 3–5 month periods, planned at least 4 months in advance.

These strategies embody the notion of a programme's value. A programme's value is often related to the perceived impact of an advertisement with a slot during its broadcast. The higher a programme's audience, the higher the publicity cost to insert an advertisement in the programme. In this case study we consider audience data from the Italian television market. By magnitude and composition, this is one of the most complex television markets in the world and it therefore represents an important example for other markets too. In the Italian television market there are six leading channels, and several smaller channels; most of these smaller channels are local but some are national. All six leading channels are national, as they reach almost 100% of the country. Three are owned by the state: rai1, rai2, rai3. The other three are owned by a private company called Mediaset: rete4, canale5 (can5), italia1 (ita1). Although the real competition is between Mediaset and the state, each owning three channels, the individual channels have a degree of autonomy, so it makes sense to talk about competition between them all.

Data on the television audience, at regional level and national level, is provided in Italy by an institutional company called Auditel. Auditel selects a panel – a stratified sample of viewing families – to represent the different geographic, demographic and sociocultural characteristics of the national population. The

Applied Data Mining. Paolo Giudici
© 2003 John Wiley & Sons, Ltd   ISBNs: 0-470-84679-8 (Paper); 0-470-84678-X (Cloth)

selected individuals remain on the panel for a period of about five years; each year about 20% of them are replaced. Each television in the house of a panel family is fitted with an electronic meter. The meter continually records viewing data: whether the television is on and to which channel it is tuned. The panel consists of 5000 families, containing a total of 15 000 individuals, and data is collected from 8000 television meters. It is one of the largest television audience panels in the world. The panel audience for a programme is extrapolated to the whole population using weights that reflect the representation of each population stratum in the panel. The extrapolated data is the database for our case study; we will not examine the extrapolation mechanism. Here are some indicators for measuring the audience of a channel; this case study uses the indicator called share.

- *Reach* indicates the total number of distinct (unique) visitors that, in a given time interval, have seen the channel for at least one minute.
- *Mean audience* is the sum of the number of viewers per minute divided by the number of minutes in the considered time interval.
- *Total audience* is the sum of the mean audience for all the considered channels, in the considered time interval.
- *Share* is a percentage for each channel given by the ratio of the channel's mean audience to the total audience in the given time interval.

The share of a channel is defined for a given time interval; it is the percentage of people that are watching that channel, averaged over the time interval. Here we will consider the six leading channels and put the rest into a 'residual' channel. This will give us seven channels and seven shares, which sum to 100%.

Our objective is to predict the shares of the six leading channels, for a given menu of broadcast programmes. It is difficult to predict a channel's share, because it depends on factors that can be hard to quantify, such as the preferences and habits of the viewers, and the quality of the broadcast programme. Programme quality depends on many factors besides content; two of them are programme history and coverage by other media. Many viewers enjoy a varied diet of television and show greater loyalty to a channel than to a programme or type of programme. Although this behaviour is gradually declining, it can have a considerable effect on audience share predictions and it does still exist, especially among older viewers. To summarise, our problem is to predict the shares of the six leading channels. We therefore have a predictive data mining problem aimed at predicting a multiple target, consisting of six variables, something we have not covered up to now. This data set is analysed from a Bayesian perspective in Giudici (1998).

12.2   Description of the data

We will use one year of observations from 29 November 1995 to 28 November 1996 for the hours 20:30 to 22:30, known as prime time. For every minute of these hours, the meter records the channel to which the television is tuned. The channel can be one of the six leading channels or channel 7, which contains all the rest. The data matrix consists of 366 multivariate observations; for each prime time during the considered year (a row in the matrix) it shows general and channel-specific information. The general information is the date, the day of the week (Sunday is 1 and Saturday is 7) and the total number of television viewers (in thousands). The channel-specific information is the share of each channel, the title of the broadcast programme and the type of the programme.

Table 12.1 shows an extract from the original data matrix; it contains the general information and information specific to channels rai1 and rai2. On Thursday 29 November 1995 there were, on average, 28 916 thousand people watching television (about half the country's population) during prime time: 21.7% were watching rai1, broadcasting the telefilm (TF) *Solo per il tuo bene* (Only for your love); 14.2% were watching rai2, broadcasting the film (F) *royce*. The data matrix contains similar information for the other four channels.

Now we need some more background information. The shares during prime time exhibit high variability. This is because they measure how a large total audience is distributed among the channels, which usually broadcast their better programmes in this period and generally behave according to a competitive programming strategy, instead of the counterplanning strategy they follow during the rest of the day. The high variability means that prime time shares are usually rather difficult to predict with reasonable accuracy. The six leading channels take about 92% of the television audience, so they can be treated as highly representative of the public's choices. The share of the other networks is treated as residual, and this means it is obtained by subtraction:

$$\text{share}_{7t} = 100 - \sum_{i=1}^{6} \text{share}_{it}$$

where the index $i = 1, \ldots, 6$ refers to the six main channels and the index $t = 1, \ldots, 366$ refers to the considered day.

The programme titles cannot really be used to obtain explanatory variables of the shares, as in most cases they are unique, so there is no variability on which to build a statistical analysis. Furthermore, even when a programme is

Table 12.1 Extract from the original data matrix.

	rai1	date	day	audience	shrai1	typerai1	prgrai1	rai2	shrai2	typerai2	prgrai2
1	Rai1	29/11/1995	4	28916	19.4	TF	SOLO PER IL TUO BENE	Rai2	12.9	F	ROYCE
2	Rai1	30/11/1995	5	28655	21.7	PVS	BUON COMPLEANNO LUNA PARK	Rai2	14.2	SC	CALCIO COPPA ITALIA -FIORENTINA
3	Rai1	01/12/1995	6	27957	20.2	F	ZANNA BIANCA UN PICCOLO...	Rai2	16.3	PV	I FATTI VOSTRI
4	Rai1	02/12/1995	7	24780	27	PV	SCOMMETTIAMO CHE...?	Rai2	12.1	F	OLTRE IL SOSPETTO
5	Rai1	03/12/1995	1	26880	29.4	PV	FANTASTICA ITALIANA	Rai2	13.6	F	IRRESISTIBILE FORCE
6	Rai1	04/12/1995	2	29808	23.7	F	QUALCUNO DA AMARE	Rai2	12.3	TF	L'ISPETTORE DERRICK

Table 12.2   Classification of programmes into 14 groups.

F = Film	SC = Sport (football, official league)
TF = Telefilm	SCA = Sport (football, friendly)
PV = Variety programme	SA = Sport (different from football)
PVS = Special variety programme	TSI = Italian fiction, in episodes
P = Special programme	TS = Non-Italian fiction, in episodes
PI = Information programme	TMI = Italian TV movie
D = Theatre	TM = Non-Italian TV movie

Table 12.3   Classification of the 14 groups into 5 categories.

Film: F
Tv-Movie: TF, TS, TSI, TM, TMI
Shows: PV, PVS, P
Information: PI, D
Sport: SC, SCA, SA

repeated (e.g. a show), it will never be the same programme, as it will probably have new content. We therefore need to classify programmes into homogeneous categories by programme type. This classification is a critical issue, as it affects the quality of the final predictions. Here we have the classification provided by the marketing experts of the Italian private network, who have kindly supplied the datas. For each combination of day and channel, the data matrix shows the programme type, as can be seen in Table 12.1. The programme classification puts each programme into one of 14 groups listed in Table 12.2.

Given the somewhat limited amount of available data, having 14 groups will mean there are too many to make accurate predictions. We therefore aggregate them into 5 groups as logically as possible, based on discussions with marketing experts. Table 12.3 shows this new classification and how it relates to the old one. There is a price to pay for this greater simplicity; it may lead to less accurate predictions because the new classes may be more heterogenous. But this danger is not entirely removed by considering finer groupings, like the original one.

We now have 6 new programme type variables, one for each channel. Each of them is a qualitative variable with 5 possible levels. To be parsimonious, we transform each of them into as many binary variables as their levels. This gives a total of $6 \times 5 = 30$ binary variables, one for each programme type and channel combination. We apply a similar binarisation to the days of the week, obtaining a total of 7 binary variables. We have therefore taken the original $6 + 1$ qualitative variables in the data matrix and replaced them with 37 binary variables. Table 12.4 shows their values for the same evenings as in Table 12.1. The share of rai2 is missing for one evening. We delete this item from the matrix as there is no obvious way to estimate it. The total number of observations is now 365.

Table 12.4 Binarisation of the qualitative explanatory variables.

	typenew1	typenew2	typenew3	typenew4	typenew5	typenew6	day
1	Tv_Movie	Film	Information	Tv_Movie	Show	Film	4
2	Show	Sport	Information	Film	Film	Film	5
3	Film	Show	Information	Tv_Movie	Show	Film	6
4	Show	Film	Film	Film	Show	Film	7
5	Show	Film	Show	Film	Show	Tv_Movie	1
6	Film	Tv_Movie	Information	Film	Film	Film	2

	film1	film2	film3	film4	film5	show1	film6	show2	show3	show4	show5	show6	sport1	sport2	sport3	sport4	sport5	sport6	tv_movie1	tv_movie2	tv_movie3
1	0	1	0	0	0	0	1	0	0	0	1	0	0	0	0	0	0	0	1	0	0
2	0	0	0	1	1	1	1	0	0	0	0	0	0	1	0	0	0	0	0	0	0
3	1	0	0	0	0	0	1	1	0	0	1	0	0	0	0	0	0	0	0	0	0
4	0	1	1	1	0	1	1	0	0	0	1	0	0	0	0	0	0	0	0	0	0
5	0	1	0	1	0	1	0	0	1	0	1	0	0	0	0	0	0	0	0	0	0
6	1	0	0	1	1	0	1	0	0	0	0	0	0	0	0	0	0	0	0	1	0

	tv_movie4	tv_movie5	tv_movie6	information1	information2	information3	information4	information5	information6	sunday	monday	tuesday	wednesday	thursday	friday	saturday
1	1	0	0	0	0	1	0	0	0	0	0	0	0	1	0	0
2	0	0	0	0	0	1	0	0	0	0	0	0	0	0	1	0
3	1	0	0	0	0	1	0	0	0	0	0	0	0	0	0	1
4	0	0	0	0	0	0	0	0	0	1	0	0	0	0	0	0
5	0	0	1	0	0	0	0	0	0	0	1	0	0	0	0	0
6	0	0	0	0	0	1	0	0	0	0	0	1	0	0	0	0

12.3 Exploratory data analysis

Exploratory analysis is essential when tackling a difficult problem like this one. We want to predict the shares of the six leading channels, so we examine the distribution of these shares over the year. Table 12.5 shows some simple summary statistics for each channel share. Notice that there appear to be two leading channels: rai1 and can5. These can be considered as the leading channels of each of the two networks (public and private); they typically compete for the leadership, and usually they can be considered as 'generalist', aiming at the general public. In the considered year, Table 12.4 indicates that rai1 had a higher overall mean share of 23.80, against 22.13 for can5. The other channels follow, with rai2 (14.76) coming before ita1 (11.73), rai3 (11.06) and rete4 (8.38). Generally, rai2 and rete4 are both targeted at a mature public, whereas rai3 and ita1 are targeted at a younger public; rai3 is more cultural than ita1. The variability of the shares, expressed by the standard deviation, varies considerably, with leading channels having a higher variability. And the wide range of the observations, expressed by the minimum and maximum shares, makes predictions rather difficult.

To understand the influence of programme type, we obtain the boxplot of each share, conditional on the programme types (Figure 12.1). There appear to be outlying observations (evenings). These manifest themselves for different channels and different programme types. The shares of the six leading channels add up to

Table 12.5 Summary statistics on the channel shares.

Variable	N	Mean	Std Dev	Minimum	Maximum
shrrai1	365	23.7915068	7.6157088	9.2000000	72.5000000
shrrai2	365	14.7591781	4.7044466	3.0000000	44.7000000
shrrai3	365	11.0575342	3.7992668	2.6000000	40.5000000
shrrete4	365	8.3783562	2.2547867	2.7000000	17.5000000
shrcan5	365	22.1252055	5.9504290	5.3000000	60.3000000
shrita1	365	11.7336986	2.9919193	3.1000000	23.4000000

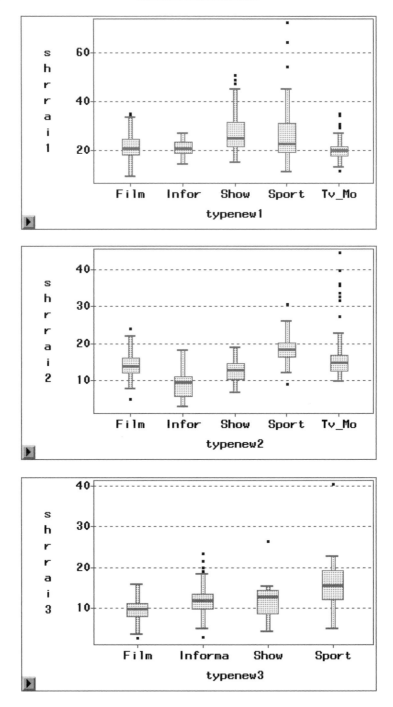

Figure 12.1 Boxplots for the six channels using the five programme types.

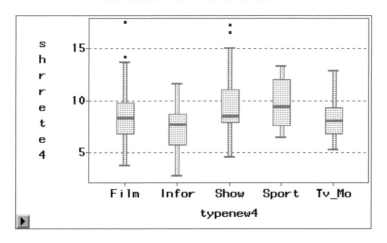

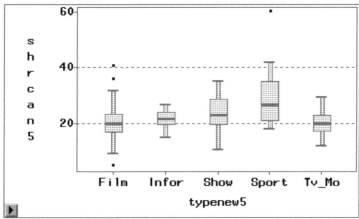

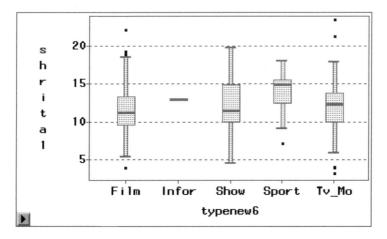

Figure 12.1   (*continued*)

a fairly stable figure of about 92%. So when there is an outlier higher than the median, other channels may have an outlier lower than the median. In any case, considering the very erratic nature of television shares, we do not remove any outliers, although removing them would improve the accuracy of the predictions. We are trying to build a model that can predict shares, whatever the menu of available programmes.

Figure 12.1 suggests the shares depend on the programme types in different ways. For instance, on rai1 Show programmes and Sport programmes seem to increase shares, with other types near the overall median. For can5 there is a similar behaviour. The other channels are more thematic; they show different effects. Generally, Sport programmes increase the shares; other programmes differ according to where they are broadcast:

- rai2 does better with Sports programmes and Tv-Movie programmes, worse with Information programmes.
- rete4, which is also rather dependent on programme types, does better with Sport programmes and Show programmes, worse with Information programmes.
- rai3, which never broadcasts Tv-Movie programmes in the considered period, does better with Sport programmes and Show programs, worse with Film programmes.
- ita1, which has a very limited amount of Information programmes, does better with Sport programmes and Tv-Movie programmes, worse with Film programmes and Show programmes.

It is very important to understand the nature of a channel – the programmes which characterise it and create its image. Table 12.6 shows the frequency distribution of the programme type variables, using our five-level classification. The channel images now begin to emerge. For instance, the distributions of rai1 and can5 are rather similar: rai1 has percentages higher than other channels on the most popular programme types, Show programmes and Sport programmes; can5 does this on Show programmes but is beaten by rai2 on Sport programmes. In the considered period, most football matches were broadcast on the public channels, and this explains the difference between rai1 and can5. The other channels are more specific, as they all differ notably.

Differences between the channels can be better understood by comparing them within the two networks, public and private. This appears to show that rai1 and can5 behave as competitive channels, with the others behaving more like counterplanners. For instance, in the public network, rai2 broadcasts a high percentage of Film programmes and Tv-Movie programmes, whereas rai3 broadcasts many Information programmes and Film programmes. In the private network, rete4 broadcasts many Film programmes, and ita1 broadcasts many Film programmes and Tv-Movie programmes. This leads to highly symmetrical planning behaviour between the two networks. Another important explanatory variable is the total audience. Variation in the total audience is usually related to specific groups of people (i.e. those who tend to be at home less often), hence it will be reflected in

Table 12.6 Distribution of the programme types by channel.

rai1	Frequency	Percent	Cumulative Frequency	Cumulative Percent
Film	103	28.22	103	28.22
Information	33	9.04	136	37.26
Show	127	34.79	263	72.05
Sport	33	9.04	296	81.10
Tv_Movie	69	18.90	365	100.00

rai2	Frequency	Percent	Cumulative Frequency	Cumulative Percent
Film	170	46.58	170	46.58
Information	9	2.47	179	49.04
Show	45	12.33	224	61.37
Sport	23	6.30	247	67.67
Tv_Movie	118	32.33	365	100.00

rai3	Frequency	Percent	Cumulative Frequency	Cumulative Percent
Film	152	41.64	152	41.64
Information	172	47.12	324	88.77
Show	17	4.66	341	93.42
Sport	24	6.58	365	100.00

rete4	Frequency	Percent	Cumulative Frequency	Cumulative Percent
Film	251	68.77	251	68.77
Information	29	7.95	280	76.71
Show	23	6.30	303	83.01
Sport	5	1.37	308	84.38
Tv_Movie	57	15.62	365	100.00

can5	Frequency	Percent	Cumulative Frequency	Cumulative Percent
Film	117	32.05	117	32.05
Information	17	4.66	134	36.71
Show	144	39.45	278	76.16
Sport	19	5.21	297	81.37
Tv_Movie	68	18.63	365	100.00

Ita1	Frequency	Percent	Cumulative Frequency	Cumulative Percent
Film	177	48.49	177	48.49
Information	1	0.27	178	48.77
Show	27	7.40	205	56.16
Sport	9	2.47	214	58.63
Tv_Movie	151	41.37	365	100.00

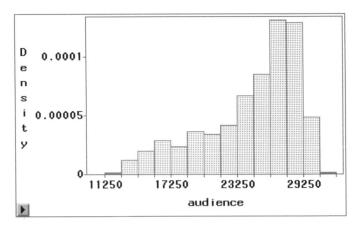

Figure 12.2   Distribution of the total audience.

changes of share. Figure 12.2 show that the distribution of the total audience is
rather asymmetric to the right; it is also extremely variable. Therefore it makes
sense to include the total audience as an explanatory variable, and we standardise
it to help with interpretation. Other variables can be derived from the data matrix.
First of all, each channel share depends not only on its own programme, but also
on the programmes broadcast by the other channels. This effect is generally less
marked, but we consider it in Section 12.4. Another relevant explanatory variable
is the day of the week. Its informative content may be included in the programme
types (which usually entail a specific day) and the total audience, but there may
also be other effects due to the day of the week. Other temporal variables may also
be included, such as the month and the season. After discussion with marketing
experts and some practical experimentation, we decide not to consider them.

   To build a statistical model, it is often important to understand which probability model can be used to describe the distribution of the response variable. Here
the response variable is a 6-variate vector of shares. The shares are continuous
quantitative variables but they have a limited range. The Gaussian distribution
is typically used to model multivariate continuous variables, yet it may not be
entirely appropriate here. This is confirmed by a closer examination of the distribution of the shares. Figure 12.3 shows the distribution of the shares of can5,
along with the Gaussian approximation and the kernel density estimate, based on
a Gaussian kernel (Section 5.2). The Gaussian curve is distant from the kernel
density estimator. But given the complexity of the analysis, it may be prudent to
use a linear model, as linear models often produce explicit results that are easy
to interpret. Since a linear model is based on the Gaussian assumption, we can
try to meet this assumption by transforming the response vector.

   When we include channel 7, others, the shares sum to 100%. They are proportions, and proportions can be transformed to a multivariate Gaussian distribution
by using the following logistic transformation. Assume there exist some explanatory variables that allow us to determine the structure of the parameter π_{it}, which

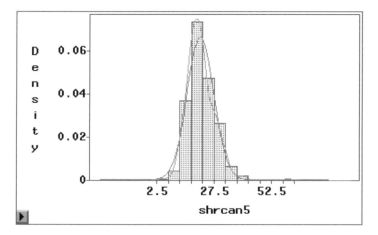

Figure 12.3   Histogram, Gaussian and kernel density estimated curves for shrcan5.

expresses the aggregated probability that each subject chooses the ith channel on the tth evening. This can be seen as a model for individual preferences. The distribution of a binary variable is defined by only two probabilities, π and $1 - \pi$. To describe a logistic transformation for a binary variable, we define a logit

$$\theta = \log \left(\frac{\pi}{1 - \pi} \right)$$

Suppose the variables are n-ary rather than binary, as in this case, where for each evening t there are seven probabilities of channel choice, which sum to 1. Then a possible logistic transformation is

$$\theta_i = \log \left(\frac{\pi_i}{\pi_7} \right) \text{ for } i = 1, \ldots, 6$$

One of the seven probabilities (here π_7, corresponding to others) is chosen as a comparison term and is therefore omitted from the analysis. We now use this transformation on the observed shares. The response variable is defined by the following transformation:

$$y_{it} = \log \left(\frac{\text{share}_{it}}{\text{share}_{7t}} \right) \text{ for } i = 1, \ldots, 6 \text{ and } t = 1, \ldots, 365$$

where y_{it} represents the logit of share$_{it}$ (share relative to the ith channel and to the tth evening).

It can be shown (e.g. Johnson and Wichern, 1982) that the previous transformation has an approximately multivariate Gaussian distribution for the 6-dimensional vector of the logit share so defined. Table 12.7 shows the values of these logit shares for the six evenings in Table12.1. It contains a logit share

Table 12.7 Logit shares for the evenings in Table 12.1.

logit1	logit2	logit3	logit4	logit5	logit6
0.8252069026	0.4171611479	0.5271620431	0	0.8096221716	0.7048432203
1.2527629685	0.8286926726	0.8901454518	0.2295744416	0.7326780193	1.2710283165
0.8774508986	0.662933402	-0.498991166	0.0578195709	1.2321436813	0.3813675565
1.4875480948	0.6849166814	0.0635134057	0.3777625056	1.5167472495	0.6427163269
1.3660916538	0.5951667722	-0.579818495	0.1484200051	1.0343700199	0.7259370034
0.804621047	0.1487452613	0.0814930343	-0.638087403	0.825498632	0.1323514515

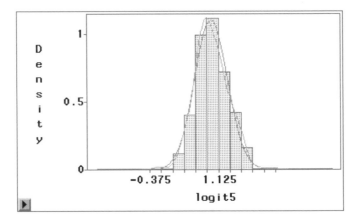

Figure 12.4 Histogram, parametric (red) and kernel density (purple) estimated curves for logitshrcan5.

equal to 0. This corresponds to a share equal to the channel 7 share for that evening (up to the second decimal place). Figure 12.4 shows the distribution of the logit shares for can5 obtained using this transformation. It exhibits a rather good approximation of the Gaussian curve, which is now very close to the kernel density estimate. The goodness of the Gaussian approximation for the logit shares can be deduced in other ways; for instance, the qq-plot after the transformation gives a remarkable goodness of fit. Figure 12.5 compares the qq-plot for the share of can5 with the qq-plot for the logit share of can5.

Logit shares help us with the statistical analysis but then they can be converted back into shares by using the following inverse transformation:

$$\text{share}_{it} = 100 \left(\frac{\exp y_{it}}{1 + \sum_{j=1}^{6} \exp y_{jt}} \right) \quad \text{for } i = 1, \ldots, 6$$

which resembles the softmax activation function used in neural networks modelling (Section 4.6).

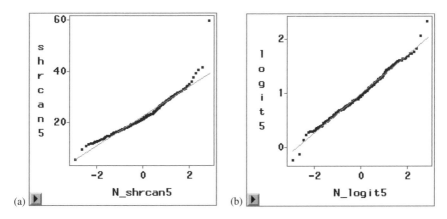

Figure 12.5 The qq-plots for (a) shrcan5 and (b) logitshrcan5.

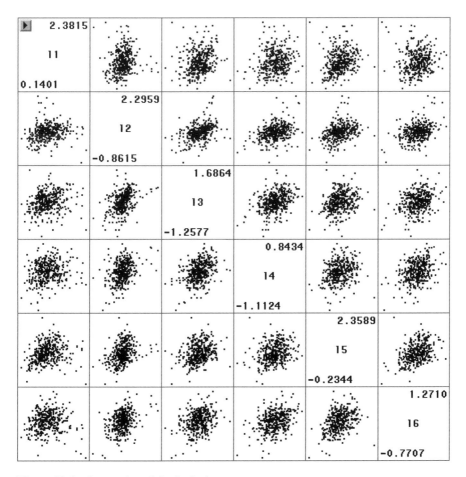

Figure 12.6 Scatterplot of the logit shares.

Table 12.8 Correlation matrix of the logit shares.

Correlation Matrix						
	logit1	logit2	logit3	logit4	logit5	logit6
logit1	1.0000	0.1400	0.1976	0.1682	0.2206	0.0445
logit2	0.1400	1.0000	0.4099	0.3387	0.3368	0.3736
logit3	0.1976	0.4099	1.0000	0.3507	0.2658	0.3330
logit4	0.1682	0.3387	0.3507	1.0000	0.2589	0.3594
logit5	0.2206	0.3368	0.2658	0.2589	1.0000	0.3751
logit6	0.0445	0.3736	0.3330	0.3594	0.3751	1.0000

Table 12.9 Partial correlation matrix of the logit shares.

	logit1	logit2	logit3	logit4	logit5	logit6
logit1	1	0.025	0.126	0.096	0.177	0.109
logit2		1	0.257	0.146	0.172	0.177
logit3			1	0.181	0.052	0.145
logit4				1	0.058	0.208
logit5					1	0.255
logit6						1

On the basis of the available logit shares, Section 12.4 considers a number of predictive models. Often, for brevity, a logit share will be indicated with l_i, with $i = 1, \ldots, 6$. First we consider the correlation structure among the logit shares, which helps us to understand the structure of the Italian television market. Figure 12.6 shows the scatterplot of the observed logit shares, and for each logit share variable it also shows the minimum and maximum observations. As expected, there is a degree of correlation between the logit shares.

To reach a firmer conclusion, Table 12.8 shows the correlation coefficients between logit shares. There are relevant correlations between logit shares, not only for the minor channels (l_2, l_3, l_4, l_6), as can be expected, but also for the can5 logit share (l_5). Table 12.9 shows the partial correlation matrix, which leads us to more accurate results on the interdependency structure between the logit shares (and in turn between the shares, as the channel 7 share is quite stable). The strongest partial correlations occur within each of the two networks: between can5 and ita1 (0.255), between rai2 and rai3 (0.257) and between rete4 and ita1 (0.208). Between networks, the strongest competition is between the two leading channels, rai1 and can5 (0.177), and also between rai2 and rete4 (0.146), rai2 and can5 (0.172), rai2 and ita1 (0.177), rai3 and rete4 (0.181), and rai3 and ita1 (0.145). These results confirm that the two leading networks compete with each other, with can5 also competing with others, in particular with rai2 and ita1. The other channels are quite interdependent and cannot simply be paired across networks; in other words, they are more exposed to the competition.

12.4 Model building

We consider two types of models that differ in their aims. First we consider a single-target model, in which the logit share (hence the share) of one channel is to be predicted, on the basis of all programme types, the day of the week and the total audience. We choose to predict can5 as it is more subject to competition. We then build a multiple-target predictive model, in which all logit shares are predicted using all the explanatory variables. So we can compare models of different kinds, we use cross-validation from the outset. We randomly partition the data set into a training data set (75% of the data) and a validation data set (25% of the observations). In this section we show, for each class of models, how to obtain a good representative model that minimises the validation error, then we compare the representative models in Section 12.5.

Our initial aim is to predict the logit share of can5, on the basis of the 30 binary explanatory variables that describe programme types, the 7 binary variables that describe the day of the week, and the continuous variable that describes the audience. We begin with a linear model. In linear models, to avoid linear dependency problems, we omit one binary variable per channel and one for the days of the week.

To select a parsimonious linear model, we follow a stepwise model selection procedure, based on pairwise model comparison F tests (Section 5.3). We choose a significancy level of 0.05. Table 12.10 summarises the stepwise procedure. The first variable that enters the model is the standardised audience. The correlation between the two is 0.3179, rather high for our data. The other significant variables inserted in the final model include whether Show programmes and Sport programmes are on can5, and variables related to programme types on other channels, in particular, whether ita1 is broadcasting a Film programme or a Tv-Movie programme. It also matters whether or not rete4 broadcasts a Film programme or an Information programme, whether or not rai1 is broadcasting an information programme, and whether or not it is a Thursday.

Table 12.10 Results from the stepwise linear model selection procedure.

Step	Effect Entered	Number DF	In	F	Prob > F
1	std(audience)	1	1	31.1124	<.0001
2	show5	1	2	29.2278	<.0001
3	film6	1	3	20.4956	<.0001
4	sport5	1	4	17.8170	<.0001
5	film4	1	5	7.0417	0.0084
6	information1	1	6	8.8123	0.0033
7	information4	1	7	4.4485	0.0359
8	thursday	1	8	5.2413	0.0228
9	tv_movie6	1	9	4.1858	0.0418
10	show3	1	10	5.4349	0.0205

Table 12.11   Parameter estimates with the linear model.

Standard
Analysis of Parameter Estimates

Parameter	DF	Standard Estimate	Error	t Value	Pr > |t|
Intercept	1	0.5582	0.0696	8.03	<.0001
AUDI_BV1	1	0.1481	0.0186	7.97	<.0001
film4	1	0.1621	0.0426	3.81	0.0002
film6	1	0.3047	0.0629	4.85	<.0001
information1	1	0.2017	0.0616	3.27	0.0012
information4	1	0.2032	0.0753	2.70	0.0074
show3	1	−0.1972	0.0846	−2.33	0.0205
show5	1	0.2249	0.0387	5.81	<.0001
sport5	1	0.3562	0.0780	4.57	<.0001
thursday	1	−0.1367	0.0543	−2.52	0.0125
tv_movie6	1	0.1498	0.0638	2.35	0.0196

To interpret these results, we look at the estimated linear coefficients in Table 12.11. It turns out that the logit share of can5 depends positively (in order of magnitude) on sports5, film6, show5, information4, information1, film4, audience and tv_movie6. It depends negatively on show3 and thursday. In other words, the estimated share of can5 is expected to increase when can5 broadcasts Sport programmes or Show programmes; when ita1 broadcasts Film programmes or Tv-Movie programmes; when rai1 broadcasts Information programmes; when rete4 broadcasts Information programmes or Film programmes. Furthermore, the logit shares increase with the audiences, by about 1.15 share points. Conversely, the estimated shares are expected to decrease when it is Thursday, or when rai3 broadcasts a Show programme. Overall this coincides with Figure 12.1: can5 takes most of its audience from Sports programmes and Show programmes, and increases it when others broadcast Films programmes or Information programmes, especially the main competitors, rai1 and ita1. The estimated intercept is quite high, and this corresponds to a strong effect of loyalty to the channel.

Next we fit a regression tree to the training data. We choose a CART tree using the variance as a measure of impurity and the mean square error in the validation set as the pruning criterion. A more parsimonious model is a regression tree similar to the CHAID tree but using the F test for model splitting, instead of the chi-squared test. But the results were poorer in terms of mean square error on the validation data set and they are not reported here.

Figure 12.7 shows the mean square error of the CART regression tree as the number of leaves increases. The optimal number of leaves is reached when the mean square error is a minimum on the validation data set; it occurs at 22. The top node of the tree specifies that the mean logit share of the training data (274 observations) is equal to about 0.99. This corresponds to a mean share of

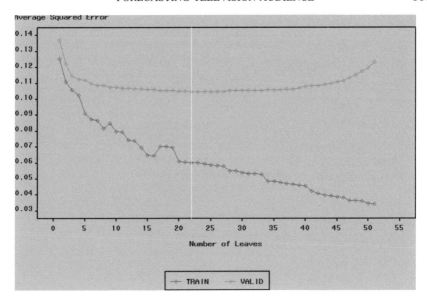

Figure 12.7 Behaviour of MSE and choice of tree configuration.

$8e^{0.99} = 21.52$, according to the definition of the logit share, and assuming a mean share for the residual channels equal to 8%. Similarly for the validation data set. The tree is first split according to whether the standardised audience is essentially positive (right node) or negative (left node). In the positive case, the resulting node has a higher mean share, about $8e^{1.08} = 23.55$; in the negative case it has a lower mean share, about $8e^{0.82} = 18.16$. A second split is done, for both nodes, according to whether or not, can5 is broadcasting a Show programme. The worst-case scenario is described by the leftmost node (no show and low audience), in which the expected share is about $8e^{0.69} = 15.95$. So far the tree results essentially agree with those from the linear model.

The whole tree, which completely describes the 22 rules leading to the terminal nodes, is given in Table 12.12. For each rule, it shows the number of observations (total) classified to be there, as well as the mean and standard deviation of the logit share for the observations in the node. It is difficult to compare the signs of the effects with the signs in the linear model, as the two models are rather different in structure. We can draw conclusions by comparing the discriminant variables. Most of the variables detected with the linear model also appear in the tree model, yet in a hierarchical form. This is the case for audience, show5, sport5, information1, film6 and tv_movie6. Other variables, such as film4, information4, show3 and thursday, do not appear here. Other effects related to the same competing channels do appear: sport3, information3, film3, show4 and sport4, as well as film2 and film1. Finally, friday, saturday and sunday appear. The overall structure of the tree seems more compatible with the image of can5 and with those of its correlated competitors (according to the correlation structure in Section 12.3).

Table 12.12 Classification rules deduced from the CART regression tree.

```
IF SHOW5 EQUALS 0
AND standardize(AUDIENCE) < -0.059023893
THEN
 N   : 44
 AVE  : 0.69386
 SD   : 0.25358

IF TV_MOVIE6 EQUALS 0
AND SHOW5 EQUALS 1
AND standardize(AUDIENCE) < -0.059023893
THEN
 N   : 25
 AVE  : 1.02851
 SD   : 0.29171

IF SATURDAY EQUALS 0
AND SHOW5 EQUALS 1
AND -0.059023893 <= standardize(AUDIENCE)
THEN
 N   : 43
 AVE  : 1.14185
 SD   : 0.29216

IF INFORMATION1 EQUALS 1
AND -0.059023893 <= standardize(AUDIENCE) < 0.6803605603
AND SHOW5 EQUALS 0
THEN
 NODE  : 25
 AVE  : 1.43764
 SD   : 0.23178

IF SPORT3 EQUALS 1
AND SATURDAY EQUALS 1
AND SHOW5 EQUALS 1
AND -0.059023893 <= standardize(AUDIENCE)
THEN
 N   : 1
 AVE  : 0.82832
 SD   : 0

IF standardize(AUDIENCE) < -0.07021096
AND INFORMATION3 EQUALS 1
AND TV_MOVIE6 EQUALS 1
AND SHOW5 EQUALS 1
THEN
 N   : 7
 AVE  : 0.655
 SD   : 0.10062
```

Table 12.12 (*continued*)

```
IF -0.07021096 <= standardize(AUDIENCE) < -0.059023893
AND INFORMATION3 EQUALS 1
AND TV_MOVIE6 EQUALS 1
AND SHOW5 EQUALS 1
THEN
 N   : 1
 AVE : 0.82146
 SD  : 0

IF SHOW4 EQUALS 1
AND INFORMATION1 EQUALS 0
AND -0.059023893 <= standardize(AUDIENCE) < 0.6803605603
AND SHOW5 EQUALS 0
THEN
 N   : 8
 AVE : 0.55035
 SD  : 0.26191

IF FRIDAY EQUALS 0
AND SPORT5 EQUALS 0
AND 0.6803605603 <= standardize(AUDIENCE)
AND SHOW5 EQUALS 0
THEN
 N   : 61
 AVE : 1.09677
 SD  : 0.23145

IF FRIDAY EQUALS 1
AND SPORT5 EQUALS 0
AND 0.6803605603 <= standardize(AUDIENCE)
AND SHOW5 EQUALS 0
THEN
 N   : 3
 AVE : 1.38847
 SD  : 0.15933

IF 0.6803605603 <= standardize(AUDIENCE) < 0.9634971743
AND SPORT5 EQUALS 1
AND SHOW5 EQUALS 0
THEN
 N   : 5
 AVE : 1.09189
 SD  : 0.28865

IF FILM3 EQUALS 1
AND SPORT3 EQUALS 0
AND SATURDAY EQUALS 1
```

(*continued overleaf*)

Table 12.12 *(continued)*

```
AND SHOW5 EQUALS 1
AND -0.059023893 <= standardize(AUDIENCE)
THEN
 N   : 4
 AVE  : 1.41927
 SD   : 0.16031

IF SPORT4 EQUALS 0
AND FILM2 EQUALS 0
AND INFORMATION3 EQUALS 0
AND TV_MOVIE6 EQUALS 1
AND SHOW5 EQUALS 1
AND standardize(AUDIENCE) < -0.059023893
THEN
 N   : 9
 AVE  : 0.80977
 SD   : 0.06078

IF SPORT4 EQUALS 1
AND FILM2 EQUALS 0
AND INFORMATION3 EQUALS 0
AND TV_MOVIE6 EQUALS 1
AND SHOW5 EQUALS 1
AND standardize(AUDIENCE) < -0.059023893
THEN
 N   : 1
 AVE  : 1.17222
 SD   : 0

IF SUNDAY EQUALS 0
AND FILM2 EQUALS 1
AND INFORMATION3 EQUALS 0
AND TV_MOVIE6 EQUALS 1
AND SHOW5 EQUALS 1
AND standardize(AUDIENCE) < -0.059023893
THEN
 N   : 5
 AVE  : 0.96288
 SD   : 0.1526

IF SUNDAY EQUALS 1
AND FILM2 EQUALS 1
AND INFORMATION3 EQUALS 0
AND TV_MOVIE6 EQUALS 1
AND SHOW5 EQUALS 1
AND standardize(AUDIENCE) < -0.059023893
```

Table 12.12   (*continued*)

```
THEN
 N   : 2
 AVE : 1.24541
 SD  : 0.21291

IF FILM6 EQUALS 0
AND SHOW4 EQUALS 0
AND INFORMATION1 EQUALS 0
AND -0.059023893 <= standardize(AUDIENCE) < 0.6803605603
AND SHOW5 EQUALS 0
THEN
 N   : 23
 AVE : 0.72516
 SD  : 0.27712

IF FILM6 EQUALS 1
AND SHOW4 EQUALS 0
AND INFORMATION1 EQUALS 0
AND -0.059023893 <= standardize(AUDIENCE) < 0.6803605603
AND SHOW5 EQUALS 0
THEN
 N   : 17
 AVE : 0.95977
 SD  : 0.23193

IF 0.9634971743 <= standardize(AUDIENCE) < 1.1544846418
AND SPORT5 EQUALS 1
AND SHOW5 EQUALS 0
THEN
 N   : 2
 AVE : 1.71799
 SD  : 0.13672

IF 1.1544846418 <= standardize(AUDIENCE)
AND SPORT5 EQUALS 1
AND SHOW5 EQUALS 0
THEN
 N   : 2
 AVE : 2.05309
 SD  : 0.30578
IF FILM1 EQUALS 0
AND FILM3 EQUALS 0
AND SPORT3 EQUALS 0
AND SATURDAY EQUALS 1
AND SHOW5 EQUALS 1
AND -0.059023893 <= standardize(AUDIENCE)
```

(*continued overleaf*)

Table 12.12 (*continued*)

```
THEN
  N   : 5
  AVE  : 1.6396
  SD   : 0.0795

IF FILM1 EQUALS 1
AND FILM3 EQUALS 0
AND SPORT3 EQUALS 0
AND SATURDAY EQUALS 1
AND SHOW5 EQUALS 1
AND -0.059023893 <= standardize(AUDIENCE)
THEN
  N   : 2
  AVE  : 1.39445
  SD   : 0.00816
```

Finally, we come to feedforward neural networks. We design a multilayer perceptron with one hidden layer. After some experimentation we choose to have two hidden nodes, which can be deemed to represent the public and private television networks. We choose linear combination functions and linear activation functions for the two hidden nodes. We train the network using mean square error on the validation data set. We then try an RBFs network, to capture the neighbour topology among the evenings. We choose one hidden node and make the combination function from the input nodes to the hidden node a (Gaussian) radial basis function, with equal widths and equal heights. We choose the identify function for the activation functions. The neural network models appear to perform rather similarly; the multilayer perceptron is slightly better but the RBF network is more parsimonious.

Table 12.13 shows the weights calculated using the multilayer perceptron. There are 72 weights, even though there are only 38 explanatory variables, the audience plus 37 binary variables. This occurs because rai3 has no Tv-Movie programmes, so the corresponding binary variable is dropped. Similarly, ital transmits information only once and is therefore dropped. There are also two intercept parameters (bias), one for each input, as well as one from the hidden node to the output node. Unlike with linear models, there is no need to drop further binary variables. On the other hand, there is no simple formal model selection procedure, or hypothesis testing procedure on the weights, so we can only make qualitative comments about the signs and magnitudes of the weights.

Notice that the estimated weight from the hidden nodes H_{11}, H_{12} to the output node is small but positive. It therefore makes sense to interpret the effect of the explanatory variables by looking at the sign of the coefficients from the input nodes to the hidden node. Also notice that the bias terms have rather high values, and this corresponds to the channel loyalty effect seen for the linear model. Most of the signs in the linear model match the signs in this model.

Table 12.13   Weights of the multilayer perceptron network.

	From	To	Weight
1	AUDI_BV1	H11	1.1740347772
2	AUDI_BV1	H12	0.123134213
3	FILM11	H11	0.2168710734
4	FILM21	H11	−0.003614915
5	FILM31	H11	0.1618147995
6	FILM41	H11	0.3251317677
7	FILM51	H11	−0.900685697
8	FILM61	H11	0.9334017087
9	FRIDAY1	H11	−0.091669461
10	INFORMATION11	H11	0.4018886565
11	INFORMATION21	H11	0.101447949
12	INFORMATION31	H11	0.2979551735
13	INFORMATION41	H11	0.4086658636
14	INFORMATION51	H11	0.0348085575
15	MONDAY1	H11	0.2211611959
16	SATURDAY1	H11	0.4637795148
17	SHOW11	H11	−0.178213926
18	SHOW21	H11	0.1589792454
19	SHOW31	H11	−0.420967523
20	SHOW41	H11	−0.292000262
21	SHOW51	H11	0.1495358451
22	SHOW61	H11	−0.302074523
23	SPORT11	H11	−0.367628308
24	SPORT21	H11	−0.088506097
25	SPORT31	H11	0.468554604
26	SPORT41	H11	0.3149658113
27	SPORT51	H11	1.0365237425
28	SPORT61	H11	−0.861727181
29	SUNDAY1	H11	0.0581028079
30	THURSDAY1	H11	−0.425886049
31	TUESDAY1	H11	0.2672841044
32	TV_MOVIE11	H11	−0.290958077
33	TV_MOVIE21	H11	−0.180243694
34	TV_MOVIE41	H11	−0.308903067
35	TV_MOVIE51	H11	−0.474061343
36	TV_MOVIE61	H11	0.1132854614
37	WEDNESDAY1	H11	−0.632832395
38	FILM11	H12	−0.055731218
39	FILM21	H12	−0.083121848
40	FILM31	H12	−0.073921865
41	FILM41	H12	−0.144347594
42	FILM51	H12	0.0200435139
43	FILM61	H12	−0.0349771
44	FRIDAY1	H12	0.2470090922

(continued overleaf)

Table 12.13 (*continued*)

	From	To	Weight
45	INFORMATION11	H12	0.1106999195
46	INFORMATION21	H12	−0.198466293
47	INFORMATION31	H12	−0.03354677
48	INFORMATION41	H12	0.4014440409
49	INFORMATION51	H12	0.0197488302
50	MONDAY1	H12	−0.226134652
51	SATURDAY1	H12	−0.246060203
52	SHOW11	H12	0.0688079194
53	SHOW21	H12	−0.067446329
54	SHOW31	H12	−0.472039866
55	SHOW41	H12	0.0018527931
56	SHOW51	H12	0.0462647232
57	SHOW61	H12	−0.220152292
58	SPORT11	H12	−0.220443076
59	SPORT21	H12	−0.051749183
60	SPORT31	H12	0.2625010151
61	SPORT41	H12	−0.035962957
62	SPORT51	H12	0.2103932874
63	SPORT61	H12	0.1457104861
64	SUNDAY1	H12	0.1676716269
65	THURSDAY1	H12	−0.169547437
66	TUESDAY1	H12	0.064402756
67	TV_MOVIE11	H12	0.1610823216
68	TV_MOVIE21	H12	−0.164204013
69	TV_MOVIE41	H12	0.220171918
70	TV_MOVIE51	H12	−0.138515633
71	TV_MOVIE61	H12	0.0168145323
72	WEDNESDAY1	H12	−0.137997477
73	BIAS	H11	−0.099578697
74	BIAS	H12	1.0532654311
75	H11	LOGIT5	0.0661926904
76	H12	LOGIT5	0.0489219573
77	BIAS	LOGIT5	0.864583892

We finally fit a nearest-neighbour model. For K, the number of neighbourhoods to consider in the predictions, we take different multiples of 7, coinciding with a week in our data set. This is because programmes repeat in weekly schedules. The best configuration, in terms of mean square error, occurs for $K = 28$, coinciding almost with a month.

In principle, all the previous models can be extended to the multiple-target case, but most general-purpose data mining packages, such as SAS Enterprise Miner, do not support tree models or nearest-neighbour models with multiple targets. The next section compares the following three models, to predict the 6 response variables:

- A linear model with $37 + 1$ explanatory variables (the binary programme variables plus the audience) selected through stepwise model selection with a significance level of 0.05.
- A multilayer perceptron network with $37 + 1$ input variables, one hidden layer with two hidden nodes, linear combination functions and linear activation functions.
- An RBF network with $37 + 1$ input variables, one hidden node, and a radial basis combination function from the input nodes to the hidden node, with equal widths and heights.

12.5   Model comparison

We begin with the single-target predictive problem. The models in the previous section are compared using two main measures of performance. The first one is the mean square error (MSE) of the predictions, namely, the mean of the differences between the observed and the predicted logitshares. We make this measurement on the training date set and the validation data set. The validation data set is obviously the most important, but the training data set can give an assessment of the model's goodness of fit. The second one is the correlation coefficient between the observed and predicted quantities. It measures errors in a slightly different way.

Table 12.14 shows model comparison when can5 is considered as the response target variable, for the models considered in the last section. In terms of MSE over the training data set, the CART regression tree model comes first, followed by linear regression and the two network models. The nearest-neighbour model is clearly worse than the others on goodness of fit. In terms of MSE for predictions, the CART tree is again the best model, followed by the two network models and the linear regression model. The nearest-neighbour model is again the worst.

The differences between the models are indeed slight, apart from the nearest-neighbour model. For this data set, the neighbouring structure over the input

Table 12.14   Summary of the univariate predictive models.

Model	MSE training data set	MSE validation data set	Correlation between observed and predicted
Linear regression	0.078	0.116	0.4525
CART tree	0.060	0.104	0.5066
RBF network	0.083	0.108	0.4889
MLP network	0.083	0.105	0.4933
Nearest neighbour	0.105	0.123	0.3260

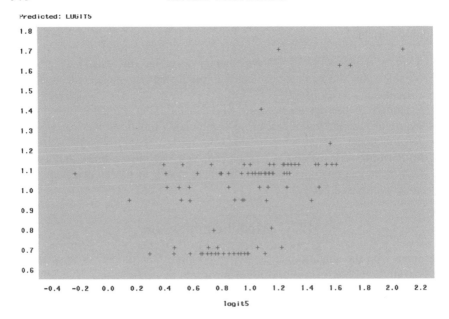

Figure 12.8 Observed versus predicted scatterplot for the CART tree (correlation = 0.5066).

variables of the different evenings is not of great help. This slightly affects the RBF network too, which is slightly inferior than the multilayer perceptron. Networks do better than the regression model, as they have probably been trained accurately, by minimising MSE over the validation data set. It may be sensible to see how they perform comparatively on a test data set, if sufficient data is available. Comparison of the correlation coefficients, over the validation data set, reflects quite well the previous ranking of the models. Figure 12.8 is a scatterplot that compares the observed and predicted logit shares for the best model, namely, the CART tree model.

We now compare models for multivariate target prediction. We compare MSEs in terms of shares, not logit shares. The two MSEs are strictly related. However, there is variability in the relationship due to the volatility of the residual shares, and this effect is stronger in the multivariate case. That is why we refer directly to shares, which we obtain by applying the inverse logistic transformation to the predicted logit shares. Table 12.15 is a summary comparison of the MSEs of the predicted shares, on the validation data set only, for each of the six channels, as well as the overall MSE obtained by averaging all squared errors. It appears that, at the overall level, the linear model performs best, followed by the MLP network and finally the RBF network. Differences appear more marked on a share scale than on a logit share scale. In particular, the linear model does considerably better for the public television channels, probably because they have a more loyal public, easier to predict in a linear way. A mean error of around 5% is considered rather good by the television market experts.

Table 12.15 Summary of the multivariate predictive models expressed as MSE of the shares on the validation data set.

Model	rai1	rai2	rai3	rete4	can5	ita1	overall
Linear network	7.95	4.43	4.74	1.90	4.94	2.81	4.84
MLP network	9.36	5.28	5.20	1.91	5.07	2.88	5.48
RBF network	9.72	5.27	5.15	1.97	5.73	2.93	5.68

Table 12.16 Comparison between observed (centre column) and predicted quantiles (right column).

Quantile			
100%	Max	41.7	30.9409
99%		41.7	29.5403
95%		31.9	28.4538
90%		29.6	27.4046
75%	Q3	25.8	25.4045
50%	Median	21.2	23.0174
25%	Q1	17.8	20.8245
10%		14.8	18.1678
5%		12.4	17.0909
1%		5.3	14.2822
0%	Min	5.3	14.2822

We then calculate the mean of all (absolute) correlations between observed and predicted shares, for each considered channel. It is 0.4739 for the linear model, 0.226 for the MLP network and 0.186 for the RBF network. This confirm the previous findings, especially the large superiority of the linear model over the neural network models. Neural networks require more data to be trained well on such a highly complex model.

The data set contains some anomalous observations, particularly for the public channels. The presence of outliers can have two effects: when they are allocated to the training data set, they bias the model fit; when they are in the validation data set, they inflate the MSE. Both occur in this case study, especially for rai1. To give a clearer picture of these effects, Table 12.16 compares the quantiles of the observed distribution and the predicted distribution of the shares of can5, under the best model, namely, the linear model. Notice how the model compresses the distribution, considerably diminishing the range. Outliers cannot be eliminated from this data set, especially because they may contain precious information on share patterns. For completeness, however, we omit the outliers and obtain about a 1% improvement in MSE over the shares.

To summarise, we have been able to build a valid predictive model for the data; this model uses information on the types of programmes broadcast by all channels, the total audience and, to a lesser extent, the date of broadcast (day of the week). The Italian television market appears to exhibit a strong channel loyalty, reflected in the high intercept (and biases) estimated by the models.

While for single response problems a regression tree seem to be the best model, followed by a neural network model, for the multiple response case a simpler linear model may be considered a very good choice.

12.6   Summary report

- *Context*: this case study concerns forecasting television shares. It may also be applied to any situations where the objective is to predict aggregate individual preferences. Here preferences were measured through the chosen television channel; more generally, this type of setting applies to any context where the data reflects consumer choices among a set of alternatives, observed repeatedly in time. Examples are choices between internet portals, videotapes or DVD rentals in a given period; brand choices in subsequent visits to a specialised shop; choice of restaurant in a given city area, in a given year, etc.
- *Objectives*: the aim of the analysis is to build a predictive rule which allows a television network to broadcast programmes which maximise audience share.
- *Organisation of the data*: the data is one year of television shares for the six leading Italian channels during prime time. Besides shares, there is information on the programme broadcast and its type, as well as on the broadcasting channel and the day of transmission. The type of a programme depends on how programmes are classified in categories; this is a fairly critical issue.
- *Exploratory data analysis*: this suggested that television shares are affected mainly by three sources of variation: the broadcasting channel, which express loyalty to the channel, the type of programme, which seems to be the driving force of individual preferences; and the day of the week, which determines what else is available to the viewers, besides watching television. This also explains why it is important to include the total audience in the analysis. The exploratory analysis also suggested that we should transform the shares into logit shares to achieve normality and lead to an easier analysis.
- *Model specification*: the objective of the analysis suggests a predictive model, and the available (transformed) data specifies that there are six potential response variables (logit shares) and a number of explanatory variables, some of which are channel specific, such as type of programme, and some not, such as day of the week and total audience. We considered predicting a single channel share and all six shares simultaneously. For the univariate problem, we considered a linear regression model, a regression tree, a multilayer perceptron, an RBF network and a nearest-neighbour model. For the multivariate problem, we considered a linear regression model, a multilayer perceptron and an RBF network. Multi-response regression trees and nearest-neighbour models were not available.
- *Model comparison*: the models were compared using cross-validation, in terms of mean square error (MSE) of the predictions, on the training data

set and the validation data set. We also considered the correlation coefficient between the observed share and the predicted share. In the univariate case, the regression tree performs best, followed by the linear model, the neural networks and the nearest-neighbour model. In the multivariate case, the linear model seems to outperform the neural network models, probably because the neural networks require more data.

- *Model interpretation*: on the basis of model comparison, it seems that simpler models, such as linear models and regression trees, do the best job for this problem. This is generally true when the available data is not sufficient to obtain correct estimates for the very large number of parameters contained in a more complex model. An overparameterised model, such as a neural network, may adapt well to the data, but its estimates may be based on very few data points, giving a rather poor predictive behaviour. This problem is further emphasised when outliers are present in the data. In this setting they cannot be removed as they may be very important for model building. In terms of business interpretability, the linear model and the regression tree (for the univariate response case) give an understandable decision rule, analytic in the case of linear models and logically deductive in the case of trees. In this type of problem, it is very important to incorporate expert judgements, such as in an expert-driven classification of programme types.

Bibliography

Agrawal, R., Mannila, H., Srikant, R., Toivonen, H. and Verkamo, A. I. (1995) Fast discovery of association rules. In *Advances in Knowledge Discovery and Data Mining.* AAAI/MIT Press, Cambridge MA.

Agresti, A. (1990) *Categorical Data Analysis.* John Wiley & Sons, Inc., New York.

Akaike, H. (1974) A new look at statistical model identification. *IEEE Transactions on Automatic Control* **19**, 716–723.

Azzalini, A. (1992) *Statistical Inference: An Introduction Based on the Likelihood Principle.* Springer-Verlag, Berlin.

Barnett, V. (1975) *Elements of Sampling Theory.* Arnold, London.

Benzecri, J. (1973) *L'analyse des données.* Dunod, Paris.

Bernardo, J. M. and Smith, A. F. M. (1994) *Bayesian Theory.* John Wiley & Sons, Inc., New York.

Berry, M. and Linoff, G. (1997) *Data Mining Techniques for Marketing, Sales, and Customer Support.* John Wiley & Sons, Inc., New York.

Berry, M. and Linoff, G. (2000) *Mastering Data Mining.* John Wiley & Sons, Inc., New York.

Berry, M. A. and Linoff. G. (2002) *Mining the Web: Transforming Customer Data.* John Wiley & Sons, Inc., New York.

Berson, A. and Smith, S. J. (1997) *Data Warehousing, Data Mining and OLAP.* Mc Graw-Hill, New York.

Bickel, P. J. and Doksum, K. A. (1977) *Mathematical Statistics.* Prentice Hall, Englewood Cliffs NJ.

Bishop, C. (1995) *Neural Networks for Pattern Recognition.* Clarendon Press, Oxford.

Blanc, E. and Giudici, P. (2002) Statistical methods for web clickstream analysis. *Statistica Applicata, Italian Journal of Applied Statistics* **14**(2).

Blanc, E. and Tarantola, C. (2002) Dependency networks for web clickstream analysis. In *Data Mining III*, Zanasi, A., Trebbia, C. A., Ebecken, N. N. F. and Melli, P. (eds). WIT Press, Southampton.

Bollen, K. A. (1989) *Structural Equations with Latent Variables.* John Wiley & Sons, Inc., New York.

Breiman, L., Friedman, J. H., Olshen, R. and Stone, C. J. (1984) *Classification and Regression Trees.* Wadsworth, Belmont CA.

Brooks, S. P., Giudici, P. and Roberts, G. O. (2003) Efficient construction of reversible jump MCMC proposal distributions. *Journal of the Royal Statistical Society, Series B* **1**, 1–37, with discussion.

Applied Data Mining. Paolo Giudici
© 2003 John Wiley & Sons, Ltd   ISBNs: 0-470-84679-8 (Paper); 0-470-84678-X (Cloth)

Burnham, K. P. and Anderson, A. R. (1998) *Model Selection and Inference: A Practical Information-Theoretic Approach.* Springer-Verlag, New York.

Cabena, P., Hadjinian, P., Stadler, R., Verhees, J. and Zanasi, A. (1997) *Discovering Data Mining: From Concept to Implementation.* Prentice Hall, Englewood Cliffs NJ.

Cadez, I., Heckerman, D. Meek, C, Smyth, P. and White, S. (2000) Visualization of navigation patterns on a web site using model based clustering. In *Proceedings of the Sixth ACM SIGKDD International Conference on Knowledge Discovery and Data Mining,* Boston MA.

Castelo, R. and Giudici, P. (2003) Improving Markov Chain model search for data mining. *Machine Learning* **50**, 127–158.

Chatfield, C. (1996) *The Analysis of Time Series: An Introduction.* Chapman and Hall, London.

Cheng, S. and Titterington, M. (1994) Neural networks: a review from a statistical perspective. *Statistical Science* **9**, 3–54.

Christensen, R. (1997) *Log-Linear Models and Logistic Regression.* Springer-Verlag, Berlin.

Cifarelli, D. M. and Muliere, P. (1989) *Statistica Bayesiana.* Iuculano editore, Pavia.

Coppi, R. (2002) A theoretical framework for data mining: the "information paradigm". *Computational Statistics and Data Analysis* **38**, 501–515.

Cortes, C. and Pregibon, D. (2001) Signature-based methods for data streams. *Journal of Knowledge Discovery and Data Mining* **5**, 167–182.

Cowell, R. G., Dawid, A. P., Lauritzen, S. L. and Spiegelhalter, D. J. (1999) *Probabilistic Networks and Expert Systems.* Springer-Verlag, New York.

Cox, D. R. and Wermuth, N. (1996) *Multivariate Dependencies: Models, Analysis and Interpretation.* Chapman and Hall, London.

Cressie, N. (1991) *Statistics for Spatial Data.* John Wiley & Sons, Inc., New York.

Darroch, J. N., Lauritzen, S. L. and Speed, T. P. (1980) Markov fields and log-linear models for contingency tables. *Annals of Statistics* **8**, 522–539.

Dempster, A. (1972) Covariance selection. *Biometrics* **28**, 157–175.

De Ville, B. (2001) *Microsoft Data Mining: Integrated Business Intelligence for e-Commerce and Knowledge Management.* Digital Press, New York.

Diggle, P. J., Liang, K. and Zeger, S. L. (1994) *Analysis of Longitudinal data.* Clarendon Press, Oxford.

Di Scala, L. and La Rocca, L. (2002) Probabilistic modelling for clickstream analysis. In *Data Mining III,* Zanasi, A., Trebbia, C. A., Ebecken, N. N. F. and Melli, P. (eds). WIT Press, Southampton.

Dobson A. J. (1990) *An Introduction to Generalized Linear Models.* Chapman and Hall, London.

Edwards, D. (1995) *Introduction to Graphical Modelling.* Springer-Verlag, New York.

Efron, B. (1979) Bootstrap methods: another look at the jackknife. *Annals of Statistics* **7**, 1–26.

Fahrmeir, L. and Hamerle, A. (1994) *Multivariate Statistical Modelling Based on Generalised Linear Models.* Springer-Verlag, Berlin.

Fayyad, U. M., Piatetsky-Shapiro, G., Smyth, P. and Uthurusamy, R. (eds) (1996) *Advances in Knowledge Discovery and Data Mining.* AAAI Press, New York.

Frydenberg, M. and Lauritzen, S. L. (1989) Decomposition of maximum likelihood in mixed interaction models. *Biometrika* **76**, 539–555.

Gibbons, D. and Chakraborti, S. (1992) *Nonparametric Statistical Inference.* Marcel Dekker, New York.

Gilks, W. R., Richardson, S., and Spiegelhalter, D. J. (eds) (1996) *Markov Chain Monte Carlo in Practice*. Chapman and Hall, London.

Giudici, P. (1998) MCMC methods to determine the optimal complexity of a probabilistic network. *Journal of the Italian Statistical Society* **7**, 171–183.

Giudici, P. (2001a) Bayesian data mining, with application to credit scoring and benchmarking. *Applied Stochastic Models in Business and Industry* **17**, 69–81.

Giudici, P. (2001b) *Data mining: metodi statistici per le applicazioni aziendali*. McGraw-Hill, Milan.

Giudici, P. and Carota, C. (1992) Symmetric interaction models to study innovation processes in the European software industry. In *Advances in GLIM and Statistical Modelling*, Fahrmeir, L. Francis, B., Gilchrist, R. and Tutz, G. (eds). Springer-Verlag, Berlin.

Giudici, P. and Castelo, R. (2001) Association models for web mining. *Journal of Knowledge Discovery and Data Mining* **5**, 183–196.

Giudici, P. and Green, P. J. (1999) Decomposable graphical gaussian model determination. *Biometrika* **86**, 785–801.

Giudici, P. and Passerone, G. (2002) Data mining of association structures to model consumer behaviour. *Computational Statistics and Data analysis* **38**, 533–541.

Giudici, P., Heckerman, D. and Whittaker, J. (2001) Statistical models for data mining. *Journal of Knowledge Discovery and Data Mining* **5**, 163–165.

Goodman, L. A. and Kruskal, W. H, (1979) *Measures of Association for Cross Classification*. Springer-Verlag, New York.

Gower, J. C. and Hand, D. J. (1996) *Biplots*. Chapman and Hall, London.

Green, P. J., Hjort, N. and Richardson, S. (eds) (2003) *Highly Structured Stochastic Systems*. Oxford University Press, Oxford.

Greenacre, M. (1983) *Theory and Applications of Correspondence Analysis*. Academic Press, New York.

Greene, W. H. (1999) *Econometric Analysis*. Prentice Hall, New York.

Han, J. and Kamber, M. (2001) *Data Mining: Concepts and Techniques*. Morgan Kaufmann, New York.

Hand, D. (1997) *Construction and Assessment of Classification Rules*. John Wiley & Sons, Ltd, Chichester.

Hand, D. J. and Henley, W. E. (1997) Statistical classification method in consumer scoring: a review. *Journal of the Royal Statistical Society, Series A* **160**, 523–541.

Hand, D. J., Mannila, H. and Smyth, P. (2001) *Principles of Data Mining*. MIT Press, Cambridge MA.

Hand, D. J., Blunt, G., Kelly, M. G. and Adams, M. N. (2001) Data mining for fun and profit. *Statistical Science* **15**, 111–131.

Hastie, T., Tibshirani, R. and Friedman, J. (2001) *The Elements of Statistical Learning: Data Mining, Inference and Prediction*. Springer-Verlag, New York.

Heckerman, D. (1997) Bayesian networks for data mining. *Journal of Data Mining and Knowledge Discovery* **1**, 79–119.

Heckerman, D., Chickering, D., Meek, C., Rountwaite, R. and Kadie, C. (2000) Dependency networks for inference, collaborative filtering and data visualisation. *Journal of Machine Learning Research* **1**, 49–75.

Hoel, P. G., Port, S. C. and Stone, C. J. (1972) *Introduction to Stochastic Processes*. Waweland Press, Prospect Heights IL.

Immon W. H. (1996) *Building the Data Warehouse*. John Wiley & Sons, Inc., New York.

Jensen, F. (1996) *An Introduction to Bayesian networks*. Springer-Verlag, New York.

Johnson, R. A. and Wichern, D. W. (1982) *Applied Multivariate Statistical Analysis*. Prentice Hall, Englewood Cliffs NJ.

Johnston, J. and Di Nardo, J. (1997) *Econometric Methods*. McGraw-Hill, New York.

Kass, G. V. (1980) An exploratory technique for investigating large quantities of categorical data. *Applied Statistics* **29**, 119–127.

Kloesgen, W. and Zytkow, J. (eds) (2002) *Handbook of Data Mining and Knowledge Discovery*. Oxford University Press, Oxford.

Kolmogorov, A. N. (1933) Sulla determinazione empirica di una leggi di probabilita. *Giornale dell'Istituto Italiano degli Attuari* **4**, 83–91.

Lauritzen, S. L. (1996) *Graphical Models*. Oxford University Press, Oxford.

Mardia, K. V., Kent, J. T. and Bibby, J. M. (1979) *Multivariate Analysis*. Academic Press, London.

McCullagh, P. and Nelder, J. A. (1989) *Generalised Linear Models*. Chapman and Hall, New York.

Mood, A. M., Graybill, F. A. and Boes, D. C. (1991) *Introduction to the Theory of Statistics*. McGraw-Hill, Tokyo.

Neal, R. (1996) *Bayesian Learning for Neural Networks*. Springer-Verlag, New York.

Nelder, J. A. and Wedderburn, R. W. M. (1972) Generalized linear models. *Journal of the Royal Statistical Society, Series B* **54**, 3–40.

Parr Rudd, O. (2000) *Data Mining Cookbook: Modeling Data for Marketing, Risk, and Customer Relationship Management*. John Wiley & Sons, Ltd, Chichester.

Quinlan, R. (1993) *C4.5: Programs for Machine Learning*. Morgan Kaufmann, New York.

Ripley, B. D. (1996) *Pattern Recognition and Neural Networks*. Cambridge University Press, Cambridge.

Rosenblatt, F. (1962) *Principles of Neurodynamics: Perceptrons and the Theory of Brain Mechanism*. Spartan, Washington DC.

SAS Institute (2001) *SAS Enterprise Miner Reference Manual*. SAS Institute Inc., Cary NC.

Schwarz, G. (1978) Estimating the dimension of a model. *Annals of Statistics* **62**, 461–464.

Searle, S. R. (1982) *Matrix Algebra Useful for Statistics*. John Wiley & Sons, Inc., New York.

Thuraisingham, B. (1999) *Data Mining: Technologies, Techniques and Trends*. CRC Press, Boca Raton FL.

Tukey, J. W. (1977) *Exploratory Data Analysis*. Addison-Wesley, Reading MA.

Vapnik, V. (1995) *The Nature of Statistical Learning Theory*. Springer-Verlag, New York.

Vapnik, V. (1998) *Statistical Learning Theory*. John Wiley & Sons, Inc., New York.

Weisberg, S. (1985) *Applied Linear Regression*. John Wiley & Sons, Inc., New York.

Weiss, S. W. and Indurkhya, N. (1997) *Predictive Data Mining: A Practical Guide*. Morgan Kaufmann, New York.

Westphal, C. and Blaxton, T. (1997) *Data Mining Solutions*. John Wiley & Sons, Inc., New York.

Whittaker, J. (1990) *Graphical Models in Applied Multivariate Statistics*. John Wiley & Sons, Ltd, Chichester.

Witten, I. and Frank, E. (1999) *Data Mining: Practical Machine Learning Tools and Techniques with Java Implementation*. Morgan Kaufmann, New York.

Zadeh, L. A. (1977) Fuzzy sets and their application to pattern classification and clustering. In *Classification and Clustering*, Van Ryzin, J. (ed.). Academic Press, New York.

Zanasi, A. (ed.) (2003) *Text Mining and Its Applications*. WIT Press, Southampton.

Zucchini, W. (2000) An introduction to model selection. *Journal of Mathematical Psychology* **44**, 41–61.

INDEX

Applied Data Mining.   Paolo Giudici
© 2003 John Wiley & Sons, Ltd   ISBNs: 0-470-84679-8 (Paper); 0-470-84678-X (Cloth)

Index compiled by Geraldine Begley